Canadian Families
Diversity, Conflict, and Change

Fourth Edition

Nancy Mandell
YORK UNIVERSITY

Ann Duffy
BROCK UNIVERSITY

NELSON EDUCATION

NELSON / EDUCATION

Canadian Families: Diversity, Conflict, and Change,
Fourth Edition

by Nancy Mandell and Ann Duffy

**Vice President,
Editorial Director:**
Evelyn Veitch

**Editor-in-Chief,
Higher Education:**
Anne Williams

Acquisitions Editor:
Maya Castle

Marketing Manager:
Amanda Henry

Developmental Editor:
Liisa Kelly

Permissions Coordinator:
Julie Pratt

Production Service:
MPS Limited, a Macmillan
Company

Copy Editor:
Karen Rolfe

Proofreader:
Dianne Fowlie

Indexer:
David Luljak

**Senior Production
Coordinator:**
Ferial Suleman

Design Director:
Ken Phipps

Managing Designer:
Franca Amore

Interior Design:
Peter Papayanakis

Cover Design:
Pamela Woodland

**Cover and Part Opener
Image:**
Masterfile

Compositor:
MPS Limited, a Macmillan
Company

Printer:
Transcontinental

**Library and Archives Canada
Cataloguing in Publication Data**

Canadian families: diversity,
conflict and change/[edited by]
Nancy Mandell, Ann Duffy.—4th ed.

Includes bibliographical references
and index.

ISBN 978-0-17-644267-5

1. Family—Canada. I. Mandell,
Nancy II. Duffy, Ann

HQ560.C3584 2010   306.850971
C2010-902938-0

ISBN-13: 978-0-17-644267-5
ISBN-10: 0-17-644267-7

DEDICATION

To our beloved colleague,
Sue Wilson,
a wonderful collaborator,
an esteemed family sociologist,
and our companion in feminist aging studies.

CONTENTS

Ann Duffy

Meg Luxton and June Corman

10 Aging Families 323

Julia Hemphill

PREFACE

Since we last updated this edited collection, Canadian families have continued to change in complicated and challenging ways. Globalization reshapes the economic and social conditions within which we work, play, and form intimate relations. Rising income gaps between the economically secure and insecure mean that families interact with the public in profoundly different ways. Fragmentation of employment and the increase in part-time and insecure jobs leave many families worried about financial matters and scrambling to provide the necessities of life. In contrast, a few financially well-off Canadian families occupy a privileged position within the social structure. All families wrestle with the social and cultural effects initiated by challenges from the persons living with disabilities, postcolonial, feminist, gay, and racial/ethnic movements.

In this dynamic context, new ways for interrogating the personal and political context of Canadians' lives demand sociological attention. *Canadian Families: Diversity, Conflict, and Change*, Fourth Edition, is intended to be a contribution to the growing debate on the direction and nature of change in family practices and policies. Each of the 10 chapters, written specifically for this collection, asks us to rethink traditional assumptions by including current empirical data and contemporary theoretical debates. Authors consider the appearance and significance of gendered and racialized encounters within and outside families that shape members' understandings of family life. Discourses of ethnicity, intimacy, and sexuality contour individual experiences of adolescence, parenting, love, and romance. Considerations of same-sex marriages, poverty, divorce, youth culture, and aging present contemporary and historically based accounts of the diverse ethnic and cultural forces affecting the many distinct ways people create family units.

In this text, we seek to present material in a clear and organized manner using accessible and jargon-free language. Students are encouraged to critically examine their own assumptions. While undergraduates will find the material easy to read and comprehend, they will also be confronted with challenging and refreshing points of view. Their lives are reflected in the narrative accounts of minority families, lesbian and gay-male families, aging families, single-parent families, and poor families. Learning objectives, chapter summaries, and boxed inserts highlight important points. Critical thinking questions, websites, suggested further reading, and a glossary are included to stimulate both individual reflection and classroom debate.

To this fourth edition, we welcome our new contributors, who bring excellent contemporary debates on emergent family topics. A core of outstanding contributors has been with us since the first edition. Over the years, their research has continued to enliven debates in a wide range of topics. All of our contributors incorporate struggles around gender, race, economics, sexuality,

disability, and violence into their analysis. We remain inspired by and apprecia-
tive of the strong theoretical and analytic perspectives of our colleagues. Their
efforts enrich and broaden our understandings of the everyday workings of
Canadian families.

The editors shared equally in the development and completion of this
fourth edition.

ACKNOWLEDGMENTS

We extend our sincere gratitude to all those who have helped us produce this
fourth edition. First, we want to extend our very heartfelt appreciation to
Franca Cece, York University, who has been a wonderful source of support and
assistance on this as well as other projects. We are very grateful for the support
from the excellent team at Nelson Education including Liisa Kelly, Maya Castle,
Susan Calvert, Ferial Suleman, Franca Amore, Amanda Henry, Debbie Yea, and
Julie Pratt, all of whom intervened at critical moments. Also, we would like to
thank our reviewers, independent scholar Ellen Faulkner and Harvey Briggs
(Algoma University). We continue to love and cherish the men and women in
our lives: Lionel, Jeremy, Marissa, and Micah, Ben and Caroline, Adam and
Jamie, Dusky, Hermana, and Mayra. Their presence sustains and enriches us.

CONTRIBUTORS

JUNE CORMAN
BROCK UNIVERSITY

June Corman is a professor of sociology at Brock University and is affiliated with the graduate program in Social Justice and Equity Studies. Her research focuses on women and work as well as restructuring and unemployment.

DEBORAH DAVIDSON
YORK UNIVERSITY

Deborah Davidson teaches sociology and social science at York University. Her teaching and research interests and publications focus on health, gender, diversity, and pedagogy. She serves on the editorial board of Sociological Research Online, the provincial board of directors for Bereaved Families of Ontario, and is chair of the Professional Advisory Committee for Bereaved Families of Ontario—Halton/Peel. She is involved in international research collaboration with colleagues in Canada and the United Kingdom, and local collaboration with colleagues at the Hospital for Sick Children in Toronto.

ANN DUFFY
BROCK UNIVERSITY

Ann Duffy is a professor in the Department of Sociology and is affiliated with the M.A. in Social Justice and M.A. in Critical Sociology at Brock University. She also teaches in Brock's Women's Studies Program. She has authored and coauthored a variety of books, chapters, and scholarly articles. Most of these publications concern some aspect of employment, women, violence, or aging. In addition, she has coedited several texts that have become popular resources in the sociology of the family, Canadian society, and work/employment. Most recently, she co-edited a text on work in the new economy entitled *Shifting Landscapes* (Nelson). She is currently principal researcher on a Social Sciences and Humanities Research Council of Canada grant examining the impact of worker displacement on workers' communities and their families.

JULIA HEMPHILL
YORK UNIVERSITY

Julia Hemphill is a PhD Candidate at York University in Toronto. Her research interests lie in social gerontology, particularly in gender, "race," and aging. She is currently involved in an ongoing Social Sciences and Humanities Research Council of Canada–funded project, "Worked to Death: Gendered and Racialized Dimensions of Retirement" with Nancy Mandell, Meg Luxton, Valerie Preston, Ann Kim, and Karen Robson. This project focuses on how economic security is gendered and racialized in late life.

SHANNON JETTE
CONCORDIA UNIVERSITY

Shannon Jette is a postdoctoral fellow at Concordia University in the Simone de Beauvoir Institute. She is interested in issues pertaining to gender, health, and the mass media, as well as cultural and historical aspects of medicine and the body. For her doctoral research, she explored the production of medical knowledge about exercise during pregnancy over the past century, illustrating the complex interplay of culture and medicine, and challenging taken-for-granted ways of thinking about the active pregnant body. Her work has been published in such journals as the *Sociology of Sport Journal*, *Sport History Review*, *Canadian Bulletin of Medical History*, and *Qualitative Health Research*.

DEBRA LANGAN
WILFRID LAURIER UNIVERSITY

Debra Langan is an assistant professor of Criminology at Wilfrid Laurier University, Brantford. She specializes in critical criminology, community/academic research partnerships, qualitative methodologies, and families and intimate relations. Debra is the recipient of the 2008 University Wide Teaching Award for full-time faculty, awarded by the Senate Committee on Teaching and Learning at York University. Her earlier work included positions as a probation officer and correctional centre program caseworker in Alberta Correctional Services and in community protocol development around violence against women in Ontario.

MEG LUXTON
YORK UNIVERSITY

Meg Luxton is a professor of Women's Studies at York University and past graduate director of the School of Women's Studies, York University. In 2002, the Canadian Sociology and Anthropology Association awarded her the Distinguished Scholar Award and recognized her coauthored book (with June Corman) as runner-up for the John Porter Book Prize. Her recent publications include book chapters and articles on unpaid work, work–family contradictions, caregiving, and aging. She is currently completing a book on caregiving practices and dilemmas in Canada.

NANCY MANDELL
YORK UNIVERSITY

Nancy Mandell is a professor of Sociology and Women's Studies at York University and chair of the Department of Sociology. Her research interests include aging, immigrant seniors, gender and race, qualitative methods, community–academic research partnerships, and schooling. Her 2008 coauthored study with Sue Wilson and Ann Duffy, *Conflict, Compromise and Choice: Canadian Women at Midlife*, examines the work, community, family, and intimate relationships of midlife women and their involvement with the women's movement.

With Robert Sweet, she has published a series of coauthored book chapters and articles on gendered social capital and parental involvement in children's schooling, especially homework. Recently, her publications have focused on feminist aging studies with particular interest in intimacy, body image, and caregiving. She is currently leading a project funded by the Social Sciences and Humanities Research Council of Canada entitled "Worked to Death: Gendered and Racialized Patterns of Economic Security among Senior Immigrants."

MAVIS MORTON
UNIVERSITY OF GUELPH

Mavis Morton is an assistant professor teaching criminology, criminal justice, and public policy in the Department of Sociology and anthropology at the University of Guelph. Her scholarship interests include violence against women, women and the law, feminist critical criminology, justice and social policy, feminist participatory action research (FPAR) and evaluation research, public sociology, and community engaged scholarship. Her previous work includes 20 years with rural and urban community partners (advocates, community committees, criminal justice and social service organizations, and government) engaging in research, education, community development, advocacy, and service coordination on issues related to violence against women and their children and other social justice issues.

JANICE RISTOCK
UNIVERSITY OF MANITOBA

Janice Ristock is an associate vice-president, Research; professor, Women's and Gender Studies; and adjunct professor in the Department of Anthropology and the Disability Studies Program at the University of Manitoba. She has gained international recognition for her research on violence in same-sex relationships and community-based research methodologies. She received a book award for No More Secrets: Violence in Lesbian Relationships from Division 44 of the American Psychological Association for making a distinguished contribution. She has authored, co-authored, and co-edited numerous books, chapters, journal articles, and government reports and is currently completing an edited collection on Relationship Violence in LGBTQ lives to be published by Routledge.

AYSAN SEV'ER
UNIVERSITY OF TORONTO

Aysan Sev'er is a professor of sociology at the University of Toronto. She is the recipient of numerous national and international awards for her work on violence against women. Her most current research focuses on extreme forms of violence against women in India and in south-eastern Turkey. She is the founding editor of the Women's Health and Urban Life Journal and the recipient of the Canadian Person's Day Award (1998), the Canadian Sociology and Anthropology Association Service Award (2001), Daughters of Ataturk Award

(2003), and the Canadian Women's Studies Book Award (2004). Her new edited book on family conflict is accepted for publication (WLU Press). Her book on honour killings in south-eastern Turkey is at the stage of academic review. She has organized numerous national and international conferences in the areas of violence against women, health, family and gender areas, and recently presented her work on honour killings in Bellagio, Italy.

CATHERINE TAYLOR
UNIVERSITY OF WINNIPEG

Catherine Taylor is an associate professor cross-appointed to the Faculty of Education and the Department of Rhetoric, Writing, and Communications. She did her Ph.D. in Cultural Studies and Critical Pedagogy at the University of Toronto. She has co-authored several books on academic writing that reflect this pedagogy and has published widely on issues of social justice such as research ethics involving marginalized populations, refusals of empathy, transgender and two-spirit people of Manitoba, and antihomophobia education. Most recently, Catherine has served as principal investigator in partnership with Egale Canada for the "First National Climate Survey of Homophobia in Canadian Schools."

VAPPU TYYSKÄ
RYERSON UNIVERSITY

Vappu Tyyskä is a professor of Sociology at Ryerson University, and Director of the MA Program in Immigration and Settlement. Her research deals with immigrant women, families, and youth, including projects on immigrant women's English language proficiency; intergenerational relations in immigrant families; and family violence in immigrant communities. Her recent work has been published in *Women's Health and Urban Life: An International and Interdisciplinary Journal*; the CERIS Working Paper series; and *Canadian Diversity/Diversité canadienne*.

BRIAN WILSON
UNIVERSITY OF BRITISH COLUMBIA

Brian Wilson is an associate professor in the School of Human Kinetics at the University of British Columbia in Vancouver. His research interests include media, consumer culture, youth, social inequality, social movements, the environment, and sport and leisure studies generally. He has published in such venues as *Youth & Society*, the *Canadian Journal of Sociology*, the *Canadian Journal of Communication*, the *Canadian Journal of Education*, the *Sociology of Sport Journal*, and the *International Review for the Sociology of Sport*. He is author of *Fight, Flight, or Chill: Subcultures, Youth, and Rave into the 21st Century* (McGill-Queen's University Press), and is currently leading a project funded by the Social Sciences and Humanities Research Council of Canada entitled "Corporate Environmentalism and the Canadian Golf Industry."

Part 1

Canadian Families in Social Context

Chapter 1

Portraying Canadian Families

Nancy Mandell

GOODBYE TO THE FAMILY DECLINE ARGUMENT

Family Myths	Family Realities
• Families are disastrous and unsuccessful.	• Families are thriving but untidy.
• Families are being discarded.	• Families are enduring, albeit in different forms.
• Families are private, individual affairs.	• Families are public, socially connected units.

LEARNING OBJECTIVES

In this chapter, you will learn that:

1. Canadian families vary by age, gender, race, sexuality, (dis)ability and class,

2. Canadian families are statistically varied,

3. traditional theories of family life no longer match the Canadian reality,

4. material conditions shape the ways Canadians construct family relationships,

5. determinism, antiracism, feminism, postmodernism and theories of personal life theorize how and why Canadians constitute families.

INTRODUCTION

Are families really in crisis or decline? Or, are they as emotionally and economically significant as ever? If we agree that individuals still desire and aspire for close personal relationships with long-lasting bonds as ways to deliver and receive care, nurturance, and affection, the real question becomes in what ways have families changed in their structure and practice. Even though families may seem like "messy puzzles," most Canadians work hard to build close, stable, and reliable unions.

Precisely because family relationships and structures remain vital to individuals and the state, we constantly debate intimacy and families—their form, their purpose, their consequences. We morally and socially regulate family behaviour by making this topic the theme of television shows and movies. *Entertainment Tonight* is full of nightly stories about individuals either obeying or defying the "rules" for intimate relations. Movies like *It's Complicated* and *Up in the Air* are morality tales reminding us of what happens to people who disregard and disrespect family units.

The ongoing argument about families and intimate relations continues in sociology as well. Carole Smart, a well-known British family sociologist, lists four ongoing, key debates in family sociology: the demise of the extended family and the rise of the nuclear family; the decline of marriage as an economic contract and the rise of companionate relationships (Stocks, Diaz, and Hallerod, 2007); the emergence of child-centredness as the role and status of children alters; and the decline of the nuclear family and the rise of fluid family practice (2007). As different forms of family arise, outdated forms decline and new debates emerge around acceptability, limitations, and boundaries of family behaviour.

The "family decline" argument comes from the structural demise of the archetypical 1950s, two-parent, heterosexual, white, middle-class family. Scholars have pointed out that this "old" form of family life actually began to change dramatically in the early 1900s and especially after the 1920s (Rotskoff, 2002). For most of the past century, the majority of Canadian families have not been able to exist on the earnings of one wage labourer, women and children have contributed to total family income, men have deserted families, and youth have stretched the law. Yet, still people declare that the decline of the intact two-parent family is responsible for our most pressing social problems. Youth crime, poverty, unwed teen mothers, and high school dropouts are attributed to family "breakdown." Coalitions to promote family values have sprung up that oppose shifts toward deinstitutionalizing marriage by opposing cohabitation, divorce, and single parenthood (Struening, 1996).

Anxiety around perceptions of family fragility reflect two trends: the fundamental untidiness of family relations and the new stresses placed on family members who cling to outdated units that are not flexible enough to adjust to contemporary demands (Coontz, 1997, 2005). Families face daily struggles to juggle the demands of two employed parents and raising children. Parents feel torn between the necessity to earn a living wage and their desire to spend time raising their children. Divorce rates have risen and male employment rates have fallen, meaning that women know it is risky to plan a life reliant on male wages. Extended schooling prolongs youth dependency, leaving far too many young adults underengaged for most of their 20s. They feel infantilized and frustrated with how long it takes to achieve economic independence.

These ongoing concerns result from shifting structural conditions including falling wages, precarious employment, and the decline of primary industries. Yet many prefer to see the shrinking of the two-parent family as both the source and solution to widespread social problems. In searching for answers to an ever-shifting landscape, odd political alliances have emerged. Conservatives support liberals when they rally behind policies designed to improve work–family balance, compress work weeks, improve work flexibility, reduce child poverty, keep the elderly in the labour force, subsidize day care, and bring in family tax credits (UNICEF, 2007). It is not that either group advocates a return to the 1960s-style traditional family—they know it is dead and gone—but both camps seem to hang onto vestiges of old ideals (Underwood, 2009).

FAMILY DISCOURSES

Even though family structures and practices have changed, "old" family ideologies persist in contemporary political and cultural debates. The fact that "ideals remain while structures collapse" amazes family sociologists who wonder how and why family discourses have achieved such power in our society. In what ways are the fundamental ideas and belief systems of particular family discourses continually attractive to individuals? What gratification and meaning do such ideas provide for those who embrace them? (Koenigsberg, 2009).

Defined as a dominant or hegemonic discourse, the grand narrative of **familialism** provides a cultural and social definition of what families are and should be. As both an ideology and a set of customary practices, familialism constitutes the "heart and soul" of our culture. We are united within society by virtue of the fact that we share this ideology or belief system (Koenogsberg, 2009). Traditionalism and familialism go hand in hand. Even though families are constructed in a wide variety of ways through the ongoing actions of their members, and even though we know that family forms shift and change over time, ideologically we cling to a set of beliefs about how families ought to behave and what members can expect to receive from intimate relationships (Gittins, 1985).

For instance, **monogamy**, the notion that one man should be married to one woman, does not exist in many cultures and, in our society, it is a principle often violated. Romantic love teaches us to believe there is one person with whom we will now spend fifty or sixty years. Yet when we go back a few hundred years, we see that the idea of love as the basis for marriage is a relatively recent idea and that, in the past, shortened life expectancies meant many were brief arrangements (Bauman, 2000 a, b).

Another hegemonic idea is that families are supposed to be nonviolent, supportive, and nurturing. Yet, abuse statistics indicate that both immediate and extended families frequently violate these standards. The 2009 movie *Precious* about an African American adolescent raped by her father and abandoned by the traditional school system revealed the underside of family life. Furthermore, Western notions of families occupying single physical spaces and of children being raised by biological mothers are contested through transnational and other mothering practices (Reyes, 2002). In our world, families are frequently ripped apart by war and migration. The 2010 earthquake in Haiti is a horrifying example of children being torn apart from parents and grandparents, as well-meaning and not so well meaning agencies moved children out of the country into new homes.

Dominant Western, white, and middle-class ideals of place, space, and intimacy turn out to be social constructions, norms that are more important as ruling ideas than they are as indicators of people's actual behaviour (Gittins, 1985). In the 1960s, families were seen as refuges from the busy world of work. Clear boundaries existed between the public world of work and the private world of the family, with masculinity being associated with the public and femininity with the private. "Real" men provided a **family wage** that supported a wife and dependent family members while "real" women stayed at home, stoking the home fires. This was an objective adopted by male trade unionists at the turn of the nineteenth century in their fight for improved wages. It is based on the argument that a wage should be sufficient to maintain a wife and children. There was considerable female support for this view—although nowadays it is often cited as a factor in explanations of women's disadvantaged position in the labour market.

Even though the reality was far from the ideal—women always contributed to household income and few men earned a family wage—the ideals remained, enshrined in romantic novels and films.

In 2010, dominant ideas of family life have been updated to take account of social changes in the economy and in personal life. While both "home" and "work" are recognized as potential sites for achieving individual autonomy and personal well-being, personal relationships in "home settings" take precedence as avenues for individuals to better themselves, to become more liberated, and to enter into life-enhancing intimate relations. Families are now supposed to function as quasi-encounter groups where individuals' deepest personal expectations can be expressed and achieved (Rotskoff 2002). Intimate relationships are supposed to provide members with psychic fulfillment as well as opportunities for self-improvement.

Yet still, the personal clashes with the collective. Individuals have to put aside their personal desires and contribute to the collective enterprise of building families and earning a living. Contemporary families are not only semi-encounter groups but also mobile economic units battling larger structural forces beyond their control. Because of the contradiction between reality and the ideal, and because social and economic conditions continue to shift, debates about the purpose and meaning of families remain. Static definitions of families represent little more than stereotypes or overarching archetypes of what society considers normative.

THEORIZING FAMILIES

Determinism

Theoretical approaches to studying family remain closely tied to contemporary political debates. Theories become ascendant and popular when what they are arguing fits with prevailing political views and empirical reality. During the post–World War II period, modernist, or what we call **determinist**, theories dominated sociology. Beginning with structural functionalism in the 1950s and closely followed by materialism or political economy, these two determinist theories see individual behaviour as a result of social structures, including social institutions, laws, and norms. Family structures are seen as determining individual behaviour within families. If something is wrong with an individual's actions, according to functionalists, the family structure is to blame and, according to materialists, the economy is the culprit. Solving family problems requires altering both family structures and the social conditions within which they exist.

For determinists, families are arenas in which members define and contextualize their assigned roles as providers, consumers, and managers of emotional and material resources (Rotskoff, 2002). Families fulfill a number of functions including attempting to secure the psychic and financial well-being of dependent children, elderly, and persons living with disabilities; socializing the young by shaping their values and behaviours so that they conform to social expectations; and providing people with an explanation of their rights and obligations within an institution in which personal identities are closely tied with family roles.

Even though broad functions of families can be delineated, there exists in any society a wide variety of ways in which family roles and relationships can be taken up and organized. How families accomplish family life is recognized as a lifelong process of socialization through which units acquire their characterization and distinction from one another. We give moral labels to certain types of families, calling them "fractured," "dysfunctional," "beloved," or "reliable" depending on how closely they approximate social norms. We then define and put into place social practices and helping institutions designed to shove and pull the so-called non-normative family back into line.

Family ideals spill over into other social institutions. Materialists argue that the closer a family approximates a middle-class, economically secure place, the more opportunity members of that unit have to "live the ideal." Studies of children's school behaviour reveals how white and middle-class ideas of performance and family support prop up achievement (Walkerdine and Lucey, 1989; Skeggs 1997; Lareau, 2003). Class, for example, produces expectations about student accomplishment. Students respond with classed, raced, and gendered school performances that are "good enough" to earn the respect of parents and community (Brah and Phoenix, 2004). Schooling studies consistently demonstrate the ways in which homes of higher social class breed efficacy in children—a belief in their ability to overcome obstacles and a knowledge of how to do so. Class assurance propels certain students through the school system and onto higher-paying jobs. In this way, the achievement of both mediocre and high-ranking students from high–social class homes ends up legitimating their child-rearing practices while, at the same time, delegitimating those of other families.

Feminism, Antiracism, and Intersectionality

Feminist, antiracist, and intersectional arguments took hold in family studies during the 1960s and 1970s, beginning with the argument that all families are social and ideological constructions. Feminism built on the materialist or political economy perspective, which critiqued structural functionalism and rendered families as problematic (Smart, 2007).

Feminists exposed women's private life as a site for the production and reproduction of oppressive and subordinate relationships. Socialist or **materialist feminists** saw women's inequality within the family as mirroring their inequality within society. Their maternal roles as nurturing caretakers pushed them away from economic independence, thus guaranteeing their dependence on male wages for subsistence. As dependent subordinates, women left themselves open to potential financial, emotional, and physical mistreatment.

Between the 1970s and the 1990s, feminist and materialist arguments influenced family studies. As women moved en masse into the labour force and made heroic attempts to balance paid and unpaid labour, theorists made equally concerted attempts to figure out how to dismantle unequal family structures. Debates about the role of social and cultural reproduction and of the unpaid work of women propping up the state blended with narratives about practical issues of arranging affordable childcare, providing care for seniors, and helping secure economically marginalized families.

Antiracist and queer theories emerged in the early 1970s from a critique of mainstream, heterosexual, white feminism. This critique extended to family sociology, which was exposed as promoting through its discourses of familialism a cultural ideal that few Canadian families experienced. Again, media was influential in paving the way to more nuanced understandings of sexual and racial/ethnic complexity. Shows such as *Arrested Development* and *Two and a Half Men* are now mainstream but in the 1970s, few would have dared to feature families with biracial children, same-sex parents, or interreligiously married parents.

As family sociology tried to build on antiracist and queer principles, theorists introduced notions of intersectionality to capture the complex interplay between structures and practices of gender, class, sexuality, age, ability, and race. **Intersectionality** claims that there cannot be an understanding of family ideology without also understanding how these structures shape family performances. As Andersen and Collins (1995) state, race, class, and gender "matter" because they structure interactions, opportunities, consciousness, ideology, and forms of resistance. McCall (2005) argued that an intersectional analysis was crucial to understanding how the projects of nationalism and colonialism were promoted through the intersection of race, class, and gender (Brah and Phoenix, 2004).

Postmodernism

Feminist theories and, more recently, theories of individualization and intersectionality, have complicated determinist theoretical framings in fascinating ways. First, recent changes in biomedical and reproductive technologies as well as the field of genetics have literally transformed the nature of kinship away from the strictly biological to more social definitions. Inheritance and relatedness are no longer biologically based; children are born of surrogates, by fertilization outside the body (in vitro fertilization), and by the use of donated third-party gametes (eggs or sperm). Who is related to whom? How? What role does biology play in forming family relationships? As the relationship between the biological and the social becomes less obvious in defining families, kinship becomes separated from biology. But, as Featherstone et al. (2006) conclude, this does not mean that most Canadian families experience postmodern kinship. For most Canadians, everyday family relations are less exotic (ibid.) and "family" still connotes biological connectedness and/or physical place (Smart, 2007).

Second, critiques of modernity have greatly influenced family studies. Concepts of liquidity, postmodernity, and individualization see the old chains of family bonds loosened as individuals focus their attention on individual agency, freedom of expression, and the search for enhancement. Women and men are praised for their individual accomplishments achieved through work or leisure or in relationships but they are not praised for subordinating their desires to those of others in their families. Family studies leapt on to the individualization bandwagon, emphasizing agency, choice, diversity, and multiplicity as key ideas fashioning postmodern families. Queer studies highlighted the existence of "families of choice"; life course theories proposed "individuation" to explain the prolongation of certain stages in the life course; and social constructionists cited the lack of emotional fulfillment in intimate relationships as an explanation for the rising divorce rate.

Theories of Personal Life   Since the beginning of the 2000s, disenchantment with postmodernity has grown. **Postmodernism** hailed the death of grand narratives. Yet the hegemonic discourse of familialism has remained a dominant cultural narrative of our time, managing to successfully reproduce and maintain itself through all forms of social and moral regulation: popular culture, state policies, changing marriage laws, and individual actions.

Not only has this discourse endured, but also attempts to discredit it have not succeeded because they have failed to capture the complexity and continuity of family life. Moreover, postmodern risk and individualization theories have been criticized as meshing too closely with the neoliberal ideologies and goals of Western capitalism (Smart, 2007). While there may be a decline in traditional regulative traditions (Pateman and Gross, 1987), there nonetheless remains a core of cultural constraints shaping family decisions. Global economies demand flexible family forms: heterosexual, gender-differentiated families are simply dysfunctional in a global economy that requires workers to be flexible, transportable, and of either sex. People still search for close connections through longstanding relationships whether they call these arrangements "marriages" and whether or not they are formally and publicly legalized. Policies propping up long-term relationships that protect the rights of involved parties and provide for dependants render state laws irrelevant. A marriage contract is often seen as dispensable and therefore doesn't guarantee anything anymore so many people simply don't bother.

Functionalist explanations of family behaviour operated on its description of the complementary and reciprocal social roles of men and women within families: men were breadwinners and women were caretakers. Once feminists and materialists discredited this claim and revealed the inequality and dysfunctionality of this system, determinism was eclipsed as the leading theoretical perspective in family sociology (Featherstone et al., 2006). Having forever altered how we understood family life, feminists and materialists were then left with a perplexing contradiction between affection and inequality. Even though families seem to be inherently unequal, people continue to flock to them. Stymied by this contradiction and devoid of fresh theoretical outlooks, studying families became unpopular and marginalized within the discipline (Smart, 2007).

Sociologists may have been temporarily stalled in theorizing families but families themselves continued to fracture and reassemble in new and innovative ways. Smart (2007) has been at the forefront in arguing for new ways to think about family life. She sees postmodern risk and individualization theories as wholly inadequate to capture the range, fluidity, and complexity of intimate relationships. Instead, she advocates focusing on family processes— what families do, rather than what they think they should do—as a way to understand the interaction between family structures and individual behaviours. Reconceptualizing family relations using terms such as "kinship," "families of choice," "multiple households," and "personal choice" represent attempts to capture family change (Smart, 2007). Focusing on family processes of embeddedness, relatedness, and connectivity reveals how individuals relate to one another and, through these interactions, create society. By understanding these family processes, we come to know the changed reality of family life (Fieldhouse, 2008). Let us now turn to an overview of some of these contemporary family processes.

CONTEMPORARY FAMILY TRENDS

When we look at a snapshot of Canadian families, we see that the norm remains legal marriage of opposite-sex partners with one or more children living at home. About 82 percent of all couple families are married, while 18 percent are common-law. The more children there are living at home, the more likely it is that the couple is married.

Of the 8.9 million families in Canada in 2006

- 39 percent were married with children at home (most two-parent units with one or more children)

- 30 percent were married with no children at home (many are baby boomers)

- 7 percent were common-law couples with children at home (longtime cohabitators who had not married)

- 9 percent were common-law couples with no children at home (first conjugal unions as a prelude to marriage).

These statistics tell us that 8 out of 10 children under 20 years of age live in a couple family (married or common-law). As the baby boomers move into retirement and live longer, obviously there are more families without children living at home.

While significant, these statistics hide the changing diversity of family life. By 2017, when Canada will celebrate its 150th anniversary, approximately one out of every five people will be members of a visible minority (95 percent of whom will live in urban areas), a greater proportion of partnerships will be cohabitating, an increasing number of families will be old, and many units will not contain children. (Statistics Canada, 2006).[1] Canadian families are increasingly urban, ethnically diverse units. The varying composition of families as well as the rapid pace of social change affecting family formation both require that we take a closer look at some of the dramatic shifts in family life.

Racialized Families

Racialization refers to processes by which individuals and groups of people are viewed through a racial lens and through a culturally invented racial framework, and come to be defined as different and are subjugated to unequal and differential treatment. How do these larger social forces shape the lives of family members?

In the 1901 Census, about 25 different ethnic groups were reported living in Canada. In contrast, in the 2006 Census, about 200 different ethnic origins were reported. In 1901, people who reported Aboriginal ancestries and British and French origins comprised the largest share of the population with the most frequent groups being English, Scottish, Irish, German, Italian, Chinese, North American Indian, Ukrainian, and Dutch. In the 2006 Census, the range of ethnic diversity is vastly wider (Daily 2006). Visible minorities now constitute over 5 million Canadians representing about 16.2 percent of the total population in Canada. Projections indicate that by 2017, about one-fifth of the total Canadian population will be visible minority (Statistics Canada, 2005).

Source countries for immigration have also changed. Thirty years ago—in 1981—68.5 percent of all recent immigrants (landed immigrants who came to Canada up to five years prior to a given census year) were born in regions other than Europe. Fully 75 percent of immigrants arriving in Canada between 2001 and 2006 belonged to a visible-minority group. Of these groups, the largest are South Asians (well over 1 million), Chinese (well over 1 million), and Black (just above three-quarters of a million) with Filipinos, Latin Americans, Arabs, Southeast Asians, West Asians, Koreans, and Japanese following.

Our Canadian family literature is woefully slight in researching, discussing, and thinking about how the complexity of family life is enriched and shaped by the wide range of languages, cultures, and backgrounds constituting family life. While we have a significant body of literature examining the gendered nature of family life, there is less information on how gender and race interact to construct family relationships (Wallis and Kwok, 2008) (see for example Box 1.1).

BOX 1.1   MAD MEN

Parenting is a result of cultural definitions of femininity, masculinity, children, and families, all of which shift over time to create new patterns and understandings. Nowhere is this more apparent than in the iconic television program *Mad Men*, which is a period piece reflecting mores and values of 1960s North America—your parents' generation! Here, men are positioned as primary breadwinners earning a "family wage," which entitles their wives to remain at home full-time caring for children. Not only do men smoke and drink at work, but also women smoke while pregnant and caring for children who, unrestrained by seatbelts, romp back and forth from the front to the back seats of cars. Single women are rarely promoted beyond secretaries in the workplace, racism deeply divides society, and homosexuality is hidden away in closets especially since so many gay men are married. We watch this program as a way to gain some understanding of how far our ideas of masculinity, femininity, work, and home have shifted in 50 years. It allows us a perspective from which to understand the ways in which contemporary gendered parenting reflects both persistently hegemonic norms while also subtly and slowly shifting traditional definitions as women and men take up new practices.

Despite the constant evolution of family norms and practices, achieving approval for new versions causes social consternation. One of the reasons for *Mad Men*'s high approval ratings lies in its portrayal of outdated ideas concerning the roles of men, women, and children in constructing families. Being able to view the "old" familialism at play in the 1960s allows us to see precisely the ways in which the "new" familialism functions. We laugh at the sole male breadwinner role, feel embarrassed by the rampant homophobia and racism, and get impatient with the subordinate position played by women. Since pernicious elements continue to exist, in family studies we aim to deconstruct contemporary versions.

Transnational Families

Immigration has altered family construction and processes. One of the most significant shifts has been the increase in transnational families. **Economic globalization**—the mass movement of peoples around the world in search of work—and capitalism—the neoliberal consolidation of global resources—force individuals to put aside their personal desires and contribute to the collective enterprise of building families and earning a living. One of the most significant consequences of economic globalization has been the increase in **transnational families**. Defined as the dispersion of families, nuclear or extended, across international borders, it results in different family members spending time in one or the other country depending on various factors. Transnational families owe their existence to the rise of communication and transportation technologies, economic transformations, and cultural features in their countries of origin.

Many people of colour, especially women, migrate to perform coerced forms of paid care work for others (Zajicek et al, 2006). Ehrenreich and Hochschild (2003) suggest there is a global care chain characterized by a series of personal links between people across the globe based on their paid and unpaid care work. Central to this the global mass movement is the relocation of married women to other countries to care for other people's children. Mothering from afar brings its own challenges, regrets, and accomplishments but it definitely leaves many families relying on "other mothering" to replace biological mothers.

The creation of transnational families, as well as transferring labour, also transfers money. Approximately 4 in 10 immigrants who arrived in Canada during 2000/2001 sent money to family or friends abroad at least once during their first four years in the country with average amounts of around $2,500 (Houle and Schellenberg, 2008). The highest proportion came from immigrants from the Philippines and Haiti with the lowest amount among those from France, the United Kingdom, and South Korea (ibid.). According to the World Bank figures for 2004, remittances represent an important source of revenue for people in developing countries, especially in Haiti, Lesotho, Jordan, Jamaica, the Philippines, and the Dominican Republic (ibid.). Men send more money than women and those between the ages of 25 to 44 are more likely to send money abroad, in higher amounts, than those in younger or older age groups (ibid.).

Partnerships Are Flourishing

About half of the Canadian population over the age of 15 was legally married in 2006, which amounts to 12.4 million Canadians (see for example Box 1.2). This figure includes both same- and opposite-sex units. Another 10.5 percent of Canadians (2.8 million) were also living in **common-law** unions.

BOX 1.2   HOOKING UP OVER THE INTERNET

Are you frequenting online dating services to find the perfect mate? The North American online dating market is expected to increase spending to $932 million in 2011(comScore, 2009). With over 900 lifestyle and dating sites online, the Internet has become big business (ibid). Flitter, Facebook, My Space, and Twitter are part of a growing use of what sociologists call information communication technologies (ICTs). The Internet has become the fastest way to reconnect households, find lost neighbours, search out ancestors, and find permanent partners.

Many individuals believe that the Internet allows them to control the dating process. Instead of hanging out in bars, or at sports events, parties, or community gatherings, they decide what sites to visit and what information to post. Information is filtered by what the site allows and by what individuals decide to disclose (Vitzthum, 2007). Many Internet dating sites match people by age, race, sexual orientation, or religion. Individuals filter the kind of person they are looking for by setting preferences for gender, sexuality, age, marital status, education, physical dimensions, and lifestyle.

Internet dating saves time. Many people do not have to time to go out and find partners. Surfing a dating site can be done alone, at home, on their own time. The movie "You've Got Mail" (1998) provides a classic example of the Internet as marriage broker. Having established an online conversation through e-mail, the two main characters—played by Meg Ryan and Tom Hanks—arrange to meet to see if they like each other in person as much as they do in virtual reality. Internet dating has opened up a global mating market. Electronic, mass communication spreads shared information, facilitating communication across borders. Through e-mails, webcasts, online chat, telephone chat through voice over Internet phones (Skype) and message boards, individuals can now hook up around the world.

This means that in 2006, the latest Canadian census, close to 60 percent of the population were in partnerships.

Many of these unions remain opposite-sex, legally married units but an increasing number are same-sex, biracial, and common-law. In Canada, there are 45,350 same-sex couples. Seventeen percent of same-sex couples are legally married, while the remaining 83 percent are living common-law. While commitment to intimate partnership remains, Canadians are freer to arrange partnerships of their choosing without fear of moral sanction.

The average age at which people first marry (28 for women and 30 for men) has grown older. Most Canadians marry once by the time they are age 50 but, even so, marriage rates are slipping across the country and especially among lower socioeconomic groups even as they are rising among the highly educated (Huston and Meltz, 2004). If individuals are not marrying their partners, then does this mean an increasing number are single for life or simply living with their partners? Both trends are occurring. More child-rearing-aged women are remaining never married while, at the same time, more couples are opting for informal living arrangements.

A few decades ago, living with an individual without being formally married was considered taboo. Yet in the past 20 years, common-law unions have more than doubled. Does this mean that cohabitation is replacing marriage? One of the reasons for the widespread emergence of cohabitation as a permanent conjugal form seems to lie in the cultural shift in attitudes toward partnership. No longer is formal marriage considered necessary as a form in which to raise children since divorce laws offer protection to those who live common-law. If we look to Quebec, an area where common-law is more widespread and acceptable, we see that nearly two-thirds (63 percent) of those whose home language was French were willing to live common-law compared with 46 percent of those who speak English at home. Reasons cited include increasing individualism, liberal views, and lower formal religious commitment (Milan, 2003).

A second consequence of living together is that it has come to be recognized as a new conjugal state, a stage in a prolonged courtship process in which individuals first live together and then go on to formally marry their partners. Reginald Bibby, a family sociologist, surveyed Canadians and discovered three reasons for the prevalence of marriage following cohabitation: the first is the feeling that *marriage signifies commitment* (93 percent), the second is *moral values* (85 percent), and the third is the *belief that children should have married parents* (77 percent). Somewhat smaller majorities of about 6 in 10 Canadians say that marriage was or is *"just the natural thing to do,"* that *financial security* is an important consideration, and that *religious beliefs* were or are a motivating factor. Relatively small numbers say that pressure from either family or friends was or is a major influence in wanting to marry (Bibby, 2004).

Gay Marriage and Parenting

According to the 2006 Census, same-sex couples represent 0.6 percent of all couples in Canada living in either marital or common-law relationships (Statistics Canada, 2006). Quebec has the largest proportion of same-sex couples and half of all same-sex couples live in three cities: Toronto, Montreal, and Vancouver (The Daily, 2010).

About 9 percent of persons in same-sex couples have children under the age of 24 living at home, a figure that no doubt underrepresents the total number of children being raised in gay families as many gay people have a child living with them even though they are not partnered (ibid.).

Canadians have unprecedented family recognition laws with legal recognition of same-sex marriage, same-sex adoption laws, and the recognition that some children have three parents (Tipper, 2009). Yet, at the same time, in parts of Canada hostility remains toward queer parents, those who identify as lesbian, gay, bisexual, transgender, transsexual, or queer (LGBTTQ) (ibid.). Unbelievably, apparently half the population continues to believe that gays and lesbians should be denied the right to parent (ibid.).

Interreligious Unions

As cultural diversity increases across the country, so too do interreligious unions. In 1981, only 15 percent of Canadian couples intermarried but by 2001, this figure increased to 19 percent of couples (cohabiting or married). This means that approximately 2.7 million Canadians had a partner from a different religious group. The two largest religious groups in Canada are Protestants and Catholics. Thus, it is not surprising that over half, or 1.3 million people, of the religious intermarriages were between these two groups. Rates of Jewish intermarriage have doubled from about 9 percent in 1981 to around 17 percent in 2001 (The Daily, Oct. 3, 2006).

Groups who have arrived in Canada between 1991 and 2001—mostly Muslims, Hindus, and Sikhs—are less likely to intermarry, maintaining instead the strong marital traditions of their countries of origin. Muslims who do interreligiously marry are likely to choose a Catholic partner (Clarke, 2006).

Choosing a Partner

Even though courtship has altered, men and women cite fairly traditional reasons as being important in choosing partners. First, homogeneity reigns, meaning "like tend to marry like." We still choose partners from a narrow geographic area, from similar racial/ethnic groups, from similar religious backgrounds, and from comparable educational backgrounds (South, 1991).

Both sexes are what Crompton (2005) calls "mercenary" in their approach to marriage in that women and men would prefer to marry someone who earns more money and has more education than themselves but would not really consider accepting someone who has trouble keeping a steady job, has children, or has been married already.

Women generally want a wealthy, socially stable man and men want an attractive younger woman with whom they are able to have children. Other factors—such as being of a different religion, much younger, not good looking, or having less education—fall somewhere in between and assume more or less importance depending on the attractiveness of the candidate's other qualities (Crompton, 2005). Reality television show such as The Bachelor are popular because they reveal these partnership choices.

Mature Singles Who Do Not Expect to Marry

Single refers to being never married, widowed, divorced, or separated. Mature singles who have chosen to remain single represent two distinct groups: the "seriously single" who are committed to remaining single and the rest who stay single for other reasons (Connidis, 2010).

Singlism refers to the stereotyping and discrimination of people who are single including those who are divorced, widowed, or who have never been married. Since marriage represents the foundation of North American society and politics, the resulting system of discrimination against the nonmarried pervades social, economic, and cultural beliefs. Cultural attitudes associate "single" with loneliness, homosexuality, and/or a personal defect that prevents a single person from achieving marriage. State policies discriminate against single persons through increased tax burdens, decreased social security benefits, and wage disparities.

Singlism refers to a largely uncontested set of beliefs—familialism—which assumes that the sexual partnership is the one truly important peer relationship and that people who have such relationships are happier and more fulfilled than those who do not (DePaulo and Morris, 2005). In fact, people who are single, especially women who have always been single, fare better than the ideology would predict because they do have positive, enduring, and important interpersonal relationships.

The persistence of singlism remains perplexing given the growth in the number of singles. In 2002, of the 1.1 million mature singles in Canada, about half—550,000—did not expect to marry. This group is similar to mature singles who do plan to marry but they differ in some key ways: many are lone parents, their incomes tend to be lower, and they tend to be less well educated. Men and women who do not believe that being part of a couple is important hold unconventional views of marriage and family and are therefore less likely to seek out unions (Crompton, 1994).

If not married by their early 50s, women are 13 times more likely to never marry than unmarried women aged 35 to 39. This does not mean that this group of "never marrieds" have not lived in conjugal relationships or common-law nor does it mean that they do not value couplehood. Research consistently shows that the vast majority of Canadians continue to hold very traditional views about love, marriage, and having children (Vanier Institute, 2004). Most mature single women and men have lived with others and even though they do not expect to marry, they still rate being part of a couple as "important" or "very important" to their happiness, more so than actually being married (Crompton, 2005).

Why Have Kids?

Since 2000, the fertility rate in Canada has been on a slight rise, due to the increasing number of women over age 30 having children. But even still, as a small nation, Canada does not produce enough children to replace our current population, meaning we rely heavily on immigration to replenish the population. Current trends suggest that, on average, women in Canada will have 1.59 children over the course of their lives. The number of children per family has dropped (only 10 percent of all families have three or more children living at home) but having children remains a priority (Ruddick, 1995).

Children are not economic assets to families as they may have been in the past. Estimates are that to raise a child to age 18 costs about $250,000! Given how expensive children are and how conflicted parents seem to be in attempting to juggle paid and unpaid labour, why have children? According to Robert

Glossop (2008), former director of the Vanier Institute, people have children to satisfy certain kinds of emotional and psychological needs and desires including passing on family traditions, intergenerational sharing of values, transmission of particular ways of life, intimacy and attachment, and having someone who survives us and thus remembers us.

Despite promises for cost-effective childcare and increased flexibility in work–family balance, the state continues to see children as a private, personal matter (Glossop, 2008).Whatever the costs, hardships, or delights children bring, parents remain responsible for their well-being, including their education and launching to adulthood.

Older Mothers

Women are delaying childbirth. Thirty years ago, the average age for first-time mothers was 22 years. Now the average age is 28 years. The trend toward higher maternal ages means that the fertility rate among women aged 30 to 34 is now higher than it is for women aged 25 to 29 (Wheeler, 2008). Moreover, 8.9 percent of women aged 40 to 44 are mothers of preschool children, reflecting the rising education level of women across the country (Vezina and Turcotte, 2009). Occupations with the highest proportion of older mothers with preschool children are those that require a high level of skill and education, including physicians, dentists, veterinarians, judges, lawyers, and Quebec notaries (ibid.).

Aside from increasingly higher levels of education, what else accounts for delayed childbirth? Other factors include finding a partner and securing employment. The economic restructuring that began in the 1970s and was exacerbated by the 2008–09 recession tends to decrease the availability of well-paying jobs for men in the resource processing and manufacturing sectors while increasing the number of less well paying service sector jobs populated largely by females (Wheeler, 2008).

The shift toward higher maternal age has significant implications for health and development (Bushnik and Garner, 2008). Studies have found that delayed motherhood is associated with higher educational achievement, less involvement in crime, less substance abuse and mental health problems at age 18, and more nurturing and stable home environments. In short, advanced maternal age has a positive impact on the life opportunities available to offspring. However having children after age 35 exposes children to more prenatal and perinatal risk factors.[2]

Childless-by-Chance and by Choice

While 7 percent of Canadians aged 20 to 34 stated in the 2001 General Social Survey that they did not intend to have children (child-free by choice), an even greater number of women—by a ratio of almost two to one—become childless by circumstance (Wheeler, 2008). The longer a woman waits before having a first child, the less likely a second child becomes because the odds that she will become infertile in the meantime increase.

Childless-by-chance families have received very little attention in the literature largely because we have yet to grapple with the effects of delayed first-time motherhood. Of those childless by circumstance, sexually transmitted diseases (STDs) of chlamydia and gonorrhea account for the largest proportion of acquired infertility followed by endometriosis, a condition that increases with age.

In 2006, Canadians adopted 1,535 children from abroad, a drop from previous years. Each year in Canada, there are about 1,700 public adoptions (public agency matches a child with you; there are long waits and no fees) and 1,000 private adoptions (you find a child or a birthmother chooses you with the help of a private agency; it is difficult to find healthy newborns and the process can be very costly) that take place.[3]

Single Mothers

While 62 percent of children live with two parents, lone-parent families are on the rise, 80 percent of which are female headed (Statistics Canada, 2006). In the past, single mothers were often poor due to their relative youth, lack of access to male wages, and their lower earnings in the labour force. But older motherhood and higher postsecondary educational achievement levels acquired by women have begun to pay off in the form of higher earnings (Statistics Canada 2008). Even so, the vast majority of single-earner households struggle to make ends meet and single moms face considerable hurdles in juggling work and family demands.

Can Men Mother?

In 2000, the federal government extended parental leave from six months to one year. One in 10 fathers now takes a formal employment leave to be home with his newborn, which is a statistically and socially significant change (Marshall, 2006). Approximately one in 10 fathers takes parental leave while in Quebec, about 50 percent of fathers take some time off through the province's unique offering of three to five weeks of paternity leave or "daddy's days" as they are called (Marshall, 2008).

In 2009, Andrea Doucet asked "Can men mother?" She defines parenting responsibility as being composed of three components: emotional, community, and moral. Emotional parenting includes nurturing tasks as it entails knowing and responding to others' needs; community responsibility refers to the administrative tasks of organizing, scheduling, and planning children's extra-domestic activities; and moral responsibility refers to individuals' feelings of how they should and ought to act as parents (ibid.).

According to Doucet (2009), there are gender differences in parenting. Men parent emotionally in ways largely indistinguishable from women except that they actively promote children's independence; even though men are especially involved with children's sports, they are more likely to leave the administration of children's activities to women unless forced or enabled to do so; and to feel responsible for, and judged by, their contributions to family earnings.

Even though household labour is less gendered than before, daily participation rates for housework continue to be significantly higher for women than for men (Sussman and Bonnell, 2006). Changes in the daily participation rate for core housework (meal preparation, meal cleanup, indoor cleaning, and laundry) are the most noticeable—40 percent to 59 percent for men and 88 percent to 85 percent for women. The proportion of some men doing some housework daily, such as making sandwiches for lunch, vacuuming, or taking out the garbage, increased from 72 percent in 1986 to 79 percent in 2005 (ibid.).

Two-Earner Households

More than 75 percent of families with children under the age of 18 have two working parents (Marshall, 2009). This means that only 15 percent of all couples have only the husband as the sole earner and 5 percent have the wife as a sole earner. More wives are now the primary breadwinners. In 1967, only 11 percent of wives earned more than their husbands did but by 2003, this proportion had tripled to nearly 29 percent (Statistics Canada, 2006).

Primary-earning wives are more likely to be better educated, be slightly older than their husbands, be employed full time and have more years of experience (ibid.). Average family incomes before income taxes are lowest for those with no earners ($41,700). Family incomes rise to an average $54,200 for families where the wife is the only earner and $66,800 if the husband is the only earner. When the two spouses have earnings, family incomes jump to $85,900.

Immigrant Families

Immigration has always been, and continues to be, vital to Canada's economic and cultural well-being. Roughly two-thirds of Canada's population growth comes from net international migration, which will account for virtually all net labour force growth by 2011 (Zietsma et al., 2008).

Lifetime earnings are closely related to education levels. In 2007, 37 percent or 1.2 million immigrants of core working age (25 to 54) had a university degree compared with only 22 percent of their Canadian-born counterparts. Overall, children of immigrants tend to achieve higher levels of education than children of Canadian-born parents. Asian youth, except for Filipinos, for example, have higher rates of obtaining a university degree by age 34 than most youth of European origin. University completion rates ranged from over 65 percent for youth of immigrant parents from China and India to 24th among second-generation German and Central and South American youth. In comparison, about 28 percent of children of Canadian-born parents had completed university by the time they were aged 25 to 34 (Daily, 2002).

Despite these high rates of education, university-educated immigrants aged 25 to 54 who arrived in Canada within the previous five years were less likely to be employed in 2007 than their Canadian-born counterparts

(Ostrosky, 2008). In 2007, the employment rate for these newcomers was 75.3 percent, much lower than the average of 90.7 percent for their Canadian-born, university-educated counterparts (Picot, Hous, and Coulombe, 2007).

Creating family requires secure and stable employment. Yet the economic welfare of immigrant families remains precarious despite their higher levels of education and their arrival as members of the skilled immigrant class. This situation has worsened for our most recent immigrants. Of those who arrived during the early 1990s, about 65 percent entered low income (were below the LICO) at some point during their first 10 years in Canada, largely during their first year in Canada.

Very recent immigrants (those who have been in Canada five years or less) who landed between 2001 and 2006 had the most difficulty integrating into the labour market even though they were more likely than the Canadian-born population to have a university education (Zietsma et al., 2008). In 2006, the national unemployment rate for these immigrants was 11.5 percent, more than double the rate of 4.9 percent for the Canadian-born population. The longer immigrants remain in the country, the better they fare in the labour market and the more the gap narrowed between them and Canadian-born workers (ibid.). Newcomers, it seems, need more time to adjust to labour market demands.

The employment rate for core working-age immigrants is well below that of their Canadian-born counterparts and the gap continues to rise (Ostrovsky, 2008). Of those who are employed, it is the more established immigrants, namely those who have been in Canada for more than 10 years, who experience employment growth. Similar to the Canadian-born, most employment growth for immigrants aged 25 to 54 was in the service sector. However, immigrants found jobs in transportation, accommodation, and food services while the Canadian-born were more likely to find jobs in public administration, profes-sional, scientific, and technical services as well as finance, insurance, real estate. and leasing (ibid., 2008). University-educated immigrants of core working age had the largest gains in immigrant employment. Among the various age groups, older immigrants aged 55 and over posted very strong gains while youth immigrants aged 15 to 24 had employment rates similar to the Canadian-born (Gilmore, 2008).

How do second-generation immigrant children fare? According to Palameta (2007), who examined income data for young men and women born in Canada to two immigrant parents between 1967 and 1982, the results are mixed. Young women with two immigrant parents had significantly higher hourly and annual earnings than young women with Canadian-born parents from 1999 to 2004. In contrast, young men, especially some visible-minority men with two immigrant parents, seemed to have a significant disadvantage in earnings compared to their peers with Canadian-born parents. By following this cohort, Palameta was able to see that young women retained their eco-nomic advantage because by the time they had reached ages 22 to 34, less than half of them were married and only about one-third had a child through birth or adoption. Interestingly, in contrast, over 60 percent of those with Canadian-born parents had been married and about half had had children. Visible-minority status seems to have no effect on the earnings of young second-generation women while it does seem to directly affect that of visible-minority men. Everything else being equal (education, jobs, location), their earnings were significantly lower than those of young men with Canadian-born parents (Palameta, 2007).

Rising Household Debt

Even with women taking on more hours in the paid labour force, household savings rates are at all-time lows. Rising household debts are creating financial instability in many Canadian households (Sauve, 2009). Spending has risen much faster than incomes as spending increased twice as fast (+24.4 percent) and total debt increased more than six times faster than incomes (+71 percent). In 2008, average hourly earnings were basically at the same level they were in the mid-1990s (ibid.). The 11.6 percent rise in average household income between 1990 and 2006 comes from more families members working longer hours (ibid.).

The severe recession in 2008–09 continues to plague families. With pension funds shrinking, employment opportunities decreasing, and costs continuing to rise, many households will collapse under the weight of escalating household debt (Lochhead and Tipper, 2009). Moreover, 7 out of 10 Canadians do not have a budget, according to a Bank of Montreal national survey, nor do they consider the current economic downturn sufficient incentive to create one (Nares, 2009). Sauve (2009) raises a fascinating question by asking whether and to what extent changes in public/government spending have affected spending and debt patterns within households. When spending is examined between 1999 and 2004, Canadians spent 45 percent more on education (mostly tuition) and 32 percent more on extended health care insurance and more on personal care, recreation, household furnishings, tobacco and alcohol, food, clothing, and shelter. As Sauve asks,

> If households are spending more on education, it is quite simply because governments are spending less. Did we really eliminate government deficit spending in the lead up to this recession, or did we simply "shift" it to the household level?

Adult Children Returning Home

"Boomerang kids" refers to young adults who return to their family home after an initial departure (Marshall, 2006). Added with the group who never leave for any extended period of time, there are also a sizeable number of young adults (about 60 percent aged 20 to 24) who live with their parents well into their 20s. Delayed transitions to adulthood are particularly common among males. Explanations for delayed departure include prolonged higher education, accumulation of debt, the temporary nature of jobs often held by young people, divorce, loss of employment, delayed formation of couples, the high cost of rent in urban areas, and changes in values and preferences (Turcotte, 2006a).

There has been much speculation about why adult children do not leave home upon adulthood or why some return home. Being unable to find stable employment has led to an increasing number of Canadians aged 20 to 29 living with their parents (43.5 percent in 2006) compared to their counterparts 25 years earlier (27.5 percent) (ibid.). A 2005 study by Statistics Canada shows that the "number of temporary jobs is clearly on the rise among newly hired employees," rising from 11 percent in 1998 to 21 percent in 2004 (Morissette and Johnson, 2005).

Another suggestion is that they do so to save money to buy a house. However, Turcotte (2006b) finds that there is little correlation between returning home at age 25 and the likelihood of owning a home in their 30s. The age at which adult children leave seems statistically significant. According to Turcotte (2006b), about two-thirds (67 percent) of young adults who leave the parental home at age 18 or 19 report owning their own home in their 30s. The proportion is almost three-quarters (74 percent) for those who leave at age 24 or 25. Among those who do not leave until they are 28 or 30 years old, about 61 percent own their own homes in their 30s. Beyond age 25, the later the age of departure, the lower their probability of being a homeowner in their 30s.

Fractured Families

Individuals continue to invest in marriage despite the odds of its success. Of those couples who married in 2004, close to 38 percent of marriages are expected to end in divorce before the 30th year of marriage. Cohabitation is even more risky with more than 50 percent of ending in dissolution within five years (Milan, 2003). Remarriages have a higher divorce risk than first marriages (Cherlin, 2009).

Nearly one in two divorces in Canada involves dependent children. About 10 percent of all Canadian children under the age of 12 are living in a stepfamily. What sort of contact do fathers have with their nonresident children? According to a recent Statistics Canada study (Oct. 29, 2007), about half of children up to the age of 11 saw their fathers frequently; 27 percent saw him at least every week, while 22 percent saw him every two weeks. The remainder (19 percent) had no paternal visits but had some contact by phone or mail. Two years after the initial data were gathered, researchers posed the same questions and found an interesting pattern: for about half the children, the frequency of paternal visits had altered. Fathers who regularly visited their children seldom lost contact while "absent" fathers in the first phase rarely initiated regular visits two years later (Ambert, 2005).

One extenuating factor is the frequent remarriage of fathers and mothers. Most formed unions following separation, often with individuals who also have children from an earlier union. Close to half of these newly constituted unions go on to have children of their own. Fathers who were less involved with their original children and start second families seem to invest more with the children with whom they live at the expense of those with whom they no longer live (Statistics Canada, 2007). However, fathers who were involved with their children following separation continue to be involved with their children regardless of whatever new family commitments they take on.

Aging Families

An aging tsunami is beginning to sweep the country. In 2006, over 4 million Canadians were over the age of 65. One out of every seven Canadians is now a senior citizen. Within a decade, seniors will outnumber children under age 14. The graying of the population derives from two revolutions: the longevity revolution and the declining birth rate. The average Canadian woman now has 1.5 children, far below replacement rate for the population. At the same time, average life expectancy has risen to 77.7 for men and 82.5 for women (Statistics Canada, 2006). There are over 1 million Canadians over the age of 80 and the proportion of frail elderly is expected to continue to climb.

Aging families represent a significant new family form about which we know very little. The elderly world is largely female, economically insecure, and single. Along with being financially strained, elderly families encounter caregiving issues. Research on care work indicates that senior women care for dependent senior men while dependent senior women are often institutionalized (Mandell and Wilson, 2010). Left understudied are care exchanges among grandchildren and grandparents, the emotional reciprocity involved in caregiving, the places and spaces within which care is provided, and the practical implications of providing care for the aging population.

Widowhood

Women and men are disadvantaged differently upon the death of a spouse. While both groups suffer emotionally, senior women are far more likely also to suffer financially than are senior men. Within the first year of widowhood, women's incomes decline by as much as 15 percent. Thereafter, senior widows, at every age, see their incomes decline continuously in the five years following the death of their husbands. In contrast, among men who lose their wives, five years after widowhood, their incomes were 5.8 percent higher than in the year before widowhood (The Daily, 2006). Loss of pension income plays a large role in the drop of widows' income while for widowers, loss of wives' income played a larger role in any decline in total family income they experience following the death of their partner (ibid.).

In a fascinating long-term study of the effects of psychological stress, the National Population Health Survey found that women aged 65 or older who had experienced significant psychological stress in the prior eight years were far more likely to die regardless of age, family and financial stress, level of education, major chronic diseases, smoking, weight, and use of alcohol.

Psychological stress includes frequent feelings of sadness, worthlessness, and hopelessness. Men seemed more vulnerable to the effects of chronic, degenerative conditions, notably heart diseases and cancer (Statistics Canada, 2009).

THE FUTURE OF CANADIAN FAMILIES

Families remain important to Canadians as long as they retain the freedom to construct them in ways that suit their needs and desires. This includes not marrying, not necessarily having children, cohabitating or marrying same-sex partners, raising children alone, and foregoing biological families in lieu of friends (Bibby, 2004). Moreover, the population's age structure shapes family structures. For example, the closure of many elementary schools is directly related to the decline in the youth and young adult populations in the 1990s and the declining number of families being formed (Sauve, 2003). The notion of "working to death" (Mandell et al., 2010) comes from the increase in the number of aging workers remaining in the labour force well past the "traditional" retirement age of 65 years. With the aging population, family questions will arise as to the types of communities of care that may evolve in the future to resolve questions of intimacy, resource sharing, and caregiving.

CONCLUSION

Canadian families have shifted in function and form over the past few decades. Yet, theories about family formation seem to be taking longer to catch up to changes in family life. In this chapter, we have introduced some basic statistical trends outlining contemporary family life with the hope that students will focus on these recent trends in order to gain a better understanding of the diversity and complexity of Canadian families. We need to look to these trends as a way to predict future behaviour and to ensure that policy decisions reflect consistent patterns. Families never stay the same. Fortunately, they change shape and direction in order to reflect societal, cultural, and personal demands. In this way, understanding family change provides us with a solid grasp of larger social trends. In the rest of this book, authors concentrate on certain outstanding issues in family life in order to demonstrate emergent trends. We hope you enjoy reading these next chapters!

Summary

- Canadian families are diverse units.
- Families change formation and structure as material conditions alter.
- Nuclear families have almost disappeared.
- Traditional ideologies of families are no longer relevant.
- Age, gender, race, sexuality, (dis)ability, and economics continue to shape family structures and relationships.

Notes

1. With a population of 33.8 million in 2009, 80 percent of Canadians live in urban areas, two-thirds of whom live in six urban areas: Toronto, Montreal, Vancouver, Ottawa-Gatineau, Calgary or Edmonton.

2. Advanced maternal age is significantly associated with a higher proportion of children considered late achievers in sitting up by themselves and well as scoring lower on motor and social development scales at ages 0 to 1 and 2 to 3. They also had lower positive behaviour scores at ages 4 and 5.

3. There are also about 66,000 children in foster care and about 22,000 of those children are considered permanent wards (i.e., Crown wards in which the rights of the parents have been terminated by the courts) (Family Helper; Adoption and Fertility, http://www.familyhelper.net).

Critical Thinking Questions

1. Draw up a list of family members whom you communicate with and see, how often you communicate with or see them, under what circumstances, and how close to you they live. Include all forms of communication such as e-mail, texting, phone calls, and visits.

2. Draw up a list of personal and social issues with which you are currently or have recently dealt. With whom do you discuss these issues? To whom do you turn for support? How many of these people are family members? Why or why not would you seek out a family member? What does this tell us about the function of families?

3. Define both the old and the new familialism.

4. Theorizing families is a political and social process. Define this statement. Provide examples from three different theoretical perspectives to prove your thesis.

5. Choose three contemporary family trends that have led to the emergence of new family forms. Point out the ways in which these patterns have changed the nature of Canadian families.

Websites

Families Count—Profiling Canada's Families, 4th edition, eBook
http://www.vifamily.ca
   This book is available as an ebook on the Vanier Institute website. This is one of the Vanier Institute's most popular data books on Canadian families. Full of interesting and up-to-date information on all the latest trends on family patterns and trends, it contains a wealth of charts, tables, and commentary identifying trends, successes, and challenges facing contemporary families.

International Day of Families
http://www.un.org/esa/socdev/family/IDF.html
> May 15th is the International Day of Families as declared by the United Nations General Division for Social Policy and Development. This global, annual day reveals the significance of families in society by promoting knowledge of issues related to families around the world.

The Lesbian, Gay, Bisexual, Transgender, Queer Parenting Website
http://www.lgbtqparentingconnection.ca
> To learn more about queer parenting, check this website for advice, resources, and references.

National Family Week
http://www.frp.ca
> Since 1985, the Canadian government has celebrated National Family Week by proclaiming it an official week. This website contains useful and up-to-date information on Canadian families.

OECD Family Database
http://www.oecd.org/els/social/family/database
> This international database provides cross-national indicators on the situation of families and children across the globe, including family outcomes and family policy.

Suggested Readings

Daniel Dagenais. 2008. *The (Un)making of the Modern family.* Vancouver: University of British Columbia Press.
> Translated into English by Jane Brierley, this important contribution explores contemporary trends shaping postmodern families in Quebec and the rest of Canada. Deconstructing old myths and stereotypes, the book tackles central questions of the work–family boundary, parenting, gender and sexuality, the conjugal relationship, and the French Canadian family.

Rachel Epstein (Ed). 2009. *Who's Your Daddy? And Other Writings on Queer Parenting.* Toronto: Sumach Press.
> This is an edited collection of 38 pieces of writing and interviews on various aspects of queer parenting. Through its wide assortment of contributions, the depth, richness, and tensions involved in queer parenting are revealed.

Charles B. Hennon and Stephan M. Wilson (Eds). 2008. *Families in a Global Context.* New York: Routledge.
> This diverse edited collection contains articles on family life in 17 countries including providing a rich comparative and detailed view of the complexity and significance of family life around the world.

Janet Stocks, Capitolina Diax, and Bjorn Hallerod. 2007. *Modern Couples Sharing Money, Sharing Life.* New York: Palgrave Macmillan.

A collection of essays written by a collaborative research team from Spain, Sweden, and the United States who did an international qualitative comparative study on how couples share their lives and manage their finances.

References

Ambert, A-M. 2005. "Cohabitation and Marriage: How Are They Related?" The Vanier Institute of the Family. http://www.vifamily.ca (accessed April 19, 2010).

Andersen, M.L. and P.H. Collins. 1995. *Race, Class and Gender: An Anthology,* 2nd ed. Belmont, CA: Wadsworth.

Bauman, Z. 2000a. *Liquid Love: On the Frailty of Human Bonds.* Cambridge, UK: Polity Press.

Bauman, Z. 2000b. *Liquid Modernity.* Cambridge, UK: Polity Press.

Bibby, R. 2004. *The Future Families Project: A Survey of Canadian Hopes and Dreams.* Ottawa: The Vanier Institute of the Family. December 2004. http://www.vifamily.ca/library/publications/futured.html (accessed March 23, 2010).

Brah, A. and A. Phoenix. 2004. "Ain't I a Woman? Revisiting Intersectionality." *Journal of International Women's Studies,* 5(3), 75–86.

Bushnik, T. and R. Garner. 2008. "The Children of Older First-Time Mothers in Canada: Their Health and Development." *Statistics Canada.* Catalogue no. 89-599-M-No. 005: Ottawa.

Cherlin, A. J. 2009. *The Marriage-Go-Round.* New York: Alfred A. Knopf.

Clarke, W. 2006. "Interreligious Unions in Canada." *Canadian Social Trends,* 82, 17–27.

ComScore, 2009. *The comScore 2009 Digital Review of the Year: A Recap of the Year in Canadian Digital Marketing.* http://www.comscore.com/layout/set/popup/Press_Events/Presentations_Whitepapers/2010/2009_Canada_Digital_Year_in_Review (accessed April 26, 2010).

Connidis, I.A. 2010. *Family Ties and Aging,* 2nd ed. Los Angeles: Pine Forge Press.

Coontz, S. 1997. *The Way We Really Are: Coming to Terms with America's Changing Families.* New York: Basic Books.

Coontz, S. 2005. *Marriage, a History: How Love Conquered Marriage.* New York: Penguin.

Crompton, S. 1994. "Adults Living Solo." *Perspectives on Labour and Income,* 6(4), 30–36.

Crompton, S. 2005. "Always the Bridesmaid: People Who Don't Expect to Marry." *Canadian Social Trends,* 77: 2–8.

The Daily, 2002. "Group Differences in Educational Attainment among the Children of Immigrants." *Analytical Studies Branch Research Paper Series,* http://www.statcan.gc.ca/dai-quo/index-eng.htm (accessed January 5, 2010).

The Daily, 2006. "2006 Census: Ethnic Origin, Visible Minorities, Place of Work and Mode of Transportation." http://www.statcan.gc.ca/daily-quotidien/080402/dq080402a-eng.htm (accessed January 5, 2010).

The Daily, 2010. "More Same-sex Couples Being Counted." http://www.statcan.gc.ca/dai-quo/index-eng.htm (accessed January 5, 2010).

DePaulo, B. and W.L. Morris. 2005. "Singles in Society and in Science." *Psychological Inquiry*, 16(2 and 3), 57–83.

Doucet, A. 2009. "Can Men Mother? Or Is Mothering Essentially Female?" *Transition*, 39(1), 1–5.

Ehrehreich, B. and A.R. Hoschschild (Eds.). 2003. *Global Woman: Nannies, Maids and Sex Workers in the New Economy*.

Family Helper. *Adoption and Fertility*. http://www.familyhelper.net (accessed January 5, 2010).

Featherstone, K., P. Atkinson, A. Bjaradwaj, and A. Clarke. 2006. *Risky Relations: Family, Kinship and the New Genetics*. New York: Berg.

Fieldhouse, P. 2008. "Eating Together: The Culture of the Family Meal." *Transition*, 37(4), 3–6.

Gilmore, J. 2008. "The 2008 Canadian Immigrant Labour Market: Analysis of Quality of Employment."

Gittens, D. 1985. *The Family in Question: Changing Households and Familiar Ideologies*. London, UK: Macmillan.

Glossop, R. 2008. "We Are What Survives Us: An Interview with Dr. Robert Glossop." *Transition*, 38(4), 9–14. Gordonsville, VA: Henry Holt and Company.

Houle, R. and G. Schellenberg. 2008. "Remittance Behaviours among Recent Immigrants in Canada." *Perspectives on Labour and Income*, 20(3), 27–37. http://dsp-psd.pwgsc.gc.ca/collection_2007/statcan/71-606-X/71-606-XIE2007001.pdf (accessed April 19, 2010).

Huston, T.L. and H. Melz. 2004. "The Case for (Promoting) Marriage: The Devil Is in the Details." *Journal of Marriage and the Family*, 66(4), 943.

Koenigsberg, R. 2009. "After Postmodernism: The Death and Resurrection of Grand Narratives." http://www.ideologiesofwar.com (accessed January 5, 2010).

Lareau, A. 2003. *Unequal Childhoods: Class, Race and Family Life*. Berkeley: University of California Press.

Lochhead, C. and J. Tipper. 2009. "What's up with Household Debt?" *Transition*, 39(2), 1–4.

Mandell, N. and S. Wilson. 2010. "Intergenerational Care Work: Mothering, Grandmothering and Eldercare," pp. 21–42 in C. Krull and J. Sempruch (Eds.), *Diversifying the Model*,

Diversifying the Approach: The Work–Family Debate Reopened. Vancouver: University of British Columbia Press.

Mandell, N., J. Hemphill, A. Kim, M. Luxton, V. Preston, and K. Robson. 2010. *"Worked to Death": Gendered and Racialized Forms of Economic Security among Senior Immigrants in Canada,* paper presented to the Canadian Sociology Association Annual Meeting, Concordia, Montreal, June.

Marshall, B. 2006. *The Boomerang Age: Transitions to Adulthood in Families.* New Brunswick and London: AdlineTransaction.

Marshall, K. 2008. "Father's Use of Paid Parental Leave." *Perspectives on Labour and Income,* 20(3), 5–13.

Marshall, K. 2009. "The Family Work Week." *Perspectives on Labour and Income,* 21(2), 43–50.

McCall, L. 2005. "The Complexity of Intersectionality." *Signs: Journal of Women in Culture and Society,* 30(3), 1771–1800.

Milan, A. 2003. "Would You Live Common-law?" *Canadian Social Trends,* 3, 2–6.

Morissette, R. and A. Johnson. 2005. "Are Good Jobs Disappearing in Canada?" *Analytical Studies Branch Research Paper Series,* Statistics Canada, Catalogue no. 11F0019, no. 239.

Nares, P. 2009. "Making Sense of Money." *Transition,* 39(2), 10–12.

Ostrovsky, Y. 2008. "Earnings Inequality and Earnings Instability of Immigrants in Canada." *Analytical Studies Branch Research Paper Series,* Catalogue no.:11F0019MWE.

Palmetta, B. 2007. "Economic Integration of Immigrants' Children." *Perspectives on Labour and Income,* 19(4), 31–42.

Pateman, C. and E. Gross. 1987. *Feminist Challenges: Social and Political Theory.* Boston: The Northeastern University Press.

Picot, G., F. Hous, and S. Coulombe. 2007. "Chronic Low Income and Low-Income Dynamics among Recent Immigrants." *Analytical Studies Branch Research Paper Series,* Number 294. 11F0019MIE. http://www.statcan.gc.ca/bsolc/olc-cel/olc-cel?lang= eng&catno=71-606-X (accessed January 5, 2010).

Reyes, A. 2002. "I'm Not Mad, I'm Postcolonial, a Woman, and a Mother: Introduction." pp.1–31 in Angela Reyes (Ed.). *Mothering across Cultures: Postcolonial Representations.* Minneapolis: University of Minnesota Press.

Rotskoff, L. 2002. *Love on the Rocks: Men, Women and Alcohol in Post-World War II America.* Durham, NC: University of North Carolina Press.

Ruddick, S. 1995. *Maternal Thinking: Towards a Politics of Peace.* Boston: Beacon.

Sauvé, Roger. 2003. *Canadian Age Trends and Transitions to 2016.* Summerstown, ON: People Patterns Consulting.

Sauvé, R. 2009. "The Current State of Canadian Family Finances 2008 Report." Ottawa: Vanier Institute of the Family. http://www.vifamily.ca/library/cft/fam fin08.pdf (accessed January 2, 2010).

Skeggs, B. 1997. *Formations of Class and Gender: Becoming Respectable.* Thousand Oaks, CA: Sage.

Smart, C. 2007. *Personal Life.* Malden, MA: Polity.

South, S.J. 1991. "Sociodemographic Differentials in Mate Selection Preferences." *Journal of Marriage and the Family,* 53(4), 928–40.

Statistics Canada, 2005. *The Daily,* March 22, "Canada's Visible Minority Population in 2017." http://www.statcan.gc.ca/daily-quotidien/050322/dq050322b-eng.htm (accessed March 23, 2010).

Statistics Canada, 2007. "Frequency of Contact between Separated Fathers and Their Children." *The Daily,* October 29, 2007. http://www.statcan.gc.ca/dai-quo/index-eng.htm (accessed January 5, 2010).

Statistics Canada, 2008. "The Employment Growth among Lone Mothers in Canada and the United States, 1980 to 2000." http://www.statcan.gc.ca/dai-quo/index-eng.htm (accessed January 5, 2010).

Statistics Canada, 2009. "Predictors of Death in Seniors." *Statistics Canada,* Catalogue no. 82-003-SIE.

Statistics Canada. 2006. *Census Trends, 2006 Census,* Catalogue Number 97-553-XCB2006007.

Stocks, J., C. Diaz, and B. Hallerod. 2007. *Modern Couples Sharing Money, Sharing Life.* New York: Palgrave Macmillan.

Struening, K. 1996. "Feminist Challenges to the New Familialism: Lifestyle Experimentation and the Freedom of Intimate Association." *Hypatia: A Journal of Feminist Philosophy,* 11(1), 135–154.

Sussman, D. and S. Bonnell. 2006. "Women as Primary Breadwinners." *Perspectives on Labour and Income,* 18(3), 20–28.

Tipper, J. 2009. "In Other Words: An Interview with Rachel Epstein." *Transition,* 39(1), 9–11.

Turcotte, M. 2006a. "Parents with Adult Children Living at Home." *Canadian Social Trends,* 2–10.

Turcotte, M. 2006b. "Staying at Home Longer to Become Homeowners." *Canadian Social Trends,* 32–36. Statistics Canada Catalogue No. 11-008.

Underwood, N. 2009. "The Real Mommy War." *Transition,* 39(1), 6–8.

UNICEF. 2007. "Report Card 7, Child Poverty in Perspective: A Comprehensive Assessment of the Lives and Well-Being of Children and Adolescents in the Economically Advanced Nations." Geneva, Switzerland: Innocenti Research Centre.

Vanier Institute of the Family. December 2004. *The Future Families Project: A Survey of Canadian Hopes and Dreams.* http://www.vifamily.ca/library/publications/futured.html (accessed August 25, 2009).

Vezina, M. and M. Turcotte. 2009. "Forty-year-old Mothers of Pre-school Children: A Profile." *Canadian Social Trends*, 88, 34–45.

Vitzthum, V. 2007. *I Love You, Let's Meet: Adventures in Online Dating*. New York: Little, Brown.

Walkerdine, V. and H. Lucey. 1989. *Democracy in the Kitchen: Regulating Mothers and Socializing Daughters*. London, UK: Virago Press.

Wallis, M. and S. Kwok. 2008. *Daily Struggles: The Deepening Racialization and Feminization of Poverty in Canada*. Toronto: Canadian Scholar's Press.

Wheeler, M. 2008. "Braving the No-go Zone: Canada's Sub-replacement Fertility Rate. *Transition*, 38(4), 3–8.

Wikipedia. 2010. "Online Dating Service" (accessed April 19, 2010).

Zajicek, A., T. Calasanti, C. Ginther, and J. Summers. 2006. "Intersectionality and Age Relations: Unpaid Care Work and Chicanas" in T.M. Calasanti and K.F. Slevin (Eds.), *Age Matters: Realigning Feminist Thought* (pp. 175–197). New York and London: Routledge.

Zietsma, D. 2007. *The Canadian Immigrant Labour Market in 2006: First Results from Canada's Labour Force Survey*, Ministry of Labour, 71-606-XIE2007001.

Chapter 2

Rethinking Intimate Questions: Intimacy as Discourse

Debra Langan and Deborah Davidson

LEARNING OBJECTIVES

In this chapter, you will learn that:

1. taken-for-granted, ideological assumptions are embedded in popular notions of "intimacy" in Western society,

2. much of the literature on intimacy has involved descriptions of gender differences and therapeutic approaches to dealing with these differences,

3. understanding intimacy as discourse offers alternative ways to approach questions around intimacy,

4. Intimacy Discourse has implications for men and women's lived experiences.

INTRODUCTION

In Western society, we think of love as a driving force for romantic relationships. Literature treats **romantic love** as something we find difficult to define. Even though we may not agree on a definition of "love," most of us can cite examples of relationships in which we were romantically "in love." Romantic love justifies marriage and partnerships, incites legal contracts, and validates sexual activity within or outside marriage. We are socially conditioned to think of love as liberating and as the answer to dissatisfaction with being single (Langford, 1999). We value the 'couple' (Langford 1999, p. xi) as the most basic intimate relationship and valorize romantic love as "a means of salvation" (Langford, 1999, p. 153).

While love is conceptualized as a driving force in creating and maintaining romantic relationships, **intimacy** is widely understood as a desirable *goal* for romantic relationships. Yet intimacy seems difficult to achieve, as the extensive self-help literature reveals. Sociological literature on families and partnerships largely fails to include a consideration of intimacy. In this chapter, we challenge the taken-for-granted, **ideological assumptions** that characterize the most widely held beliefs on intimacy. We argue for a broader understanding of "intimacy" that incorporates and critiques dominant intimacy discourse that is popular in contemporary Western society. Dominant discourse emphasizes the importance of developing intimacy in romantic relationships. It neither questions intimacy as a desirable goal nor considers alternative ways in which intimacy might be experienced. Our critique is important because **Intimacy Discourse** has different but equally profound implications for the expectations and lived experiences of men and women. Women take up most of the **intimacy work** in relationships, while men are criticized for their lack of attention to intimacy.

IDEOLOGICAL ASSUMPTIONS ABOUT INTIMACY

"Intimacy" is rarely defined or problematized.[1] However, the "taken-for-granted" assumptions about "intimacy" that appear in popular culture and that are enshrined in ideologies contain the following themes:[2]

- Intimacy is a desirable, subjective experience.
- Intimacy is achieved in romantic relationships.
- Romantic relationships are also sexual relationships.
- Sexual relating is restricted to one monogamous couple relationship.
- Intimacy is linked to **heteronormativity** (i.e., heterosexual relationships are the "natural" home for intimacy).
- Intimacy naturally develops in the evolution of a healthy relationship.
- Intimacy develops over time.
- Intimacy requires "mutual self disclosure and an appreciation of others' unique qualities" (Jamieson, 1999, p. 477).
- In order for intimacy to be achieved, propinquity (i.e., being physically close) is necessary.[3]

These assumptions ignore the *contextual features* of interactions or relationships, such as current practices, historical locations, transnational realities, or the pressures of day-to-day life in contemporary, high-tech societies. Rather than uncritically accepting these prescriptions, we present an intimacy critique similar to Adrienne Rich's (1980) critique of "compulsory heterosexuality." Rich suggests that our ideas about intimacy are conflated with heterosexual romance, and this dramatically restricts the ways in which we think about, and engage in, relationships with others. Following Rich, we argue that heterosexuality continues to be framed as a "natural" sexual orientation, which limits our field of possible partners and presents heterosexual romance as our greatest "adventure, duty and fulfillment" (Rich 1980, p. 654).

GENDER DIFFERENCES IN THE QUEST FOR INTIMACY

He was a boi. She was a girl. Can I make it any more obvious?

—*Avril Lavigne, 2002, from her song, "Sk8ter Boi" on her CD, Let Go.*[4]

Gender shapes private love relationships. The desire for intimacy is not equally shared, and the contouring of intimate relations varies for women and men. Not only do the above lyrics by 2003 Juno award winner Avril Lavigne highlight this notion of boys and girls as "obviously" different, but the song implies that, because of their sex difference, boys and girls will "obviously" be romantically, and/or sexually, attracted to one another. So, how do women and men differ? Adie Nelson and Barrie W. Robinson's review of the literature reveals "males tend to be more idealistic about love than are females . . . [who] . . . are more realistic, pragmatic, and practical about the nature and power of love" (2002, p. 279). But it seems that the "tables turn" once women have "acknowledged being in love, [for then] women tend to experience the emotions of their relationship more intensely than do men" (Dion and Dion, 1973; Kanin et al., 1970 in Nelson and Robinson, 2002, p. 279). Once they are involved in romantic relationships, women want intimacy and understanding through the self-disclosure of feelings. In contrast, men want independence, sex, and nondisclosure of "feelings" (Cancian, 1987; Duncombe and Marsden, 1993; Hare-Mustin, 1991; Hite, 1987; Mansfield and Collard, 1988; Tannen, 1997; Tavris, 1992; Wood, 1997). Women prefer to be more "connected," while men prefer to be more autonomous and withdrawn.

Some contemporary researchers challenge these findings, suggesting they reinforce and replicate traditional gender norms. Reis, Senchak, and Solomon (1985) found the desire for intimacy is situationally bound. They compared male and female evaluations of the criteria constituting intimate interactions; their labelling of interactions; whom they select for intimate interactions; and their preference for intimate interactions. They concluded that "males are capable of interacting as intimately as females when the situation makes it desirable to do so . . . [however] males are relatively more likely to choose not to interact intimately . . . despite an equivalent capacity for intimacy" (1985, pp. 1215–216).

Anthony Giddens (1992) agrees that men have the capacity for interacting intimately. He argues that couples are experiencing what he labels "a transformation of intimacy" that is fostering more equality both in personal relationships and at the structural level. Our increasing preoccupation with bodies and sexuality accounts for this transformation of intimacy, and signals a move toward what he calls "the pure relationship." According to Giddens, women are the driving force behind these changes.

While these findings are appealing, other critics wonder if heterosexual relationships have equalized to the extent that Giddens suggests (Jamieson, 1999). Undoubtedly, the widely shared cultural belief is that both men and women want equality and intimacy. For example, consider the success of reality romance television shows that showcase women picking their favourite men (e.g., *The Bachelorette*) and men picking their favourite women (e.g., *Joe Millionaire*). As illustrated in the excerpt taken from *The Bachelorette*: Episode Guide (Box 2.1), Charlie, who has "a career in finance," is described as having a vulnerable side

BOX 2.1 *THE BACHELORETTE*: EPISODE GUIDE

ST. LOUIS WITH CHARLIE

Charlie arrives in St. Louis, and is greeted by Trista. They go for a date in the park, and reconnect. Trista confesses it feels great with Charlie no matter what they do, and Charlie asks her if he's her boyfriend. They then go to meet Trista's family . . .

They head into the living room and get to know Charlie a little better, talking about Charlie's career in finance; Charlie explains he thinks he's at a crossroads in his life. They go off to dinner with a bowl filled with questions that Trista's mom has written, with the idea of randomly picking questions out of the bowl.

Charlie takes their questions in stride, and reveals that he's a morning person, is comfortable if his wife made more money than him, and has no issue staying at home to be a Mr. Mom. . . . Trista's father can clearly see that they are a couple, and at ease with each other, and Trista's stepmother thinks he would be truly devoted to Trista. Charlie feels he's done well with her parents, and feels good about his chances; Trista thinks her family really liked Charlie.

In the limo back to Trista's, she tells Charlie that she needs the freedom to be intimate with Ryan, so she can learn who's best for her; she tells Charlie she's totally with him, but she also has feelings for Ryan. Charlie understands what she is saying, and is OK with it. They then enter her room for some much needed privacy.

Next . . .

[St. Louis with Ryan is next, and we are left to imagine what happened in Trista's room!]

Source: *The Bachelorette: Episode Guide*, February 2003, ABC. http://abc.go.com/primetime/bachelorette (accessed October 4, 2003).

("He thinks he's at a crossroads in his life") and as striving for equality in his relationships with women (He would be "comfortable if his wife made more money than him, and has no issue staying at home to be a Mr. Mom"").

Shows like *The Bachelorette* provide details of couples' interactions, allowing us to engage as voyeurs of couples' intimacy and thus gain information, often titillating, that we otherwise would not possess. In the excerpt (Box 2.1), the sense is that Trista and Charlie are becoming intimate by talking with one another, exchanging personal information (Trista also clarifies how she feels about Charlie and another suitor, Ryan), and ultimately retiring to Trista's room "for some much needed privacy." The account suggests that their interaction was romantic, openly communicative, and perhaps sexual in nature, some of the assumptions that accompany the popular notion of what it means to achieve intimacy.

THERAPEUTIC ANALYSES OF INTIMACY

Therapeutic analyses of intimacy elaborate how gender differences manifest in interaction. These analyses take up the project of offering solutions to address the behavioural outcomes of gender differences. Like the gender difference analyses, most of this therapeutic literature focuses on interactions within heterosexual couple relationships. The most popular theme is that men and women fail to have intimacy because they are unable to communicate effectively and satisfactorily. Failure to communicate causes conflict, unhappiness, and sometimes dissolution (Tannen, 1997). Even when men and women try to reinforce intimacy, their efforts often result in a **failure of intimacy**. According to Tannen, "Trying to trigger a symmetrical communication, they end up in an asymmetrical one" (1997, p. 190).

Because of this asymmetry, women feel that men lack "emotional participation" in the relationship. Women are irritated when men intellectualize, but do not appear to experience, emotion. This commonly reported "problem" conveys a particular idea of what qualifies as legitimate "emotional" involvement and signals a set of assumptions condoned by the therapeutic community. This analysis is gendered in that men's "emotional needs" (perhaps, for example, the emotional need to intellectualize) are discounted while women's emotional needs are prioritized. Moreover, women's needs are privileged over those of men. That is, there is a privileging of a specific way of relating, one "way" (the woman's way) that is condoned as better than another "way" (the man's way). Doherty (1991) labelled this analysis "deficit model of manhood." It has important implications for therapeutic interventions because it signals how "problems" are socially constructed and addressed.

Women who experience a lack of intimacy typically become turned off by sex (Duncombe and Marsden, 1993). Since the men's desires for sex are no longer being met, the conflict in couple situations intensifies. The therapeutic responses from counsellors, typically psychologists and social workers, help couples in therapy resolve their difficulties and learn new ways of working toward intimacy. Case Study 2.1, "Cheryl and Rob" typifies the therapeutic approach by addressing barriers to mutual self-disclosure and issues of sexuality. In this case study, a counsellor works with a couple, and encourages the man to emotionally participate more (i.e., become more intimate) in the relationship. The result is an enhancement of the woman's desire for and participation in sex. (The Critical Thinking Questions at the end of this chapter will help you to analyze the case study using the theories on intimacy.)

DISCOURSE ANALYSIS

Some theorists, therapists, sociologists, and postmodernists question traditional conceptions of intimacy by suggesting a theoretical framework within which they can be critiqued. Discourse analysis, a type of social constructionism that has emerged within postmodernism, provides a useful way to analyze intimacy. According to Weingarten (1991, p. 288), discourse

1. consists of ideas and practices that share common values

2. reflects a specific world view

3. constrains what we can feel, think, and do

CASE STUDY 2.1   CHERYL AND ROB

It was February 14, and Cheryl was very excited. She and Rob had been dating for almost a year now, and they were about to celebrate their first Valentine's Day together. They had talked about getting married someday. Cheryl met Rob at the door, and told him that she had a surprise for him. "Come into the kitchen!" she coaxed. "Sure" he replied, glancing nervously at his watch. "What's going on?" he asked. Cheryl pointed to the table, set for two with flowers and lit candles in the centre. "I thought we could have a romantic dinner together, just the two of us. I've been cooking all day! You sit down, and I'll open the wine" she said. "But I thought we were going to the bar," said Rob. "I told the guys that we'd meet them there at six. We can grab something to eat when we get there."

Cheryl went to the table, pulled out a chair, and sat down. She suddenly felt sick to her stomach. "When we talked about what we were going to do on Valentine's Day," she said, "I thought we agreed that we were going to spend some time together, alone. Now you are telling me that you've made plans to go to the bar, with the guys! Some Valentine's Day this is going to be!" she retorted, as tears filled her eyes. "You haven't even given me a card!" she cried. Rob seemed surprised. "When we talked about what we were doing tonight, we said that we were going to have dinner together, so when the guys called, I said that we would join them, so it's not like I'm going out without you! Come on, Cheryl, let's go and have a good time. Don't ruin it by making me feel guilty!" By now, Cheryl was really crying. Rob hated it when she cried, and he reconsidered his position. Maybe he was being insensitive. There were many times during the past year when they had had similar arguments, and it was always such a drag.

Rob looked at his watch again. There was still time to solve this. It was only 5:30. At this point, Cheryl got up from the table to go to the stove. Dinner needed her attention or it would all be ruined. As she walked across the room, Rob reached out to Cheryl and put his arms around her. His embrace made her feel hopeful and she stopped crying. Maybe this wouldn't be such a bad Valentine's Day after all. Maybe her plan for dinner and a romantic evening would go ahead. Then Rob began to unbutton Cheryl's blouse, moving his hands across her breasts. Disbelieving, she pulled back. He then put one hand between her legs. Cheryl began to cry uncontrollably and sat down again on the chair. "I don't get it," was all that Rob could say.

Over the next few weeks, things got worse between them. It seemed like they couldn't talk anymore, even when Rob tried to pay more attention to Cheryl. Their relationship seemed doomed to fail. When Cheryl suggested that they see a counsellor at the University Centre, Rob reluctantly agreed. The counsellor told them that they had been doing a "dance" that had to stop. Cheryl, he said, had been what therapists called a "pursuer" who was trying to establish intimacy and Rob had been a "distancer," trying to avoid intimacy. The therapist explained that they would need to change the way in which they related to one another in order to achieve intimacy in their relationship. In the days that followed, they tried to take the counsellor's advice. Cheryl stopped trying to create romantic situations, and focused more on her schoolwork, and her female friendships. Rob stopped initiating sex, and instead tried to be more emotionally sensitive toward Cheryl. Rob really missed the sex, but as things started to get better between them, Cheryl began to feel better about their relationship and began to initiate sex.

4. shapes our experience

5. evolves through collective conversations people have about their lives.

Barbara Hudson also emphasizes the complexity of discourse:

> Discourse is not just a unity of themes, or a grouping of knowledge, a professional termi-
> nology or a set of concepts, but an interrelationship of themes, statements, forms of
> knowledge, and ... positions held by individuals in relation to these (1984, p. 33).

DISCOURSE ANALYSIS APPLIED TO INTIMACY

There are two main discourses on the subject of intimacy (Weingarten, 1991).
The first discourse is called the "Individual Capacity Discourse" and involves the
idea that achieving intimacy depends upon an individual's ability to talk about
his or her private thoughts and feelings of intimacy. The second discourse, called
the "Quality of Relatedness Discourse," involves the idea that intimacy grows out
of long-term, committed relationships; it does not depend on the characteristics
of the individual (Weingarten 1991, p. 292). Weingarten maintains that both of
these discourses work against people's ability to engage in intimate interactions
for the following reasons: The Individual Capacity Discourse suggests that the
self is a coherent entity, and Weingarten argues that the self is socially constructed through narratives, and this means that individuals sometimes may have
the capacity to be intimate, and sometimes may not (Weingarten, 1991, p. 289).
The Quality of Relatedness Discourse suggests that a "relationship" is a static
entity, rather than a series of evolving interactions, giving the impression that
your relationship either is or is not intimate. Weingarten posits that an understanding of self and relationships as more fluid phenomena would better reflect
people's fluctuating potentials for, and experiences of, intimacy.

Weingarten's conceptualization of intimacy challenges the aforementioned heterosexist, couple-oriented assumptions. She advocates thinking of
intimacy as taking place at the level of interactions, so that the potential for
intimate (as opposed to "nonintimate") relating, increases. By locating intimacy firmly within the context of interaction, Weingarten moves beyond
essentialist depictions of what is and isn't intimate, and who is and isn't intimate. Her approach allows for a range of interactions to count as intimate, and
broadens the possibilities with respect to how intimacy can be achieved. She
argues, "Intimate interaction occurs when people share meaning or co-create meaning and are able to coordinate their actions to reflect their mutual meaning-
making" (1991, p. 287). In addition to co-creating meaning, Weingarten notes
the importance of coordinating action. For example, "people select a range of
activities as ones in which it is likely that intimate interaction will occur
between themselves and the people who participate with them" (1991,
p. 292). Viewed in this way, any activity can be intimate if those involved in the
activity are both co-creating meaning and coordinating action. To illustrate,
Weingarten offers the following specific experiences (see Box 2.2).

BOX 2.2   WEINGARTEN'S EXPERIENCES OF INTIMACY

Experience 1:   My second child had serious health problems at birth and we didn't know if she was going to live or die. I was also very sick after the birth, and asked my father, who lives in a distant city, to wait to visit until I felt better. Waiting was stressful and difficult for him. After three days, I felt well enough to have him come to see us, and he did. He looked at me, looked at the baby, sat in a chair, and promptly fell asleep.

Experience 2:   Several years ago, my husband and I had a particularly wonderful vacation. Each in excellent health, we hiked and read and kept a running conversation. We were each talking about topics that were of great intellectual, political, and emotional interest to us. One day, late in the afternoon, I began talking with him about thoughts that I had about my own funeral. With as much laughter as tears, we planned my funeral.

Experience 3:   Recently, my 11-year-old daughter had minor surgery that necessitated general anesthesia. In the aftermath, she had a lot of discomfort, and over the course of the several hours I was with her, my attention faltered and I felt impatient and bored. Her surgeon had insisted that she and I could go to a play that evening, and because she was eager to do so, we went. During intermission, out on the lawn on this lovely summer's evening, she began vomiting, and she vomited more than I have ever seen in my whole life. Both of us got covered with her vomit. Just as she started to feel better, but before either of us was clean, and on the periphery of a group of what I can only imagine must have been horrified spectators, we began to laugh, and then roar until we had trouble standing up.

Source: Excerpted from Kathy Weingarten. 1991. "The Discourses of Intimacy: Adding a Social Constructionist and Feminist View," *Family Process*, 30(3): 295–296.

Conceptualizations that challenge taken-for-granted assumptions about intimacy move away from heterosexist understandings to include lesbian, gay, transgender, and transsexual relating. The experience of marginalization for gays impedes their desire to achieve intimacy (Meneses, 2000), particularly in cultures that hold static definitions of gender identity (i.e., you are either male or female). When same-sex couples are compared to heterosexual couples, emotional intimacy is more salient for women than it is for men, regardless of sexual orientation. Schreurs and Buunk (1996) argue that lesbian relationships are characterized by greater emotional intimacy than are heterosexual relationships. In the latter, women compromise their desire for intimacy. Mackey et al. (2000) reported a similar finding in their study of whites, blacks, and Mexican-Americans, with Catholic, Jewish, and Protestant religious backgrounds. They found that, regardless of racial or religious identity, women in lesbian relationships, compared to their heterosexual and gay counterparts, are more likely to report that psychologically intimate communication characterized their relationships. Carroll et al. (1999)

reached a different conclusion in their argument that there are no differences in intimacy (which they refer to as "relational connectedness") when heterosexual, gay, and lesbian couples' perceptions are compared.

The links between intimacy and sexuality are explored in literature researching gay and lesbian relationships. This line of inquiry challenges the assumption that sexual activity is a prerequisite for the achievement of intimacy. Similar to heterosexual relationships, same-sex relationships can be sexual, but lack intimacy. For example, a collection of essays on the masculine gay subculture in Greenwich Village (New York City) during the late 1970s suggests that, like heterosexual men, gays during this period lacked the required emotional skills to maintain long-term, emotionally intimate relationships (Bhugra, 1997). Most of the studies that report on intimacy within gay subculture have focused on the relationship between AIDS (either having AIDS, or the threat of AIDS), sexual activities, and gays' desire for intimacy. A common finding is that unsafe sex practices (e.g., not using a condom) symbolize love and trust within a relationship, and are inspired by the desire for intimacy by gay partners (Sandstrom 1996; Flowers et al., 1997; Diaz and Ayala, 1999; Cannold et al., 1995; Martin and Knox, 1995; Fontaine, 1995; Powell-Cope, 1995; Robinson, 1994; Paradis, 1991).

Other analyses point to the ways in which lesbians often enjoy intimacy in their friendships with and/or without being sexual (e.g., Weinstock and Rothblum, 1996; Diamond, 2000). For example, in Case Study 2.2: "Marcia

---

CASE STUDY 2.2   MARCIA AND MARTHA

"Martha McPheeters and Marcia Munson request the pleasure of your company at their 21st Anniversary Party. . . . We are celebrating 21 years of open love, uncommitted sex, firm friendship, and wild adventures."

As we read over the invitation, we knew that our friends would focus on the phrase "uncommitted sex." Because we have both been in open relationships, various lesbian communities have seen us as "loose women" over the years. But sex, though fun, has never been central to our relationship. First of all, we have been friends. The words that inspired us most were "wild adventures." Both of us have done plenty of wilderness travel over the last two decades, but very little of it has been together. As we embarked on the adventure of planning our anniversary party two months away, we dreamed of seeing more wild landscapes together in the future.

. . . From the start we knew we wanted to each wear evening gowns for part of the night and tuxedos for the rest of the party. Political discussions of butch/femme, butch/butch, femme power, and gender-bender got pushed aside once we realized comfort was the real issue. Marcia would start out in a tux, Martha in a dress. To get everyone's attention we would switch, right before our non-commitment ceremony.

To help us celebrate open love, we each planned to bring a date to our anniversary party. We wanted to emphasize the point that we were not, nor had we ever been, a couple . . .

Source: Marcia Munson. 1996. "Celebrating Wild Erotic Friendship: Marcia and Martha," pp. 124–132 in Jacqueline S. Weinstock and Esther D. Rothblum, eds., *Lesbian Friendships for Ourselves and Each Other*. New York: New York University Press.

and Martha," we read of two lesbians who enjoy intimacy in their relationship together and who are sometimes sexual and at other times not sexual with one another. In addition, they are also nonmonogamous, and not always living in close physical proximity, thus challenging two other assumptions about the prerequisites for intimacy. Gabb points to the ways in which those who identify as lesbian engage in relationships that challenge the normalcy of (hetero)sexuality: "Lesbian sexual narratives, because they do not operate with what is seen to be 'natural,' displace the sexual as the determining factor of love, and support the postmodern academic analyses that posit friendship as the primary source of emotional support" (2001, p. 318). Furthermore, Gabb argues that lesbians are far more likely than heterosexuals to retain relationships with past sexual partners.

Adrienne Rich deconstructs the heterosexual/lesbian distinction, and highlights the importance of intimacy among women generally. She speaks of the "lesbian continuum," referring to a range of women who identified "many forms of a primary intensity between and among women, including the sharing of a rich inner life . . . " (1980, p. 649). Her vision of a lesbian continuum is much more inclusive than the phrase might suggest: "[W]omen exist on a lesbian continuum, we can see ourselves moving in and out of this continuum, whether we identify ourselves as lesbian or not" (1980, p. 651). Similarly, Esther Rothblum (1999) argues that a shift in emphasis from lovers to friends more accurately reflects the realities of lasting commitment within most adult lives, regardless of sexual orientation (in Gabb, 2001, 318). Jessie Bernard (1985) has also noted the importance of both male and female same-sex relating, which she argues "is more **homophilic** (i.e., based on friendship) than homosexual." "Such woman-to-woman and man-to-man relatedness grows through communicational sharing as well as through joint problem solving" (Wynne and Wynne, 1986, p. 390). For example, in the television show *Sex and the City*, the primacy of the women stars' friendships in the show illustrates the ways in which homophilic intimacy can characterize relationships between women. The main characters discuss their sexual experiences in detailed ways that would normally be shared (if at all) between sexually intimate partners (www.tv.com/sex-and-the city/show/456/summary.html). As Lee notes, "[this] show actually serves to sever connections between sex and intimacy; here sex is not the most intimate of communications" (2007, np).

While intimacy may also be present in nonsexual friendships between men, there is a prevailing negative social stigma for heterosexual men's friendships to be perceived as intimate. One case in point is the phrase, "no homo," used in hypermasculine Hip Hop culture when black male friends are nearing, or experiencing, a point of emotional intimacy (see http://www.racialicious.com/2007/06/11/no-homo-black-male-intimacy). By declaring "no homo," they signal noninvolvement in anything that might be construed as same-sex, sexual, intimacy.

Research on lesbian families supports the argument that love is not biologically determined, and that its "natural" home is not exclusively in heterosexual, nuclear families. Love is seen as an elective property. Romantic love between adults is not afforded a privileged position to mother–child(ren) love or to love and intimacy that is developed in friendships. Rather, mother–child(ren) relationships and/or friendships gain legitimacy as possibly the only, and/or the most important, love relationship(s) in a woman's life.

In her analysis of lesbian families, Gabb focuses on intimacy in the lesbians' relationships with their children. She highlights the mother–child(ren) relationship as "a positive and active response to the inherent failings of heterosexual love" (Langford, 1999 in Gabb 2001, p. 315). Gabb argues that traditional discourses of love stratify our emotions and intimate relations into socially prescribed categories, wherein "mature love" (read adult love) is conflated with sex and desire (2001, p. 313). This "stratification of intimacy" means that adult "love" experiences have become privileged over mother–child(ren) love experiences. Focusing on mother–child(ren) relationships "challenges the binary logic that underpins heterosexual society and makes evident the artificiality of competing hierarchies of love" (2001, p. 314). Lesbian families with children provide an opportunity to witness the disruption of this "stratification of love." Gabb argues that mother–child(ren) relationships are important sites for intimacy irrespective of sexual orientation. An appreciation of love within all mother–child(ren) units suggest that women have an innate need for intimacy, and that these needs can be fulfilled through their relationships with their children (2001, p. 316). Of course, the "rules of engagement" differ (i.e., rules demand that mothers do not have sexual relationships with their children) (Gabb, 2001, p. 317), but Gabb's research shows that sex is not necessary for the achievement of love and intimacy.

These kinds of critical analyses make room for innovative conceptualizations of who can be involved in creating intimacy and of who can constitute "family" (Gabb, 2001, pp. 324–25). Legislative changes in Canada also pose profound challenges to traditional ideas about who "legitimately" constitutes a family. In June 2003, the Ontario appeals court ruled as unconstitutional Canada's heterosexual-only definition of marriage, thereby legalizing gay marriages. This court decision marked significant social change that will undoubtedly enhance possibilities for elective relationships.

In addition to contesting heterosexist assumptions, Weingarten's approach, because it casts intimacy as contingent on the sharing of meaning-making, allows for more than two people to be involved in the creation of an intimate interaction (Weingarten 1991, p. 295). This approach challenges the idea that intimacy is achievable only in monogamous, couple relationships. For example, Williams and Guendouz's study of sheltered retirement community residents shows how, "in the absence of heart to heart intimacy," the image of solidarity and symbolic intimacy in intergenerational family relationships is established through talking about family achievements and the frequency and quality of contact with their grandchildren (2005, p. 453, 462–463). Information on support groups (e.g., Alcoholics Anonymous, bereavement groups, etc.) supports the idea that more than two individuals can come together and create intimate interactions. More radical is the idea that people establish intimacy in ways that do not involve interpersonal relationships with other people. As Gabb (2008, p. 1) notes,

> Some people form spiritual affinities, through communities of faith and/or immaterial relationships with dead loved ones (Kellaher, Hockey et al. 2006). Others are investing in cross-species relationships, wherein pets are seen as a consistent repository and source of intimacy (Bonas, McNicholas et al. 2000). For many, objects, such as keepsakes (Finch and Mason 2000; Smart 2007), and activities, such as gardening (Bhatti and Church 2004; Milligan, Gatrell et al. 2004), provide emotional comfort and affective rewards.

QUESTIONING THE DOMINANT DISCOURSE ON INTIMACY

All the analyses of "intimacy" presented thus far are premised on the assumption that intimacy is an innate, desirable goal for romantic relationships. This point is difficult for us to imagine otherwise, or for many of us to appreciate, for we have been socialized to accept, without question, the value of intimacy.[5] By understanding how families, sex, and intimacy have changed over time, we can appreciate the way in which "intimacy" as a historical, social construction has come to be valued in contemporary society. In what follows, we begin to question the importance placed on intimacy in Western culture by arguing that intimacy is discourse.

Although some of the aforementioned analyses (e.g., Weingarten, 1991; Jamieson, 1999; Gabb, 2001) profess to offer a discursive analysis of intimacy, what they really offer are different ways to describe intimacy: they do not question the dominant discourse on intimacy per se. A critical analysis focuses on the way in which language contributes to the cultural construction of intimacy, and questions how "intimacy" as a type of discourse (hereafter we offer as "Intimacy Discourse")[6] has shaped both our ideas about what is important in romantic relations, and our behaviour in romantic relations.

What we offer as dominant "Intimacy Discourse" involves the ideological assumptions that were outlined at the beginning of this chapter. In brief, intimacy is an innate human need that can be achieved through mutual self-disclosure and the appreciation of the other's unique qualities in romantic, sexual, couple relationships characterized by propinquity. When understood as a discourse, "intimacy" is no longer viewed in this essentialist way. Intimacy is no longer a need or a state of being. Rather, as discourse, intimacy is framed as a cultural and historical construction that is "mediated by social processes . . . [and] . . . inextricably linked to the other discourses—discourses of gender, power, domination, and sexuality" (Weingarten 1991, p. 287). Intimacy Discourse conveys particular ideologies that are connected to power and that are embedded in language (Fairclough, 1989, p. 2).

Weingarten observes that whether or not an interaction is defined as intimate depends upon the availability of discourses of intimacy. She notes that people are able to invest in discourses if they have been exposed to them. Our access to discourses depends, in great part, on the discourses that are popular at any given point in history. Once we have access to a discourse, we can invest in it to varying degrees. The dominant Intimacy Discourse, as we have presented it, is the one that most people have access to most of the time.

This discourse, we believe, demands thoughtful interrogation because of the implications that it has for women and men.

HISTORICAL EVOLUTIONS OF FAMILIES, SEXUALITY, AND INTIMACY

Understanding the historical development of ideas provides insight into how Intimacy Discourse has come to be culturally valued. Charles Lindholm describes how expectations and beliefs about romantic love develop out of specific cultural backgrounds and historical trajectory (1998). Drawing on cross-cultural analyses, Lindholm demonstrates that "the beloved is very rarely the person one marries, and reproduction and romantic attraction usually do not coincide" (1998, p. 246). For example, in Victorian times, sexual desire was not fulfilled in middle-class marriage; rather, married women were expected to remain virginally pure, and married men were expected to satisfy their sexual passions with prostitutes. Sexual contact between husband and wife was seen as "an unfortunate necessity of marriage" (1998, p. 247).

Prior to the Industrial Revolution, family members lived and worked together; "intimacy," as it is commonly understood, characterized all aspects of their daily relations. Wynne and Wynne draw on the historical analysis of Gadlin (1977) and note that in earlier times, ". . . people's lives were completely intertwined in close physical proximity . . . persons were intertwined in every waking and sleeping moment. . . . Under such circumstances, self-disclosure did not take place in isolated rare moments, but as a part of the continuous stream of life experiences" (Wynne and Wynne, 1986, pp. 388–389). Family relations were based on work and economics, such that each family member had a specific task and contribution, their activities were closely coordinated, and one member was subordinated to another (Beck-Gernsheim, 1999). As a result, family members were exposed to similar experiences, pressures, and common efforts, resulting in what Elizabeth Beck-Gernsheim calls "an obligation of solidarity" (1999, p. 58).

The Industrial Revolution

In the 19th century, the Industrial Revolution transformed family relationships from "obligations of solidarity" (Beck-Gernsheim, 1999, p. 58) to "obligations of individualism." Rapid urbanization and industrial development severed the world of work from the world of home (Beck-Gernsheim, 1999, pp. 56–58). The family no longer functioned mainly as an economic unit, for men became chiefly employed outside the home, in the public realm. Women, on the other hand, were relegated to home and children, in the private sphere, and women became dependent on men's earnings. Thus the family's relationship to work and economics changed because individuals within families assumed their own relationships with the labour market—men were paid for their work; women were not. Furthermore, the rise of the welfare state brought social control mechanisms such as pension and welfare, giving some protection and material assistance to those in need. Individuals no longer had to rely as much on their families as they had historically (Beck-Gernsheim, 1999, p. 58).

Wynne and Wynne's evaluation of this historical transformation showed "changes in social structure brought disconnectedness between both persons and the parts of an individual's life. One result . . . was the painful loss of what had previously often been onerous: As a result of the changes, intimacy became recognized as a 'need' when it became more difficult to achieve" (Wynne and Wynne, 1986, p. 389). It is interesting to note Wynne and Wynne's argument that the origin of intimacy as a need resulted from the *loss* of *too much* intimacy ("the painful loss of what had previously often been *onerous,*" italics ours). If, in pre-industrial times, the intimacy (although not a linguistic concept at that time) was often onerous, one might expect that when familial relations individualized and became less intense (i.e., less onerous), people would have become relieved of, rather than in need of, intimacy. This kind of hearkening back to "the good old days" is a phenomenon noted by Stephanie Coontz in her book, *The Way We Never Were* (1992). She notes the tendency for people to romanticize past familial relations, even when there is abundant evidence to the contrary.

An analysis of intimacy as discourse renders irrelevant the question of the extent to which people have "needed" or "experienced" intimacy, and focuses instead on how, as economic conditions changed and familial relations individualized, the notion of "intimacy" was "born" and socially constructed in historical portrayals. As noted previously, discourses evolve relative to changing social conditions and the collective conversations people have about their lives.

The Sexual Revolution

A historical analysis of developments in love and sex since the 1960s (Wouters, 1998) further contextualizes our notions about intimacy in contemporary society. From the 1920s onward, the desexualization and desensualization of love began a reversal to asexualization of love and an eroticization of sex. Until the mid-century, gender differences in how love was interpreted were apparent in what Cas Wouters calls the "lust balance"— a social code that represented a lust-dominated sexuality for men and a romantic love- or relationship-dominated sexuality for women.[7] In the 1950s, the notion of female sexual pleasure and gratification gained attention, followed by a diminution in fear of sexuality in the 1960s. Wouters uses the concept of "lust balance" to "focus on the relationship between sex and love . . . the attempt to find a satisfying balance between the longing for sex and the longing for love" (1998, p. 189). Wouters's analysis demonstrates the growing empowerment of women during the last 50 years, and the growing trend for women to exercise more agency in making individualistic choices with respect to their sexuality. Still, these changes have not meant that the "lust balance" has completely equalized. Traditional romantic ideologies, as evidenced in Intimacy Discourse, have continued to perpetuate gendered ideologies and practices that reinforce inequality in the sexual arena, even as women's sexuality has become more liberated. As will become apparent later in this section, these changes in sexuality are in keeping with the ways in which family relations have become increasingly individualistic.

Contemporary Society

According to Lindholm, in our contemporary society, romantic love occupies an ambiguous place in our thoughts (1998). While love is not necessarily sexual, it often assumes a sexual nature, or is thought to lead to sexual involvement. "Love is akin to a religious experience—a vision of the beloved other as a unique, transcendent and transformative being who can 'complete' one's own life . . . the fountainhead of all that is beautiful, good, and desirable" (1998, pp. 247–248).

Other historical analyses of the family support the argument that the rise of individualism has had a major impact on the relations among members of the same family. Beck-Gernsheim (1999) argues that the family is acquiring a new historical form, less obliged to external, imposed rules, and more elective in nature. Similarly, Gabb (2001) argues that familial relations have increasingly become relationships of choice. Jamieson notes, "Individuals are in fact restructuring friendships into 'voluntaristic and altruistic bonds of disclosing intimacy': developing networks that support or even usurp the former emotional privilege afforded to 'the family'" (in Gabb, 2001, p. 319). The rise in divorce and remarriage rates signals that love and family relations have become more elective in nature, and the promise to love another "until death do you part" becomes suspect. Similarly, the proliferation of other-than heterosexual families illustrates the trend toward choice in the construction of new forms of family relationships that have no social "blueprint" in place. For example, Gabb points to the ways in which lesbian mothers and their children exercise agency in the development of strategies for dealing with situations. "Living outside the social scripts of traditional family life, individuals are given no choice but to construct a series of identity kits for immediate assembly and equally instant dismantling" (Gabb, 2001, p. 323).

Another alternative approach is seen in "virtual" intimacies that characterize transnational family relationships (Wilding, 2006, p. 125). For example, e-mail "provides a sense of transcending time and space, which contributes to a perception of intimate connectedness . . . that improv(es) over-all quantity and quality of contact . . ." (Wilding, 2006). Parrenas's study of Filipino mothers and their young adult children examined "the challenges to the achievement of intimate familial relations, . . . 'transnational communication' refer[ring] to the flow of ideas, information, goods, money and emotions" (2005, p. 317). This "transnational intimacy" seeks to maintain "a sense of connection" with children through phone calls, shared bank accounts, letters, and e-mail (Yeoh et al, 2005, pp. 309–310). "By 'being there,' mothers attempt to achieve a semblance of intimate family life across borders" (Parrenas, 2005, pp. 333–334), and often overcompensate by performing a transnational version of "intensive mothering" (Hays, 1996 in Parrenas 2005, p. 323). Wilding argues that transnational families' experiences with virtual forms of communication are wrought with contradiction: "The inability to have face-to face contact is sometimes made even more poignant by the fact that long-distance communication has made the relationship feel so much more intimately connected" (2006, p. 139). The above examples signal how "the contours of a '**post-familial family**' are taking shape" (Beck-Gernsheim, 1999, p. 54).

So, how do changing family relations impact the quest for intimacy? As noted previously in our discussion of the impact of the Industrial Revolution, the usual response in the literature to this question is that without the traditional structures of imposed family relations in place, individuals "may find meaning and emotional warmth in the mutuality of romantic relationships" (Lindholm, 1998, pp. 255–256). "The couple is idealized as the ultimate refuge against the hostile world, and functions as the necessary nucleus of the atomized social organization" (Lindholm, 1998, pp. 255–256). Beck-Gernsheim makes a similar argument: "Individualization and choice in family relations 'fosters a longing for the opposite world of intimacy, security and closeness'" (Beck-Gernsheim, 1999, p. 67).

It is important to note the ways in which this historical portrayal is discursively constructed. We are presented here with the case that, because of increasing individualization, the family has become "a haven in a heartless world" (Lasch, 1977), suggesting that the onset of the need for intimacy resulted from the rise of individualism and the resulting weakened social ties among family members. This explanation is reminiscent of Durkheim's analysis of "anomie."[8] Berger and Kellner (1964) have offered a similar analysis of intimate relations in their description of marriage as protection against anomie. The research on gender difference can be used to further elaborate this argument by highlighting the notion that it is women, not men, who appear to have this inherent need. Social structural changes and one's location within the social structure are used to explain why there is a need for intimacy, and who within the society manifests this need. The reasoning is tautological—society evolves to meet needs, and these changes create new needs that lead to societal evolutions, which lead to new needs, etc. The question that emerges from all of this is: do we accept the idea that society has "needs"?

The "need" theory is dispelled when we move to an analysis of how Intimacy Discourse serves to perpetuate patriarchal relations. The historical record suggests that "intimacy" was an unspoken state of affairs in familial relations prior to the Industrial Revolution. With the Industrial Revolution and the increasing autonomy of family members, people longed for "the good ol' days" (Coontz, 1992), and discursively constructed depictions of past familial relations as harmonious, and present familial relations as lacking. Intimacy, even though reportedly it had been onerous, became a valued cultural construction, and the notion of a need for intimacy, with all of the ideological assumptions previously detailed in this chapter, developed. Individualism and intimacy are conceptualized here as binary opposites (as noted above, in the words of Beck-Gernsheim (1999), "a longing for the opposite world of intimacy," italics ours) both in the historical portrayals and, we would argue, in everyday discursive constructions. We can begin to see the lack of fit between discourses of individualism and intimacy within contemporary society. These are competing discourses: Individualism Discourse demands independence, while Intimacy Discourse demands interdependence.

While Intimacy Discourse perpetuates idealized notions of the family, and romantic couple relationships more generally, as locations for us to seek refuge, it fails to acknowledge the broader societal contexts in which these now exist. Although a complete elaboration of the societal contexts is not possible here,[9] the changing nature of employment provides one example of the demands that characterize our day-to-day living. Dual-career marriages are the norm rather than the exception (Wynne and Wynne, 1986, p. 341; Mandell and Duffy, 2004, p. 20), and research shows that long work hours for men and women compromise time for family (Roxburgh, 2006; Jacobs and Gerson, 2004). This scenario puts added pressures on family members to manage a myriad of domestic affairs that traditionally were the exclusive domain of the women (primarily the mothers) in the family. Thus, for families to be successful interpersonally, together they must create sophisticated ways in which to negotiate and plan the allocation of tasks and roles within the household, and this requires ingenuity and cooperation (Wynne and Wynne, 1986, p. 386). As Wynne and Wynne note, "[Men and women] have no models from the immediately preceding generation for resolving the division of tasks and authority . . ." (1986, p. 392) and struggle to find ways to successfully deal with these "uncharted territories."

Another social context that has dramatically changed contemporary society involves the technological revolution of the past 20 years. Widespread use of the Internet during this period has fostered new possibilities for intimate relating, in addition to the example of transnational families cited previously. For example, Internet match-making services facilitate finding a mate; Facebook connects people who otherwise would not have been connected; and cell phones apprise others of the personal minutiae of day-to-day life, either through phone conversations or text messaging. Still, digital technologies have added to the complexity of achieving intimacy among family members, because they oftentimes take the place of opportunities for in(ter)person(al) relating (Henline, 2006). In households where digital technologies abound, it is not uncommon for family members to be concurrently engaged with these kinds of technologies: one person may be searching the Internet, while another gets caught up on e-mail, while another chats on MSN, while another engages with "friends" across the globe through virtual gaming systems. Although the technological devices are connecting the family members with other people, arguably they are also serving to disconnect the family members with one another. Whether or not you agree with this analysis will depend, in large part, upon your age. The persistent use of computers, e-mail, Internet, iPods, gaming systems, and cell phones tends to be perceived as "normal" for those of the digital generation (i.e., those who have grown up with these forms of technology), but for older family members who recall pre-computer times, these practices frequently represent intrusions into family intimacy.

INTIMACY WORK FOR WOMEN

Feminist critiques have asserted that romantic love "traps women in false expectations and psychologically crippling demands" (Evans 1998, p. 265) such that in heterosexual relationships, "love" as an ideology is one of the primary means through which women are subordinated to men (e.g., Gabb, 2001; Jackson, 1993; Rich, 1980). Critics argue that women invest more in love and give more affection than they receive (de Beauvoir, 1972; Firestone, 1972), and that they are overburdened with domestic responsibilities. Women become "everybody's Mummy" (Langford, 1999, p. 88). As Langford notes, while initially love seems like a shared project, women end up submitting and men withdrawing: ". . . Eventually the heroine finds herself deciding what the hero should have in his sandwiches while he shows more interest in his computer" (Langford, 1999, p. 87). The literature on gender differences supports the idea that men and women cannot meet one another's needs, and that it is women who become the victims of love (Gabb, 2001, p. 316).

Intimacy Discourse promotes particular expectations as to how primary relationships should be realized and reinforces patriarchal relations. As noted by Duncombe and Marsden (1993), gender differences in emotion behaviour result in differences in "emotion work," (or as we have named it more specifically here, "intimacy work"). "In heterosexual couple relationships, women express men's unwillingness to do emotion work necessary to maintain the relationship, and they point to the unspoken assumption that women will take on this work" (Duncombe and Marsden, 1993, p. 222). As we have argued, women tend to "buy into" Intimacy Discourse, and engage in an inordinate amount of "intimacy work," expending considerable time and energy to pursue the ideological, and frequently unrealizable, dream of intimacy.

Rich argues that "[t]he ideology of heterosexual romance . . . [is] beamed at [girls] from childhood out of fairy tales, television, films, advertising, popular songs, [and] wedding pageantry" (Rich, 1980, p. 645). Throughout maturation, girls are bombarded with messages that perpetuate heterosexuality and they become inundated with the notion of intimacy as a goal in romantic relationships. Ads abound for "intimate apparel" as the key to securing a (male) partner. Advice columns in magazines reinforce the idea that it is up to the woman to create situations in romantic relationships that will entice, and then retain, a man. Valentine's Day, roses, and candlelit dinners (Jackson, 1993, p. 207), wine, sexy lingerie, and readiness for sexual intimacy are just some of the "tickets" to successful intimacy, and therefore, a successful relationship. As discussed previously, television programs provide supposedly "close up and personal" insights into what individuals will do together, even in "intimate moments," in any number of situations. This illusion arguably has become as alluring as the intimacy that is sought through in-person interactions (see Wilson, 1999 on a "celebration of fakery"). This is not to say that we do not challenge television portrayals of intimacy. Most of us argue that we "know" what we see on TV is not really "real." Still we are influenced by the allure of intimacy that is suggested.

EXPERIENCING CONTRADICTORY INVESTMENTS

Dominant discourses on love and intimacy impact women at the level of experience in complex and contradictory ways. For many, the idea of Intimacy Discourse, while it makes sense intellectually, is counterintuitive to their own experiences of, or aspirations for, intimacy in a relationship. Similarly, many resist theories that point to inequalities as impediments to intimacy, because to acknowledge this is to surrender a valued belief in our culture that we are "all equal." They also allude to the "fact" that they have been less than successful in this regard.[10] When we have suggested that gender "inequalities" impede the development of intimacy, the overwhelming response from these same women is the rejection of inequality as the culprit. Contradictions, then, can be seen within people's discursive productions (i.e., gender differences both *are*, and *are not*, impediments).

Contradictions are also evident in people's investments in discourse and the material circumstances of their relationships. Many couples attest to intimacy in their relationships; however, these claims may not fit in large part with their lived experiences together as a couple. According to Jamieson, therapeutic understandings, or discourses on the achievability of intimacy, are reflected in everyday "talk," even though these "truths" about intimacy do not coincide with people's everyday experiences. Couples often overlook their inequalities and define their relationships as intimate even though they are contributing differentially to the maintenance of their relationships (Jamieson, 1999, p. 484).

Frigga Haug et al. also point to contradictions when they describe how women take pleasure in simultaneously submitting to and resisting their subjection and oppression: "they saw themselves taking pleasure in the very process of being trained into particular dominant structures rather than feeling tyrannized by them" (1987, p. 81). Haug et al. did not arrive at this analysis of contradictions easily, and point to [their] "own [initial] incapacity to see two sides at once; for us, women were either victims, or active agents who could never be seen as subordinate" (1987, p. 145). Haug et al.'s reflections on their analytic process highlight the ways in which we tend to look for consistency in others' subject positions.

CONCLUSION

As mentioned at the outset, we are arguing for a conceptualization of intimacy as discourse, similar to the way in which Adrienne Rich argues for a conceptualization of "heterosexuality" as an institution. Rich outlines her reason for doing so: "To take the step of questioning heterosexuality as a 'preference' or 'choice' for women—and to do the intellectual and emotional work that follows—will call for a special kind of courage in heterosexually identified feminists, but . . . the rewards will be great: a freeing-up of thinking, the exploring of new paths, the shattering of another great silence, new clarity in personal relationships" (1980, p. 649). We hope that our critique of Intimacy Discourse will achieve similar ends.

While we are not suggesting that you abandon the quest for intimacy in your lives, we *are* arguing that it is prudent to reflect on ways to understand intimacy, the contradictory and fluctuating nature of investments in discourses on intimacy, and the social importance that is placed on achieving intimacy in romantic relationships. Perhaps it is useful to distinguish between the *experience* of intimacy and the *quest* for that experience. The "quest for intimacy" can mean, particularly for women, an inordinate amount of work that is possibly aimed at a subject who is not similarly oriented toward the same goal. While intimacy, however you define it, may constitute an enjoyable emotional experience, working hard on getting it can be a misspent use of time and energy, especially in relationships that are characterized by inequality. As Bittman and Lovejoy (1993) argue, a lot of creative energy is used to disguise inequality rather than to undermine it (in Jamieson, 1999, p. 485).

The harder one strives to create intimacy, the more elusive it is. Wynne makes this point: "preoccupation with intimacy as a goal, as with simultaneous orgasm, interferes with its attainment and also distracts, at the very least, from attention to other forms of relatedness" (Wynne, 1985, p. 311 in Wynne and Wynne, 1986, p. 385). Therefore, to make the achievement of intimacy a primary goal may be to automatically undermine its possibility. In Box 2.3, we make a number of suggestions that we hope will help you think critically about your own, and others', social experiences.

BOX 2.3 APPLYING CRITICAL ANALYSES

We suggest the following:

1. Work individually and collectively toward social change that would rectify social inequalities (since equality seems to be a key feature for achieving intimacy in relationships). Wynne and Wynne argue that experiences of intimacy are associated with deepened mutuality in families that work collaboratively on home and work issues (1986, pp. 386–387).

2. Seek intimacy in places other than romantic, heterosexual relations, since men tend to be uninterested in achieving intimacy, and other relationships can offer intimacy.

3. Seek intimacy through other than in-person interaction (through online communities, through memories, through pets).

4. Reconceptualize intimacy as achievable through other than mutual, interpersonal, self-disclosure (e.g., through activity-based interactions).

5. Lessen the cultural importance placed on intimacy and make something other than the achievement of intimacy a primary goal. Wynne and Wynne (1986) make the following point in this regard: "professionals in the marital and family field should take the leadership in challenging the enshrinement of 'intimacy' as the primary goal" (p. 392 in Weingarten, 1991, p. 302).

Summary

- Intimacy is a desirable goal in romantic relationships that is based on a number of ideological assumptions.

- Most of the literature on intimacy reflects these assumptions, and focuses on gender differences in the desire for intimacy and therapeutic approaches to the conflicts caused by these differences.

- Critical analyses broaden our notions of how, where, or with whom intimacy can be realized, and consider how intimacy is experienced in nonromantic interactions; gay and lesbian relationships; friendships; adult–child relationships; nonmonogamous relationships; noncoupled relationships; and long-distance relationships.

- Intimacy Discourse came into being following the Industrial Revolution, as family relations became individualized and elective.

- Intimacy Discourse perpetuates patriarchal relations—women invest time and energy in "intimacy work" in relationships, men are faulted for not contributing to "intimacy work."

- Intimacy Discourse is an idealized way of relating that is difficult to achieve because of competing demands that characterize life in contemporary society.

- Our investments in Intimacy Discourse are complex and contradictory.

- Think critically about ways to understand intimacy and to question the social importance that is placed on achieving intimacy in romantic relationships.

Notes

1. Wynne and Wynne (1986, p. 384) are one exception. In their article: "The Quest for Intimacy," they define intimacy as *a subjective relational* experience in which the core components are *trusting self-disclosure* to which the response is *communicated empathy*" (italics in the original). Later in that article, they note, "intimacy is not so much a *process* as it is the subjective corollary of any of the more basic relational processes" (1986, p. 386).

2. Fairclough defines ideologies as "common sense assumptions which are implicit in the conventions according to which people interact linguistically, and of which people are generally not aware . . ." (1989, p. 2).

3. Research on Internet relationships is challenging the notion of propinquity as necessary for the development of intimacy; still it is a common assumption within the literature, and in the society more generally.

4. SK8ER BOI Words and Music by Avril Lavigne, Lauren Christy, Scott Spock and Graham Edwards. © 2002 Warner-Tamerlane Publishing Corp., Rainbow Fish Publishing, Mr. Spock Music, Hollylodge Music, WB Music Corp., Ferry Hill Songs, TIX Music and Copyright Control. All Rights for Rainbow Fish Publishing, Mr. Spock Music and Hollylodge Music Administered by Warner-Tamerlane Publishing Corp. All Rights for Ferry Hill Songs and TIX Music. Administered by WB Music Corp. All Rights Reserved. Used by Permission.

5. In fact, it was not until we were well advanced in our research for this chapter that we came to question the taken-for-granted assumption that the quest for intimacy was a "good thing."

6. The phrase, "Intimacy Discourse" has been purposefully capitalized to emphasize the idea that "Intimacy Discourse" (as opposed to "intimacy") has an empirical reality, and to convey the sense of importance that this discourse has on subjectivity.

7. Wouters took the term from Norbert Elias who used it in a wider sense, i.e., the whole lust economy (Wouters, 1998).

8. Durkheim studied suicide rates among various groups and concluded that the more socially integrated groups had lower rates of suicide. Groups that were not as socially integrated experienced what he called "anomie" and this was a factor in their higher suicide rates.

9. See Rubin, 1983 and Gergen, 1991 (noted in the References at the end of this chapter) for an analysis of the hectic, complex nature of contemporary society and the implications for social relationships.

10. While working on this chapter, when asked by other women about the topic of the chapter, we would say, "It's about love and intimacy." Typically, they reacted by saying things like, "Oh! I sure could stand to read that

when you're done!" or, "I could really use that!" typically followed by some joking that suggested, in our opinion, that women felt as if they had "failed" to achieve an ideal level of intimacy in their heterosexual relations with their partners.

Critical Thinking Questions

In Case Study 2.1: "Cheryl and Rob," a couple encounters problems in their relationship.

1. In terms of "gender difference" theorizing, what is the source of Cheryl and Rob's problems?

2. From a therapeutic perspective, how can their problems be solved?

3. How might critical analyses of intimacy as discourse explain Cheryl and Rob's problems?

4. To what extent is the social context of Cheryl and Rob's relationship considered in this case study (i.e., what factors might improve or interfere with their efforts to achieve intimacy, and are these addressed)?

5. Considering this case study as a text, what ideological assumptions about intimacy are perpetuated? What ideological assumptions are challenged?

Websites

The Oprah Winfrey Show and Intimacy

www.oprah.com/search.jsp?query=intimacy&resultsPerPage=20&sortBy =Relevancy&filtrType=&filterBy=&page=1&x=0&y=0

> The links on this site are good examples of how dominant ideological assumptions about intimacy are reinforced in popular culture.

The Relationship Institute

www.stevesolomonphd.com/workshop-ads-couples-therapy-services .html#workshopscouplesoutsd

> This website advertises how to "love intimately" through workshops offered by "the relationship institute" for couples who wish to "learn how to keep [their] relationship thriving and loving."

Matchmaking

www.eHarmony.ca

> This website is a good example of how the Internet makes possible alternative ways of seeking romantic/intimate relationships. "eHarmony does the matching for you based on 29 Dimensions^{TM} of personality that are scientifically-based predictors of long-term relationship success" (www.eHarmony.ca).

Suggested Readings

Jacqui Gabb. 2008. *Researching Intimacy in Families.* Balingstoke: Palgrave Macmillan.
  Gabb explores the topic of intimacy through various theoretical and
  methodological lenses.

Kenneth Gergen. 1991. *The Saturated Self: Dilemmas of Identity in Contemporary Life.*
New York: Basic Books.
  Gergen provides an analysis of contemporary Western society that highlights the way in which technology has increased the complexity of
  everyday experience.

Adrienne Rich. 1980. "Compulsory Heterosexuality and Lesbian Existence."
Signs 5(4): 631–660.
  In this groundbreaking article, Rich interrogates heterosexuality as a
  political institution based in patriarchy, and argues that while heterosexual coupling and marriage are presumed to be the "sexual preference" of
  "most women," this choice is bound by sex roles and social prescriptions
  for women that are born out of economic necessity.

Lillian B. Rubin. 1983. *Intimate Strangers: Men and Women Together.* New York: Harper
and Row.
  Rubin notes the ways in which the social institutions have changed the
  social roles and responsibilities of men and women, and how this has
  resulted in a contradiction: a lack of fit between the old dreams and the
  new realities of romantic relationships.

References

Beck-Gernsheim, Elizabeth. 1999. "On the Way to the Post-Familial Family: From a
  Community of Need to Elective Affinities," pp. 53–79. In Mike Featherstone (Ed.),
  Love and Eroticism. London: Sage.

Berger, P.L. and H. Kellner. 1964. "Marriage and the Construction of Reality." *Diogenes*, 1–23.

Bernard, Jessie. 1985. "The Marital Bond vis à vis the Male Bond and the Female
  Bond." *Newsletter of the American Family Therapy Association* 19: 15–22.

Bhatti, M. and A. Church. 2004. "Home, the Culture of Nature and Meanings of
  Gardens in Late Modernity." *Housing Studies,* 19(1): 37–51.

Bhugra, Dinesh. 1997. "Coming Out by South Asian Gay Men in the United Kingdom."
  Archives of Sexual Behavior, 26: 547–557.

Bittman, M. and F. Lovejoy. 1993. "Domestic Power: Negotiating an Unequal Division
  of Labour within a Framework of Equality." *Australian and New Zealand Journal of
  Sociology,* 29: 302–321.

Bonas, S., J. McNicholas, et al. 2000. "Pets in the Network of Family Relationships: An
  Empirical Study." In A. Podberscek, E. Paul, and J. Serpell (Eds.), *Companion Animals
  and Us* (pp. 209–236). Cambridge, UK: Cambridge University Press.

Cancian, F.M. 1987. *Love in America: Gender and Self Development.* New York: Cambridge University Press.

Cannold, Leslie, Bill O'Loughlin, Geoff Woolcock, and Brian Hickman. 1995. "HIV as a Catalyst for Positive Gay Men's Desire for Clarification, Enhancement and Promotion of Intimacy in Significant Relationships." *Journal of Psychology and Human Sexuality,* 7: 161–179.

Carroll, Lynne, Natalia Hoenigmann-Stovall, Joseph A. Turner, and Paula Gilroy. 1999. "A Comparative Study of Relational Interconnectedness, Merger, and Ego Development in Lesbian, Gay Male, and Heterosexual Couples." *Journal of Gay and Lesbian Social Services,* 9: 51–67.

Coontz, Stephanie. 1992. *The Way We Never Were: American Families and the Nostalgia Trap.* New York: Basic Books.

De Beauvoir, S. 1972. *The Second Sex.* Harmondsworth: Penguin.

Diamond, Lisa M. 2000. "Passionate Friendships among Adolescent Sexual-Minority Women." *Journal of Research on Adolescence,* 10: 191–209.

Diaz, Rafael M. and George Ayala. 1999. "Love, Passion and Rebellion: Ideologies of HIV Risk among Latino Gay Men in the USA." *Culture, Health and Sexuality,* 1: 277–293.

Dion, K.L. and K.K. Dion. 1973. "Correlates of Romantic Love." *Journal of Consulting and Clinical Psychology,* 41: 51–56.

Doherty, William J. 1991. "Beyond Reactivity and the Deficit Model of Manhood." *Journal of Marital and Family Therapy,* 17: 29–32.

Duncombe, Jean and Dennis Marsden. 1993. "Love and Intimacy: The Gender Division of Emotion and 'Emotion Work': A Neglected Aspect of Sociological Discussion of Heterosexual Relationships." *Sociology,* 27(2): 221–241.

Evans, Mary. 1998. "'Falling in Love with Love Is Falling for Make Believe': Ideologies of Romance in Post-Enlightenment Culture." *Theory, Culture & Society,* 15(3–4): 265–275.

Fairclough, Norman. 1989. *Discourse Analysis.* Cambridge: Polity Press.

Finch, J. and J. Mason. 2000. *Passing On: Kinship and Inheritance in England.* London: Routledge.

Firestone, S. 1972. *The Dialectic of Sex.* London: Paladin.

Flowers, F. Paul, Jonathan A. Smith, Paschal Sheeran, and Nigel Beail. 1997. "Health and Romance: Understanding Unprotected Sex in Relationships between Gay Men." *British Journal of Health Psychology,* 2: 73–86.

Fontaine, Michele M. 1995. "Issues of Isolation and Intimacy for the HIV Infected, Sexually Addicted Gay Male in Group Psychotherapy." *Journal of Psychology and Human Sexuality,* 7: 181–190.

Gabb, Jacqui. 2001. "Querying the Discourses of Love: An Analysis of Contemporary Patterns of Love and the Stratification of Intimacy within Lesbian Families." *European Journal of Women's Studies,* 8(3): 313–328.

Gabb, Jacqui. 2008. "The Boundaries of Intimacy: What Constitutes Intimacy and an Intimate Relationship?" Working Paper. http://www.persons.org.uk/ptb/persons/pil/pil2/gabb%20paper.pdf (accessed April 21, 2008).

Gadlin, H. 1977. "Private Lives and Public Order: A Critical View of the History of Intimate Relationships in the United States." In G. Levinger and H.L. Raush (Eds.), *Close Relationships: Perspectives on the Meaning of Intimacy.* Amherst: University of Massachusetts Press.

Gergen, Kenneth. 1991. *The Saturated Self: Dilemmas of Identity in Contemporary Life.* New York: Basic Books.

Giddens, Anthony. 1992. *The Transformation of Intimacy: Sexuality, Love and Eroticism in Modern Societies.* Cambridge: Polity Press.

Hare-Mustin, R.T. 1991. "Sex, Lies, and Headaches: The Problem Is Power." In T.J. Goodridge (Ed.), *Women and Power: Perspectives for Therapy.* New York: W.W. Norton.

Haug, Frigga et al. 1987. *Female Sexualization: A Collective Work of Memory.* London: Verso.

Henline, Branden Hayes. 2006. *Technology Use and Intimacy Development in Committed Relationships: Exploring the Influence of Differentiation of Self.* A Dissertation in Marriage and Family Therapy. Texas. Texas Tech University. http://dspace.lib.ttu.edu/bitstream/handle/2346/1298/Henline_Branden_Diss.pdf?sequence=1 (accessed April 8, 2010).

Hite, S. 1987. *Women in Love: A Cultural Revolution in Progress.* New York: Alfred A. Knopf.

Hudson, Barbara. 1984. "Femininity and Adolescence." In A. McRobbie and M. Nava (Eds.), *Gender and Generation.* London: Macmillan.

Jackson, S. 1993. "Even Sociologists Fall in Love: An Exploration in the Sociology of Emotions." *Sociology,* 27: 201–220.

Jacobs, Jerry A. and Kathleen Gerson. 2004. *The Time Divide: Work, Family, and Gender Inequality.* Cambridge, MA: Harvard University Press.

Jamieson, Lynn. 1999. "Intimacy Transformed? A Critical Look at the 'Pure Relationship.'" *Sociology,* 33(3): 477–494.

Kanin, E. J., K.R. Davidson, and S.R. Scheck. 1970. "A Research Note on Male–Female Differentials in the Experience of Heterosexual Love." *The Journal of Sex Research,* 6: 64–72.

Kellaher, L., J. Hockey, et al. 2006. "Blowing in the Wind? Identity, Materiality, and the Destinations of Human Ashes." *Journal of the Royal Anthropological Institute,* 12(4): 881–898.

Langford, Wendy. 1999. *Revolutions of the Heart: Gender, Power and the Delusions of Love.* London: Routledge.

Lasch, C. 1977. *Haven in a Heartless World. The Family Besieged.* New York: Basic Books.

Lee, Katherine Hyunmi. 2007. "'Hello Lover': Commodification, Intimacy, and Second-Wave Feminism on Sex in the City." *Americana: The Journal of American Popular Culture* (1900–present) 6, 2. http://www.americanpopularculture.com/journal/articles/fall_2007/lee.htm (accessed March 24, 2010).

Lindholm, C. 1998. "Love and Structure." *Theory, Culture & Society*, 15: 243–263.

Mackey, Richard A., Matthew A. Diemer, and Bernard A. O'Brien. 2000. "Psychological Intimacy in the Lasting Relationships of Heterosexual and Same Gender Couples." *Sex Roles* 43: 201–227.

Mandell, Nancy and Ann Duffy. 2004. "Explaining Family Lives," pp. 3–30. In Nancy Mandell and Ann Duffy (Eds.), *Canadian Families: Diversity, Conflict, and Change*. Toronto: Thomson-Nelson.

Mansfield, Penny and Jean Collard. 1988. *The Beginning of the Rest of Your Life?* London: Macmillan.

Martin, James I. and Jo Knox. 1995. "HIV Risk Behavior in Gay Men with Unstable Self-Esteem." *Journal of Gay and Lesbian Social Services*, 2: 21–41.

Meneses, Ines. 2000. "Intimacy, Norm and Difference: Gay Modernity in Lisbon; Intimidade, norma e diferenca: a modernidade gay em Lisboa. *Analise Social*, 34: 933–955.

Milligan, C., A. Gatrell, et al. 2004. "'Cultivating Health': Therapeutic Landscapes and Older People in Northern England." *Social Science & Medicine*, 58(9): 1781–1793.

Munson, Marcia. 1996. "Celebrating Wild Erotic Friendship: Marcia and Martha," pp. 124–132. In Jacqueline S. Weinstock and Esther D. Rothblum (Eds.), *Lesbian Friendships for Ourselves and Each Other*. New York: New York University Press.

Nelson, Adie and B.W. Robinson. 1995. "The Quest for Intimacy," pp. 231–248. In Adie Nelson and B.W. Robinson (Eds.), *Gender in the 1990s: Images, Realities, and Issues*. Scarborough: Nelson Canada.

———. 2002. *Gender in Canada*. Toronto: Pearson Education Canada.

Paradis, Bruce A. 1991. "Seeking Intimacy and Integration: Gay Men in the Era of AIDS." *Smith College Studies in Social Work*, 61: 260–274.

Parrenas, Rhacel. 2005. "Long Distance Intimacy: Class, Gender and Intergenerational Relations between Mothers and Children in Filipino Transnational Families." *Global Networks*, 5, 4: 317–336.

Powell-Cope, Gail M. 1995. "The Experiences of Gay Couples Affected by HIV Infection." *Qualitative Health Research*, 5: 36–62.

Reis, Harry T., Marilyn Senchak, and Beth Solomon. 1985. "Sex Differences in the Intimacy of Social Interaction: Further Examination of Potential Explanations." *Journal of Personality and Social Psychology*, 48: 1204–217.

Rich, Adrienne. 1980. "Compulsory Heterosexuality and Lesbian Existence." *Signs*, 5(4): 631–60.

Robinson, C. Sean. 1994. "Counseling Gay Males with AIDS: Psychosocial Perspectives." *Journal of Gay and Lesbian Social Services*, 1: 15–32.

Rothblum, Esther. 1999. "Poly-Friendships," pp. 71–83. In Marcia Munson and Judith P. Stelboum (Eds.), *The Lesbian Polyamory Reader: Open Relationships, Non-Monogamy, and Casual Sex*. New York: Harrington Park Press.

Roxburgh, Susan. 2006. "'I Wish We Had More Time to Spend Together . . .': The Distribution and Predictors of Perceived Family Time Pressures Among Married Men and Women in the Paid Labor Force." *Journal of Family Issues*, 27(4): 529–533.

Rubin, Lillian B. 1983. *Intimate Strangers: Men and Women Together*. New York: Harper and Row.

Sandstrom, Kent L. 1996. "Relationships of Gay Men Living with HIV/AIDS." *Symbolic Interaction*, 19: 241–262.

Schreurs, Karlein M.G. and Bram P. Buunk. 1996. "Closeness, Autonomy, Equity, and Relationship Satisfaction in Lesbian Couples." *Psychology of Women Quarterly*, 20: 577–592.

Smart, C. 2007. *Personal Life*. Cambridge: Polity Press.

Tannen, Deborah. 1997. "You Just Don't Understand." In Estelle Disch (Ed.), *Reconstructing Gender: A Multicultural Anthology* (pp. 186–191). Toronto: Mayfield.

Tavris, C. 2003, February. *The Mismeasure of Women*. New York: Simon and Schuster.

The Bachelorette: Episode Guide—ABC. http://abc.go.com/primetime/bachelorette (accessed October 4, 2003).

Weingarten, Kathy. 1991. "The Discourses of Intimacy: Adding a Social Constructionist and Feminist View." *Family Process*, 30: 285–305.

Weinstock, Jacqueline S. and Esther D. Rothblum. 1996. *Lesbian Friendships for Ourselves and Each Other*. New York: New York University Press.

Wilding, Raelene. 2006. "'Virtual' Intimacies? Families Communicating across Transnational Contexts." *Global Networks*, 6, 2: 125–142.

Williams, Angie and Jacqui Guendouz. 2005. "Constructing Family Relationships: Intimacy, Harmony and Social Value in Accounts of Sheltered Retirement Community Residents." *Journal of Aging Studies*, 19: 453–470.

Wilson, Robert. 1999. "Playing and Being Played: Experiencing West Edmonton Mall," pp. 82–90. In Lynne Van Luven and Priscilla L. Walton (Eds.), *Pop Can: Popular Culture in Canada*. Scarborough: Prentice Hall Allyn and Bacon Canada.

Wood, J. 1997. *Gendered Lives: Communication, Gender, and Culture*, 2nd ed. Belmont: Wadsworth.

Wouters, Cas. 1998. "Balancing Sex and Love since the 1960s Sexual Revolution." *Theory, Culture, and Society*, 15: 187–214.

Wynne, L.C. 1985. "Mutuality and Pseudomutuality Reconsidered: Implications for Therapy and a Theory of Development of Relational Systems." In D. Schwartz, J. Stacksteder, and Y. Akabane (Eds.), *Attachment and the Therapeutic Process* (pp. 81–116). New York: International Universities Press.

Wynne, Lyman C. and Adele R. Wynne. 1986. "The Quest for Intimacy." *Journal of Marital and Family Therapy*, 12(4): 383–394.

Yeoh, Brenda S.A., Shirlena Huang, and Theodora Lam. 2005. "Transnationalizing the 'Asian' Family: Imaginaries, Intimacies and Strategic Intents." *Global Networks*, 5(4): 307–315.

Chapter 3

Canadian Youth Culture: Consumption, Resistance, and Rave

Brian Wilson and Shannon Jette

LEARNING OBJECTIVES

In this chapter, you will learn that:

1. the history of the term "youth" helps to demonstrate the evolution of the rift between teen and parent generations,

2. the cultural activity of youth has been interpreted by sociologists in various ways,

3. youth interpret the cultural activities in which they participate in complex ways,

4. new media technologies enable new forms of peer interaction among young people, while offering unique potential for social resistance and civic participation,

5. media and popular culture are central in the everyday lives of young people.

INTRODUCTION

The cultural activities of young people inspire both fascination and concern. Mass media reports often include stories about school bullying, drug abuse, teen pregnancy, race-related violence, and gang membership. Activities such as skateboarding and snowboarding, formerly alternative leisure pursuits for youth, have entered mainstream culture through televised events such as the "X-Games" (i.e., extreme sport games) and are often the focus of news segments that describe the lifestyles of highly committed participants. Marketers enamoured with the teen demographic devise ultra-appealing commercials and advertisements in hopes of wooing young consumers into buying sneakers, clothes, video games, soft drinks, and other items.

Those who study youth and **youth culture** have identified a number of problems with these portrayals and product positionings. Some researchers argue that youth are too often depicted in overly simplistic and deceiving ways in mass media reports. These critics suggest that young people are frequently portrayed as either menaces to society who need to be disciplined or incarcerated, or as troubled, unstable "at risk" adolescents who require serious help and protection—while the mundane, everyday activities and behaviours of most youth are seldom acknowledged (Acland, 1995; Wilson, 2006). Still other commentators suggest that youth are not given enough credit for their ability to critically interpret media and advertising (Rushkoff, 1996; Jette et al., 2007). These scholars assert that youth are too often viewed as passive, impressionable, and easily influenced by the "evils" associated with popular culture (e.g., violence in movies; ads for high-priced sneakers). Underlying many of these apprehensions is the worry that mass media and associated cultural influences are threatening the role of the family and community as primary socialization agents (Furlong and Cartmel, 2007).

Emerging from this myriad of concerns is a series of questions about youth, culture, and society. These include

- What are the various meanings of the term "youth"?

- What do young people do with their time beyond the spectacular and problematic activities that receive so much attention?

- How can the leisure preferences and cultural involvements of young people be explained?

- To what extent are youth passive "dupes" who uncritically accept the media messages they are exposed to?

- To what extent are these same youth active and informed consumers of information and culture?

- How can an understanding of youth activity help us understand the contemporary Canadian family?

With the goal of engaging these topics and questions, we have organized this chapter into the following four sections. In the first section, we describe and consider the range of ways that the term "youth" has been defined and the cultural meanings that the concept has taken on. The second section is a discussion and overview of patterns of leisure activity that have been identified within large-scale research on youth in Canada. This is followed, in the third section, by an exploration of the range of ways that young people's activities have been interpreted and explained by scholars who study youth and culture. In the fourth section, a case study of the **rave** subculture in southern Ontario is presented and used as a departure point to help us describe and interrogate some of the theories of youth outlined in section three. The rave case is also used to illustrate our argument that youth are a complex and diverse group that negotiate, understand, and interpret the various cultural influences they encounter in different ways at different times. We conclude the chapter with a summary of key points and a reflective assessment of contemporary work on youth culture and its relationship to the family.

WHO ARE YOUTH?: A SOCIAL HISTORY OF THE TERM AND ITS MEANINGS

Although in contemporary Western society the term "youth" refers broadly to a transition stage between childhood and adulthood that is characterized by distinct physical, psychological, and social developments (c.f. Coleman, 1992), current understandings of "youth" are quite different from those of earlier generations. Authors such as Tanner (2001), Tyyskä (2001), and Gillis (1974) describe how, prior to the Industrial Revolution in the early 1800s, conceptions of "youth" were akin to what we now think of as "young adulthood." Tanner (2001), in his work on youth and deviance in Canada, explains how in pre-industrial Europe, different age groups were far more integrated in work and leisure than in contemporary times, and how in medieval France especially, children as young as 7 years old worked alongside adults. Kline (1993) elaborates on this point:

> [during medieval times, the] objects that children handled were no different to the cultural objects that adults had, and children's lives were essentially no different from those of adults. The whole community shared work and leisure as well as games, songs, and tales (p. 46).

Thus, working-class children were expected to contribute to the maintenance of the household from almost the time they could walk. This adult status extended into nonwork activities such that "children were present at, and participated in, all the great ceremonies and rituals of the life cycle—including death" (Tanner, 2001, p. 24).

The Industrial Revolution was a pivotal time in the development of the notion of "youth." Two key social changes occurred at this time that ultimately served to increase the transition period between childhood and adulthood. First, there was a general shift from an agrarian to an industrial lifestyle, with many families in both European and North American societies migrating from their homes in the countryside to burgeoning urban centres. Second, there was a shift from a tradition of home-based work and family businesses to factory work (Tanner, 2001). In these new circumstances, young people quickly became a threat to the employment of male industrial workers. Fearful of losing their jobs, these male workers began to lobby through their trade unions to restrict the employment of children. At approximately the same time, humanitarian groups, largely made up of members of the middle class, began to oppose the use of children in the mines and factories on the basis that the working conditions were too severe and that the young were being exploited. This combination of factors resulted in the passage of legislation in Canada from the 1880s onward that restricted the use of child labour (Tanner, 2001; Tyyskä, 2001).

This legislation had a profound effect on the role of young people in Western society and the ways in which youth were perceived. Unemployed working-class youth who had been displaced from the factories and mines throughout the 19th century began to populate the streets of major North

American and European cities. While many attempted to earn a living by selling newspapers or matches, some of the displaced youth began to steal in order to survive (Tanner, 2001). Members of the middle class, increasingly disturbed by the work and leisure activities of this newly formed youth group, successfully lobbied for compulsory education as a means of civilizing and controlling these "ruffians." Tyyskä (2001), for example, notes, "the first public schools were aimed not only at creating a literate population, but at raising a patriotic citizenry and instilling into 'idle youth' habits valuable in the workforce, such as obedience and punctuality" (p. 29).

This connection between delinquency and adolescence was not restricted to lower-class street youth. In fact, conventional thinking in psychology and psychiatry at the time was that rebellion was a natural part of adolescent development. G. Stanley Hall, an early 20th-century psychologist, was at the leading edge of this work and was well known for his belief in an association between a young person's biological development and their inclinations toward deviant behaviour. Adams (1997), in her study of Canadian youth and societal perspectives on sexuality, acknowledges that while Hall's work linking biological changes with deviant behaviour during adolescence (i.e., puberty) still informs much work on youth today, these perspectives have led many to adopt the deceiving and problematic view that youth-related deviance was somehow "natural." As she explains:

> [Acknowledging that] Hall's conceptualization of adolescence as a stressful, instinct-driven, transitional stage between childhood and adulthood has yet to be completely overturned . . . [Hall's ideas] fit nicely into common-sense discussions of puberty as the grounds of the "youth problem," a perspective made evident in the 1940s and 1950s by some of the strategies used to regulate juvenile delinquency, strategies based on efforts to control adolescent sexuality (Adams, 1997, pp. 46–47).

A consequence of these concerns/panics about the behaviour of all youth was the development of federal controls and legislation, such as the Juvenile Delinquency Act of 1908, that were intended to prevent youth from being pulled into the delinquent lifestyle to which they were supposedly "predisposed." For example, in 1912, the city of Vancouver passed a curfew law that prohibited any person under the age of 16 from being out in public between the hours of 9 p.m. and 6 a.m. without the accompaniment of an adult.

The Emergence of the Teen and Teen Market

Of particular relevance to this chapter's discussion of the activities of contemporary youth are a series of post–World War II developments that were associated with the emergence of a "teen" culture—a culture of youth intricately linked to consumer and popular culture. The most notable of these societal changes, according to Hall and Jefferson (1976), was the sharp increase in the birth rate from 1945 onward (i.e., the "baby boom") that meant an increase in the proportion of young people in the population and a related rise in the

number of youth enrolled in schools. Other relevant trends included the elimination of unskilled jobs in increasingly technologically sophisticated business
environments, and the return of soldiers to positions previously held by youth.
The net result of these changes was that teenagers were now spending more
years in school and in isolation from the adult workforce. What this also meant
was that an increasing number of young people spent an increasing proportion of their youth in age-specific peer groups. A key consequence of these
developments was the increased opportunity for and impression of a distinct
"youth-specific" culture. Elaborating on this point, Adams (1997) described
how the psychologists, psychiatrists, physicians, sociologists, and journalists
of the time further reinforced these perceived differences:

> Teenagers were new and interesting. Those who took an interest in them created specialized
> niches for themselves in their various fields of study. So, for instance, psychiatrists and psy-
> chologists alike undertook studies to determine the boundaries of normal teenage develop-
> ment . . . Journalists and sociologists made mileage out of explaining teenagers to their
> elders, as did education film houses like the National Film Board . . . While adults
> were informed about a strange and baffling culture, teens were enlightened about appropri-
> ate modes of behaving (p. 43).

Equally significant in this context was that the discretionary spending of
youth during these years was on the rise, a development that did not go unno-
ticed by businesses and advertisers. The result was the emergence of a "targeted" teen consumer (Hebdige, 1988). Rock and roll, teen magazines,
records, clothing, and other items were being marketed exclusively toward
this younger demographic. At the same time that this new teen market was
being exploited, the perceived gap between the parent/adult generation and
the new youth culture had become as wide as ever. As Hall and Jefferson
(1976) put it, "the arrival of the whole range of distinctive styles in dress and
rock-music cemented any doubts anyone may have had about a 'unique'
younger generation" (p. 20).

This increasing cultural separation between adults and youth led to a new
sense of trepidation about "out of control," hedonistic youth consumers who
were embracing the pleasures associated with youth-oriented rock and roll
music, dances, fast food, and "outrageous" clothing styles. When this new
panic about teens "having too much fun" is considered in conjunction with
existing concerns about youth delinquency (along with the perception of a
"naturally" psychologically underdeveloped adolescent noted earlier), it
becomes easy to see just how fluid, complex, and ambiguous the notion of
youth had become.

Youth and Culture into the 21st Century

From the 1950s to the present, these links between business, advertising, and
teenage consumer culture solidified. This evolution is largely attributable to the
increasing sophistication of the advertising industry. Evidence of this

youth–advertiser connection is the development of the term "tweens" during the 1990s. Tweens, the 9- to 14-year-old youth demographic, are now distinct from the 15- to 19-year-old "teens," a separation that is useful for advertisers attempting to more effectively target youth (Clark and Deziel, 1999). The "tween" segment, in particular, has become the object of marketing research given tweens' tremendous purchasing power. In 2005, for example, they spent an estimated $2.9 billion of their own money on food, entertainment, and clothing, while influencing about $20 billion in household purchases through "kidfluence" (the influence young people have over household purchases) (YTV, 2007).

This final point is important because it raises questions not only about the ways that contemporary youth are spending their time and about their relationships with consumer culture, but also about the nature of their ties with the "parent/adult generation" in the 21st century. That is to say, it would seem that the adult world would be less relevant to the lives of teens who spend an increasing amount of time in youth-oriented educational settings, and who live in an increasingly consumption-driven and media-saturated world. Of course, to a certain extent this is only speculation. Until the actual meanings that young people give to their activities are considered (and potential for youth to be critical of and able to distance themselves from advertising images accounted for), we cannot speak decisively about Canadian youth and culture. For similar reasons, more information is needed about the variety of activities youth are involved in. In the following sections, we work through some of the existing research and theory on these topics with the goal of clarifying these issues.

What Are Canadian Youth Doing?: Leisure Participation Patterns In and Outside the Home

In this section we provide a broad overview of the most common leisure activities and consumption habits of Canadian youth, as reported by Canadian teenagers over the past several years. In doing this, we draw heavily on the work of Reginald Bibby (2009) and his book *The Emerging Millennials: How Canada's Newest Generation Is Responding to Change and Choice*. Bibby's book includes an exemplary synopsis of the activities of Canadian teens, drawing on 11 nationwide surveys of teens (aged 15 to 19) and adults spanning the years 1975 through 2008. In the process of doing this research, about 16,000 young people (and 10,000 adults) were surveyed or interviewed. While we recognize that such an overview cannot possibly do justice to the diversity of young Canadians and their activities, this "big picture" does provide a platform from which to discuss the centrality of various popular culture-related activities in the lives of youth.

Teen Trends and Cultural Activity: Bibby's Big Picture

According to the findings reported in Bibby's book, in 2008, the top three daily activities for Canadian teens, both male and female, were using the computer (99 percent), watching television (96 percent), and listening to music

(87 percent). Number four on the list was using a cell phone (54 percent), although more females reported carrying out this activity than males (60 as compared to 48 percent). Ranking fifth was text messaging at 44 percent (51 percent for female and 37 percent for males). On a daily to weekly basis, about 75 percent of males indicated they play video/computer games, an activity reported by only 25 percent of females. Four in ten females read books they want to read, as compared to three in ten males, and 35 percent of youth reported playing an instrument or working on music on a weekly basis (Bibby, 2009). Attending a movie was the most popular activity on a monthly basis (Bibby, 2009).

Computer   As discussed above, using the computer ranked as number one on the list of top daily activities and, significantly, the computer-related activities of accessing Facebook and using e-mail followed up at number six and seven, respectively, suggesting that Canadian youth spend a great deal of time online. Indeed, 98 percent of the young people surveyed by Bibby (2009) reported using computers at least one hour a day, with 50 percent indicating that they are on the computer at least two hours a day, 30 percent for three to four hours per day, and close to 20 percent for five or more hours a day. Little gender differentiation was reported, although females said they received greater enjoyment from using e-mail than males (57 as opposed to 45 percent) while males reported higher levels of enjoyment from playing video/computer games (67 percent and 26 percent) (Bibby, 2009).

Given the amount of time spent online, it is perhaps not surprising that a study conducted by the Media Awareness Network found evidence to suggest that about 94 percent of Canadian youth have Internet access from home, a marked increase from 79 percent in 2001 (Steeves, 2005). Moreover, the points of access to networked spaces appear to include more than computers, as around half of youth with cell phones are reportedly able to use the phone to surf the Internet (44 percent) and text message their friends (56 percent). The numbers provided by Bibby (2009) and the Media Awareness Network (Steeves, 2005) suggest that Canadian youth are "connected youth." According to Steeves (2005), the online environment is such an integral part of the lives of young Canadians that they do not see the Internet as a distinct entity or environment. Instead, "it is simply one more space in which they live their lives, connecting with friends, pursuing interests, figuring out what it means to be a teenager and a grown-up . . . To them the Net has become wallpaper, seamlessly blending with the social spaces they inhabit in the real world" (p. 4).

In 2001, it was reported that the three favourite websites of Canadian youth aged 13 to 17 were the e-mail websites hotmail.com and yahoo.com and the music-download website napster.com (Environics Research Group, 2001), while the top three online activities were playing and downloading music (57 percent), e-mail (56 percent), and surfing for fun (50 percent) (Environics

Research Group, 2001). A more recent analysis of the top 500 favourite websites of Canadian youth indicates that youth typically like to spend time on gaming sites (20 percent) and streaming/multimedia sites (20 percent), followed by special interest sites (18 percent), shopping sites (14 percent), and TV channels (8 percent) (Steeves, 2005). The top five sites of females aged 13 to 17 were Addicting Games, eBaumsworld, Neopets, Miniclip, and Nexopia while the top five sites of their male counterparts were Addicting Games, eBaumsworld, Miniclip, Newgrounds, and eBay (Steeves, 2005).

Television   Viewing television is reported as the second most popular daily activity of teens. According to Bibby (2009), 96 percent of young people in Canada watch television for an hour or more every day (or at least have their televisions on in the background while sitting at their computers), about 60 percent watch television at least two hours a day, 30 percent for three to four hours a day, and just under 10 percent watch television for five or more hours per day, with little or no significant difference between males and females.

It is important to remember here that when youth spend time in front of the television set, they are exposed not only to the programs they are watching, but also to advertising and commercials. In fact, Canadian youth cite television as the key influence on their purchase decisions, whether they buy the good themselves or ask their parents to buy it for them (Health Canada, 2000). In the same way, Canadian youth are exposed to an abundance of American-based programming and culture, with U.S.–based television being the primary source of television programming for Canadian teenagers (Health Canada, 2000). Adding to this, the websites that youth tend to frequent are commercial sites that have been designed to sell products, reinforce branding, or advertise to youth (Steeves, 2005). According to the Media Awareness Network, Canadian youth encounter a great deal of advertising while on the Internet as almost all of the top 50 sites identified by the survey participants include marketing material (Steeves, 2005). Interestingly, over three-quarters of kids who play product-centred games think they are "just games," not "mainly advertisements." Awareness of the commercial nature of these games rises with age, from 18 percent of kids in Grade 4 to 31 percent in Grade 11 (Steeves, 2005). Interestingly, Bibby (2009) reports that only one in four young people regard advertising as having a high level of influence on them.

Friends, Family, and Cultural Activity   While it is apparent that popular culture, especially mediated forms, plays a central role in the lives of Canadian teenagers, friends play a large part as well. When asked to rank important sources of enjoyment, the top answer for both males and females was friends (95 percent). In addition, when given a list of characteristics and asked to indicate how personally important each one was, friendship ranked first (86 percent) with freedom coming a close second (85 percent) (Bibby, 2009). Furthermore, 86 percent of Canadian youth perceive friends as having "a great deal" of influence in their lives and finally, when faced with a serious problem, "friends" was the second choice (31 percent) for teens to turn to after family (35 percent) (Bibby, 2009). Bibby notes that over the past decade, there has been a remarkable increase in the number of close friends that teens say they have. In 2000, 52 percent indicated that they had four or more close friends while in 2008, the number had grown to 72 percent. Moreover, there has been a decrease in the percentage of youth who have no close friends, as well as those who have one, two, or three close friends. "Right across the board," explains Bibby, "the number of close friends is up" (p. 31). Bibby goes on to suggest that the obvious explanation for the increase in the number of friends who are perceived to be "close" lies with technology:

> Teens can readily pursue friendships by going on-line and accessing any number of interactive websites, led, in 2008, by Facebook—accessed at least once a week by 74% of females and 66% of males. Sites like Skype enable them to turn on their webcams and see and be seen by the person with whom they are speaking. And multi-functional cell phones, of course, provide them with any number of audio, video, camera and recording possibilities (p. 32).

According to Bibby, additional evidence that websites contribute to expanded friendship links is that the number of young people involved in "Internet friendship groups" now almost matches the number who are involved in sports groups. "In fact," explains Bibby, "Internet social ties represent the no. 1 group activity for females (48%) and the no. 2 group activity for males (41%)."

EXPLAINING YOUTH CULTURAL ACTIVITY

It is clear from Bibby's research and the work of others that popular culture (e.g., popular media, music, games) plays a central role in the lives of Canadian youth (see Box 3.1). It would also be fair to suggest that while parents remain an important part of young people's lives, relationships with and approval from peers and friends are immensely important to youth. These trends and findings are the inspiration for many sociologists who attempt to understand how leisure and popular culture influence young people. In the following section we outline some of the key theoretical perspectives that speak to these trends and findings. As will become evident, these perspectives are somewhat diverse, with some scholars portraying youth as passive and impressionable consumers of various forms of popular culture, and others viewing youth as reactive and proactive agents who sometimes symbolically use cultural activities such as listening to music and dancing, as well as stylistic expressions (e.g., embodied in hairstyles, clothing, and body alterations like piercing and tattooing) in order to (1) resist "mainstream" influences and authority; (2) react to feelings of marginalization or disaffection; and/or (3) negotiate their ever-evolving identities.

BOX 3.1   SATELLITE CHILDREN: ETHNIC IDENTITY, FAMILY, AND LEISURE

According to Tsang et al. (2003), the term "satellite children" was first used in the late 1980s "to describe children whose parents are Chinese immigrants to North America [mainly from Hong Kong and Taiwan] and who have returned to their country of origin after immigration" (pp. 359–360). Typically, the father returns to the home country to ensure financial security for the family, while the mother and children remain in Canada. Because the family is separated by an "immense geographical distance" (p. 360), irregular visits occur and, as a result, the separated couples are commonly referred to as astronauts. Using a similar analogy, the children are referred to as "satellite children."

A crucial point made by the researchers is that ethnic identity is not something that people are born with. That is to say, it is something that is "socially constructed." For instance, some respondents reported that they are still Chinese even though they live in Canada, others classified themselves as Chinese-Canadians, and still others felt confused about the issue of ethnic identity. Furthermore, the acculturation process was found to be unique and differentiated for each respondent, although in most cases leisure activities and consumer items were crucial in the negotiation of ethnic identity. For instance, Chinese shopping malls, with karaoke bars, video rental shops, teahouses, and cinemas were credited with allowing satellite children to stay in touch with their culture of origin. Respondents in the study also reported that they are able to maintain a connection with their roots through local Chinese media structures, including Chinese TV and radio stations, newspapers, and magazines. Many respondents also felt that electronic communication technology such as the Internet, mobile phones, and e-mail "contributed to the ease of personal and cultural connections with the country of origin" (p. 373), especially with parents. Finally, it was noted that with the absence of parental guidance, peer influence became increasingly important in the development of ethnic identity among satellite children.

In short, the growth of Chinese communities and institutions in Canada, as well as the use of communication technology, enable satellite children to exist in a "hybrid cultural environment" (p. 377) that is a mixture of the host culture and the culture of origin. Furthermore, satellite children "are part of the growing ethnic population that created this new cultural milieu and contributed to its rapid development" (p. 377). Thus, instead of merely being conditioned and shaped by the existing Canadian culture, satellite children use leisure activities and consumption to actively create a new environment that eases their transition into Canada and helps them to cope with an altered family structure.

Passive Youth and the Culture Industry

Implicit in many arguments that have been put forth about the negative impacts of, for example, video games and advertising on young people is the view that youth are "social dupes" who uncritically consume popular culture. This perspective of youth and consumers is not new. In fact, it is part of a long history of cultural criticism and writing that presumes that audiences (youth and others) have great difficulty resisting the evils of popular film and television. The most notorious proponents of this view were the social thinkers and theorists associated with the **Frankfurt School of Social Research**. The Frankfurt School, whose origins can be traced back to Germany in 1923, was best known for the critiques of modern capitalism put forth by the school's associates, especially

Theodor Adorno, Max Horkheimer, and Herbert Marcuse. Members of the school fled to the United States (New York and California, in particular) in response to the rise of the Nazi party in Germany and the increasing intolerance to any ideas that were inconsistent with party ideology. What is especially interesting about this move is that the Frankfurt School's members, in escaping the Nazi ideologies of intolerance and control, found in America an extremely developed and sophisticated form of "control through culture" that formed the basis of subsequent work on the topic (Strinati, 1995).

This Frankfurt School's critique of the power of "mass culture" (e.g., mass-mediated advertising, Hollywood film) emphasized the ways that commodity producers indirectly but forcefully manipulate consumer desires (Horkheimer and Adorno, 1972; Marcuse, 1964). Horkheimer and Adorno (1972), in their revered book *Dialectic of Enlightenment*, describe how pro-capitalist ideologies are supported through and within the "culture industry," the industry of technologies, commodities, and entertainments that impose wants and needs for material satisfaction on the "passive" consumer. According to the authors, within the culture industry, industrialized, mechanized, and standardized cultural products are given a seemingly individual character—a character that masks the reality of mass production, and, in turn, manipulates and subjugates the individual. For example, a television advertisement for a mass-produced product might be marketed in ways that lead consumers to think they will "stand out from the crowd" if they only purchase that item. Horkheimer and Adorno (1972) suggested, "in the culture industry the notion of genuine style is seen to be the aesthetic equivalent of domination" (pp. 129–130). In this way, the culture industry creates a homogenous culture of "social dupes," who, in being fascinated by and enamoured with elements of popular culture such as Hollywood film and consumer items, have been lulled into an uncritical acceptance of present conditions (i.e., where identity is created and negotiated through consumption). Since the "concepts of order which it [the culture industry] hammers into people are always those of the status quo" (Adorno, 1991, p. 90), the masses—with youth being the most impressionable of the lot—are deceived into conformity and a loss of consciousness. That is to say, a life guided by and given meaning through the consumption of products and entertainment comes to be a taken-for-granted and unrivalled way of life.

Acknowledging that this portrayal of the Frankfurt School is necessarily brief and oversimplified, it is important to point out that there have been many critics of the school's view of the culture industry and the consumer over the years. Most pertinent to this chapter is the concern expressed by authors who feel that the Frankfurt School did not give sufficient credit to consumers—consumers who might well interpret popular culture-related messages and items in ways not intended by industry producers. As Douglas Kellner (1995) argued:

> The Frankfurt School position that all mass culture is ideological and debased, having the effects of duping a passive mass of consumers, is . . . objectionable . . . [One should]

allow for the possibility that critical and subversive moments could be found in the artefacts of the culture industries . . . In addition, one should distinguish between the encoding and decoding of media artefacts, and recognize that an active audience often produces its own meanings and uses for products of the culture industries (pp. 29–30).

Many researchers have provided analyses of popular culture that responded to and contradicted those of the Frankfurt School. John Fiske (1989a, 1989b), in his books *Reading the Popular* and *Understanding Popular Culture*, celebrated the capacities of consumers who, for example, use shopping malls in empowering and resistive ways (e.g., by hanging out in the mall, but not shopping). Albert Cohen (1955), in his foundational research on youth and deviance, described how working-class youth who do not have the resources to measure up against "the middle-class measuring rod"—a status system essentially defined by academic and occupational achievement (and, by association, ownership of desirable consumer goods)—create their own "oppositional" value system (e.g., where disrespecting middle-class values come to be revered within the subcultural group).

Active Youth and Symbolic Resistance

It was at the **Centre for Contemporary Cultural Studies** (CCCS) at the University of Birmingham, England, in the 1970s that a core of researchers and theorists developed a still-influential approach for understanding the ways that youth proactively respond to the power of mainstream culture and their related feelings of marginalization. Central to their analysis was the concept of **hegemony**, a term developed in the early 20th century by Italian revolutionary Antonio Gramsci (1971). Hegemony, in simple terms, refers to the ways that groups in power (e.g., upper classes) are able to maintain their privileged position by developing strategies that ensure that marginal/oppressed groups consent to their power. By creating education systems that favour the status quo (e.g., that maintain standards oriented to the middle class), and by supporting the dissemination of media messages that both stigmatize groups that do not conform (e.g., youth) while maintaining a system of consumption that benefits only the most powerful, hegemony is maintained. As you might expect, for those who study hegemony and popular culture, research often focuses on how much input powerful groups have into the messages that are dispersed through mass media (e.g., by looking at relationships between media producers and big business) (see Box 3.2).

At the same time that Gramsci described the power of dominant groups and classes, he more optimistically recognized the possibility for **counter-hegemony**, that is, the potential for marginal groups to fight back against the forces that oppress them. It was this potential for counter-hegemony that inspired the arguments made by those at the CCCS, who interpreted the spectacular and sometimes offensive styles and activities of youth subculture members to be proactive responses to these youths' marginalized positionings (i.e., positionings as both "youth" and "working class"). For example, Dick Hebdige (1979), in his classic

BOX 3.2   RACE, INTERPRETATION, ADVERTISING, AND YOUTH CULTURE

In the late 1980s and early 1990s, mass media reports about the "power of sneaker commercials" over youth began to surface. The impetus for these reports was a series of high-profile reports of violence over sneakers in the United States and Canada, including a well-documented case where one youth killed another for his Air Jordan Sneakers (Telander, 1990). A study by one of the authors of this chapter and his colleague considered the extent to which athletic apparel advertisements featuring celebrity icon athletes actually influenced young male basketball fans' perceptions of what is "cool" and the extent to which these youth felt they "needed" sneakers to "be cool" (Wilson and Sparks, 1996, 1999). An important addendum to this study was that the celebrity icon athletes (basketball players) in the commercials were in almost all cases African-American. For this reason, Wilson and Sparks focused on the ways that "black" youth in Toronto and "nonblack" youth in Vancouver interpreted these commercials (using small focus group interviews in each city). The researchers found that the black youth were extremely enamoured with many of the sneaker commercials and the athletes featured in these commercials, and were clear about the importance of the name-brand (e.g., Nike) sneaker as a style marker in their culture. It was also pertinent, though, that while appreciating the commercial and admitting to its influence, these same youth were also critical of the ways that blacks are portrayed in television, suggesting that there should be more "positive" nonathlete portrayals of blacks. Conversely, the nonblack youth, who also enjoyed the commercials and admired the celebrity athletes, did not consider the sneakers to be as central to their cultural identities or as crucial in the construction of a "cool" persona among peers. As strikingly, these youth were largely uncritical of or ambivalent to the ways that blacks are portrayed in mass media. That is to say, unlike the black youth, for whom race-related issues (as they relate to African American portrayals in particular) were a central part of their everyday lives, for the nonblack youth, these concerns were not something they had thought much about—although the authors also found that some nonblack youth appeared to learn about race from television. Conclusions offered by Wilson and Sparks (1996, 1999) in their two articles on the topic that are especially pertinent to this chapter are (a) that young people are a complex group who interpret media in a variety of ways, depending on their cultural experiences and their social locations (i.e., their race and gender-related identities; and their positioning as basketball fans living in different parts of Canada) and (b) that youth audiences are both critical (e.g., the black youth noticing the ways that African-Americans are portrayed in media) and impressionable (e.g., both youth groups enjoying the sneaker commercials, the nonblack youth in some cases appearing to learn about race from television).

book *Subculture:The Meaning of Style*, described how youth who were members of subcultures such as the punk rockers and skinheads were expressing dissatisfaction with the status quo through style. That is to say, by dyeing their hair blue or purple, wearing intentionally torn clothes, adorning themselves with safety pins as nose-rings, and listening to music by bands like the Sex Pistols (a band whose lyrics challenged and mocked powerful institutions such as the British monarchy), these youth were making purposeful attempts to challenge the sensibility of the establishment—or, as the title of another CCCS-based book relays, they were "resisting through rituals" (Hall and Jefferson, 1976).

It is important to acknowledge, however (as the CCCS members did), that these challenges were largely symbolic or "magical," and were not direct political challenges to authority. This concession could be interpreted in at least two ways. On one hand, it could mean that youth subcultures are not truly counter-hegemonic in the sense that their activities in no way alter the conditions that these young people are living with. In fact, it would seem that dominant groups would not be opposed to this kind of resistance because it would appear that young people "have a voice," when in reality existing social conditions that favour the privileged remain intact. On the other hand, to say that these activities do not "make a difference" is to be insensitive to the ways that young people are at least temporarily empowered by participation in alternative cultural activity. In the same way, it is important to consider that youth involvement in symbolically resistant subcultural activity is evidence that young people are active and critical recipients of cultural messages that circulate through, for example, mass media and educational settings. Paul Willis (1990) and Angela McRobbie (1994) are two authors who have specifically discussed how young people actively subvert aspects of consumer culture by, for example, illegally recording music or purchasing secondhand clothing.

Research and theory out of the CCCS has been subject to a series of criticisms (c.f., Blackman, 2005; Bennett and Harris, 2004). Most notably, CCCS-based theorists have been accused of "celebrating" the capacity of young people to resist mainstream cultural influences. That is to say, some critics argue that the youth depicted in some of the CCCS's work are given too much credit for their ability to think critically and respond proactively. Still others (who work in what has come to be termed the "postsubculture" tradition) have convincingly made the case that we have entered an era where the term "subculture" is less relevant than in the past because it refers to a somewhat unified group—a group organized around a shared set of perspectives, activities, and relationships. According to postsubcultural theorists, contemporary youth are often members of various cultural groups, frequently move between these groups, and are less committed to any one group. Andy Bennett (1999), a leading proponent of this argument, feels that the term "neo-tribe" captures the essence of the groups that contemporary youth belong to—youth whose cultural identities are more fluid and complex than those referred to by theorists at the CCCS.

Another issue identified by critics is that spectacular subcultures like punk rockers and skinheads are only a small sample of youth today, and that the everyday activities of young people might not be subversive in the ways described by some members of the CCCS (the work of Willis and McRobbie noted above notwithstanding). A related concern is that the research seemed to assume that all punks or skinheads interpreted their activities in the same way. As sociologists such as Young and Craig (1997) (who studied skinheads in Calgary) suggest, subculture members, while sharing broad philosophies, often participate in subcultures for quite different reasons and interpret their subcultural activities in distinct ways.

This understanding of youth subcultures as groups of young people who share many perspectives and cultural activities, but who also interpret cultural items (such as clothing) and media messages in somewhat diverse ways is, in our view, a more balanced approach to explaining and describing relationships between youth and culture. At the same time, we acknowledge that in the current historical moment, youth have varying forms of membership within subcultures (some are committed members, others are more transient subcultural interlopers), and that subcultures take on various forms (some are local and well organized; others are global, virtual, and diffuse).

In the next section, we explore these views of youth and subcultures through a case study of the rave subculture in southern Ontario that took place in the mid- and late-1990s, referring to findings from research conducted by Wilson (1999, 2002a, 2006), one of the authors of this chapter. Following this, Wilson also describes some of the findings from his research as a way of explaining some of the theories of youth cultural activity described here. The section concludes with a discussion of the political potential of rave (and youth subcultures more generally) in an age of Internet communication.

RAVE IN SOUTHERN ONTARIO: A CASE STUDY AND REFLECTIVE ACCOUNT

"Rave" is a culture of youth whose members are renowned for their interest in computer-generated "techno" music, use of amphetamine drugs, and attendance at all-night dance parties known as "raves (see Box 3.3)." Over the course

BOX 3.3   RAVE, TECHNOLOGY, AND GLOBALIZATION

The rave subculture is also a "pro-technology" subculture. Ravers advertise their parties over the Internet, often engage in chatroom discussions about upcoming and previous rave parties and about music, and enjoy and sometimes create music that is largely computer-generated. In some cases, virtual and real rave parties are held, where "online ravers" interact in chatrooms with those sitting at computers at an actual party, while observing the event and hearing the music through webcams and web-audio technology. In an article that I wrote with Michael Atkinson, we suggested that "online and offline" life for ravers had become increasingly blurred (Wilson and Atkinson, 2005). In fact, some DJs who play at rave parties will bring an entire "set of music" on their laptop computer, to be played for the raver audience.

Unlike many previous subcultures that were antitechnology, ravers celebrate technology (Kellner, 1995) and, as Greener and Hollands (2006) suggest in their study of the "psy-trance" community (psy-trance is an electronic music genre associated with rave and dance parties), Internet technology has supported the evolution of a global subculture. In an article I wrote with Ben Carrington that compared the British house music scene and the Canadian rave scene, we similarly discussed ways that various communication technologies supported the globalization of the rave scene. We described how the connections ravers form with other members of their subculture who live in other parts of the world—and the information they glean about rave scenes in other places from "surfing the Net"—inspire international travel to dance parties (Carrington and Wilson, 2002).

of my research on the southern Ontario rave scene from 1995 to 1999, I attended raves; interviewed ravers, rave-DJs, and rave party promoters; and read daily comments that appeared on rave-related newsgroups of which I was a member. In my Ph.D. dissertation (Wilson, 1999) and in a subsequent article and book (Wilson, 2002a, 2006), I reported findings from my research and, in conducting a sociological analysis of these findings, considered the extent to which raver-youth were either actively resisting aspects of mainstream culture (e.g., creating an alternative "neo-hippie" set of values in the rave) or passively participating in the scene (e.g., mindlessly escaping into the dance party and a drug-induced haze).

In essence, I found that although ravers shared a range of activities and perspectives, they also tended to participate in and interpret their experiences in diverse ways. At times this diversity manifested itself as differences between ravers, while other times it appeared that raver perspectives changed over time, as subculture members learned more about their scene. For example, many youth were aware of and generally supported the rave-related values articulated through the acronym **PLUR**, "Peace-Love-Unity-Respect." These values were operationalized in some of the following ways:

- The "pick-up" culture that defines many dance clubs was less evident in rave, where ravers seldom "hit on" one another in the same way that people do at clubs, preferring to dance and listen to music.

- The macho norms of intimidation that are commonplace in many dance clubs are frowned upon in the rave. When strangers bump into one another on the dance floor, often an apology and friendly gesture or conversation will follow (instead of a scowl or physical confrontation).

- Uninhibited "communal" dancing to heavy and fast-beated techno music was viewed as a way for ravers to "connect with one another" through ritual. When ravers are moving together to the music and, if they choose to do drugs, feeling the positive effects of the amphetamine drug Ecstasy (a drug that apparently allows people to lose inhibitions while giving them energy to dance), they are said to be "feeling the vibe." Many ravers claim that by feeling the vibe through this music and dance ritual, they are able to lose preconceptions about people—a state and perspective that at least partially explains why rave culture is also thought to be open to and accepting of all races and ethnicities, and to be especially empowering for women (c.f., Pini, 1997).

For many of the youth I interviewed, rave culture was an alternative youth movement that was, for them, an escape from and a reaction against a mainstream culture where people are intolerant of one another and are poor communicators, and where day-to-day life is so intense that "letting go" is almost impossible.

Of course, not all ravers were this reflective about the meaning of their rave experiences, nor were they necessarily motivated by the "countercultural" possibilities of rave. Some of these youth viewed raves as places to go after the bars closed. At times, these "drop-in" ravers were known to be either ignorant of or disrespectful of the informal norms of interaction in rave. Other youth viewed raves as little more than safe spaces to use drugs, a perspective frowned upon by "authentic" ravers who see drug use as only one component of an integrated ritual of dancing and music listening. Still others came to raves in hopes of "picking up" for a "one-night stand," a practice usually associated with more conventional nightclubs. One raver in the study labelled these disrespectful interlopers into the scene "toxic ravers," as a way of describing their effects on the culture and environment. The increased number of "outsiders" attending rave parties was a point of concern for many committed/"authentic" long-time ravers, who were upset about how, with the increased popularity of rave as a topic of discussion in mass media and a "style" adopted by advertisers, people have begun to attend raves because it is the "cool" thing to do, not because of a desire to be part of a PLUR-inspired community (Wilson, 2002a, 2006).

In broad terms then, many youth attended raves for several different reasons. At the same time though, and as pertinently, many "committed" ravers described how their views on rave changed over their "careers" as a subculture member. For example, a number of interviewed members of the culture talked about how, when they first entered the rave scene, they were enamoured with the music, drugs, and sense of community. As time went on though, some explained that they began to see that rave was actually more "political" than they thought, with rave promoters competing for raver-dollars and not always acting in the best interest of the community/participants (e.g., overcharging for bottled water, a necessary resource for those engaged in intense, all-night dancing). Others noticed some of their friends becoming too "into" the drug aspect of the scene and noticed how the "nonrave" lives of these peers were being negatively impacted. Others realized that the rave community was much more fragmented than they originally thought, with some ravers looking down on other ravers because of the specific type of techno music they listened to or the clothes they wore. The most common complaint was that rave was becoming too "commercialized," and that the alternative lifestyle they were seeking was not attainable in a rave scene that was now marketed in mainstream magazines and by money-hungry promoters. Certainly this latter view is a more cynical understanding of the scene, but it certainly represents the perspective of many ravers who became disillusioned over their subcultural careers (Wilson, 2002a, 2006).

Using Rave to Help Us Understand Youth Cultural Activity

It was clear from the research that rave was viewed and used in a variety of ways by the young people who participated in it. That is to say, rave represented, depending on to whom you talked and when you talked to them, anything from a weekend escape and "good party" to a proactive form of resistance and social movement. For example, some youth might attend raves because they saw a flashy "rave flyer" advertising what looked like a fun time, but did not view their participation as being a meaningful symbolic statement about or escape from an "overregulated and oppressive" mainstream culture. Conversely, many ravers were dedicated to and supported the rave PLUR philosophy. These ravers often would not only attend raves, but also put up rave websites promoting PLUR-related views, and throw (sometimes nonprofit) raves with titles such as "Good Vibes" or "Unification of a Peaceful Nation." Many others, who were somewhere "in between" these extreme positionings, would express an awareness of rave values and would adhere to and enjoy the norms of interaction in raves, but considered themselves to be only weekend ravers not very committed to the subculture.

In other words, some youth were passive consumers of the rave party and music, akin to the consumers described by the Frankfurt School theorists (if we view more mainstream raves as leisure activities for mass consumption). On the other hand, some youth were proactive and committed participants in a culture that, for them, embodied countercultural values and symbolically challenged aspects of "the mainstream" that they find distasteful. Through the lens of CCCS theorists, these youth would be "resistant," using culture as a form of expression and potential disruption. Of course, there were also youth who inhabited a "middle ground," attending raves sometimes and adhering to rave norms when they do attend, but without a firm or long-term commitment to the scene or the countercultural ideology.

Although it is useful to outline these theoretical positionings, it is also important to point out that theorists committed to understanding the "hegemony" of the mainstream (e.g., the power of those who support the pro-commercialism values that ravers resist), would argue (cynically) that the symbolic resistance of ravers, even in its most proactive form, in no way alters the existing conditions of oppression or feelings of marginalization that some youth experience and resist. In other words, while some youth are empowered by their participation in rave, their "resistance," according to some theorists, is meaningless in the big picture.

Beyond Symbolic Resistance: Youth, Internet Culture, and Collective Action

With the rise of Internet communication in the mid- and late-1990s, some sociologists began to rethink these ambivalent views on youth resistance and participation in rave. Authors like Kahn and Kellner (2003, 2004), Meikle (2002), and Darntell (2006) argued that the Internet—as an inexpensive communication tool that supports interaction and information sharing on a global scale—offers a resource to young people interested in sharing ideas and concerns with others, and possibly organizing around and collectively responding to social and political issues. The renowned protests that took place in Seattle in 1999 at the World Trade Organization (WTO) meetings are commonly referred to in this context because the Internet was shown to support this unprecedented activist response to concerns about capitalist globalization. As Kahn and Kellner (2003) describe:

> [Prior to the WTO meetings] many Web sites contained anti-WTO material and numerous mailing lists used the Internet to distribute critical material and to organize the protest. The result was the mobilization of caravans throughout the US to take protestors to Seattle, many of whom had never met and were recruited through the Internet ... In addition, protests occurred throughout the world, and a proliferation of anti-WTO material against the extremely secret group spread throughout the Internet (p. 305).

The "Battle in Seattle" signalled for many commentators the emergence of a more politically oriented (sub)culture of young people that was distinct from the "symbolically resistant" and "passive" youth featured in previous research (cf., Wall, 2007). Put another way, young people, who historically have been limited in their access to the resources that are needed to support coordinated and widespread forms of collective action now have relatively easy access to this seemingly "democratizing medium" (Wilson and Hayhurst, 2009). Juris and Pleyers (2009), in their recent article on "young global justice activists," describe the subcultural practices associated with protests such as Seattle as "**alter-activism**," and emphasize the importance of new information and communication technologies for the development of "alter-activist" networks that enable various forms of political action and participation.

The rave example we have been working with remains pertinent here if we consider how the group's relationship with new forms of technology (especially the Internet) might support the politically oriented activities of some members of the group—such as the protest against "anti-rave" laws in Toronto (Hier, 2002), the antiwar demonstrations by rave community members in Vancouver, and the rave party dedicated to raising awareness about homophobia in San Francisco (Fritz, 1999; Wilson 2006).

CONCLUSION

In this chapter we described how youth have increasingly developed a cultural life separate from the "parent/adult generation," outlined a striking (albeit unsurprising) trend that mass media and popular culture have become an integral part of young people's lives, and discussed some ways that youth cultural activity has been explained. In working through these explanations, we referred to sociological theories developed by the Frankfurt School of Social Research and the Centre for Contemporary Cultural Studies in Birmingham, England, that theorized about young people's relationships with popular culture, peers, and the parent/adult generation. The rave subculture was used as a case study to interrogate some of these approaches and to ultimately argue that youth should be viewed as a diverse group who understand their social and cultural world in a range of ways, and that their perspectives change as they gain new experiences.

In reflecting on the developments, ideas, and assertions of this chapter on existing literature focused on contemporary youth, it seemed to us that much of what is written about young people's fascination with popular culture and the impacts of these fascinations on the family is quite negative. As noted earlier, authors such as Furlong and Cartmel (2007) suggest that as youth become increasingly connected to the outside world through global media, they also come to be aware of social problems in ways that previous generations were not. In the same way, these authors suggest that in spending time in the world of global media (and not within more conventional local peer- and family-oriented groups), there is a weakened "sense of community" for young people, and, for this reason, youth feel more "on their own" than ever before.

While we agree that there is reason to be concerned, we also suggest that recent developments are not unconditionally negative. For example, the Internet has been described in some instances as a forum where young people, especially marginalized youth, can connect with one another, experience a sense of belonging that was missing in their "offline" lives, and express themselves in creative and productive ways (e.g., websites for bullied youth to attain information and get advice from peers about how to best deal with problems at school) (cf., Wilson, 2002b). Others see the Internet as a communication tool that enables forms of civic participation among a generation commonly considered apolitical and apathetic (Juris and Pleyers, 2009). In fact, the younger generation's literacy in computers and other media could be considered testament to their ability to adapt to new social and cultural circumstances in ways that many adults cannot or do not (Rushkoff, 1996). With these ideas in mind, Don Tapscott (1998), author of *Growing Up Digital: The Rise of the Net Generation*, offers a more optimistic approach to family relations in a society where young people's lives are intricately linked with media and technology. Tapscott argues that in order "to break down the walls between generations" there is a need to work toward more open and communicative families. Central to Tapscott's (1998) argument is that this openness is possible only if parents "understand the potential of new media" and, crucially, accept the part that it plays in youth culture (pp. 249–250). We would add to this that it is also important to recognize the diversity of ways young people interpret media and experience peer cultural relationships. In this way, parents and researchers can work toward a better understanding of youth and youth culture and, in turn, move away from a situation where young people are commonly stigmatized and demonized.

Summary

- Youth are a complex and diverse group that negotiate, understand, and interpret the various cultural influences they encounter in different ways at different times.

- Conceptions of youth have changed through history; after World War II, a youth (teen) culture emerged linked to consumer and popular culture.

- In the 21st century, popular culture, which targets youth—music, television, computer activities, movies—and is enjoyed with friends, plays a central role in the lives of Canadian teenagers.

- There is a long history of analysts viewing youth as passive, uncritical consumers of popular culture; more recently, theorists and researchers have articulated a perspective that suggests youth are active, critical recipients of cultural messages and may explicitly resist the dominant culture.

- Youth literacy with aspects of the new technology—the use of computers and other media—promotes connection and community among youth and allows for the possibility of enhanced communication between generations if parents accept it as an integral part of youth culture.

- An examination of contemporary Canadian rave subculture suggests a diversity of youth groups—those who are simply passive consumers of the rave party and music as well as those who are proactive and committed to a countercultural challenge to mainstream values.

- The Internet—a communication technology known for supporting various forms of political action among youth activists—is now recognized as a resource that allows young people to do more than "symbolically resist."

Critical Thinking Questions

1. What does it mean to say that the term "youth" is "socially constructed"?

2. Are youth more susceptible to the influences of popular culture than adults?

3. Why are youth often portrayed as either "troubled or troubling" in mass media reports?

Websites

Media Awareness Network
http://www.media-awareness.ca/english/index.cfm
> This site provides resources and support for those interested in media literacy programs for youth. It includes links to several special initiative projects that the Media Awareness Network has undertaken with the goal of advancing our understanding of key media literacy-related issues, including Internet safety for young people.

Health Canada: Division of Childhood and Adolescence Webpage
http://www.phac-aspc.gc.ca/dca-dea/index-eng.php
> This webpage contains a range of information about issues to do with youth, children, identity, and health issues.

Suggested Readings

Mary Louise Adams. 1997. *The Trouble with Normal*. Toronto, ON: University of Toronto Press.

> Adams's book is one of the few recent Canadian books to consider youth culture with a specific focus on the historical construction of gender and heterosexuality in the lives of youth. Adams's book includes a useful discussion of the recent history of the social category "youth."

Andy Furlong and Fred Cartmel. 2007. *Young People and Social Change: New Perspectives*. Berkshire, UK: Open University Press.

> Furlong and Cartmel's book includes an excellent discussion of social and societal changes into the 21st century and how these changes impact and offer unique challenges for young people. The book discusses social change and youth in relation to education, the labour market, family and patterns of dependency, leisure, health, crime, and politics.

Julian Tanner. 2010. *Teenage Troubles: Youth and Deviance in Canada*. Don Mills, ON: Oxford University Press.

> This is a most comprehensive examination of deviance-related approaches to the study of youth in Canada.

References

Acland, C. 1995. *Youth, Murder, Spectacle: The Cultural Politics of "Youth in Crisis."* Boulder: Westview Press.

Adams, M. 1997. *The Trouble with Normal: Postwar Youth and the Making of Heterosexuality*. Toronto: University of Toronto Press.

Adorno, T. 1991. *The Culture Industry*. London: Routledge.

Bennett, A. 1999. "Subcultures or Neo-tribes?: Rethinking the Relationship between Youth, Style and Musical Taste." *Sociology*, 33(3): 599–617.

Bennett, A. and K. Harris, eds. 2004. *After Subculture: Critical Studies of Subcultural Theory*. New York: Palgrave.

Bibby, R. 2001. *Canada's Teens: Today, Yesterday, and Tomorrow*. Toronto: Stoddart.

Bibby, R. 2009. *The Emerging Millennials: How Canada's Newest Generation Is Responding to Change & Choice*. Lethbridge, AB: Project Canada Book.

Blackman, S. 2005. "Youth Subcultural Theory: A Critical Engagement with the Concept, Its Origins and Politics, from the Chicago School to the Postmodern." *Journal of Youth Studies*, 8(1), 1–20.

Carrington, B. and B. Wilson. 2002. "Global Clubcultures: Cultural Flows and 'Late Modern' Dance Music Culture." In M. Ceislik and G. Pollock, eds., *Young People in a Risk Society: The Restructuring of Youth Identities and Transitions in Late Modernity* (pp. 74–99). Aldershot, Hampshire, UK: Ashgate Publishing.

Clark, A. and S. Deziel. 1999. "How Teens Got the Power." *Maclean's*, 112(12): 42–47.

Cohen, A. 1955. *Delinquent Boys*. Glencoe: The Free Press of Glencoe.

Coleman, J. 1992. "The Nature of Adolescence." In J. Coleman and C. Warren-Adamson, eds., *Youth Policy in the 1990s: The Way Forward* (pp. 8–27). New York: Routledge.

Dartnell, M. 2006. *Insurgency Online: Web Activism and Global Conflict*. Toronto: University of Toronto Press.

Environics Research Group. 2001. *Young Canadians in a Wired World: The Students' View*. Prepared for the Media Awareness Network and the Government of Canada.

Fiske, J. 1989a. *Reading the Popular*. Boston: Unwin Hyman.

———. 1989b. *Understanding Popular Culture*. Boston: Unwin Hyman.

Furlong, A. and F. Cartmel. 2007. *Young People and Social Change: New Perspectives*. Berkshire, UK: Open University Press.

Gillis, J. 1974. *Youth and History*. New York: Academic Press.

Gramsci, A. 1971. *Selections from the Prison Notebooks*. New York: International Publishers.

Greener, T. and R. Hollands. 2006. "Beyond Subculture and Post-Subculture: The Case of Virtual Psytrance." *Journal of Youth Studies*, 9(4): 393–418.

Hall, S. and T. Jefferson. 1976. *Resistance through Rituals: Youth Subcultures in Post-War Britain*. London: Hutchinson.

Health Canada. 2000. *Youth Public Opinion Research Study: Secondary Analysis of Current Market Research on Youth Ages 7–19*. http://www.hc-sc. gc.ca/hppb/socialmarketing/2/youth/youth_e.pdf (accessed July 28, 2003).

Hebdige, D. 1979. *Subculture: The Meaning of Style*. London: Methuen.

———. 1988. *Hiding in the Light*. London: Routledge.

Hier, S. 2002. "Raves, Risk and the Ecstasy Panic: A Case Study in the Subversive Nature of Moral Regulation." *Canadian Journal of Sociology*, 27(1): 33–57.

Horkheimer, M. and T. Adorno. 1972. *Dialectic of Enlightenment*. Trans. John Cummings. New York: Herder and Herder.

Jette, S., B. Wilson, and R. Sparks. 2007. "Female Youth Interpretations of Smoking in Film." *Qualitative Health Research*, 17(3): 323–339.

Juris, J. and G. Pleyers. 2009. "Alter-activism: Emerging Cultures of Participation Among Young Global Justice Activists." *Journal of Youth Studies*, 12(1): 57–75.

Kahn, R. and R. Kellner. 2003. "Internet Subcultures and Oppositional Politics" (pp. 299–313). In D. Muggleton and R. Weinzierl, eds., *The Post-Subcultures Reader*. New York: Berg.

———. 2004. "New Media and Internet Activism: From the 'Battle of Seattle' to Blogging." *New Media & Society*, 6(1), 87–95.

Kellner, D. 1995. *Media Culture: Cultural Studies, Identity and Politics between the Modern and the Postmodern*. New York: Routledge.

Kline, S. 1993. *Out of the Garden: Toys, TV, and Children's Culture in the Age of Marketing*. New York: Verso.

Marcuse, H. 1964. *One-Dimensional Man*. Boston: Beacon Press.

McRobbie, A. 1994. *Postmodernism and Popular Culture*. London: Routledge.

Meikle, G. 2002. *Future Active: Media Activism and the Internet*. New York: Routledge.

Pini, M. 1997. "Women and the Early British Rave Scene." In A. McRobbie, ed., *Back to Reality: Social Experience and Cultural Studies* (pp. 152–169). Manchester: Manchester University Press.

Rushkoff, D. 1996. *Playing the Future: How Kids' Culture Can Teach Us to Thrive in an Age of Chaos*. New York: HarperCollins.

Steeves, V. 2005. *Young Canadians in a Wired World (Phase II): Trends and Recommendations*. Ottawa, ON: Media Awareness Network.

Strinati, D. 1995. *An Introduction to Theories of Popular Culture*. London: New York: Routledge.

Tanner, J. 2001. *Teenage Troubles: Youth and Deviance in Canada*. Scarborough: Nelson Canada.

Tapscott, D. 1998. *Growing Up Digital: The Rise of the Net Generation*. Toronto: McGraw-Hill Ryerson.

Telander, R. 1990. "Senseless." *Sports Illustrated* (May 14), pp. 36–38, 43–44, 46, 49.

Tsang, A., H. Irving, R. Alaggia, S. Chau, and M. Benjamin. 2003. "Negotiating Ethnic Identity in Canada: The Case of the 'Satellite Children.'" *Youth and Society*, 34(3): 359–383.

Tyyskä, V. 2001. *Long and Winding Road: Adolescents and Youth in Canada Today*. Toronto: Canadian Scholars' Press.

Wall, M. 2007. "Social Movements and Email: Expressions of Online Identity in the Globalization Protests." *New Media & Society*, 9(2): 258–277.

Willis, P. 1990. *Common Culture*. San Francisco: Westview.

Wilson, B. 1999. "Empowering Communities or Delinquent Congregations?: A Study of Complexity and Contradiction in Canadian Youth Cultures and Leisure Spaces." Unpublished doctoral dissertation, McMaster University, Hamilton, Ontario, Canada.

———. 2002a. "The Canadian Rave Scene and Five Theses on Youth Resistance." *Canadian Journal of Sociology*, 27(3): 373–412.

———. 2002b. "The 'Anti-Jock' Movement: Reconsidering Youth Resistance, Masculinity and Sport Culture in the Age of the Internet." *Sociology of Sport Journal*, 19(2): 207–234.

———. 2006. *Fight, Flight, or Chill: Subcultures, Youth, and Rave into the Twenty-First Century*. Montreal and Kingston: McGill-Queen's University Press.

Wilson, B. and M. Atkinson. 2005. "Rave and Straightedge, the Virtual and the Real: Exploring On-line and Off-line Experiences in Canadian Youth Subcultures." *Youth & Society*, 36(3): 276–311.

Wilson, B. and L. Hayhurst. 2009. "Digital Activism: Neo-Liberalism, the Internet, and 'Sport for Youth Development.'" *Sociology of Sport Journal*, 26(1): 155–181.

Wilson, B. and R. Sparks. 1996. "'It's Gotta Be the Shoes': Youth, Race, and Sneaker Commercials." *Sociology of Sport Journal*, 13(4): 398–427.

———. 1999. "Impacts of Black Athlete Media Portrayals on Canadian Youth." *Canadian Journal of Communication*, 24(4): 589–627.

Young, K. and L. Craig. 1997. "Beyond White Pride: Contradiction in the Canadian Skinhead Subculture." *Canadian Review of Sociology and Anthropology*, 34(2): 175–206.

YTV. 2007. *Decoding Tween Influence*. Conducted by Decode and commissioned by Corus Media. http://www.corusmedia.com/ytv/docs/2008/YTV_Kidfluence_2007.pdf (accessed May 16, 2009).

Chapter 4

Immigrant and Racialized Families

Vappu Tyyskä

LEARNING OBJECTIVES

In this chapter, you will learn that:

1. racialized and immigrant families in Canada are diverse, based on socioeconomic, regional, rural/urban, and other considerations,

2. colonialism brought on significant changes in Aboriginal and black families, through the imposition of the European nuclear family model,

3. colonialism, racialization, and globalization continue to influence the family lives of Canadian immigrants and racialized groups,

4. racialized and immigrant families need to be understood with reference to age (generational) and gender hierarchies,

5. racialized and immigrant families exhibit resiliency amid adverse conditions.

INTRODUCTION

Canadians, particularly those who live in the large urban centres of Toronto, Montreal, and Vancouver, pride themselves in the diversity of this nation.

The numbers are certainly impressive: in 2006, immigrants to Canada came from over 200 ethnic backgrounds, compared to 25 in 1901 (Citizenship and Immigration Canada, 2007), with 89 languages currently spoken among them (Gordon, 2005).

But would it surprise you to hear that, in fact, the diversity we now celebrate pales in comparison to the 17th century? At the time of the arrival of the colonizers, the **Aboriginal** population of the Western hemisphere had inhabited the area for approximately 30,000–40,000 years, and around 500,000 of them lived in what is now Canada, with estimates ranging from 221,000 to 2 million (Royal Commission, 1991). In this hemisphere, approximately 2,000 languages were spoken (Crawford, 1995), and 60 still exist in Canada today (Statistics Canada, 2008), falling within the 12 distinct language families that were documented from the times of first colonial contact (Cook and Howe, 2004).

These startling statistics are an important starting point for the discussion of racialized and immigrant families. For it is **colonialism** and the steady arrival of peoples from across the world that continue to shape Canadian family lives. It is impossible to speak of families without reference to the population diversity of historical and contemporary Canada. In the sections to follow, the history and legacy of colonialism will be outlined, with examples drawn to illustrate the family lives of selected populations among the hundreds that form the totality of Canadian family life.

The main focus of this chapter is **racialization**, or "processes by which racial meanings are attached to particular issues" (Murji and Solomos, 2005, p. 3). More specifically, racialization refers to

> . . . ways of thinking about race as well as to institutional processes that give expression to forms of ethno-racial categorization. An important issue . . . concerns the ways in which the construction of race is shaped historically and how the usage of that idea forms a basis for exclusionary practices. The concept therefore refers both to cultural or political processes or situations where race is invoked as an explanation, as well as to specific ideological practices in which race is deployed (Murji and Solomos, 2005, p. 3).

Therefore, this chapter will emphasize how the racialization process in Canada shapes the institutional context of family life and, in turn, affects the daily lives of families.

COLONIALISM AND ABORIGINAL FAMILIES

Colonialism is defined as the economic and political domination of a region and its people by a foreign power (Green, 1995). Historically, the process of colonial expansion into Asia, Africa, and the Americas by Europeans spanned from the 15th to the 19th century (Wilde, 2007). The early entrants to colonial explorations were France and Denmark, followed by the British and Dutch. Later imperial nations included Germany, Italy, and Belgium. In the colonial wars in North America, England assumed Canada after warfare with France (Wilde, 2007; McElroy, 2004).

Upon arrival on this continent, colonizers met different groups of Aboriginal peoples. With some, they extended contact through trade and community relationships. Despite the diversity among North American Aboriginal peoples, they shared some distinctive characteristics. Early settler and missionary accounts describe Aboriginal communities based on foraging, hunting, fishing, horticulture, and agriculture. The earliest societies were nomadic or semi-nomadic, characterized by a collective work effort with minimal hierarchies (particularly in eastern Canada) and a generalized sharing of resources. Everyone participated in the work involved with food collection or production as soon as they were able. Children and young people were gradually integrated into adult activities which were generally divided by gender. Members of the community were responsible for the education of the young in their daily practices, aimed at ensuring material and cultural survival

(Wotherspoon, 1998, p. 47). Old Jesuit records of Huron life also show that children were treated with kindness, and harsh punishment was not generally used. Both women and men participated in child care (Anderson, 1987).

By and large, Aboriginal peoples valued ties to the extended kin group rather than the nuclear family, and had strong norms about reciprocity and gift giving in their kin groups, and beliefs about humans as spiritually linked to all life forms around them. The division of labour was based on age and gender, with adult women providing the bulk of foodstuffs by collecting plant foods whereas men tended to be responsible for hunting as a less predictable food source (Benoit, 2000). Though not matriarchal (implying power held by women over men), the family systems of the Huron in the 17th century tended toward **matriliny** (accounting for family relations through female kin) and matrilocal residence (consisting of clans headed by women, with men moving in with their wives' clan). Matrilineal clans were of crucial importance in the small-scale agricultural societies in North America (Benoit, 2000; Anderson, 1987). For example, among the 17th century Huron Indians in Canada, matrilineal kin organization worked to create relatively egalitarian gender relations, despite separate spheres of activity for women and men. Through a matrilineal kin structure, Huron women both provided the bulk of the sustenance of their communities and also had significant say over how those resources were spent. They also had political power in the matrilineal clans, including say over the election of leaders (Anderson, 1987).

The family lives of the Huron are documented in some detail in the Jesuit writing of the time. According to these records, as summarized by Mees (1997), the Huron had a flexible understanding of family and sexual relationships. Sexual expression, including intercourse, was considered a normal part of life soon after puberty, and individuals had the right to multiple sexual partners. If a young woman got pregnant outside marriage and if she had multiple sexual partners, she would choose the man from among her lovers who would be known as the child's father. This system encouraged matrilineal kin relations because only the mother would be known with certainty. When individuals wanted to marry, parents and relatives had to approve of the choice. Marriages were monogamous and divorces were approved of but usually only before the couple had children. Families would get involved to keep couples with children together. Because of matrilineal clans and women's food production, women were not dependent on men for their livelihood and therefore divorces were relatively easy. Men, who were more reliant on their wives for food sources, were not as likely as women to seek divorce. By all accounts, family violence was rare, due to the relatively egalitarian gender relations (Anderson, 1987).

Whereas the diverse North American Indian populations lived in relatively benign environments and had a wide range of foodstuffs, the Arctic Inuit and Inupiat lived in more hostile conditions where eking out a livelihood was much harder. The Inuit shared some features with the Huron, in their economic and kin organization. Inuit kin relations were flexible, allowing for easy regrouping for gathering, hunting, and fishing, based on seasonal availability of food in the harsh Arctic climate. As among the Huron, there was no private property or land ownership among the Inuit. Marriages were monogamous, and women enjoyed access to and support from their own families. However, the traditional Inuit and Inupiat had a more rigid division of labour by gender: men doing the hunting and fishing, while women looked after children, prepared foods, and engaged in some supplementary food gathering and making of clothing. Due to the precariousness of livelihood in the Arctic that men's status was elevated; daily hunting trips posed such risks to men's survival that they needed to establish a sense of control over their situation. They did this by reliance on the supernatural and by exerting control over their families, women, and children. Thus, these Arctic societies had a patriarchal organization, exhibited in violence against women, though factors such as women's access to their kin may have tempered this somewhat (Bonvillain, 2001).

The analyses of traditional Huron by Anderson (1987) and others rely on the **political economy perspective**. Central to the political economy (also referred to as the Marxist or materialist) theory is an analysis of the links between the economy and family forms (Renzetti and Curran, 1999; Armstrong and Armstrong, 1988; Gaskell, 1993). According to this theory, economic systems that are based on ownership of private property tend to be less egalitarian than those where there is no private property. Feminist theorists have clarified how the issue of economic power links to gender inequality: where private property exists, it tends to be controlled by men, resulting in patriarchy (men's power over women and children). Since there was no private property among the Huron, and both women and men contributed to the economy and their families, this society tended toward both economic and gender equality. In contrast, our contemporary society can be described as capitalist (based on the ownership of the economy by a relatively small elite group) and patriarchal because of mostly male-owned private property and associated gender inequalities. In this system, the capitalist class benefits from the domestic work of women who are primarily responsible for families and household work and are also exploited as an inferior category to men in the wage labour force. **Socialist feminists** add to this classic political economy (or Marxist view) by addressing how it is not only the capitalists but also men as a group who benefit from this gender division of labour. Men benefit directly from women's work at home, in more free time and a range of services. They also benefit by getting better work positions and pay in the wage labour force. Thus, the **double day** of paid and unpaid work for women is a feature of patriarchal capitalism (Tyyskä, 2006a; also see Krahn and Lowe, 2002).

In sum, there was variation in the precolonial family lives and gender relations of Aboriginal societies. Records of contact with traditional Aboriginal peoples generally reveal all family members' contributions toward common good. The lack of private property, mutual reliance on extended kin, and relative gender equality (particularly in the case of the Huron) seem near idyllic, particularly when we compare precolonial lives to the postcolonial period, through several centuries of colonization.

Postcolonial Family Lives

The decimation of Aboriginal populations through European contact is well documented. Warfare, displacement, and the many European diseases that the colonizers brought with them shrank the Canadian Aboriginal population to 102,000 by the 1871 Census (Royal Commission, 1991). The centuries that followed initial contact were marked by **internal colonialism**, characterized as the continuing subjugation of the Aboriginal peoples and their being defined as racially inferior. Thus, racialization is an inherent part of colonialism and consists of the "**othering**" of the population depicted as inferior in biology and in culture (Green, 1995).

One element of the racialization process of Canadian Aboriginal peoples was their homogenization (Green, 1997). Not only are the numbers of Aboriginal individuals fewer due to their decimation, but also the number of populations was reduced to three, through official categorization. Despite the rich diversity of languages and cultures, official statistics collect information for only three main categories of Aboriginal populations: North American Indian (First Nations), Inuit, and Métis. Métis live largely in Western Canada, and are a direct product of colonization; they are the descendants of Canadian Indian women and European male colonizers who married Native women (Métis National Council, 2009).

Colonization seriously disrupted Aboriginal kin relations. European colonizers either reinforced or introduced more rigid economic and gender inequalities among Aboriginal peoples. Trading relations generally benefited men whose status was elevated while women's status was reduced. Colonizers, and particularly the missionaries they brought with them, gradually enforced European standards of family behaviour on the Aboriginal population, including stricter gender divisions and age hierarchies including harsher treatment of children (Benoit, 2000; Bonvillain, 2001; Anderson, 1987).

One of the biggest devastations inflicted on Aboriginal families was the **residential school system**, which was imposed on the First Nations and the Inuit. Through this system, children were taken away from their families to be "schooled" by non-Aboriginals (McCue, 2009). First Nations critics explain that this practice effectively destroyed these children's links to their families, communities, and culture. The residential school system was put in place in Canada in the last two decades of the 19th century and continued past the mid-20th century, with most of the residential schools closing by the 1960s (Crawford, 1995; Wotherspoon, 1998, p. 48; Henry, Tator, Mattis, and Rees, 2000, pp. 125–127), and the last one closing as recently as in 1996 (Health Canada, 2007).

By the time the last of the schools closed, there had been losses of life due to poor conditions, malnourishment, and disease. There had also been denigration of culture as Aboriginal children were torn from their families and put into institutions aimed at "educating" and "civilizing" them. It has been mated that there were no educational benefits to at least half of the childre. who went through the residential school system (Henry, Tator, Mattis and Rees, 2000, pp. 125–27). Instead, these youth faced harsh discipline for offences such as speaking their own language, and were allowed to see their families only a few times a year (Wotherspoon, 1998, p. 48). Lois Gus recalls his life in a Canadian residential school for Native children (Wotherspoon, 1998, p. 49, in Tyyskä, 2008, p. 32):

> Normally, in a Native family, a child is allowed to learn by trial and error, with love and support being freely given. My experiences in residential school were a sharp contrast to this. There, our natural curiosity was impeded by the outlook of nuns, who had no experience in life and no experience as a parent … There were very few times you could enjoy life as it was so regimented. There was no freedom of thought or expression allowed. Everyone had to conform to a rigid set of standard rules: pray, learn, pray, obey, pray, eat, pray.

Survivors of this repressive system gradually came forward to reveal the extent of the physical, psychological, and sexual abuse they suffered. Compensation was slow in coming and the outcome was an offensively low amount ($24,000) offered to the survivors by the Canadian government (Tyyskä, 2008). An apology was finally issued by Prime Minister Stephen Harper in the House of Commons on June 11, 2008 (Inuit Tapiirit Kanatami, 2008).

The cultural isolation engendered by residential schools meant that generations of young people were lost to their families through nontransmission of traditional ways of making a living (Fiske and Johnny, 1996, pp. 230–232), and through the loss of a common language that would be customarily passed on orally from elders to the young. Cook and Howe (2004) found that 43 of the 55 spoken Aboriginal languages in their study have fewer than 1,000 speakers, and, of those, 17 have 100 speakers or fewer. According to another study (Norris, 1998), as of 1996, only three of Canada's Aboriginal languages (Cree, Ojibway, and Inuktitut) had large enough populations to be considered truly secure from the threat of extinction in the long term.

Since the 1871 Census, the Aborginal populations have rebounded. According to the 2006 Census, the total Aboriginal population numbers 1,172,790, nearly 4 percent of the Canadian population. The Inuit are the smallest group, with around 50,485 people, and the Métis number around 389,785. The largest category is the 698,025 North American Indians. Though a large proportion (40 percent) of First Nations people still live on reserves, just over half (54 percent) of the Aboriginal population is urban (Statistics Canada, 2008).

Notably, Aboriginal populations are significantly younger than non-Aboriginals. While 31 percent of the general Canadian population consists of children and youth under 24 years of age, the percentage is 48 for Aboriginal peoples. The median age of Aboriginal people is 27 and 40 for the non-Aboriginal population (Statistics Canada, 2006a, p. 6). Aboriginal groups have higher than average birth rates, and children are more likely than non-Aboriginal people to live with one parent or with a grandparent (Statistics Canada, 2008).

The young age of the Aboriginal population means that the trend toward population growth will continue once the young generations reach child-bearing age. There are projections that by 2017, Aboriginal youth could make up 24 percent of all youth aged 20 to 29 in Manitoba, 40 percent in Saskatchewan, 48 percent in Yukon, and 58 percent in the Northwest Territories. Nunavut, the territory of the Inuit, is already 80 percent Aboriginal insofar as the age category of 20 to 29 is concerned (Statistics Canada, 2008).

Canadian Aboriginal groups share similarities based on colonial history, and continue to bear the consequences of internal colonialism and racialization in reduced and young populations that continue to live in economically dire conditions with associated multiple problems—poor health, substance abuse, and suicide—that amount to much lower quality of life than that among the general population. Among the sad statistics about Aboriginal lives is deeply ingrained poverty, with one child in four living in poverty (Public Service Alliance of Canada [PSAC], 2008). Aboriginal people are four times as likely as Canadians in general to live in a crowded dwelling and three times as likely to live in a home in need of repairs (Statistics Canada, 2006a: 6). Among the First Nations, more than half are unemployed; nearly half (43 percent) of the children lack basic dental care; youth suicides are five to eight times the Canadian rate (and the Inuit's are six times the Canadian rate); and Aboriginal people are eight to ten times more likely than other Canadians to suffer from developing-countries' diseases (e.g., tuberculosis) (PSAC, 2008).

The colonial legacy of large-scale pauperization and alienation experienced by Native communities is shown in the prevalence of family violence, which is estimated to be several times higher than in the general Canadian population. In 2004, Aboriginal women were three and half times more likely to suffer some form of spousal violence than non-Aboriginal women (Brzozowski, Taylor-Butts and Johnson, 2006). In the late 1990s, some studies found that 40 percent of children in some northern communities were victims of family violence, and about half of females and one-third of males had been sexually victimized by a family member (Department of Justice Canada, 2008).

These long-standing disruptions amount to a **disenfranchisement** of Aboriginal families who then became targets for government intervention. Large numbers of children have been taken away from parents who were deemed unfit to look after them and from grandparents who were deemed too old (LaBoucane-Benson, 2005). Especially through the 1960s and 1970s, large numbers of Native children were removed from their families to be cared for by white foster homes. The outcome was the "removal of almost an entire generation of children" and a disruption of intergenerational continuity. The system was gradually changed, and Native communities have gained more control over what to do with their children and youth. However, this does not solve the larger problems of unemployment and poverty that are at the root of the problem (Duffy and Momirov, 1997, 73, 184–185; also see Trocmé, Knoke, and Blackstock, 2004).

Many of the foster homes that children ended up in turned out to be abusive and exploitive, and other children were lost through adoption by non-Aboriginal families. These continuing practices amount to "child abduction" in the eyes of the Aboriginal critics, and have resulted in long-term ill consequences for the youth, measured in loss of cultural identity, substance abuse, and incarceration (LaBoucane-Benson, 2005; see also Duffy and Momirov, 1997, pp. 73, 184–185).

The current living arrangements (see Table 4.1) reflect the significant differences in Aboriginal families compared to non-Aboriginal families. Aboriginal children are much less likely to be living with two parents, twice as likely to be living with one parent (either mother or father), and higher proportions live with grandparents, other relatives, or with nonrelatives.

Despite the severely disrupted family lives of Aboriginal peoples, some authors (LaBoucane-Benson, 2005) caution against the continuing use of a deficit perspective on Aboriginal families, implying that they are lacking only in the basic requirements enjoyed by other families. Given the multiple changes in those families brought on by urbanization and changing economies, it is time to turn attention to the strengths of these families. LaBoucane-Benson (2005) points out that the concept of family **resiliency** is more appropriate, referring to families that thrive even if they have been exposed to severe adversity (Luthar, Cicchetti, and Becker, 2000, in LaBoucane-Benson, 2005, p. 9). The American-based National Network for Family Resiliency (2009, p. 3) defines resiliency as "the ability to bounce back from stress and crisis . . . Individuals, families, and communities demonstrate resiliency when they build caring support systems and solve problems creatively."

Table 4.1 **LIVING ARRANGEMENTS OF ABORIGINAL AND NON-ABORIGINAL CHILDREN AGED 14 YEARS AND UNDER, CANADA, 2006**

Living Arrangements of Children	Aboriginal Population (percent)	Non-Aboriginal Population (percent)
Total—children aged 14 years and under	100	100
Total living with at least one parent	93	99
Living with two parents	58	82
Living with a lone mother	29	14
Living with a lone father	6	3
Living with a grandparent (no parent present)	3	0.4
Living with another relative	4	0.5
Living with nonrelatives	0.4	0.2

Source: Statistics Canada. 2006a. *Aboriginal Peoples in Canada in 2006: Inuit, Métis, and First Nations, 2006 Census.* Catalogue No. 97-558-XIE.

In Aboriginal families, the sources of this resiliency are found in the belief in interconnectedness of all living things, and in the centrality of the family and community. Aboriginal communities are focusing rebuilding their families through "community healing" (Castellano, 2002). Castellano (2002) summarizes the current situation as one of hope (Box 4.1).

BOX 4.1   HOPE FOR ABORIGINAL FAMILIES

Aboriginal families assume a variety of forms. Extended family networks in rural communities and reserves continue to provide a stable reference point for younger members who relocate in pursuit of education and employment opportunities. Nuclear families, two-generation families in households of parents and children, are increasingly the unit of family organization in both rural and urban communities. As Aboriginal community membership becomes more heterogeneous in ethnic origin and cultural practice, there is a vigorous movement to conserve and revitalize traditional languages, teachings, and ceremonial practice. Formal associations and informal networks are emerging to support this move to traditionalism, deliberately embracing norms of "sharing and caring" and extending spiritual and practical support to those made vulnerable by family breakdown. Some call these voluntary communities "families of the heart." Spontaneous and self-directed efforts to heal from the effects of trauma, past and current, constitute perhaps the most hopeful sign of what the future holds for Aboriginal families. However, because of the interdependence of individuals, families, and communities, individual effort must be complemented by collective effort to eliminate the structural disadvantage evidenced in statistics on income, education, and health. The challenges differ between urban and rural settings, and among subgroups of the Aboriginal population. However, there is a common theme in Aboriginal community effort: Institutions that share responsibility with families to protect children, deliver education, promote and restore health, and preserve order must be responsive to the culture and identity of Aboriginal citizens. Public policies have historically been intrusive and often destructive, generating alienation from mainstream institutions and distrust of "white" professionals. There is a strong movement to re-establish Aboriginal control of public services not only in governance but also in health, education, and justice (Castellano, 2002).

Source: Castellano, Marlene Brant. 2002. *Aboriginal Family Trends. Extended Families, Nuclear Families, Families of the Heart.* Vanier Institute of the Family. Retrieved May 27, 2009 from http://www.vifamily.ca/library/cft/aboriginal .html#Healing.

BLACK FAMILIES AND THE COLONIAL LEGACY

The year 2007 saw the 200th anniversary of the abolition of the slave trade in the British Empire (Span, 2002, p. 113). The slave trade was an inextricable part of colonialism, and spanned from 1441 till the 19th century when slavery was officially abolished in the new world (Africa Reparations Movement [ARM], 2007; Wilde, 2007; McElroy, 2004). Historians estimate that anywhere between 12 and 50 million slaves were forcibly transported from Africa, 10–20 percent dying along the way (BBC World Service, 2007; National Archives, UK, 2007).

Canada was also a part of the **Atlantic slave trade**, having built at least 60 slave ships for the British slave trade (Cooper, 2007, p. A15). The first African slave, given the name Olivier de Jeune, arrived in Quebec in 1628 (Walker, 1985, p. 8). Although New France had officially abolished slavery, it was practised by the French and the English until the early 1800s. Until the late 1700s, almost all Canadian blacks were slaves, mostly in domestic service to white colonizers (Walker, 1985, p. 8; Thomson, 1979, p. 17–18, 96). In 1760, black and Indian slaves in Quebec numbered around 4,000 (Thomson, 1979, p. 96). Slaves were generally treated harshly, subjected to public whippings or death sentences for attempts to flee or for any misdemeanours (Thompson, 1979, p. 18–19).

The consequences of the Atlantic slave trade for families are summarized in this way:

> The Atlantic Slave Trade generated a huge parasitical infrastructure. The trade's pattern skewed the family profile, sundered kinship relations, crippled monogamous customs, dramatized upper-class **polygyny**, strengthened patriarchy, and lowered the status of women in society (Munford, 2008).

More is known about black American than Canadian slaves and their families. Based on research about the United States, we know that a large proportion of these millions of kidnapped Africans were children and youth who were seen to be more controllable as slaves than the older age groups (Perkins, 2005, p. 6–19). They were ripped out of the security of their families, transported across the world, stripped of their African names and had English names imposed, and put to work in dehumanizing conditions. Children born to slaves in America were kept with their mothers and typically separated from their fathers who were kept in male quarters by the slave owners. Their mothers had to work in the fields from morning till night and saw little of their children who were kept in plantation nurseries. These young slaves grew into servitude and were brought up to accept their miserable condition (Perkins, 2005, p. 6–19). Slave owners deliberately kept the young slaves separated from the older ones so they wouldn't consider running away or rebelling (Perkins, 2005, p. 14–16). Young female slaves were subjected to their owners' sexual exploitation, and essentially that of any white male, their most important function being "that of breeding children" (Perkins, 2005, p. 14; also see Campbell, Miers, and Miller, 2005).

What little is known of black Canadian slaves and their families indicates that they faced similar problems. They were considered sub-human by the British and the French, with Catholic nuns and priests having a hand in the slave trade. In Nova Scotia, emancipated blacks were, in fact, compelled to indenture themselves to the white population because the plots of land allocated to them were too small to sustain them. The fear of slavery was palpable; once a black man was sold into slavery, the same fate befell his wife and children (Winks, 1971, in Christensen and Wienfeld, 1993, pp. 32–33). Though the circumstances were harsh, families tended to stay together. The reputation that black couples gained for "temporary or casual" relationships was in fact rooted in racism: marriages performed by black ministers were considered illegal (Mannette, 1984, in Christensen and Wienfeld, 1993, p. 33).

Even as slavery was gradually abolished in the British Empire, the general image of servitude remained (Thomson, 1979, pp. 19, 98; Walker, 1985, pp. 80–90; Tyyskä, 2008), a part of the racialization process that accompanies colonialism and is a legacy in the postcolonial era. As in the case of the continuities between today and the colonial era for Aboriginal peoples, Cooper (2007, p. A15) argues that the significance of the slave trades remains today for blacks. She says

> institutionalized racist practices, anti-black racism, the colour line, colonialism, African underdevelopment and also that of former slave societies in the New World, duplicity of western governments, white supremacy, economic disadvantage, racialization of black peoples, and psychic distance between black and white have all been identified as legacies of the slave trade and slavery.

After abolition of slavery, different groups of black people continued to arrive in Canada. They included the so-called **Black Loyalists** who escaped to Nova Scotia, New Brunswick, and Ontario from slavery in the United States ((Walker, 1985, pp. 8–11; Thomson, 1979, p. 89); and a group that arrived on Vancouver Island in 1858–59 (Walker, 1985, p. 11–12). Though the "underground railroad" that secretly brought fugitive slaves to safety in Canada is generally a source of pride for Canadians, the black people who arrived here faced racism and discrimination (Walker, 1985, pp. 12–14; Thomson, 1979, pp. 21–22). Many of them returned to the United States, or travelled to Africa and the West Indies (Walker, 1985, pp. 8–9; Thomson, 1979, p. 98).

Like their American counterparts, Canadian blacks faced the worst available jobs (Hill, 1981) and their children attended separate schools. Separate schools were in place well into the 20th century and, in the case of Alberta, into the 1960s (Thomson, 1979, pp. 20, 99–106), only to be dismantled after the **civil rights movement** led to human rights legislation through the 1960s and 1970s (Walker, 1985, pp. 16–18; see also Tyyskä, 2008).

In 1961, there were approximately 12,000 blacks in Canada, and their numbers increased over the next two decades with immigrants from the West Indies (nearly 150,000) and Africa (50,000) (Thomson, 1979, p. 105). By 1981, the population numbered around 200,000, with 40,000 (15 percent) descendants of the arrivals from the previous centuries (Walker, 1985, pp. 17–19). As immigration patterns have changed in the last few decades (see below), blacks have continued to immigrate to Canada from all parts of the world. The current black population of approximately 783,800 represents 2.5 percent of the total Canadian population, the third-largest racialized minority group in Canada, after South Asians and Chinese (Statistics Canada, 2006a). In terms of origins, *over one-half (52.0 percent) of the Black visible minority group reported Caribbean origins, and another 42.4 percent reported African origins. Black visible minorities also reported British Isles origins (11.6 percent), Canadian origin (10.9 percent) and French origins (4.1 percent) (Statistics Canada, 2006a).*

Although black families come in many varieties, they are nearly three times more likely than families on average, to be of a single-parent variety. This is commonly considered a consequence of family instability, poverty, racism, and discrimination (Christensen and Weinfeld, 1993, p. 41; Calliste, 1996, pp. 252–259). Studies show a pattern similar to that among Aboriginal peoples in that due to their higher likelihood of single-parent households and the associated higher rates of poverty, black families have been subjected to excessive attention by welfare and child protection agencies, and are unduly stigmatized. A part of the ethno-centric tendency is the lack of understanding of specifically Caribbean family patterns, which are more likely than white North American families to be extended and woman-centred in structure (Christensen and Weinfeld, 1993, p. 34). This is one of the many patterns among black families, rooted in the diversity of origin. As will be discussed in the segment on immigrant families below, different cultures and places of origin challenge the tendency toward mere general conclusions about any racialized or immigrant population.

One of the challenges for black families living in a racist society is how to raise children to be physically and emotionally healthy (Calliste, 1996, pp. 262–264). Parents play a crucial role in mediating the negative messages and images about blackness, through "**racial socialization**," which is a socialization process focused on developing children's and youths' pride in themselves and their group (Calliste, 1996; Codjoe, 2006). Some researchers suggest that ethnic/racial identity develops in four stages: (1) ethnic/racial unawareness in early childhood; (2) ambivalence in adolescence, often characterized by preference for mainstream norms and a distancing from one's group; (3) an emergence in late adolescence and early adulthood, i.e., individuals seek connections to their origins and groups; and (4) ethnic/racial incorporation in the adult years, in which any identity conflicts are resolved (Hébert, 2001, p. 160). Regardless of whether this stage theory is applied strictly, the process of racialized identity development is likely to be gradual and marked by periods of difficulty for individuals and their families.

In sum, black families in Canada are varied, including the earliest arrivals through slavery and their descendants, and continuing through the last century with arrivals from Africa, the Caribbean, France, and the British Isles. Currently, only about one in ten blacks is Canadian-born. Thus, black families are culturally and linguistically varied although they share the legacy of colonialism and racialization in a larger than usual component of single parents and in the challenge of raising children in a racist society.

IMMIGRANT FAMILIES

Canada is a major immigrant-receiving nation, admitting up to 250,000 entrants annually, with the foreign-born forming just over 11 percent of the Canadian population (Liu and Kerr, 2003, p. 115). In 2007, a total of 236,758 people arrived in Canada as permanent residents (CIC, 2007). However, one less known but noteworthy fact about Canada is that it admits people under the **temporary foreign worker** status in higher numbers than under the permanent resident category. In 2007, 115,470 first-entry temporary foreign workers were admitted while there were 201,057 previously admitted temporary foreign workers (CIC, 2008). The significance for families is that temporary foreign workers cannot bring their spouses, children, or other family members to Canada under the temporary work visa conditions, and they endure long separations from their families while making a living in Canada. These families fall under the category of transnational families, to be discussed below.

Permanent residents arrive under three main categories: **economic class** (including a number of economic-status determinants and programs), **family class**, and protected persons (including those arriving under humanitarian and compassionate grounds). In 2007, 55.4 percent (131,248) of immigrants were economic immigrants and their dependants; 28.0 percent (66,230) were in the family class; 11.8 percent (27,956) were protected persons; and 4.7 percent (11,201) were granted permanent resident status on humanitarian and compassionate grounds (CIC, 2007). Applicants in the large skilled-worker category of the economic class are assessed based on six selection factors, with a 100 points maximum in total (each factor's maximum points are indicated in parentheses): education (25); ability in English and/or French (24); experience (21); age (10); arranged employment in Canada (10); adaptability (10) (CIC, 2009). The discussion here is focused on the economic and family class arrivals.

Significantly, there has been a shift in the source countries for immigration from the British and other European migrants who were selected in the 19th century and most of the 20th century. In the last quarter of the 20th century, Canada underwent changes in immigration legislation, with a consequent influx of immigrants from non-European countries who now make up 78.5 percent of all immigrants entering Canada (See Table 4.2) (Momirov and Kilbride, 2005, p. 99; Ambert, 2006, pp. 89–91).

Recent immigrants to Canada tend to be from racialized groups: over half are Asian, with three of the largest groups being Chinese, South Asians, and blacks (CIC, 2007). Most permanent residents settle in three provinces, Ontario (47 percent), Quebec (19.1 percent), and British Columbia (16.4) (CIC, 2007), and in large urban centres (Toronto, Montreal, Vancouver, Calgary, and Winnipeg (CIC, 2007), each with a slightly different balance of racialized immigrants. For example, the largest groups in Toronto, Vancouver, and Montreal are South Asians, Chinese, and blacks, respectively.

Table 4.2   **THE TOP TEN SOURCE COUNTRIES OF CANADIAN IMMIGRANTS, 2007**

Country	Number of Immigrants
People's Republic of China	27,014
India	26,054
Philippines	19,064
United States	10,450
Pakistan	9,547
United Kingdom	8,128
Iran	6,663
Republic of Korea	5,864
France	5,526
Columbia	4,833

Source: "Facts and Figures 2007–Immigration Overview: Permanent and Temporary Residents," Canada – Permanent residents by top source countries. http://www.cic.gc.ca/english/resources/statistics/facts2007/permanent/12.asp. Reproduced with the permission of the Minister of Public Works and Government Services Canada, 2009.

Canadian government information about racialized categories is based on official employment-equity category of "visible-minority status," defined as "persons, other than Aboriginal persons, who are non-Caucasian in race or non-white in colour" (CIC, 2006b). As in the case of the Aboriginal categories, the visible-minority categorization reduces the number of possible statuses and identities, reflecting the colonial homogenization process of **othered** populations. Indeed, the United Nations Committee on the Elimination of Racial Discrimination recently criticized the use of the term **"visible minority"** by Canada because it implies that those so classified are "the other" and that there is homogeneity of experiences among them. Canadian Race Relations Foundation (CRRF) recommends that the term be replaced with "racialized" persons or groups "because it better reflects the realities of racism" (CRRF, 2007).

According to the 2006 Census, 5,068,100 people were racialized minorities, accounting for 16.2 percent of Canada's total population, an increase from 13.4 percent in 2001 and 11.2 percent in 1996 (CIC, 2006b). Though 75 percent of current racialized minorities are immigrants, the remaining 25 percent have been Canadians for at least a generation, and many have long-standing histories in Canada. Notably, the proportion of Canadian immigrants born in countries outside Europe has risen steadily, from 68.5 percent in 1981 to 83.9 percent in 2006 (CIC, 2006b), reflecting the increasing racialization of immigrants and contributing to increasing racial diversification of the population.

Economic Conditions

The weight put on education in the Canadian permanent resident category is reflected in the permanent resident population: almost twice as many immigrants aged 25 to 54 (40 percent) hold university degrees, relative to the Canadian-born population (Momirov and Kilbride, 2005; Frenette and

Morissette, 2005), and 37 percent of the 1.2 million immigrants in the core working age group (25 to 54) have a university degree compared to the same age group of those Canadian-born (Gilmore, 2008).

The challenges and stresses that newcomer families face include poverty, isolation, and loss of occupational status (Seat, 2000; Anisef and Kilbride, 2000; Kilbride et al., 2001). Canadian research summarized by Tyyskä (2007) shows that (1) immigrants experience economic difficulties for several years after immigration (Liu and Kerr, 2003); (2) recent immigrants perform more poorly than those who arrived in Canada before the 1990s (Statistics Canada, 2006c); and (3) that immigrants with degrees do not fare as well as Canadian-born degree holders, especially (4) if race is taken into account (Li, 2001).

Racialized status has consequences for the economic foundations of immigrant families. Those of European ancestry fare better in the labour market than those from Africa, Asia, and Latin America. Some of the poor economic outcomes of these immigrants are due to lack of official language proficiency, and the purported lack of "Canadian experience" (Momirov and Kilbride, 2005; Boyd and Norris, 2000). Consequently, Canadian immigrant families (defined as those who arrived within the last 10 years), most of whom are racialized, have much higher rates of poverty than the general population, approximately 39 percent in the 2001 Canadian Census (Canadian Council on Social Development, 2003; also see Liu and Kerr, 2003). At 21.5 percent in 2004, the incidence of low income among new immigrants was over twice that of nonimmigrants, including earlier immigrants and native-born Canadians (Human Resources and Skills Development Canada, 2007). Their poor economic conditions create difficulties in finding affordable housing and accessing needed health care, education, and training (Statistics Canada, 2005a, Shields, 2004), and result in low home ownership rates (Statistics Canada, 2005b). These difficulties have deepened since the 1990s (Shields, 2004; Frenette and Morissette, 2005).

Gender Relations

Because of the general tendency of men to be primary breadwinners, immigrant men are overrepresented in the principal economic class (77 percent) while there are more women in the family class (60 percent) (Momirov and Kilbride, 2005: 101). Generally, immigrant men are more likely to work for pay than women, while unemployment rates are high for almost all immigrant women, regardless of origin or time of arrival in Canada. Unemployment rates are highest among very recent immigrant women from Africa, South Asia, and West Central Asia and the Middle East (Ontario Council of Agencies Serving Immigrants [OCASI], 2006). In 2006, immigrant women's employment rate was 56.8 percent compared to 78.5 percent among Canadian-born women (Statistics Canada, 2006b).

However, there is evidence that at least some immigrant women may find full-time employment faster than immigrant men because the latter tend to accept any type of employment (Ali and Kilbride, 2004; Momirov and

Kilbride, 2005; Grewal, Bottroff, Hilton, 2005; Creese, Dyck, and McLaren, 1999). While some researchers suggest that women's employment may lead toward more gender-egalitarian gender and family relations (Haddad and Lam, 1988; Jain and Belsky, 1997; Anisef et al., 2001), more studies suggest that women's employment may put unwelcome pressure on men to take on more domestic responsibilities and that they may suffer loss of self-esteem as they lose their traditional breadwinner role (Ali and Kilbride, 2004; Momirov and Kilbride, 2005; Grewal, Bottroff and Hilton, 2005; Creese, Dyck and McLaren, 1999).

Though there is a temptation to assume that all immigrants are "traditional" and the industrialized West is "modern" in gender relations, we must avoid oversimplification. Large numbers of immigrants come from urban environments in which their premigration living conditions, including family and gender relations, are similar to the range found in Canada overall (Walton-Roberts and Pratt, 2003: 5; Man, 2003; Shahidian, 1999; Tyyskä, 2003b).

Notably, because of the "**points system**" (see above) of Canadian immigration, many immigrants originate from comfortable middle- or upper-class and educated backgrounds. For example, Guida Man's (2003) study of Chinese women who immigrated to Canada after the points system was instituted shows that though many of them are educated female professionals, most of them came to Canada as dependants under the family class of immigrants. This resulted in significant life changes as they became stay-at-home wives, dependent on their husband's income for the first time in their lives, a situation that some enjoy and others feel trapped in. Similarly, a study of educated South Asian women revealed feelings of a loss of honour over having to do physical work after immigration, something that was performed by domestic servants before migration (Grewal, Bottroff, and Hilton, 2005).

In many families, immigrant and nonimmigrant alike, the husband/father holds more power (Tyyskä, 2002a, 2002b; 2003a). One significant aspect lies in the interpretation of familial power arrangements by women themselves. One of the contributions of **antiracist feminism** (e.g., Abbott and Wallace, 1997) regards the realization that racialized women may see the family as a refuge from the oppression they face in the outside world. Rather than wanting to escape from the nuclear family, they may want to protect their right to have one, and will consequently be sympathetic to their husband's right to a traditional domestic life, whether accompanied with domestic inequalities or not (Momirov and Kilbride, 2005, p. 104; Moghissi, 1999).

Antiracist feminists have added racialization to our understanding of economic and family relations (see above for the political economy and socialist feminist theories). The double day of work—a central feature in the oppression of women—gains an added dimension when examined in the context of immigration and racialized minority status. For example, Mianda (2004, in Tyyskä, 2006a) outlines the experiences of one specific group of racialized immigrants: African immigrant women in Montreal. Without the help from extended family who were left behind upon migration, and experiencing racism in employment, these women struggle to involve their husbands in a more equitable domestic division of labour to alleviate the stresses of a double day of work. At the same time, they feel alienated from white Canadian women whose stereotypical notions about "Third World Women" hinder the development of women's general networks of support.

Intergenerational Relations

Research on immigrant parents and their **second-generation children** has revealed some main areas of concern related to family relationships. Box 4.2 captures some of the issues from the point of view of one group of Sri Lankan Tamil youth in Toronto.

BOX 4.2   VOICES OF IMMIGRANT YOUTH

The following quotes from a study by Tyyskä (2006b) capture some of the difficulties and dilemmas of Sri Lankan Tamil youth as they reflect on their families and parents. These young people show significant insight into the difficult conditions they and their parents face upon immigration and settlement, including changing family composition (from extended to nuclear family; negotiating work–family balances; and intergenerational differences in expectations from family members.

> They are working. They just say ok that this is not a country to chill with your family and everything. They think work, money is a big problem. So basically that's the main issue. Basically money problems. You are working 24/7. There's no time for family (Male, 19) (p. 21).

> Well, it was pretty hard for them at first getting a permanent job. It's still hard because it's very hard with three girls. There is not much time for anything anymore, I'm always working. And they don't get paid a lot either so they're pulling it together but we are better fit than when we first came to Canada, and we're better off now (Female, 13) (p. 30).

> I think he expects more because he changed his lifestyle for us, so he wants it in return (Female, 13) (p. 20).

> We're away from our family members and we need to help each other out more and we can't ask our neighbours and our cousins don't live across the street. Say back home when you were small, you could've easily gone to my next door neighbour's house or my aunt's house while my parents had to go out, but now it's not like that because we don't have relatives across the street or next door. We have to do everything ourselves (Female, 17) (p. 23).

> I think it's because of the generation gap and the way they were raised. They were raised 40 or 50 years ago in Sri Lanka and I was raised ten years ago in Canada. So morals change every decade and that would be one. Some parts of them, they still hold on to some values that they learned when they

(continued)

(continued)

> were child[ren]. Things like what girls should do and what boys should do and what they should wear. But for us, everything is changed. It's not the same—what girls should do here is not the same as what girls should do there. So, I think the generation gap—how we are raised (Female, 18) (p. 27).
>
> What my parents expect from me, is—no matter what culture you are, no matter what religion you are—one thing that child should do for their parents, is to uphold the family name and honor. When I go in public, I wouldn't do anything to cause my family any dishonor. So I would behave properly (Female, 18) (p. 20).
>
> Canada is very different from my country so down there it's a different way of living, we can't just be living like how we lived down there. So my mom had to change her ways here (Male, 17) (p. 20).

Many immigrant parents feel that their parenting is challenged in a number of ways (Fuligni and Yoshikawa, 2003; Noivo, 1993; Tyyskä, 2005, 2006, 2008). Poverty alone creates situational and systemic obstacles that undermine attentive and nurturing parental behaviours (Beiser, Hou, Kasper, and Who, 2000). Parental struggles to make a living and negotiate new conditions for spousal relations may result in less time for children. Parents often cite their children's futures as a reason for immigrating. Their fears that economic hardships may be repeated in their children's lives often result in pressure on their children in education and career planning (Creese et al., 1999; Tyyskä, 2005, 2006; Beiser et al., 2000; Dhruvarajan, 2003; Fuligni, 1997; Li, 1988; Noivo, 1993).

In addition to education and career planning, immigrant parents express concern with their children's peer relations and social behaviour (Wong, 1999; Wade and Brannigan, 1998), dating and spouse selection patterns (Dhruvarajan, 2003; Mitchell, 2001; Morrison, Guruge, and Snarr, 1999; Zaidi and Shuraydi, 2002), and retention of culture (James, 1999). Immigrant youth often feel torn between their desire to fit in with their peers and their desire to meet their parents' expectations (Tyyskä, 2003b, 2006). The areas listed are often sources of contention in families, and are referred to as the **"generation gap"** between immigrant parents, whose reference point is the world they left behind, and their children, who are subjected to **acculturation** to Canadian norms and values (Tyyskä, 2005, 2006, 2008).

Language differences can result in family problems. Children often learn the official language faster than their parents, due to the influence of schools and peers. One problem area is that language differences can disrupt intergenerational communication and transmission of culture and identity (Anisef et al., 2001; Bernhard, Chud, Lefebvre, and Lange, 1996). Second, there are problems with regard to children's role as **"cultural brokers"** in their parents' dealings with mainstream social institutions (schools, hospitals, social services) and culture. The situation may result in unwanted role and authority reversals, leaving parents feeling unable to be proper heads of the household, and stressing children who themselves are undergoing significant adjustments to a new environment (Ali and Kilbride, 2004; Creese et al., 1999; Momirov and Kilbride, 2005; Tyyskä, 2005, 2006).

This role reversal may not be the only one that affects the immigrant family. Shifts in maternal and paternal work and family roles and authority patterns add to the general dislocation of familial patterns (Ali and Kilbride, 2004; Anisef et al., 2001; Creese et al., 1999; Grewal et al., 2005; Haddad and Lam, 1988; Jain and Belsky, 1997; Momirov and Kilbride, 2005; Shimoni, Este, and Clark, 2003; Tyyskä, 2005, 2007, 2008). The resulting tensions have been found to contribute, in part, to the onset or increase in severity of family violence against women and children (Creese et al., 1999, p. 8; MacLeod and Shin, 1993; Smith 2004; Tyyskä, 2005, 2008; Wiebe, 1991).

While spousal gender relations are subject to renegotiation among immigrants, so are gender issues among children. In some immigrant communities, parental expectations of male and female children are quite different (Tyyskä, 2003b). Adolescent boys have been found to have much more freedom of movement and decision-making power than their sisters (Anisef and Kilbride, 2000; Anisef et al., 2001; Dhruvarajan, 2003; Handa, 1997; Shahidian, 1999, p. 212; Tyyskä, 2001, 2006, 2007, 2008). Parental concerns for their children differ: concerns for daughters relate predominantly to premarital sexuality and dating, while fears for sons include their potential involvement with drugs and violence (Anisef et al., 2001; Shahidian, 1999; Tyyskä, 2006b, 2007, 2008).

Muslim and Asian families are more protective than Western cultures over their children and particularly their daughters (Aapola et al., 2005, pp. 93–94). The fear of cultural identity loss, combined with the fear of losing their children, has pushed many parents toward conservative sexual norms (Shahidian, 1999, pp. 200–201). Girls are seen to hold a special place as "**cultural vessels**" in these immigrant communities, and their conduct can bring either pride or shame on the family and the community. North American studies (Handa, 1997; Tyyskä, 2006b; also see Aapola et al., 2005, pp. 94–95) document that some young immigrant women may live dual lives, hiding aspects of their daily activities outside their homes from their parents, in order to live up to the conflicting demands of their families and their mainstream peers. Since mothers are held responsible for children's socialization, and particularly for the socialization of daughters into culturally acceptable behaviours, there are indications that there may be heightened mother–daughter conflict in some immigrant families (Shahidian, 1999, p. 212; Dyck and McLaren, 2002, p. 9; Tyyskä, 2006b). Nevertheless, this is not a uniform reaction across immigrant groups. For example, Tyyskä (2003b) found a continuum from traditional (protective) to modern (permissive) gender and intergenerational relations in the Iranian immigrant community in Toronto.

More attention is being paid of late to second-generation immigrant youth, or Canadian-born offspring of immigrant parents. Typically, their lives and relationships with their parents have been seen through the lens of the "acculturation thesis," which measures degrees to which immigrants adapt to the host society. According to this thesis, acculturation is seen as a natural progression in which each successive immigrant generation adopts more of the "behaviours, rules, values, and norms of the host society" (Boyd and Norris, 2000, p. 138, in Tyyskä, 2001, pp. 105–106). In more recent sociological literature, there is a shift in the interpretation. It is recognized that the **multiple** and **"hybrid"** identities among youth (Gordon, 1999) may come into conflict with their parents' cultural expectations (Karakayali, 2005; Tyyskä, 2003a). Acculturation as adaptation to the receiving society is no longer seen as the only possibility. Youth may embrace a range of identities and cultural markers from their parental culture and from the environment around them (Tyyskä, 2006b).

Family Violence

Above, some main aspects of Aboriginal family violence were highlighted, with attention to the issue of stigmatization, manifested in the overrepresentation of Aboriginal children in the child welfare system. Though we should not underestimate the extent of the problem in these communities, we also note that racialized and immigrant communities are faced with differential treatment and interpretation of violence and its root causes.

On the one hand, a typical approach found among the public and the media is the **"cultural model,"** which proposes that some immigrant communities are inherently more violence-ridden than Canadian-born families. This view is based on a selective look at specific communities that are seen to be particularly traditional in terms of gender relations and age hierarchies (Menjivar and Salcido, 2002; MacLeod and Shin, 1993; Maiter, Trocmé, and George, 2003; Dinshaw, 2005). Based on the approach taken in this chapter, this stigmatization of the immigrant population is one feature of the process of racialization, and does not necessarily capture the diverse experiences in the immigrant population. Furthermore, at present we have insufficient studies to determine the prevalence of family violence in any specific immigrant community, compared to the Canadian-born population.

On the other hand, the concept of **"social determinants of health"** has been used to capture how multiple environmental stresses of immigration and settlement lead to physical and mental health problems, and may be more obstacles to the overall healthy functioning of the whole family unit (Ali and Kilbride, 2004; (Beiser, Hou, Hyrnan, and Tousignant, 2002; Grewal, Bottroff, and Hilton, 2005; Beiser, Hou, Kasper, and Who, 2000). Family violence is increasingly recognized as an important health issue. Accordingly, one of the models of family violence within immigrant communities is a **"structural model,"** proposing that violence in immigrant families is a reaction to the multiple challenges of immigration and settlement, including language barriers, unemployment, poverty, lack of housing, isolation, and racism (Tyyskä, 2008; Preston, 2001; Wiebe, 1991; Kinnon, 2002; Bui and Morash, 1999; Menjivar and Salcido, 2002; Martin and Mosher, 1995; McLeod and Shin, 1993; Dinshaw, 2005).

Among the stressors leading to violence are also the significant shifts in families' internal roles and power relationships upon immigration. For example, the comparatively easier employability of women and teen children over men in some immigrant communities may cause shifts in gender and age hierarchies that result in family conflict and violence (Smith, 2004; Jiwani, 2001; MacLeod and Shin, 1993; Wiebe, 1991; Creese, Dyck, and McLaren, 1999, p. 8). There is an arguable link between loss of employment status and an elevation in the level of male/father aggression in some immigrant families (Tyyskä, 2005, pp. 127–128).

Alternately, family violence may have been present but may possibly escalate upon immigration (Martin and Mosher, 1995; MacLeod and Shin, 1993; Tyyskä, 2005, 2008; Pratt 1995). Family violence may also become more pervasive but hidden, as members of an extended family may have been left behind and are unable to provide support to end violence or to protect specific family members from violence (Morrison, Guruge, and Snarr, 1999; Tyyskä, 2008).

Because of the associated stigma, many immigrant communities react defensively at the suggestion that family violence is a problem in their communities. Solutions in this area require sensitivity from the service-providing sector, and a full involvement of the communities in question, which can offer the best ways of alleviating the problems (Preston, 2001; Wiebe, 1991; Kinnon, 2002; Bui and Morash, 1999; Menjivar and Salcido, 2002; Martin and Mosher, 1995; MacLeod and Shin, 1993; Dinshaw, 2005).

Transnational Families

Many immigrant groups do not limit their kin relations to the traditional nuclear family but count numerous extended kin as important members of the closest family (Creese, Dyck, and McLaren, 1999, p. 7). Though some families are fortunate enough to arrive as multigenerational units (Noivo, 1993), many families arrive sequentially, with one adult arriving first, followed by a spouse, children, and/or other family members. As identified in Box 4.2 by one of the youth, some immigrant communities experience a real loss of extended family members who traditionally help raise children and alleviate many daily stresses (Anisef et al., 2001; Tyyskä, 2002b, 2003b).

Because of serial separations and reunifications of families over their migration history, we can now clearly identify **transnational families**, or "families that live some or most of the time separated from each other, but yet hold together and create a feeling of collective welfare and unity" (Bryceson and Vuorela, 2002, p. 3–7, in Sorensen, 2005). Transnational families result from global migrations in which adults look for work for themselves and education for children (Ambert, 2006, pp. 110–112; Panagakos, 2004; Waters, 2002; Benhard, Landolt, and Goldring, 2008). "**Astronaut families**" and "**satellite children**" are other terms used in relation to transnational families, capturing the idea that spouses or children may experience prolonged absences and separation in the migration process, sometimes lasting for years (Waters, 2002; Shahidian, 1999, p. 201; Cohen, 2000).

Not surprisingly, spousal relationships are subject to the multiple stresses of transnational living. Lengthy separations often result in extramarital relations (Shahidian, 1999, p. 201; Cohen, 2000), couples growing apart, and a host of negative emotions including jealousy, hostility, depression, and indifference (Cohen, 2000). For example, Man (2003) found that experiences may be contradictory. One the one hand, many of the Chinese women living in "astronaut" families in Vancouver experienced spousal estrangement, jealousies, and affairs over time. On the other hand, some wives found an improvement in their marital relationships and a reduction in their domestic workloads because their husband's income meant that they could afford hired household help. Yet some also spoke of the loss of extended family members in helping with child care.

Transnational parent–child relationships are also stress-ridden. One type of transnational family in Canada is women who arrive under the Foreign Immigrant Domestic Program (FIDP), from developing countries such as the Philippines and the Caribbean nations (Bakan and Stasiulis, 1996; Arat-Koc, 1997). These women leave their children behind to come and work as low-wage domestics and nannies, in order to escape the poverty created in their home countries by the legacy of colonialism and expanding global economic exploitation (Ambert, 2006, p. 111; Bakan and Stasiulis, 1996; Arat-Koc, 1997).

Since mothers are held primarily responsible for their children, they face serious social disapproval if they leave them behind as they search for better opportunities abroad (Bernhard, Landolt, and Goldring, 2005, 2008; Ambert, 2006, p. 112). Because of the difficult conditions for family reunification under immigration regulations, by the time children are reunited with their parents, families face a lot of adjustment issues, including children's anger, fear of abandonment, or jealousy of siblings who may have accompanied the immigrating parent. Re-establishing a parental connection and authority with children may be difficult because of the separation. The children may experience a double loss because they are first separated from their parents and now face another separation from a familiar caregiver (Bernhard, Landolt, and Goldring, 2005, pp. 16–19; Cohen, 2000; Ambert, 2006, pp. 111–112).

Family members may engage in multiple migrations, making it difficult to manage relationships with those family members who are present and with those who live at a distance. One aspect of the latter includes **remittances**, or money and gifts sent to family members who still live in the country of origin

(International Policy Coordination [IPC], 2004). Some estimates put the total value of Canadian remittances to Central America, the Caribbean, and South America at US$3.38 billion (IPC, 2004), with average annual remittances per immigrant ranging from CAN$500 to $3,000 (Houle and Schellenberg, 2008). The importance of remittances to receiving families and economies of their countries is enormous, amounting to a significant portion of these countries' GNP (Houle and Schellenberg, 2008). In this way, transnational family networks are contributing to the global economy, founded on colonial and postcolonial economic exploitation of the developing world by corporations of the industrialized North.

There is no denying that many immigrant families face seemingly insurmountable challenges. It is equally evident that most of these families are managing their lives quite well, creating new patterns and dealing with their lives as they unfold in new environments. As in the case of Aboriginal peoples, researchers have pointed to the usefulness of the concept of "resiliency" with regard to immigrant families (Rink and Tricker, 2005; Ryan and Hoover, 2005; Kwak, 2003; Suárez-Orozco and Carhill, 2008). The resiliency approach overcomes the tendency in general social scientific research to pathologize immigrant families by focusing on the "negative fall-out from [their] migratory experience" (Suárez-Orozco and Carhill, 2008, p. 89). Resiliency is aimed at uncovering "assets" and "buffers" that protect family members from the negative effects of challenging circumstances. As indicated, the term "resiliency" can be applied to the levels of the individual, the family, and the community (Rink and Tricker, 2005; Suárez-Orozco and Carhill, 2008). Generally, the notion of resiliency brings attention to the need to develop supports in areas where they are needed (Ryan and Hoover, 2005). It also addresses the issue of **agency**, or the capacity of individuals and groups to take initiative even if the power relations are not in their favour.

CONCLUSION

The lives of racialized and immigrant families are shaped by major interlinking social forces and processes of colonialism, racialization, and **globalization**. The consequences include the demographics of age and gender structures of families; the health consequences, including family violence; the restructuring of family units, including single parenting and the separation and keeping together of extended families; and difficulties in securing a reasonable standard of living, manifested in poverty and associated challenges to daily life. Though we must avoid the homogenization of all racialized and immigrant families, these characteristics apply to many of them, given the legacy of colonization for Aboriginal and black families, and given the current makeup of the general immigrant population.

While the depiction of racialized and immigrant families as marginal and struggling can be stigmatizing, more recent researchers are utilizing the concept of family resiliency, capturing the resourcefulness of marginalized families amid seemingly insurmountable adversities. The resiliency of immigrant families is manifested in many aspects of their lives, including the fact that, despite their economic hardship, they manage to send much-needed remittances to help their families remaining in countries of origin. At the same time, Aboriginal families are developing community healing strategies to turn back the tide of family and community dysfunction.

We need to recognize differences based on socioeconomic, regional, rural/urban, and other considerations when examining the diverse family lives of racialized and immigrant communities. The experiences of middle-class and well-to-do immigrants, though challenging in dealing with cultural differences and family fragmentation, are qualitatively quite different from those who are less well-off financially and have fewer options. Similarly, the urbanization process among Aboriginal peoples has resulted in a wider range of family experiences than would seem possible if we take into consideration only the most impoverished segments living on reserves and/or remote locations. The community healing processes in Aboriginal communities are premised on the recognition of this present-day diversity of the population.

Many racialized and immigrant families have undergone significant shifts in their structure, exemplified in the imposition of the nuclear family model on Canadian Aboriginal peoples whose grandparents are not deemed by mainstream agencies as acceptable caregivers to children, and whose families are more likely to be single parenting due to the lingering ill effects of colonialism and displacement. The nuclear family model is also evident in the forcible separation of immigrant families from their mutual support networks when members of extended families are differentially processed during the immigration process. Fragmentations in family life are traumatizing and cannot be blamed on family dysfunction but on the conditions of living in a racialized society. Thus, transnational families are not voluntary but are created by economic and social conditions that prevail globally and that force adults to migrate in search of employment and other opportunities. Just as, historically, "unstable" black families were an invention of racist practices that denied official married status to black couples, discriminatory and ethnocentric policies and practices continue to create continuing challenges for immigrant families.

As this chapter has also illustrated, experiences of family life are quite different for separate family members, based on their position in age- and gender-based family hierarchies. Customary patterns of family life are unsettled through immigration and settlement. Family members face new requirements of themselves, resulting in often difficult renegotiation of family relations. Women may find themselves having to be (primary) breadwinners while men's wage-earning status may diminish, resulting in ripple effects in terms of sharing of domestic work and child care. Much is expected from children and youth who themselves deal with cultural and other adjustment issues and may be required to help their parents with theirs, as cultural brokers. Intergenerational and gender-based difficulties may escalate to conflict and even violence. It is remarkable that despite living in such a pressure cooker, many immigrant families are doing well and are managing their lives and relationships successfully.

Summary

- Canadian family diversity was reduced through colonialism and the homogenization of the Aboriginal population.

- Colonization disrupted the family lives of Aboriginal and blacks, who were disenfranchised and socially constructed as dysfunctional.

- The promise of a new country is not fulfilled for many immigrant families whose lives are characterized by poverty and other challenges.

- Gender and intergenerational relations in immigrant families are disrupted upon immigration and settlement, resulting in challenges for the integration of individual family members and the family as a whole.

- Family violence in immigrant and racialized families is often viewed as a cultural phenomenon whereas it is more likely to be a result of racist and ethnocentric policies and ideologies.

- In theorizing about immigrant and racialized families, they should be perceived as resilient rather than be stigmatized as deficient.

Critical Thinking Questions

1. In what ways have colonialism, globalization, and racialization shaped the experiences of racialized and immigrant families?

2. To what extent do gender and generation (age) characterize family relations in immigrant and racialized families?

3. How has the state contributed to the creation of immigrant, Aboriginal, and racialized families?

Websites

Statistics Canada
http://www12.statcan.ca/english/census06/analysis
> The Statistics Canada website provides a lot of baseline statistical information, including detailed information on, and analyses of the results of the most recent census (2006), in terms of Aboriginal peoples, immigration, ethnicity, and race.

Citizenship and Immigration Canada
http://www.cic.gc.ca
> The Citizenship and Immigration Canada website gives information about the different immigration and temporary resident categories, and criteria for selection.

The Vanier Institute of the Family
http://www.vifamily.ca/library/publications/publications.html
> The Vanier Institute of the Family is a well-known research institute that provides many reports and statistics related to racialized and immigrant families in Canada.

Suggested Readings

Judith K. Bernhard, Patricia Landolt, and Luin Goldring. 2008. "Transnationalizing Families: Canadian Immigration Policy and the Spatial Fragmentation of Care-Giving Among Latin American Newcomers." *International Migration*, pp. 1–29. https://tspace.library.utoronto.ca/handle/1807/16701 (accessed April 13, 2010).
> This article gives an orientation and background to the topic of transnational families in the global and Canadian context, while illustrating the difficulties experienced by transnational mothers through interviews with Latin American mothers in Canada.

Patti LaBoucane-Benson. 2005. *A Complex Ecological Framework of Aboriginal Family Resilience*. University of Alberta, Centre of Canadian Studies, pp. 1–18. http://www.cst.ed.ac.uk/2005conference/papers/LaBoucane-Benson_paper.pdf (accessed March 30, 2010).
> This is a fresh take on the often stigmatizing view of Aboriginal families as problem-ridden and dysfunctional. Instead, against a backdrop of the history of Aboriginal family life, the author proposes that these families should be looked at through the lens of family resiliency, giving them credit for managing well under severe stresses.

Vappu Tyyskä. 2006. *Teen Perspectives on Family Relations in the Toronto Tamil Community*. CERIS Working Paper #45. Toronto: CERIS—The Ontario Metropolis Centre. **http://ceris.metropolis.net/research-policy/wkpp_list.htm (accessed April 13, 2010).**
> This working paper gives an overview of the main issues in intergenerational relations between parents and youth in immigrant families, and provides the results (including many quotes) from interviews with Sri Lankan Tamil youth regarding their relationships with their parents.

References

Aapola, S., M. Gonick, and A. Harris. 2005. *Young Femininity. Girlhood, Power and Social Change*. London: Palgrave McMillan.

Africa Reparations Movement. 2007. *A Brief Chronology of Slavery, Colonialism and Neo-colonialism*. http://www.arm.arc.co.uk/CronOfColonialism.html (accessed March 30, 2010).

Ali, M. and K.M. Kilbride. 2004. *Forging New Ties: Improving Parenting and Family Support Services for New Canadians with Young Children.* Ottawa: Human Resources and Skill Development Canada.

Ambert, Anne-Marie. 2006. *Changing Families. Relationships in Context.* Canadian Edition. Toronto: Pearson.

Anderson, Karen. 1987. "A Gendered World: Women, Men, and the Political Economy of the Seventeenth-Century Huron." In Heather Jon Maroney and Meg Luxton (Eds.), *Feminism and Political Economy. Women's Work, Women's Struggles* (pp. 121–138). Toronto: Methuen.

Anisef, P. and K.M. Kilbride. 2000. *The Needs of Newcomer Youth and Emerging "Best Practices" to Meet Those Needs.* Toronto: Joint Centre of Excellence for Research on Immigration and Settlement.

Anisef, P., K.M. Kilbride, J. Ochocka, and R. Janzen. 2001. *Parenting Issues of Newcomer Families in Ontario.* Kitchener: Centre for Research and Education in Human Services and Centre of Excellence for Research on Immigration and Settlement.

Arat-Koc, Sedef. 1997. "From 'Mothers of the Nation' to Migrant Workers." In Abigail B. Bakan and Daiva Stasiulis (Eds.), *Not One of the Family. Foreign Domestic Workers in Canada* (pp. 53–79). Toronto: University of Toronto Press.

Armstrong, Pat and Hugh Armstrong. 1988. "Women's Work in the Labour Force." In Arlene Tiger McLaren (Ed.), *Gender and Society: Creating a Canadian Women's Sociology* (pp. 275–315). Toronto: Copp-Clark Pitman.

Bakan, Abigail D. and Daiva Stasiulis. 1996. "Structural Adjustment, Citizenship, and Foreign Domestic Labour: The Canadian Case." In Isabella Bakker (Ed.), *Rethinking Restructuring: Gender and Change in Canada,* pp. 217–242. Toronto: University of Toronto Press.

BBC World Service. 2007. *The Story of Africa. Slavery.* http://www.bbc.co.uk/worldservice/specials/1624_story_of_africa/page49.shtml (accessed April 13, 2010).

Beiser, Morton, Feng Hou, Irene Hyrnan, and Michael Tousignant. 2002. "Poverty, Family Process and the Mental Health of Immigrant Children in Canada." *American Journal of Public Health,* 92(2): 220–228.

Beiser, Morton, Feng Hou, Violet Kasper, and Samuel Who. 2000. *Changes in Poverty Status and Developmental Behaviour: A Comparison of Immigrant and Non Immigrant Children in Canada.* Hull: Applied Research Branch, Strategic Policy Division. Human Resources Development Canada.

Benoit, Cecilia. 2000. "Women's Work and Social Rights in the Pre-Capitalist Era." In Cecilia M. Benoit (Ed.), *Women, Work, and Social Rights. Canada in a Historical and Comparative Perspective* (pp. 26–47). Scarborough: ON: Prentice-Hall Allyn and Bacon Canada.

Bernhard, Judith K., Patricia Landolt, and Luin Goldring. 2005. *Transnational, Multi-local Motherhood: Experiences of Separation and Reunification Among Latin American Families in Canada.* Toronto: CERIS Working Paper No. 40. http://ceris.metropolis.net/frameset_e.html (accessed April 1, 2010).

Bernhard, Judith K., Patricia Landolt, and Luin Goldring. 2008. "Transnationalizing Families: Canadian Immigration Policy and the Spatial Fragmentation of Caregiving among Latin American Newcomers". *International Migration*, pp. 1–29. https://tspace.library.utoronto.ca/handle/1807/16701 (accessed April 13, 2010).

Bernhard, J.K., M.L. Lefebvre, G. Chud,, and R. Lange. 1996. "Linguistic Match between Children and Caregivers in Canadian Early Childhood Education." *Canadian Journal of Research in Early Childhood Education*, 5(2) 202–222.

Bonvillain, Nancy. 2001. *Women and Men. Cultural Constructs of Gender*. 3rd ed. Upper Saddle River, NJ: Prentice Hall.

Boyd, Monica and Doug Norris. "Demographic Change and Young Adults Living with Parents, 1981–1996." *Canadian Studies in Population*, 27(2): 267–281.

Bryceson, Deborah and Ulla Vuorela (Eds.). 2002. *The Transnational Family: New European Frontiers and Global Networks*. New York: Berg, 2002.

Brzozowski, Jodi-Anne, Andrea Taylor-Butts, and Sara Johnson. 2006. "Victimization and Offending among the Aboriginal Population in Canada." *Juristat*. Canadian Centre for Justice Statistics, June.

Bui, H. and M. Morash. 1999. "Domestic Violence in the Vietnamese Immigrant Community: An Exploratory Study." *Violence Against Women*, 5(6): 769–795.

Calliste, Agnes. 1996. "Black Families in Canada: Exploring the Interconnections of Race, Class, and Gender." In Marion Lynn (Ed.), *Voices. Essays on Canadian Families* (pp. 243–270). Toronto: Nelson Canada.

Campbell, Gwyn, Suzanne Miers, and Joseph C. Miller. 2005. "Women in Western Systems of Slavery: Introduction." *Slavery and Abolition*, 26(2): 161–179.

Canadian Council on Social Development. 2003. *Census Shows Growing Polarization of Income in Canada*. Ottawa: Canadian Council on Social Development. http://www.ccsd.ca/pr/2003/censusincome.htm (accessed March 30, 2010).

Canadian Race Relations Foundation (CRRF). 2007. *CRRF Responds to UN Body's Criticism of the Use of "Visible Minorities."* http://www.crr.ca/content/view/538/592/lang, english (accessed March 30, 2010).

Castellano, Marlene Brant. 2002. *Aboriginal Family Trends. Extended Families, Nuclear Families, Families of the Heart*. Vanier Institute of the Family. http://www.vifamily.ca/library/cft/aboriginal.html#Healing (accessed March 30, 2010).

Christensen, Carole P. and Morton Weinfeld. 1993. "The Black Family in Canada: A Preliminary Exploration of Family Patterns and Inequality." *Canadian Ethnic Studies*, 25(3), pp. 26–44.

Citizenship and Immigration Canada (CIC). 2007. *Facts and Figures*. http://www.cic.gc.ca/english/resources/statistics/menu-fact.asp (accessed March 30, 2010).

Citizenship and Immigration Canada (CIC). 2008. *Fact and Figures.* http://www .cic.gc.ca/english/resources/statistics/menu-fact.asp (accessed March 30, 2010).

Citizenship and Immigration Canada (CIC). 2009. *Application for Permanent Resident. Federal Skilled Worker Class.* http://www.cic.gc.ca/ENGLISH/pdf/kits/guides/EG7.pdf (accessed March 30, 2010).

Codjoe, H. 2006. "The Role of an Affirmed Black Cultural Identity and Heritage in the Academic Achievement of African-Canadian Students." *Intercultural Education,* 17(1), 33–54.

Cohen, Rina. 2000. "Mom Is a Stranger: The Negative Impact of Immigration Policies on the Family Life of Philipina Domestic Workers." *Canadian Ethnic Studies,* 32(3): 76–89.

Cook, Eung-Do and Darin Howe. 2004. "Aboriginal Languages of Canada." Chap. 9 in W. O'Grady and J. Archibald (Eds.), *Contemporary Linguistic Analysis,* 5th ed. Toronto: Addison Wesley Longman, 294–309.

Cooper, A. 2007. "The Invisible History of the Slave Trade." *Toronto Star,* March 25, p. A15.

Crawford, J. 1995. "Endangered Native American Languages: What Is to Be Done, and Why?" *The Bilingual Research Journal,* 19(1), 17–38.

Creese, Gillian, Isabel Dyck, and Arlene McLaren. 1999. *Reconstituting the Family: Negotiating Immigration and Settlement.* Vancouver: RIIM Working Paper 99–10.

Department of Justice Canada. 2008. *A Review of Research on Criminal Victimization and First Nations, Métis and Inuit Peoples 1990 to 2001.* http://www.justice.gc.ca/eng/pi/rs/ rep-rap/2006/rr06_vic1/rr06_vic1.pdf (accessed April 13, 2010).

Dhuravarajan, V. 2003. "Hindu Indo-Canadian Families." In M. Lynn (Ed.), *Voices. Essays on Canadian Families,* 2nd ed (pp. 301–328). Toronto: Nelson Canada.

Dinshaw, F. 2005. *Elder Abuse: South Asian Women Speak Up.* Toronto: COSTI Immigrant Services.

Duffy, Ann and Julianne Momirov. 1997. *Family Violence: A Canadian Introduction.* Toronto: J. Lorimer.

Dyck, Isabel and Arlene Tigar McLaren, 2002. *Becoming Canadian? Girls, Home and School and Renegotiating Feminine Identity.* Vancouver: RIIM.

Fiske, J.A. and R. Johnny. 1996. "The Nedut'en Family: Yesterday and Today." In M. Lynn (Ed.), *Voices. Essays on Canadian Families* (pp. 225–242). Toronto: Nelson Canada.

Frenette, Marc and René Morissette. 2005. "Will They Ever Converge? Earnings of Immigrant and Canadian-Born Workers Over the Last Two Decades." *International Migration Review,* 39(1): 228–258.

Fuligni, Andrew J. 1997. "The Academic Achievement of Adolescents from Immigrant Families: The Roles of Family Background, Attitudes, and Behaviour." *Child Development,* 68(2): 351–363.

Fuligni, A.J. and K. Yoshikawa. 2003. "Socioeconomic Resources, Parenting, and the Child Development Among Immigrant Families." In M. Bornstein and R. Bradley (Eds.), *Socioeconomic Status, Parenting, and Child Development* (pp. 107–124). Mahwah, HJ: Lawrence Erlbaum Associates.

Gaskell, Jane. 1993. "Gender Equity in the Curriculum." In James Curtis, Edward Grabb, and Neil Guppy (Eds.), *Social Inequality in Canada. Patterns, Problems, Policies* (pp. 233–244). 2nd ed. Scarborough, ON: Prentice Hall Canada.

Gilmore, J. 2008. *The Canadian Immigrant Labour Market in 2007.* The Immigrant Labour Force Analysis Series. http://dsp-psd.pwgsc.gc.ca/collection_2008/statcan/71-606-X/71-606-XIE2008003.pdf (accessed April 21, 2010).

Gordon, Everton. 1999. *Separation, Reunification and the Hybridization of Culture: A Study of Caribbean Immigrant Families in Toronto.* Toronto: MA Thesis, York University.

Gordon, Raymond G., Jr. (Ed.). 2005. *Ethnologue: Languages of the World,* 15th ed. Dallas: SIL International. http://www.ethnologue.com (accessed April 1, 2010).

Green, Joyce. 1995. "Towards a Détente with History: Confronting Canada's Colonial Legacy." *International Journal of Canadian Studies* 12, Fall. http://sisis.nativeweb.org/clark/detente.html (accessed April 1, 2010).

Grewal, Sukhdev, Joan Bottorff, and Ann Hilton. 2005. "The Influence of Family on Immigrant South Asian Women's Health." *Journal of Family Nursing,* 11(3): 242–263.

Haddad, T. and I. Lam. 1988. "Canadian Families—Men's Involvement in Family Work: A Case Study of Immigrant Men in Toronto. *International Journal of Comparative Sociology,* 29(3–4): 269–81.

Handa, Amita. 1997. "Caught Between Omissions: Exploring 'Culture Conflict' Among Second Generation South Asian Women in Canada." PhD Thesis, University of Toronto.

Health Canada. 2007. *Indian Residential Schools.* http://www.hc-sc.gc.ca/fniah-spnia/services/imdiresident/index-eng.php (accessed April 2, 2010).

Hébert, Y. 2001. "Identity, Diversity, and Education: A Critical View of the Literature." *Canadian Ethnic Studies,* 32, 111–125.

Henry, F., C. Tator, W. Mattis, and T. Rees. 2000. "Racism in Canadian Education." In F. Henry, C. Tator, W. Mattis, and T. Rees (Eds.), *The Colour of Democracy. Racism in Canadian Society,* 2nd ed. (pp. 231–261). Toronto: Harcourt Brace and Company.

Houle, René and Grant Schellenberg. 2008. *Remittance Behaviours of Recent Immigrants in Canada.* Ottawa: Statistics Canada. http://dsp-psd.pwgsc.gc.ca/collection_2008/statcan/11F0019M/11F0019MIE2008312.pdf (accessed April 2, 2010).

Human Resources and Skills Development Canada. 2007. *A Study of Poverty and Working Poverty among Recent Immigrants to Canada.* http://www.hrsdc.gc.ca/eng/publications_resources/research/categories/inclusion/2007/sp_680_05_07_e/page04.shtml (accessed April 2, 2010).

International Policy Coordination (IPC). 2004. *Remittances: A Preliminary Research.* Ottawa: Citizenship and Immigration, with research from Analysis and Research Division of Canadian International Development Agency (CIDA), March.

Inuit Tapiirit Kanatami. 2008. *Inuit Receive Apology to Survivors of Residential Schools with Great Relief.* http://www.itk.ca/media-centre/media-releases/inuit-receive-apology-survivors-residential-schools-great-relief (accessed April 2, 2010).

Jain, A. and J. Belsky. 1997. "Fathering and Acculturation: Immigrant Indian Families with Young Children." *Journal of Marriage and Family,* 59: 873–883.

James, Carl E. 1999. *Seeing Ourselves: Exploring Race, Ethnicity and Culture,* 2nd ed. Toronto: Thompson Educational Publishing.

Jiwani, Y. 2001. "Intersecting Inequalities: Immigrant Women of Color Who Have Experienced Violence and Their Encounters with the Health Care System." Vancouver: Feminist Research, Education, Development, and Action Centre.

Karakayali, Nedim. 2005. "Duality and Diversity in the Lives of Immigrant Children: Rethinking the 'Problem of the Second Generation in Light of Immigrant Autobiographies.'" *Canadian Review of Sociology and Anthropology,* 42(3): 325–344.

Kilbride, K.M., P. Anisef, E. Baichman-Anisef, and R. Khattar. 2001. *Between Two Worlds: The Experiences and Concerns Of Immigrant Youth in Ontario.* Toronto: Joint Centre of Excellence for Research on Immigration and Settlement.

Kinnon, D. 2002. *Community Awareness and Response: Abuse and Neglect of Older Adults.* Ottawa: National Clearinghouse on Family Violence.

Krahn, Harvey and Graham S. Lowe. 2002. *Work, Industry, and Canadian Society,* 4th ed. Toronto: Thomson Nelson.

LaBoucane-Benson, Patti. 2005. *A Complex Ecological Framework of Aboriginal Family Resilience.* University of Alberta, Centre of Canadian Studies, pp. 1–18. http://www.cst.ed.ac.uk/2005conference/papers/LaBoucane-Benson_paper.pdf (accessed April 2, 2010).

Li, Peter. 1988. *Ethnic Inequality in Class Society.* Toronto: Thompson Educational Publishing.

Li, Peter S. 2001. "The Market Worth of Immigrants' Educational Credentials." *Canadian Public Policy,* 27(1): 23–38.

Liu, Jeanye and Don Kerr. 2003. "Family Change and Economic Well-Being in Canada: The Case of Recent Immigrant Families with Children." *International Migration,* 41(4): 113–140).

Luthar, S. S., D. Cicchetti, and B. Becker. 2000. "The Construct of Resilience: A Critical Evaluation and Guidelines for Future Work." *Child Development,* 71(3), 543–562.

MacLeod, L. and M. Shin. 1993. *'Like a Wingless Bird . . .' A Tribute to the Survival and Courage of Women Are Abused and Who Speak Neither English nor French.* Ottawa: National Clearinghouse on Family Violence.

Man, Guida. 2003. "The Experience of Middle Class Women in Recent Hong Kong Chinese Immigrant Families in Canada." In Marion Lynn (Ed.), *Voices: Essays on Canadian Families* (pp. 271–300). Toronto: Thomson Nelson.

Maiter, S., N. Trocme, and U. George. 2003. "Building Bridges: The Collaborative Development of Culturally Appropriate Definitions of Child Abuse and Neglect for the South Asian Community." *Affilia: Journal of Women and Social Work*, 18(4), 411–420.

Martin, D. and J. Mosher. 1995. "Unkept Promises: Experiences of Immigrant Women with the Neo-Criminalization of Wife Abuse." *Canadian Journal of Women and the Law*, 8: 3–44.

McCue, Harvey. 2009. "Native People, Education." *Canadian Encyclopedia Historica*. http://www.thecanadianencyclopedia.com/index.cfm?PgNm=TCE&Params= A1ARTA0005646 (accessed April 2, 2010).

McDonald, P.L., J.P. Hornick, G.B. Robertson, and J.E. Wallace. 1999. *Elder Abuse and Neglect in Canada*. Toronto: Butterworths.

McElroy, W. 2004. *West Africa and Colonialism*. Fairfax, Virginia: The Future of Freedom Foundation. http://www.lewrockwell.com/mcelroy/mcelroy55.html (accessed April 2, 2010).

Mannette, Joy A. 1984. "'Stark Remnants of Blackpast': Thinking on Gender, Ethnicity and Class in 1780s Nova Scotia." *Alternate Routes*, 7: 102–33.

Mees, Mary C. 1997. "Teach Them The Moral Way Of Living: The Meeting Of Huron Sexuality And European Religion." Loyola University, New Orleans: *The Student Historical Journal 1997–1998*. http://www.loyno.edu/~history/journal/1997-8/ Mees.html (accessed April 2, 2010).

Menjivar, C. and O. Salcido. 2002. "Immigrant Women and Domestic Violence: Common Experiences in Different Countries." *Gender and Society*, 16(6): 898–920.

Métis National Council. 2009. *Who Are the Métis?* http://www.metisnation.ca/who/index.html (accessed April 2, 2010).

Mianda, Gertrude. 2004. "Sisterhood versus Discrimination: Being a Black African Francophone Immigrant Woman in Montreal and Toronto." In Marlene Epp, Franca Iacovetta, and Frances Swyripa (Eds.), *Sister or Stranger? Immigrant Women, Ethnic, and Racialized Women in Canadian History* (pp. 266–284). Toronto: University of Toronto Press.

Mitchell, Barbara. 2001. "Ethnocultural Reproduction and Attitudes Toward Cohabiting Relationships." *Canadian Review of Sociology and Anthropology*, 38(4): 391–414.

Moghissi, Haideh. 1999. "Away from Home: Iranian Women, Displacement, Cultural Resistance and Change." *Journal of Comparative Family Studies*, 30(2): 207–218.

Momirov, Julianne and Kenise Kilbride. 2005. "Family Lives of Native Peoples, Immigrants and Visible Minorities." In Nancy Mandell and Ann Duffy (Eds.), *Canadian Families: Diversity, Conflict and Change* (pp. 87–110). Toronto: Thomson Nelson.

Morrison, Lynn, Sepali Guruge, and Kymberly A. Snarr. 1999. "Sri Lankan Tamil Immigrants in Toronto: Gender, Marriage Patterns, and Sexuality." In Gregory Kelson and Debra DeLaet (Eds.), *Gender and Immigration* (pp. 144–162). New York: New York University Press.

Munford, Clarence J. 2008. *Atlantic Slave Traffic. An Uneven Development of African Societies.* http://www.nathanielturner.com/atlanticslavetraffic.htm (accessed April 2, 2010).

Murji, Karim and John Solomos. 2005. *Racialization: Studies in Theory and Practice.* London: Oxford University Press.

National Archives, UK. 2007. *Slavery. How Did the Abolition Acts of 1807 and 1866 Effect Slavery?* London: National Archives.

National Network for Family Resiliency, CSREES-USDA. n.d. "Family Resiliency: Building Strengths to Meet Life's Challenges." http://www.extension.iastate.edu/Publications/EDC53.pdf (accessed April 21, 2010).

Noivo, Edite. 1993. "Ethnic Families and the Social Injuries of Class, Migration, Gender, Generation and Minority Status." *Canadian Ethnic Studies*, 23(3): 66–76.

Norris, Mary Jane. 1998. "Canada's Aboriginal Languages." *Canadian Social Trends* (Winter): 9–16.

Ontario Council of Agencies Serving Immigrants (OCASI). 2006. *Statistics Canada on the Immigrant Labour Market.* http://www.ocasi.org/index.php?qid=950 (accessed April 2010).

Panagakos, Anastasia. 2004. "Recycled Odyssey: Creating Transnational Families in the Greek Diaspora." *Global Networks*, 4(3): 299–311.

Perkins, U.E. 2005. *Harvesting New Generations: The Positive Development of Black Youth*, 2nd ed. Chicago: Third World Press.

Pratt, A. 1995. "New Immigrant and Refugee Battered Women: The Intersection of Immigration and Criminal Justice Policy." In *Wife Assault and the Canadian Criminal Justice System. Issues and Policies* (pp. 84–104). Toronto: Centre for Criminology, University of Toronto.

Preston, B. 2001. *A Booklet for Service Providers Who Work With Immigrant Families: On Issues Relating to Child Discipline, Child Abuse and Child Neglect.* Ottawa: National Clearinghouse on Family Violence.

Public Service Alliance of Canada (PSAC). 2008. "PSAC Statement on National Aboriginal People's Day June 21, 2008." http://www.psac.com/what/humanrights/aboriginalsolidarity-e.shtml (accessed April 2, 2010).

Renzetti, Claire M. and Daniel J. Curran. 1999. *Women, Men, and Society.* Toronto: Allyn & Bacon (pp. 3–13).

Rink, E. and R. Tricker. 2005. Promoting Healthy Behaviors among Adolescents: A Review of the Resiliency Literature. *American Journal of Health Studies*, 20(5): pp. 39–46.

Royal Commission on Aboriginal Peoples. 1991. *Report of the Royal Commission on Aboriginal Peoples.* Ottawa: Indian and Northern Affairs Canada.

Ryan, C.A. and J.H. Hoover. 2005. *Reclaiming Children and Youth*, 14:22, 117–119.

Seat, R. 2000. *Factors Affecting the Settlement and Adaptation Process of Canadian Adolescent Newcomers 16–19 Years of Age.* Toronto: Family Service Association of Toronto.

Shahidan, Hammed. 1999. "Gender and Sexuality Among Immigrant Iranians in Canada." *Sexualities*, 2(2): 189–222.

Shields, J. 2004. "No Safe Haven: Markets, Welfare, and Migrants." *CERIS Working Paper 22* (January 2003): 1–39. A Report of the Joint Centre of Excellence for Research on Immigration and Settlement (CERIS)—Toronto. http://ceris.metropolis.net/frameset_e.html (accessed April 2, 2010).

Shimoni, E., D. Este, and D. Clark. 2003. "Paternal Engagement in Immigrant and Refugee Families." *Journal of Comparative Family Studies*, 34(4): 555–571.

Smith, E. 2004. *Nowhere to Turn? Responding to Partner Violence Against Immigrant and Visible Minority Women*. Ottawa: Department of Justice, Sectoral Involvement in Departmental Policy Development (SIDPD).

Sorensen, Ninna Nyberg. 2005. "Transnational Family Life across the Atlantic: The Experience of Colombian and Dominican Migrants in Europe. Presentation at the International Conference on 'Migration and Domestic Work in a Global Perspective' (May 26–29). Wassenar, The Netherlands.

Span, C.M. 2002. "Educational and Social Reforms for African American Juvenile Delinquents in 19th Century New York City and Philadelphia." *Journal of Negro Education*, 71(3), 108–117.

Statistics Canada. 2005a. "Longitudinal Survey of Immigrants to Canada: A Portrait of Early Settlement Experiences." Cat. No. 89-614-XIE.

Statistics Canada. 2005b. "Decline in Homeownership Rates Among Immigrant Families." *The Daily*, February 3.

Statistics Canada. 2006a. "Canada's Ethnocultural Mosaic, 2006 Census Highlights." http://www12.statcan.ca/english/census06/analysis/ethnicorigin/highlights.cfm (accessed April 2, 2010).

Statistics Canada. 2006b. "Canada's Changing Labour Force, 2006 Census: The Provinces and Territories." http://www12.statcan.ca/english/census06/analysis/labour/ov-cclf-29.cfm (accessed April 2, 2010).

Statistics Canada. 2008. "Aboriginal Peoples in Canada in 2006: Inuit, Métis, and First Nations, 2006 Census." Cat. No. 97-558-XIE.

Suárez-Orozco, C. and A. Carhill. 2008. "Afterword: New Directions in Research with Immigrant Families and Their Children." *New Directions in Child and Adolescent Development*, 121: 87–104.

Thomson, C.A. 1979. *Blacks in Deep Snow: Black Pioneers in Canada*. Don Mills, ON: James Dent & Sons (Canada).

Trocmé, Nico, Della Knoke, and Cindy Blackstock. 2004. "Pathways to the Overrepresentation of Aboriginal Children in Canada's Child Welfare System." *Social Service Review* (December): 1–28.

Tyyskä, Vappu. 2001. *Long and Winding Road: Adolescents and Youth in Canada Today*. Toronto: Canadian Scholars Press.

Tyyskä, Vappu. 2002a. "Report of Key Informant Interviews—Toronto. Improving Parenting and Family Supports for New Canadians With Young Children: Focus on Resources for Service Providers" (unpublished).

Tyyskä, Vappu. 2002b. "Report of Individual Interviews with Parents—Toronto. Improving Parenting and Family Supports for New Canadians With Young Children: Focus on Resources for Service Providers" (unpublished).

Tyyskä, Vappu. 2003a. "Report of Focus Groups with Newcomer Parents. Improving Parenting and Family Supports For New Canadians with Young Children: Focus on Resources for Service Providers" (unpublished).

Tyyskä, Vappu. 2003b. "Solidarity and Conflict: Teen-Parent Relationships in Iranian Immigrant Families in Toronto." In Marion Lynn (Ed.), *Voices. Essays on Canadian Families*, 2nd ed (pp. 312–331). Toronto: Nelson Canada.

Tyyskä, Vappu. 2005. "Immigrant Adjustment and Parenting of Teens: A Study of Newcomer Groups in Toronto, Canada." In Vesa Puuronen, Jarna Soilevuo-Grønnerød, and Jatta Herranen (Eds.), *Youth—Similarities, Differences, Inequalities*. Joensuu, Finland: Joensuu University, Reports of the Karelian Institute, No. 1/2005.

Tyyskä, Vappu. (Ed.). 2006a. *Action and Analysis: Readings in Sociology of Gender*. Toronto: Nelson Thomson.

Tyyskä, Vappu. 2006b. "Teen Perspectives on Family Relations in the Toronto Tamil Community."CERIS Working Paper No. 45. March 2006.

Tyyskä, Vappu. 2007. "Immigrant Families in Sociology." In Jennifer E. Lansford, Kirby Deater-Deckard, and Marc H. Bornstein (Eds.), *Immigrant Families in Contemporary Society* (pp. 83–99). New York: The Guilford Press.

Tyyskä, Vappu. 2008. *Youth and Society. The Long and Winding Road*, 2nd ed. Toronto: Canadian Scholars' Press.

Wade, Terrance, J. and Augustine Brannigan. 1998. "The Genesis of Adolescent Risk-Taking: Pathways through Family, School and Peers." *The Canadian Journal of Sociology,* 23(1): 1–20.

Walker, J.W.S. 1985. *Racial Discrimination in Canada: The Black Experience*. Ottawa: Canadian Historical Association. Historical Booklet No. 41.

Walton-Roberts, Margaret and Geraldine Pratt. 2003. "Mobile Modernities: One South Asian Family Negotiates Immigration, Gender and Class." Vancouver: RIIM Working Paper No. 03–13.

Waters, Johanna L. 2002. "Flexible Families? 'Astronaut' Households and the Experiences of Lone Mothers in Vancouver, British Columbia." *Social and Cultural Geography*, 3(2): 17–134.

Wiebe, K. 1991. *Violence Against Immigrant Women and Children: An Overview of Community Workers*, 2nd ed. Vancouver: Women Against Violence Against Women/Rape Crisis Centre.

Wilde, R. 2007. "The European Overseas Empires." *About: European History*. http://
europeanhistory.about.com/od/colonimperialism/a/ovoverempires.htm
(accessed April 2, 2010).

Winks, Robin W. 1971. *The Blacks in Canada: A History*. New Haven and London: Yale
University Press [Montreal: McGill-Queen's University Press].

Wong, Siu Kwong. 1999. "Acculturation, Peer Relations, and Delinquent Behaviour of
Chinese-Canadian Youth." *Adolescence*, 34(133): 107–119.

Wotherspoon, T. 1998. *The Sociology of Education in Canada: Critical Perspectives*. Toronto: Oxford
University Press.

Zaidi, Arshia and Muhammad Shuraydi. 2002. "Perceptions of Arranged Marriages by
Young Pakistani Muslim Women Living in Western Society." *Journal of Comparative
Family Studies*, 33(4): 37–57.

Part 2

Living Inside Families

Chapter 5

LGBTQ Families in Canada: Private Lives and Public Discourse

Catherine Taylor and Janice Ristock[1]

LEARNING OBJECTIVES

In this chapter, you will learn that:

1. LGBTQ people and their family structures are diverse,

2. the lingering impact of homophobia and transphobia structures Canadian society,

3. assimilation and integration are in tension in the progress that we make,

4. the discursive territory that LGBTQ families occupy in Canadian society is complex.

INTRODUCTION

In many ways, same-sex rights are family rights. Most of the changes that have decriminalized same-sex life over the last 40 years, and brought an array of federal and provincial laws into conformity with the Canadian *Charter of Rights and Freedoms*, can be seen as family-rights issues. Family relationships and the typical activities associated with such relationships—sex, marriage, divorce, adoption, parenting, custody, hospital visitation rights, inheritance rights—are now legally protected rights in Canada for lesbian, gay, and bisexual (LGB) people. Canada is a world leader in same-sex family rights, and there is now (almost) no official distinction between heterosexual and same-sex couples when it comes to their family life. (The only legal grounds for discrimination now are religious, with religious officials maintaining the right not to perform same-sex weddings, and the right to make statements that would otherwise be subject to criminal prosecution under hate propaganda law [see Box 5.1].)

However, LGB people continue to experience social discrimination in all aspects of their family lives. Although many religious people do support same-sex marriage and same-sex families, often the source of oppression is socially conservative faith communities that have historically demonized "homosexuality" as a damnable sin that must be punished in order to protect the institution of the family from crumbling. Current secular versions of their arguments drop the allegations of sin and focus their opposition to same-sex rights on the

BOX 5.1 LGBTQ FAMILY RIGHTS TIMELINE IN CANADA

1967	Pierre Trudeau, then Justice Minister of Canada, declares, "There's no place for the state in the bedrooms of the nation."
1969	Consensual homosexual sex in private between two adults 21 or over is decriminalized.
1977	Quebec becomes the first large jurisdiction in the world to protect citizens from discrimination of the basis of sexual orientation.
1992	Conservative Justice Minister Kim Campbell announces the end of a ban on gay and lesbian people serving in the armed forces.
1995	The Supreme Court of Canada rules that "sexual orientation" should be "read in" to the 1982 Canadian *Charter of Rights and Freedoms*.
1995	Ontario court rules in favour of gay and lesbian couples' adoption rights.
1996	Sexual orientation is added to the Canadian *Human Rights Act*.
1996	The Canadian Psychological Association opposes discrimination against lesbians and gay men and supports same-sex marriage and same-sex couples parenting.
1999	The Supreme Court of Canada rules that gay and lesbian couples should have same rights as heterosexual common-law couples.
2005	Canada becomes the fourth country in the world (preceded by the Netherlands, Belgium, and Spain) to legalize same-sex marriage.

claim of social necessity. Ethicist Margaret Somerville (2003), for example, whose views have been widely covered by Canadian mainstream and Christian media, argues against legalizing same-sex marriage this way:

> I do not believe that we should change the definition of marriage to include same-sex couples. My reasons go to the nature of marriage as the societal institution that represents, symbolizes and protects the inherently reproductive human relationship. I believe that society needs such an institution. . . .

In contrast, Lloyd Axworthy (former Minister of Foreign Affairs) described the impact of Canada's "Cadillac" Charter of Rights this way on the occasion of the Supreme Court of Canada's ruling in favour of legalizing same-sex marriage:

> "This country began to change in a remarkable way. We had a culture of rights" that led to protection of rights for women, Aboriginal people, and gay men and lesbians. ... We should take an enormous amount of exuberance" from the Supreme Court's ruling.[2]

To Axworthy, the occasion was "a moment of joy"; to Somerville, an attack on the family. Debates within Canadian society still occur. Some people maintain that same-sex family rights must be sacrificed for the greater good lest our nation be led down a slippery slope into social chaos, with men abandoning their children and perhaps marrying animals. Others argue that, in a diverse nation committed to protecting human rights, everyone deserves protection, not just the majority, and that respecting same-sex families will strengthen the institution of marriage and protection of children, not undermine it.

It may seem strange, more than 40 years after Trudeau's famous proclamation, and years after the legal battles have been won, to find that people's right to marry or to be parents is still the subject of heated debate in public discourse. But as important as the law is in establishing the grounds on which life is conducted in a society, it is only one of many institutions involved in influencing the progress of social justice movements; as Henry David Thoreau (1849) famously observed, "Law never made men [sic] a whit more just." LGBTQ family rights are still contested through competing discourses of "family values" and "human rights," with socially conservative forces maintaining that LGBTQ family rights are opposed to family values, and progressive forces maintaining that LGBTQ family rights are human rights.

The passion fuelling the public debate over the personal family life of a small minority population can be understood through sociological analysis. Through this lens, families are seen as not just a few people spending their lives together; they are an "Ideological State Apparatus" (ISA) in Louis Althusser's (1971) sense of a social institution that reflects and maintains particular power arrangements, and are enmeshed in our cultural, legal, and economic systems and structures. ISAs such as the family are focal points of *discourse* systems in Michel Foucault's sense of the term as interconnected language patterns, institutional features, and social practices that both reflect and reinforce the *status quo* (McHoul and Grace, 1993). While debate continues over what goes on in "the bedrooms of the nation," what is at stake, then, is not simply the social legitimacy of LGBTQ families. That is surely at stake, but so is the social legitimacy of arguably the most powerful discourse system in the history of the world: compulsory heterosexuality, and the rigidly circumscribed gender roles it has maintained (the same people who oppose same-sex marriage also support the innate superiority of traditional gender roles where women raise children and men provide for them).

Above all, then, family is not only a group of caring people living together but also a key institution of society that is the focus of a great deal of formal and informal regulation. To its opponents, it does not matter how loving LGBTQ families might be, or how much evidence social scientists offer that their children are happy and productive; what matters is that LGBTQ families exist in defiance of the argument that society desperately needs to keep heterosexual marriage compulsory. This obviously begs the question, "What are they so afraid of?" The answer of anti-LGBTQ people is usually some version of, "Social chaos—irresponsible fathers—abandoned children." Sociology offers a more complicated answer: "redistribution of power—rupture of discourse systems that structure some straight people's self-concept and social identity—withdrawal of consent to the current arrangement of power."

Further complicating the rosy picture presented by the clear trajectory of the legal timeline from criminalization to equality is the fact that this country has yet to grapple with the legal issues associated with the different-but-related topic of transgender rights: the right to live outside traditional gender conventions of male masculinity and female femininity. While the *Charter of Rights* has been established as protecting **lesbian, gay, and bisexual** people from discrimination on the grounds of sexual identity, Transgender and Transsexual people are not yet protected from discrimination on the grounds of gender identity. *The Globe and Mail* has described transgender rights as "poised to become the fourth great human rights movement, following the fights against racism, sexism, and homophobia" (Armstrong, 2004, p. F6).

Thus it remains necessary, in a country that leads the world in same-sex legal rights, to have a chapter that focuses on the particular issues confronting queer families, and to ask the question, What will it take to uproot the discourses of homophobia and transphobia from their institutional moorings in religion, education, medicine, and media, and rearticulate LGBTQ family rights as not just "human rights" but "family values"?

TERMS USED

As important as it is in all academic work to use the right terms and understand them clearly, it is particularly important in the area of same-sex family studies, for a couple of reasons. First, any terms having to do with "homosexuality" have a history of extremely negative usage that can muddy our conceptions. Second, most people are heterosexual and may be unfamiliar with current language usage on LGBTQ issues. Before going on then, we will clarify some terms—and trouble others (see Box 5.2).

The term "LGBTQ" is used throughout this chapter. Although some people use "gay" as an umbrella term meaning "everyone who identifies as not heterosexual," such usage has been critiqued as "always, already" signifying "gay men." The use of

BOX 5.2   DISCOURSES AT WORK IN THE LIFE OF LGBTQ FAMILIES

Compulsory heterosexuality:	the system of thought that says heterosexual relationships are the only good and natural ones, and that all other kinds of relationships ought to be suppressed for the good of society. Compulsory heterosexuality works in part by prescribing strict gender roles for men and women. All discourses involve value-laden systems of thought, people who believe in those values (or at least say they do), social practices that reflect them, and language practices that repeat them. What makes this discourse especially powerful in our culture is that it has been reinforced by the key institutions of law, medicine, education, religion, and the state. Each of these institutions has been useful to compulsory heterosexuality by extending rewards and punishments, both symbolic and material, for heterosexual compliance and LGBTQ infractions.

(continued)

(continued)

Heteronormativity:	another name for the discourse of compulsory heterosexuality. The term "heteronormativity" draws attention to the "norming" functions of the language conventions, institutional structures, and social practices that assume and enforce (only) heterosexuality as normal.
Homophobia:	a system of thought that supports compulsory heterosexuality by representing same-sex relationships as sinful, unnatural, and generally inferior to straight ones. Homophobia used to be reinforced by all the key institutions of society through measures such as silence about LGBTQ lives in the school system, condemnation in religion, and prohibition in law. It is still very active, though in much reduced form, through the continued efforts of socially conservative faith communities.
Transphobia:	a system of thought that supports the conventional gender roles of compulsory heterosexuality by characterizing any sign of masculinity in biologically female people or femininity in biologically male people as unnatural. Transphobia has been used to maintain heterosexuality in part by persecuting LGBTQ people through such police practices as arresting women found wearing fewer than three "gender-appropriate" articles of clothing and in part through blanket representation of conventional gender roles in popular culture.
Family values:	a system of thought developed by socially conservative faith communities that signifies "family values" as "straight, conventionally gendered married people with children." This discourse has been used in a range of faith communities and media campaigns to oppose progress in LGBTQ family rights.
Human rights:	a system of thought that says all human beings deserve to be treated with equal dignity and accorded equal rights. A key idea of human rights discourse is that marginalized populations need the active protection of the State. Human rights discourse is central to the Canadian *Charter of Rights* and provincial human rights codes, and features prominently in public school education. It is historically rooted in philosophy and law, and has become especially powerful as an official movement in response to the gross abuses of human rights in World Wars I and II.
LGBTQ rights/same-sex rights:	a system of thought that says LGBTQ people are human beings and deserve equal rights. This discourse is in conflict with the discourse of family values, in which LGBTQ rights are depicted as (undeserved) "special rights."

"LGBTQ" reminds us that we are also talking about lesbians, bisexuals, transgender, and queer people. We acknowledge that even "LGBTQ" is problematic in some ways, in that it, too, homogenizes very different social locations, identities, and experiences. Further, the community is ethnically diverse with different systems of gender, sexuality, and family; differing sites of possibility and obstacles; and different terms of self-identification. As social theorist Michel Foucault (1982) pointed out, any attempt at representation or "naming" is dangerous, because every inclusion potentially excludes as well. Some people use an even longer acronym such as LGBTT2IQ2 (to include Transsexual, Two- Spirit, Intersex, and Questioning people). Others add an asterisk like the one used in search terms to remind us to use LGBTQ as an inclusive term, not a closed one: LGBTQ* (see Box 5.3).

We do not use the term "homosexual" or "homosexuality" except in quotation marks because of their historical usage in legal and medical discourse as extremely pejorative terms denoting immorality and mental illness. Most LGBTQ people do not identify with those terms and have deliberately stopped using them (just as, for example, black people generally avoid "Negro").

BOX 5.3   TERMINOLOGY

These definitions are not fixed and are always changing in meaning in society. Readers should be aware that many individuals might have different definitions for their own identities, which are theirs to define.

LGBTQ: an acronym for "lesbian, gay, bisexual, transgender, transsexual, two-spirit, queer and questioning" people.

anti-oppression work: work that is committed to ending oppressive hierarchal social relations and larger systems of oppressions such as racism, sexism, classism, and heterosexism.

bisexual: a person who is physically and emotionally attracted to both genders or who expresses fluidity in his or her attraction to a particular gender.

come out: identify oneself as LGBT or Q. Coming out is a multifaceted process that involves realizing one's own LGBT or Q identity and can include disclosing that identity to family members, friends, teachers, employers, or the media.

gay: a man who is physically and emotionally attracted to other men. It can also be used to describe men and women who have primarily same-sex desires.

gender-variant: those who identify their gender outside the gender binary system of male and female, who may be fluid with gender presentation, or who simply may not conform to conventions of gender identity or gender expression for their birth sex.

(continued)

(continued)

gender-based analysis:	an analysis that focuses on gender relations and how sexism and patriarchy operate. In the field of violence this analysis would examine the strong pattern of male violence against women.
heterosexism:	the assumption that everyone is or should be heterosexual and that only heterosexual relationships are natural, normal, and worthy of support. These assumptions are systemic and institutionalized.
heterosexual:	a person who is physically and emotionally attracted to people of the opposite sex and not to people of the same sex.
homophobia:	the negative attitudes, stereotypes, and prejudices that still exist in society about individuals who are not heterosexual. It is most often directed at LGBTQ people or people perceived as LGBTQ but is also used to harass heterosexual individuals.
intersex:	a general term used to cover many different situations in which a person is born with reproductive or sexual anatomy that does not seem to fit typical definitions of male or female. Often they are subjected to surgical procedures as newborns or in early infancy to remove sexual ambiguity. These procedures can negatively alter and affect their adult lives.
intersectionality:	an analytical framework used to understand the way multiple identities (for example, gender, race, class, sexuality) shape people's experiences of oppression and privilege. The analysis exposes the different types of discrimination and disadvantage that occur as a consequence of multiple identities.
lesbian:	a woman who is physically and emotionally attracted to other women.
queer:	a formerly derogative term that has been reclaimed in a positive way to reflect the diversity and breadth of sexual and gender identities. Sometimes used as an umbrella term to include anyone who is not heterosexual or conventionally gendered, it can also include people who are attracted only to the "opposite" sex but who reject the term "heterosexual" as oppressive and refuse to identify with it.
questioning:	a person who is unsure of his or her sexual orientation or gender identity.
straight:	a person who is sexually and emotionally attracted to someone of the so-called "opposite" birth sex; "heterosexual."
transgender or trans:	a person who feels their gender identity as man or woman does not match their biological sex or who rejects the binary gender system altogether and prefers not to be identified in its terms. Trans is also sometimes used by people who "play" with gender-crossing without feeling any deep inner sense of discomfort with the assumption of male masculinity. "MtF" (male-to-female) and "FtM" (female-to-male) are two of the common ways trans people describe themselves.

(continued)

(continued)

transphobia:	the negative attitudes, stereotypes, and prejudices that exist about individuals whose gender identity or gender expression does not conform with the gender traditionally assigned to their biological sex.
transsexual:	a person who experiences intense personal and emotional discomfort with his or her assigned birth sex. Some transsexuals pursue treatments (i.e., sex reassignment surgery and/or hormone therapy) to physically alter their body to correspond with what they feel their true sex is.
Two Spirit:	some Aboriginal people identify themselves as Two Spirit rather than as lesbian, gay, bisexual, or transgender. Historically, in many Aboriginal cultures two-spirit persons were respected leaders and medicine people. Two-spirit persons were often accorded special status based upon their unique abilities to see the world from both male and female perspectives.

DEFINING LGBTQ FAMILIES

To define LGBTQ families is to try to pin down a diverse group of people who do not fit the conventional and traditional social definition of family as a married man and woman and their children. As the website of "Family Pride Canada" suggests, LGBTQ families are not so easy to define. They may be "nuclear, chosen, blended, extended" and they include

- queer parents—lesbian, gay, bisexual, trans

- prospective queer parents—coming out, just out, long out, far out

- our partners—same-sex, married, common-law, ex-

- our children—adopted, biological, non-biological, fostered, step-, grand-.

Thus, "families" mean different things to different LGBTQ people and may include a range of forms from same-sex couples without children, gay or lesbian single parents with their biological children and a close group of chosen friends, or married same-sex partners with adopted children. The diversity of LGBTQ families reveals "the" family as a social construction that we can create and define in many ways. This is in contrast to the traditional, and no longer accurate, view of the family as that fixed nuclear entity that we either have or do not.

Of course, it is equally fictional to imagine a boundary line with straight families on the one hand and LGBTQ families on the other. The truth is that we live together. There are straight people in families headed by LGBTQ people; LBGTQ children and youth in families with straight parents and siblings; and extended families that include straight and LGBTQ aunts, uncles, and cousins. While "chosen" families of close friends can be liberating and positive spaces, some LGBTQ people still experience hostility, discomfort, and rejection by

members of the families they were born or adopted into, and a great many LGBTQ people never "come out" to their own parents and siblings, who prefer to assimilate them into their family portrait as bachelors and spinsters.

CENSUS CANADA FAMILY PORTRAIT STATISTICS

Census Canada conducts a survey periodically to gather demographic information about the population for budgetary planning and program development purposes. The 2001 survey asked people for the first time to identify whether they were in a same-sex couple. The 2006 Census found that same-sex couples represented only 0.6 percent of all couples in Canada, or 6 out of 1,000, when we know from a wide number of other studies that the proportion of LGBTQ people in the population is roughly 10 percent, or 100 out of 1,000. The 2006 survey also asked people to identify whether they were in a same-sex marriage and enumerated 7,465 married couples; again, this number is far lower than we should expect, given that 12,438 same-sex weddings were officially performed and registered between 2003 and 2006. Although the census results, at least for unmarried couples, are likely drastically affected by LGBTQ people's historically justified reluctance to being officially identified by the state, they nevertheless offer an interesting snapshot:

- The number of people who reported being in a same-sex couple increased dramatically between 2001 and 2006: 32.6 percent, or roughly five times the rate of increase in people identifying as being in a heterosexual couple.

- In total, the census enumerated 45,345 same-sex couples, of whom 7,465, or 16.5 percent, were married couples.

- Slightly more than half the married couples (53.7 percent) were men.

- Just under 1 in 6 female couples (16.3 percent) had children under 25 living in the home, and fewer than 1 in 30 male couples (2.9 percent).

- Same-sex couples were more likely to have children if they were married: 1 in 4 female married couples (24.5 percent versus 14.6 percent) had children, and 1 in 11 male couples (9 percent versus 1.7 percent).

- Half of all same-sex married couples lived in Canada's largest three largest cities, Montreal (18.4 percent), Toronto (21.2 percent), and Vancouver (10.3 percent).

- Same-sex couples tended to be younger than straight couples, with a much smaller proportion of seniors aged 65 or more (3.8 percent same-sex versus 16 percent straight) (Statistics Canada, 2008, 2009).

How are we to understand these numbers? Several observations can be made.

First, the dramatic 32.6 percent increase in same-sex couples is more likely attributable to more people feeling that it was safe to be officially recognized as LGBTQ than to an increase in actual numbers of couples. At the time of the 2001 survey, same-sex marriage was being vigorously denounced by many Canadian politicians and governments. Alberta had just passed Bill 202, which said the province would use the "notwithstanding clause" to opt out of the *Charter of Rights* were Canada to legalize same-sex marriage. The Ontario government declared it would not recognize same-sex marriages. British Columbia and Toronto asked the courts to clarify whether the ban on same-sex marriage contravened the *Charter*. The 2006 survey was done one year after the reassuring legitimization of same-sex couples that occurred when same-sex marriage was legalized in 2005.

In regard to the gender differences reported: The slightly higher numbers of married men than women needs to be understood in the context of the overall population, where some studies suggest that men are significantly more likely than women to be LGBTQ. (The Census has not asked people to identify their sexual identity.) The higher proportion of female than male couples with children may or may not reflect women's greater desire to have children, but also the greater likelihood of mothers than fathers to have custody of children from a previous heterosexual relationship, and of course the gender-specific ability of women to bear a child conceived in a variety of circumstances (sex with a man, artificial insemination, rape). The differential impact of marriage on men's and women's likelihood of having children could be similarly explained.

Are people in same-sex couples actually more likely to be young than people in straight couples? Perhaps; the progress in same-sex rights has certainly made living in a same-sex couple more viable in recent years, but it has also made reporting that one is doing so to the state less scary. It may be true that there are disproportionately few older same-sex couples, but it may also be the case that older people are less likely to trust the state with the knowledge that they are LGBTQ.

What would account for so many married same-sex couples living in Canada's largest metropolitan areas? Historically, LGBTQ people have migrated from rural areas and small towns to big cities to escape discrimination and find communities of other LGBTQ people. While many LGBTQ families live very openly in big cities and encounter little discrimination in their personal and public lives, that is usually not the case for small-town families.

Finally, the small proportion of married to unmarried couples compared to the proportion among straight people might reflect a continuing wariness of being officially recognized as LGBTQ. However, it may also reflect resistance to being assimilated into an institution that had long been a bastion of absolute discrimination against LGBTQ people and still represents an unfairly restrictive definition of what counts as a respectable relationship in this country. And it may reflect a heteronormatively framed census question that did not match the self-concept of same-sex couples: individuals had to register their marriage as "other" and write in a description, or else check off a box indicating that they were the "husband or wife." (Statistics Canada defends the accuracy of its 2006 data collection but is testing the ungendered word "spouse" for the 2011 census) (Statistics Canada, 2008).

REGULATING LGBTQ PEOPLE IN FAMILIES

In his recent book, *Queer Inclusions, Continental Divisions*, David Rayside (2008) explores the politics of sexual diversity in Canada and the United States by analyzing three contentious areas: relationship recognition, parenting, and schooling. His analysis of change over time in the public recognition of sexual minorities shows that Canada has made substantial gains in relationship recognition and parenting while the United States has, surprisingly, made more substantial changes to the schooling system than those instituted by Canada. In this section, we explore areas of family life in Canada that are subject to formal state regulation and have inspired public debate: Should same-sex couples be allowed to keep their children? Should they be allowed to adopt? Aren't their relationships unstable and violent? Don't children need a mother and a father?

Given this context of prolonged debate over whether LGBTQ people get to marry and have children, most social science research on LGBTQ families has supported an assimilationist position that there is no significant difference between LGBTQ and straight families, and therefore no justification for differential treatment in law: if we are all the same, all just people, we all deserve a place at the table of family life; but the table itself—the laws, institutional practices, and social conventions related to family life—is just fine as it is.

However, research is increasingly paying attention to the specificity and diversity of LGBTQ families that challenges the notion that LGBTQ and straight people are the same, and argues that "normalizing" LGBTQ people has oppressive effects. The argument is that only the LGBTQ people who most closely match dominant cultural standards get to be seen as normal, which leaves many other LGBTQ people even more marginalized than before. "Normal" gets reinscribed as those LGBTQ people who are white, middle-class, able-bodied, in a long-term monogamous relationship, and conventional in gender expression. As Doreen Fumia (2007) states, "social practices that aim to separate the normal from those viewed in society as not normal ensure that some people belong and others do not" (p. 180). Research working against a normalizing impulse considers issues such as butch lesbians raising sons, queer youth as parents, and trans persons' experiences in fertility clinics (Epstein, 2009.) To integrate the real range of people signified by LGBTQ into legal, respected, Canadian society, the family table needs some modifications.

There is thus a tension between an assimilationist effort on the one hand, and on the other an effort to integrate into mainstream society by opening up spaces where people can live without suppressing our differences. This tension has also been characterized as inclusionist versus transgressive elements (Weeks, Heaphy, and Donovan, 2001). Sometimes the tension gets polarized around charges of craving normalcy on the one hand and working to undermine it on the other. But most LGBTQ families' relationships to normalcy are more nuanced than that. Hicks (2005) argues that "claims to be a 'real family' by lesbians and gay men are about legitimacy, about challenging legal and social forms of discrimination, and about asserting different ways of living intimate lives, rather than being about the desire to be 'normal'" (p. 303).

MARRIAGE

The forms of state oppression of socially marginalized people have varied historically. People marginalized by racist, sexist, and classist discourses have been denied education and employment, for example. The regulation of intimate relationships can also be oppressive. Examples include "anti-miscegenation" laws in Nazi Germany, Apartheid South Africa, and the United States, where some states prohibited marriage between people of different "races" until 1967 (Sollors, 2000); and prohibitions against marriage between impoverished people in England in the 17th century (Ingram, 1987) and between African Americans in the United States before the Civil War (Coontz, 2000). In the case of LGBTQ people, there has been an absolute prohibition on intimate relationships; hence Oscar Wilde's famous phrase, "the love that dare not speak its name." The question of relationships and how they are treated in dominant culture has therefore been of central importance to the LGBTQ rights movement. Many LGBTQ people are critical of marriage as an irredeemably racist, sexist, classist institution that has traditionally served the interests of powerful men and discriminated against others (see Box 5.4). Nevertheless, the larger struggle for formal state recognition of LGBTQ relationships has been crucial in many ways to the attainment of dignity in everyday life.

To understand the importance of this struggle, consider the history of oppression associated with LGBTQ relationships in our timeline. Before decriminalization in 1969, all same-sex relationships, whether committed long-term relationships, or casual sexual contact, were illegal. State law enforcement agencies such as the RCMP actively investigated allegations of homosexuality and raided gay bars (Kinsman, 1996). Penalties include imprisonment, loss of employment, and social ostracism. After decriminalization, people 21 years or older could have relationships, but their relationships had no legal status. This meant, for example, no parenting rights for a partner's biological children, no custody rights in the event of a breakup, no rights to visit a hospitalized partner, no pension or inheritance rights in the event of the partner's death. Their relationships had no social status either. People remained closeted in workplaces, places of worship, and health care interactions, and could face humiliating social discrimination if they came out. With the equality rights movement that fought to bring Canadian law into conformity with the Charter of Rights, mainstream homophobic discourse slowly shifted away from active persecution of LGBTQ people but still remained oppressive. It was often said of LGBTQ people that if only they

BOX 5.4   THE ANTI-MARRIAGE MOVEMENT IN THE LGBTQ COMMUNITY

Further complicating the discursive terrain of homophobia versus LGBTQ rights is that some LGBTQ are opposed to marriage on ethical grounds and want no part of it. Here is a sample of LGBTQ anti-assimilation discourse:

QUEERS AGAINST MARRIAGE

Let's remember the politics of marriage itself. The simplistic formula that claims "you're either pro-marriage or against equality" makes us forget that all forms of marriage perpetuate gender, racial and economic inequality. It mistakenly assumes that support for marriage is the only good measure of support for LGBT communities. This political moment calls for anti-homophobic politics that centralize anti-racism and anti-poverty. Marriage is a coercive state structure that perpetuates racism and sexism through forced gender and family norms. Right wing pro-marriage rhetoric has targeted families of color and poor families, supported a violent welfare and child protection system, vilified single parents and women, and marginalized queer families of all kinds. Expanding marriage to include a narrow band of same-sex couples only strengthens that system of marginalization and supports the idea that the state should pick which types of families to reward and recognize and which to punish and endanger.

We still demand a queer political agenda that centralizes the experiences of prisoners, poor people, immigrants, trans people, and people with disabilities. We reject a gay agenda that pours millions of dollars into campaigns for access to oppressive institutions for a few that stand to benefit.

We are being told marriage is the way to solve gay people's problems with health care access, immigration, child custody, and symbolic equality. It does not solve these problems, and there are real campaigns and struggles that would and could approach these problems for everyone, not just for a privileged few. Let's take the energy and money being put into gay marriage and put it toward real change: opposing the War on Terror and all forms of endless war; supporting queer prisoners and building a movement to end imprisonment; organizing against police profiling and brutality in our communities; fighting attacks on welfare, public housing and Medicaid; fighting for universal health care that is trans and reproductive healthcare inclusive; fighting to tax wealth not workers; fighting for a world in which no one is illegal.

Source: By Dean Spade and Crag Willse, *Makezine*. Retrieved 26 June 2009 from http://makezine.enoughenough.org/prop8.html.

would keep their private lives private, no one would bother them. This, of course, was a stance that ignored the many ways in which private relationships become public in their everyday intersections with institutions such as hospitals and schools. (If you have had trouble recognizing the oppressiveness of the history sketched in this paragraph, try rereading it with "straight" substituted for LGBTQ.)

It was precisely because their private lives were targets of oppression that LGBTQ people have had to wage a very public fight for state recognition of their relationships—and have to continue to fight for social recognition. The movement has encountered heated opposition from socially conservative religious and political movements at every step of the way. Although much of the opposition has finally acceded to same-sex "domestic partnerships" with full legal equality to marriage, they remain opposed to same-sex marriage itself on the grounds that ultimately marriage is for only male-female couples, leaving LGBTQ couples with equal rights (except the right to marry), but symbolically inferior. In the end, the courts and government rejected the "separate but equal" argument as specious and agreed that a country committed to human rights must support equal rights to marry.

However, religious officials have *Charter* protection to refuse to perform same-sex marriages (as they also have the right to refuse to allow women to become religious officials), a contradiction embedded in human rights discourse in Canada. The unfortunate result is that same-sex rights can be represented as opposed to freedom of religion, and religious rights can be represented as by definition opposed to LGBTQ equality, when in fact many religious people fully support LGBTQ equality. Social science research has found that socially conservative Christians and people who score higher on religiosity scales are more negative toward LGBTQ people (Holley et al., 2008), but some congregations (in Reform Judaism, the United Church, Metropolitan Community Church, Unitarian Church) perform same-sex weddings, and others bless same-sex "unions."

Divorce

Some LGBTQ marriages, like a great many straight marriages, end in divorce. Media response to this unremarkable observation highlights the ongoing context of homophobic discourse against which LGBTQ "private" lives are perceived. On September 14, 2004, the CBC News Online reported the first case of same-sex divorce: "A Toronto lesbian couple has been granted Canada's, and possibly the world's, first gay divorce." This case made headlines around the globe and once again brought to the forefront tensions between normalizing LGBTQ relationships and challenging heterosexist norms. Mainstream media accounts of this divorce were often sensationalized, indicating that the couple separated only five days after being married. (The couple had in fact been together for 10 years before marrying.) There is a tendency for the discourse of mainstream media to perpetuate pathologizing discourses surrounding LGBTQ peoples while simultaneously claiming to support equality and visibility (see Box 5.5). In this case the divorce headlines confirmed that LGBTQ marriages, like straight marriages, often end in divorce but with the added tone of moral superiority in the report that this marriage lasted only five days, thereby conjuring up the stereotype that LGBTQ people are promiscuous and their relationships unstable.

BOX 5.5   SHOCK AND CONFUSION—WITH LOVE

MADELINE RIVERS

For a very private person, this is difficult for me to share. But the lack of stories and information about transgendered partners pushes me to share my own thoughts so that others might learn.

My spouse of 12 years informed me a few months ago of his transgenderedness. I became scared and confused. Yet, celebrating his future goal of happiness, i.e., becoming his true self, eventually became easy for me to accept. It just seemed natural. Many strange things that I look back upon, I can now understand. I just thought that he was gay. Well, my own woman's intuition needs a 30-year check up because I was only half right. I see that most of our lives together has enabled us to get him/her to this point. Brent/Betty is in the safest city, at a job with the most accommodating company policies, and available support groups. Thank goodness for his high intellect that lets him think things through. If I had been approached at the beginning of our relationship, I doubt I'd have written this article.

Information, information, information. I need pamphlets, anything to see what others have felt and done. What happens to the spouse of a M2F?

I've been shoved into the rarest of rare categories. Why? Because most partners leave before the shock wears off. Did I think about it? Of course I did, I'm human; but I'm also in love with a rare and wonderful person. Brent/Betty is still the same person I've loved all these years; he/she just wants to do it in heels!

What a mind-bender! He says he loves me and his attraction is the same. So, boy/girl loves and is attracted to girl. Girl still loves boy/girl but the attraction is not natural to me. Our love for each other is the same. While he/she is dealing with gender issues, it forces me to deal with my sexuality issues. I feel like I'm in a dramatic soap opera. Living like this certainly isn't boring.

Source: Rivers, Madeline. "Shock and confusion with love," *Transforming Families: Real Stories about Transgendered Loved Ones*. Ed. Mary Boenke. 2nd ed. Oak Knoll Press, 2003. 59-60. Reproduced by permission.

Divorce is a new reality for LGBTQ couples. In most of the world and for most of Canadian history, divorce law has not applied to LGBTQ people because they could not marry. Getting a divorce brings with it all the legal and economic ramifications of dividing property and resources, which is in contrast to the different culture of many gay and lesbian relationships and social networks, where people often retained a sense of individual property ownership. The impact of the assimilative tendencies of law was felt by some Manitobans in 2004, when legislation codified the middle ground between dating and married, giving individuals who had lived as a couple for three years full common-law rights and obligations, including sharing property and pensions on dissolution of the relationship. Many long-term couples, straight and LGBTQ, who had no desire to be considered married found themselves having to have legal contracts drawn up to opt out of the provisions: the space in which people can live without state interference in their personal lives had shrunk.

PARENTING

Central to the struggle for state recognition and equal rights has been the debate over whether it harms children to be raised by LGBTQ parents. A great deal of homophobic discourse has been organized around LGBTQ adults' influence on children. Historically (and in some pockets of society, even today) people have been accused of "recruiting" children into the "lifestyle" and sexually exploiting them, and being LGBTQ was in itself sufficient cause to lose custody of one's children. With progress in the same-sex rights movements, the tack has shifted from the more outrageous accusations to a concern that having LGBTQ parents will make children LGBTQ (as though that is automatically an undesirable outcome), or that they will be somehow less well adjusted than children of straight parents.

The literature shows that neither is the case. Research on the whole is consistent in demonstrating few differences in emotional, social, and developmental outcomes between children raised by LGBTQ and by straight parents (Goldberg, 2007). Children of LGBTQ parents are neither more nor less likely to be LGBTQ themselves than children of straight parents, although they may have less anxiety about being LGBTQ if they are (Kuvulanka and Goldberg, 2009; Rose, 2003). As has often been pointed out, if parents' sexual identity were a predictor of their children's, there would be very few LGBTQ people, since the vast majority were raised by straight parents.

However, there are two issues specific to LGBTQ parents and their children. The first is of external origin: homophobic and transphobic discrimination. Such discrimination in the parents' lives can put stress on the family, just as racism or poverty in parents' lives can. Similarly, the children of LGBTQ parents can experience discrimination themselves, typically once they reach school age and are made to feel abnormal for not having straight parents. The second issue is parents disclosing their LGBTQ identity to their children, which can produce a stress from children having absorbed homophobic or transphobic attitudes from mainstream discourses. Sometimes the disclosure happens in the context of ending a relationship with the children's other parent, which presents the added stress of divorce or separation. Disclosure can also cause stress from disruption of children's bond with their parents. In particular, the disclosure that a parent is transgender and intends to transition from male to female or vice versa can result in feelings of loss or betrayal in children (White and Ettner, 2004). The daughter of a transgender parent offers this explanation:

> Your reaction depends on how you found out and also when you found out. Young children tend to adjust to change easier and might understand a parent's transition in simpler terms than older children. My four-year old sister, for example, explained that "some people are girls on the inside and girls on the outside, like you and me. Some people are girls on the inside and boys on the outside, like Dad." My reaction at 17 years old was less straight-forward as I struggled to understand what it meant for my father to become a

woman. Older youth have learned more about gender roles and what is "normal," so it can be a lot harder to handle the news. They are also navigating their own social worlds, in which having a "different" family can be a real challenge. Even KOTs [Kids of Transgender parents] whose parents transitioned when they were younger often feel pressure to be "normal" during adolescence and may struggle with their parent's identity. (Canfield-Lenfest, 2008, p. 11)

Support groups for children and youth dealing with such issues are affiliated with LGBTQ community centres in major cities in Canada.

Adoption

Like straight couples, LGBTQ couples either bring children into the family from a previous relationship, or they are already a couple when they bring children into the family. Like many single straight women and infertile straight couples, many LGBTQ people become parents through adoption. This is especially the case for male same-sex couples, who are less likely than lesbian couples to have custody of children from a previous straight relationship. In any case, if the children are not biologically theirs, they must be legally adopted or parents must gain guardian status in order for both partners to have full parental rights such as signing forms for school field trips and providing consent for medical treatments.

Canadian law no longer discriminates against same-sex couple adoption, but couples can still encounter homophobic and transphobic attitudes in the adoption process, where homophobic attitudes that LGBTQ people have an unhealthy interest in children and negative attitudes to the "opposite" sex can come into play. Hicks (2005) discusses an example of a lesbian couple wishing to adopt a girl and stating that preference; it is so common for parents to have a gender preference that there was a standard check box on the form to indicate it. Yet social workers counselled the couple to try to show that they were interested in both boys and girls to prevent the system from seeing them as too one-sided in terms of sexuality.

Apart from the challenges of helping their children to deal with homophobia and heterosexism that any LGBTQ parent might encounter, LGBTQ adoptive and step-parents may have challenges similar to those of their straight counterparts. Both straight and LGBTQ adoptive and step-parents may underestimate the amount of work involved in raising children, and be unduly optimistic about the ease of blending families. The children of both straight and LGBTQ adoptive or step-parents can feel that their families are not seen as real families by other children (although the incidence and intensity of social rejection would be worse for children with LGBTQ parents). Biological parents can feel positioned between their partner and their child, and children can feel displaced or threatened by their parents' partner. (Lynch, 2000). The situation can be complicated for LGBTQ parents though, if the parent has come out in the context of that new relationship and especially if the coming-out context involves having left the child's other (straight) parent. Since many LGBTQ people do not come to terms with their sexual identity until after they have children in a straight relationship, they may be dealing with their own discomfort about being LGBTQ and at the same time striving to come out sensitively to their children. As one parent said, "We've got all the stepfamily issues overlaid with all the coming out issues, overlaid with all the parent and child gay and lesbian issues, overlaid with all the divorce issues" (Lynch, 2000, p. 91).

Overall, then, the literature is full of evidence of the challenges faced by straight and LGBTQ parents who adopt as a couple or become step-parents to their partners' children. The context of homophobia obviously creates additional pressures, though the amount of discrimination experienced varies, with some children in socially progressive places integrating much more easily into the school culture than some children in socially conservative ones. (Lynch, 2000). It is a testament to the hard work of LGBTQ parents that the research shows their children are as happy, healthy, well-adjusted, and successful at school as the children of straight parents. As society becomes more respectful of LGBTQ families, their jobs will be easier.

Pregnancy

Single straight women and straight couples have used sperm donation to become pregnant for a variety of reasons including the lack of a male partner and a male partner's infertility. In sperm donation, donor sperm is acquired either though the parents' friendship network or through a sperm bank and transferred to the mother's cervix or uterus by artificial insemination. In vitro fertilization (IVF), where the egg and sperm are united in a test tube and then transferred to the mother's uterus, is also used, usually in cases where a medical reason precludes the mother conceiving in utero. Single lesbians and lesbian couples also use both methods. Some couples use IVF so that one mother's eggs can be fertilized with donor sperm and carried in the other mother's womb, enabling both parents to feel biologically tied to the child.

It is often assumed that lesbian relationships are completely egalitarian because they are not burdened with the male-female gender system of the larger society. Research does suggest that most lesbian couples do attempt to have an equal division of labour and to value each other's contribution equally, even in couples that self-identify in gendered ways related to masculinity and femininity, such as butch and femme (Peplau and Spalding, 2003). Many couples make a significant effort to share parenting responsibilities and create equal mother-child bonds. However, Pelka (2009) reports that the symmetry of the relationship can be challenged by pregnancy and later by the baby's greater attachment to the birth mother. Fathers in straight relationships can experience similar feelings of jealousy and unimportance in response to what developmental psychologists have identified as children's preference for their "principal attachment figure" when they are distressed. However, straight men in a heteronormative society have been socialized to expect and accept this situation, whereas lesbians may be expecting their equitable approach to their own relationship to carry over into their child's relationship to them. Further, there is no biological expectation that men will bear or nurse a child, whereas it can undermine the self-concept of a woman to watch her partner do so; the subjectivity of lesbians, too, is influenced by mainstream discourses of what it means to be a "real" woman.

School Issues

While the literature shows little difference in outcome between children raised by straight and LGBTQ parents, the children of LGBTQ parents are at risk of experiencing homophobia and transphobia once they enter into the school system, where they are unlikely to see their family structures acknowledged and where they may encounter active disrespect. "Coming out" is an issue not only for LGBTQ people, but also for their children (and their relatives and friends) who have to deal with a dominant culture that expects parents to be straight. Children can find it difficult to explain to their friends that they have two moms or dads, and as soon as they start interacting with other children at preschool or kindergarten, they have to think about how and to whom they talk about their parents. The situation can not only put stress on the child, but also potentially lead to the child's having conflicted feelings about the parents whose problematic difference from the norm has resulted in their being treated as abnormal themselves (James, 2002). Sometimes LGBTQ parents who are out in their own adult lives are more open with their children's teachers and fellow parents than their children are comfortable with. Children who feel they need to be secretive about their families may ask that only one parent take them to school or interact with teachers, and that he or she should pretend to be a single parent.

Research suggests that the pressure of homophobia on children of LGBTQ parents is compounded for adopted children, who may feel set apart from their peers on both counts. If the children or their parents in addition are in an ethnic minority at school, or there are disability issues, the alienation becomes further problematic. The support strategy of seeking out similar families with whom to share social time is more difficult to follow for families that are marginalized on multiple axes of oppression. The disabled child of colour adopted by two dads, for example, may well be the only one in the school.

LGBTQ parents may employ two main strategies to cope with homophobia (Lindsay et al, 2006): they select schools with a reputation for respecting diversity, or they remain closeted in school interactions, for example, by having only the biological parent make all contacts. Parents routinely encounter many different people in the school context who in turn have routine interactions with each other: bus drivers, traffic patrols, hall monitors, teachers, counsellors, nurses, administrators, police officers, plus other children and those children's parents and guardians. Mindful that they have no control over "schoolyard politics," parents may judge it unsafe to be open with any of these people for fear of their relationship becoming known to a homophobic or transphobic person who would ultimately cause distress to their child in some way. They may even be less open with their children when they are very young to protect them from innocently sharing stories about their home life that could trigger hostility in homophobic members of the school community. They are trying to protect their children from the heartbreaking and confusing experiences some children of LGBTQ parents have had. However, when young children are questioned relentlessly by their curious classmates about their families (as some children of LGBTQ parents have been), it is inevitable that word will get out and the results can be painful. Teachers have admonished children in front of the whole class that we do not discuss "such things" as LGBTQ Pride Marches at school, which tells the children that their families, unlike everyone else's, are not fit for polite conversation.

Whether teachers are silencing children to protect them from homophobes, or to protect themselves from backlash from homophobic parents and administrators, or because they are homophobic themselves, the result is the public shaming of the children. The children do not see their families represented in elementary school where there are a great many discussions and activities about family life. In contrast, when teachers make a point of including "two mums" or "two dads" in their references to parents, and encourage children of LGBTQ parents to share their home life just as the other children do, children feel a part of the school community.

A sign of continued conflict, and conflictedness, in Canadian public discourse occurred in 2009 in Alberta, where the Conservative government finally brought the Human Rights Act of the province into conformity with the Charter by adding sexual orientation, but at the same time proposed Bill 44 to provide parental rights to remove their children from classrooms in which sexual orientation is discussed (along with sexuality or religion) (Alberta, 2009). However, the picture is not totally bleak. As Canadian society becomes more progressive, more LGBTQ parents are able to find open, respectful school communities where they and their children can be open and feel accepted. This is more true in major urban centres than in smaller ones, and in inner-city cosmopolitan neighbourhoods than in suburbs. One study found that acceptance was higher in inner-city White Anglo middle-class educated communities than in suburban White Anglo working-class and upper-class communities and in ethnically and socioeconomically diverse communities where LGBTQ families are part of the mix rather than structurally marked as the different ones (Lindsay et al., 2006).

LGBTQ CHILDREN AND YOUTH

The majority of LGBTQ children have straight parents and can be faced with very difficult family issues. Where school-based homophobia and transphobia can be hard for the children of LGBTQ parents and can strain their family life, those children generally can go home to understanding parents who can empathize with them, advocate for them, and ensure that they do not feel completely isolated. In contrast, consider the situation of LGBTQ children who are exposed to homophobia and transphobia at school: Most of them have straight parents who have not experienced homophobia or transphobia firsthand, but more than that, most LGBTQ children and youth have not told their parents or guardians about their sexual or gender identity. These children and youth therefore cannot turn to their parents for support when they are excluded or bullied, as can children who are targets of racist or ethnic bullying.

Growing up can be a challenging and often anxiety-ridden process even when youth can turn to various people in their lives for support, guidance, and understanding, and even when their core sense of self is not the subject of widespread social prejudice. If they are experiencing harassment at school based on their ethnic or religious minority status, they can normally turn to their parents for support; if they are distressed about homophobia, they generally cannot.

LGBTQ Children and Youth at Home

Some LGBTQ children and youth are out to their parents and family members. Approximately one in five LGBTQ students who participated in the "First National Climate Survey on Homophobia in Canadian Schools" did feel very comfortable talking to at least one parent about LGBTQ issues. Another sign of solid family support is that PFLAG Canada has grown to over 70 chapters across the country. The organization is described on its website as

> born of a need by parents to help themselves and family members deal with, understand, and accept their non-heterosexual children and the new world they are thrust into when their children "come-out." Today, PFLAG Canada is the only national grassroots organization that deals with sexual orientation and gender identity issues from a family perspective, providing support, education and resources. (PFLAG, 2009)

PFLAG originally was used as an acronym for "Parents, Families and Friends of Lesbians and Gays," but the organization has dropped the name as excluding too many nonheterosexual people (for example, bisexual, transgender, Two Spirit) and now uses the acronym as a name in itself.

Despite this hopeful emergence, however, a summary of the literature on parental reactions to discovering that their child is LGBTQ confirms that children and youth are, unfortunately, probably right not to turn to their families for support (Taylor, 2008). Many youth do not disclose their LGBTQ identity because they fear destroying their relationship with their parents (Morrow, 2004). Youth are unlikely to disclose to a parent if they predict a negative response, so most studies of parental reactions are based on youth who were optimistic about coming out to them. Nevertheless, studies found that three out of four fathers and one-half of mothers react in forms ranging from disapproval, which is distressing in itself when the subject goes to one's core sense of identity, to maltreatment and disownment (Morrow, 2004). Although LGBTQ disclosures are lumped together in these studies, it can reasonably be conjectured that parental reactions to disclosures of transgender identity would be among the most hostile given the lack of public knowledge about transgender issues compared to issues of sexual orientation. A recent study of parental reactions to transgender children found negative reactions from 63 percent of fathers and 54 percent of mothers (Grossman, D'Augelli, Howell, and Hubbard, 2005).

As might be expected, socially conservative families are likely to react with hostility to disclosure (Rosario, Rotheram-Borus, and Reid, 1996; Teague, 1992), as are traditionalist religious families, who often see LGBTQ identity as an aberration of secular Western society (Newman and Muzzonigro, 1993), even when, as is the case with some First Nations in pre-contact times, the cultural group has a history of accepting non-gender-conforming people (Jacobs, Wesley, and Lang, 1997; Wilson, 1996).

Recent research on attitudes to homosexuality among religious, socially conservative, and rural populations suggests that parents from such groups would not have more positive responses to disclosure than reported in earlier studies (Eldridge, Mack, and Swank, 2006; Herek and Gonzalez-Rivera, 2006; Lewis, 2003; Olson, Cadge, and Harrison, 2006; Schulte and Battle, 2004; Stoughtenborough, Haider-Markel, and Allen, 2006). Although hostility to LGBTQ young people is common enough in dominant-culture families, families belonging to a cultural group that has been targeted by both racism and sexism can have additional sources of hostility to LGBTQ children, as reported for example by Wilson and Miller (2002) and Miller, Forte, Wilson, and Greene (2006) in their studies involving Black men who have sex with men.

Whatever hope or need brings youth to come out to their parents, feelings of loss, shame, and guilt are common after doing so (Saltzburg, 2004). Suicidal tendency among disclosers in D'Augelli, Hershberger, and Pilkington's (1998) study of more than 100 LGBTTIQ youth who had confided in their parents was more than half compared to 12 percent among the nondisclosers. Other studies report similarly elevated risks of depression and suicidality following disclosure (Hershberger and D'Augelli, 1995; Morrison and L'Heareux, 2001). The risks are compounded for youth dealing with multiple oppressions:

> Young two-spirits often leave their home communities because their sexuality is not accepted by their traditional families, only to end up in urban centres where they are discriminated against not only for their sexual preferences, but also for their race. Some experts believe that these young, two-spirit individuals are more susceptible to substance abuse problems and suicide attempts, so having access to a supportive group of likeminded people becomes very important.[3]

LGBTQ Children and Youth at School

Since the time of the minority-rights movements of the 1960s, school systems in Canada have generally embraced an "inclusive schools" philosophy that is premised on the evidence that children are happier and perform better when they feel that they belong to the school community. Efforts have been made to diversify what was once, notoriously now, a very dominant-culture or "winners take all" curriculum in which members of ethnic minorities, women, and Aboriginal people were not represented with dignity and respect. Given the very low likelihood of feeling that they are known and respected at home for who they are, it is all the more important that LGBTQ children and youth be actively supported in school.

However, this is not the case. The Climate Survey on Homophobia in Canadian Schools found that there was negligible mention of any LGBTQ topic in most schools. The survey asked 54 questions, including a set of questions gauging school attachment. Participants were asked to indicate how much they agreed or disagreed with a list of statements, some of them positive, such as "I feel like a real part of my school," and some of them negative, such as "It is hard for me to feel accepted at my school." LGBTQ students were far more likely than non-LGBTQ to agree with the negative statements. For instance, half of LGBTQ participants (50.6 percent) agreed that "It is hard for me to feel accepted at my school," compared to one in five non-LGBTQ students (19.3 percent). Similar significant differences were found with the positive statements. For example, almost half of LGBTQ participants (48.7 percent), compared to only one in five of non-LGBTQ (21.9 percent), strongly disagreed that "I can be myself at school." Transgender students were also more likely to disagree with positive comments assessing school attachment. For example, over two-thirds (69.2 percent) of transgender participants disagreed with the statement, "I feel like a real part of my school," compared to fewer than half (44.6 percent) of LGBTQ and only one-quarter (24.6 percent) of non-LGBTQ (Taylor et al., 2009).

Most schools have generic safe-schools policies that are supposed to protect all students and ensure that they feel safe at school, but the results of the Climate Survey show that this is not the case for LGBTQ students (Taylor and Peter, 2010). The following is only a sampling of the findings:

- Two-thirds of LGBTQ students feel unsafe in at least one place at their school, such as change rooms, washrooms, and hallways.

- Transgender students are especially likely to see at least one of these places as unsafe, but almost half of straight students agree that at least one part of their school is unsafe for LGBTQ students or students with LGBTQ parents.

- Over two-thirds of all participating students reported hearing expressions such as "that's so gay" every day in school. Almost half heard remarks like "faggot," "queer," "lezbo," and "dyke" daily.

- One-half of LGBTQ students reported being verbally harassed about their sexual orientation.

- Three-quarters of transgender students, more than half of LGB students, and one-quarter of straight students were verbally harassed because of their expression of gender.

- Two-thirds of LGB students and more than three-quarters of transgender students felt unsafe at school, compared to one-sixth of straight students.[4]

Among the conclusions of the report were that the situation of most LGBTQ students in Canadian high schools is difficult, and that it is particularly dire for transgender students, who are likely to be the most visibly different members of the LBGTQ community. Studies have reported that Transgender students have been asked to limit the expression of their gender variance at school, and their parents looking for support for their bullied Transgender children have been advised to ensure that their children come to school wearing gender-conventional clothes. As one mother put it, "If I said he was being teased and bullied because of the color of his skin, would you ask me to paint him?" (qtd. in Brill and Pepper, 2008, p. 161).

School system personnel will likely need cultural competence training in order to improve official responses to Transgender students and become more sensitive to the impact of everyday school practices of gender segregation such as separate lineups for boys and girls and separate gym classes. The Climate Survey found robust correlations between indicators of school attachment and inclusive safe-schools policies that explicitly deal with homophobia, and strongly recommended that all schools and school divisions develop and implement LGBTQ-inclusive safe-schools policies and programs and make them known to everyone in the school community (Taylor and Peter, 2010).

LGBTQ youth have demonstrated remarkable resilience in extremely difficult circumstances. In the absence of social acceptance and systemic integration into the life of their schools, many LGBTQ youth have developed their own support groups and lobbied their teachers and principals for official status as Gay Straight Alliances (GSAs). Other LGBTQ students, though, live very isolated lives in schools across the country. In some school divisions, teachers are prohibited by board policy from discussing LGBTQ topics. In any case, creating GSAs where LGBTQ students can go to escape homophobia and transphobia is not enough. LGBTQ students, like other students who are members of other socially marginalized and minority groups, have the right to be integrated into the life of their schools. Too many of them are not accepted for who they are by their own parents. Neither are they being served well by schools, which are failing to develop inclusive curriculum, or by governments, which could order them to do it. The Climate Survey researchers also found that a full 58 percent of straight students reported that they, too, found it upsetting to some degree to hear homophobic comments (Taylor and Peter, 2010), which suggests that there may be a great deal of passive solidarity among straight students that could be activated by supportive actions on the part of school staff.

However, fear of backlash from socially conservative parents has made school officials and ministries of education extremely reluctant to act on homophobia even though most educators acknowledge that it is a problem in their schools. These key social institutions are prepared to act "in loco parentis" on many issues, but seldom on this one, where they are acutely aware of the heated discursive context characterizing any attempts to act on what Foucault called "the last socially acceptable prejudice" (Fone, 2000). Very few school boards have developed curriculum materials and mandated their use. There have been some recent moves at the ministry level in Ontario and Newfoundland and at the school board level in a handful of divisions across the country to develop the curriculum needed to achieve LGBTQ-inclusive schools.

However, it is far more common for school officials to adopt a generic approach to inclusion by assimilation, where school policies announce respect and safety for all, and never refer to homophobia, or transphobia, or acknowledge the existence of LGBTQ students in their midst. Teachers in such schools are much more likely to intervene when they hear racist or sexist language than when they hear homophobic language, and much more likely to integrate ethnically and otherwise diverse content into the curriculum than to include LGBTQ content. The result is experiences like the following that give LGBTQ students the message that "respect for all" means "respect for all but them":

> i gave my girlfriend a simple peck on the cheek before class and was called up to the office because my principal said i was performing for boys, now i dont see how that works considering im a lesbian .... and on top of that straight couples practically have sex in the hall ways and i have never seen any actions taken i also think it is unfair that race and violence and relationships are all addressed in assemblies but there is NEVER a sexuality assembly.[5]

The situation is most extreme in religious schools, which use the special status accorded to religious freedom in the *Charter of Rights* to avoid integrating LGBTQ content. Students experience the impact of such actions this way:

> I have some friends who are devout Christians and therefore are 1000000000% against the queer community. They persistently speak against it when the issue is brought up, in the classroom, on the bus, anywhere. This is not to say that only Christians stand against the queer community, and not to say that all Christians stand against queer folk. It's just that any experiences I have had with homophobia in the school setting have involved Christians. This lends to the fact that much homophobia is due to religious beliefs and ideals.[6]

With the steady progress seen in LGBTQ rights in adult settings in the last 40 years, it is now possible for many LGBTQ adults (at least the more gender-conforming of us) to live fairly open lives with relative freedom. Adults might be tempted to think that children and youth are also benefitting from this progress. However, the school system in which children and youth spend so much of their young lives often feels mired in a more oppressive era:

In my school there is a lot of pressure for conformity and I think anyone straying outside of the norm feels very uncomfortable. Schools are not doing enough in my personal experience to conform themselves to the reality of Canadian society, meaning schools avoid dealing with issues they think may or may not exist among students. There is a lot of peer pressure and not enough is done by staff to address this. Older Canadians realize the changes in society and the acceptance of other lifestyles but this opportunity is not available to younger Canadians.[7]

LGBTQ DATING AND RELATIONSHIPS

Dating and relationships are territory that is strongly regulated in Canadian society by cultural conventions. Some LGBTQ people have their first same-sex relationships in high school. For many, though, same-sex dating begins only after they have left high school and found a social circle of LGBTQ people, often by leaving home to go to university or by moving to a larger urban centre that has a "gaybourhood" such as Denman Street in Vancouver, Wolseley in Winnipeg, Church and Wellesley in Toronto, and Rue Sainte-Catherine in Montreal.

In response to the homophobic and transphobic climate of many high schools that sends the powerful message that LGBTQ life is lived in the "uninhabitable zone" of our society, some LGBTQ youth try very hard to be straight, or at least to assimilate into straight society, by getting involved in heterosexual dating and relationships. Surveys of 30,000 youth in British Columbia conducted between 2001 and 2006 found that, compared to heterosexual peers their same age, gay and bisexual males were more than three times more likely to have been involved in a pregnancy, while lesbian and bisexual females were two to three times as likely to have been pregnant than heterosexual females (Saewyc et al., 2007). These high rates of pregnancy may reflect a lack of attention to contraception among questioning youth who are anxious to establish heterosexual credentials in their own minds or in their peer group. LGBTQ youth are sometimes unaware of the existence of other LGBTQ youth in their schools and social circles, which makes LGBTQ life seem nonviable and may lead youth to get involved in heterosexual relationships. Other research has suggested that youth follow cultural scripts as they become sexually or romantically interested in someone; for example, lesbian youth may begin a first lesbian relationship as friends because they have no cultural exposure to scripts that let them imagine a socially viable same-sex attraction (Roze and Zand, 2002, p. 90). Despite the greater visibility of LGBTQ people in the media, heterosexual relationships are dominant to the virtual exclusion of all others.

Internet Dating

Although social networking sites such as Facebook and dating sites are sometimes dismissed as a frivolous distraction from real life, the opportunities they provide for networking with other LGBTQ people represent a dramatic change in the lives of many otherwise isolated youth and adults: "in the face of practices of exclusion in their immediate physical worlds, the internet may provide the possibility of new and potentially liberating alternatives for the building of new forms of culture and community among young people" (Hillier and Harrison, 2007, p. 83). These innovations include new possibilities for finding information about LGBTQ life ranging from coming out to parents and friends to sex and intimate relationships (topics about which straight youth learn from teachers, parents, friends, and media culture). For youth coming out, Internet chat rooms provide a "dress rehearsal" space in which they can figure out how they will live their lives as LGBTQ people. The initial anonymity of Internet contact also offers a safe space in which to meet others and test out attractions. Studies show that LGBTQ men in particular make use of the Internet to meet and in some cases arrange to meet face to face (ibid., p. 85).

Relationship Violence

Dating and relationships are for the most part free of official state involvement (unless the individuals live together long enough to have common-law status). An exception is relationships in which violence occurs, triggering the state to become officially involved in private life through the institutions of law enforcement and social services.

A sensationalized headline about violence in same-sex relationships appeared in The Globe and Mail in April 2008: "A skeleton that's still in the closet: Domestic violence is more widespread among same-sex couples than straights" (Anderssen, 2008, p. F1). The two-page story was based on the results of a Statistics Canada report on violence and victimization. On the one hand, relationship violence is a serious issue and it was powerful to see the needs of a small population covered in a national newspaper, but on the other hand the headline reflected an underlying pathologizing discourse that represents LGBTQ families as not just facing issues similar to those of straight families—but issues that are even worse. This kind of mainstreaming of LGBTQ family issues serves more to exploit an already marginalized subpopulation than to integrate victims of same-sex violence into Canadian public discourse about family life, and offers little insight into the nuances, differences, and contexts of life for LGBTQ families.

This time it was more than a sensationalized headline, though: the story was based on the results of a Statistics Canada survey on violence and victimization that for the first time asked respondents to identify their sexual orientation. With its large sample size of 23,766 randomly selected respondents, it seemed authoritative, although buried in the story was the figure that only 356 of those respondents identified as gay, lesbian, or bisexual (the survey did not ask about transgender identities). The survey asked about experiences of violence in families as well as violence and discrimination in public settings. They found, not surprisingly, that gays, lesbians, and bisexuals reported higher rates of violent victimization (sexual and physical assault and robbery) and discrimination than their heterosexual counterparts. This is in fact consistent with other social science studies that report high rates of violence experienced by LGBTQ people. For example, survey research has found that 20 percent of women and 25 percent of men have experienced victimization based on their sexual orientation and another study found 60 percent of all transsexual/transgender people have been victimized by hate violence.

The headline news, though, was that Statistics Canada found that 15 percent of gay men and lesbians and 28 percent of bisexuals reported being abused by a partner in the last 5 years, in comparison to only 7 percent of heterosexuals. The message seemed clear: an impressively large Statistics Canada study had proven that LGBTQ relationships are much more violent than straight ones. The story suggested that the odds were one in six or seven of being victimized if one were in a same-sex relationship. There are many problems with these claims.

First and foremost, survey respondents were not asked if the abuse they were reporting took place within a same-sex relationship, or in an earlier, or current, straight one. So we have to ask: What do these statistics really tell us? In this study, higher rates of victimization were indeed reported by gay, lesbian, and bisexual people. But we cannot say that violence in same-sex relationships is more widespread because we do not know that the violence they reported occurred in the same-sex relationship.

Further, unlike other surveys, in this one there was no differentiation between forms of violence (physical, emotional, sexual). Nor was there any attention to gender (differing experiences of gay men, lesbians, bisexual women, and bisexual men). Buried in a footnote in the original report, and nowhere to be seen in the *Globe* story, is the disclosure that LGB female respondents were combined with LGB male respondents in this huge study because there were not enough lesbians to meet the criteria (normally 25) for conducting statistically significant analysis.

Other large comparative survey studies that include lesbians, gays, and bisexuals have paid attention to differences. A report based on the National Violence Against Women Survey (Tjaden, Thoennes, and Allison, 1999) compared intimate partner victimization rates between same-sex and opposite-sex couples. This telephone survey, with a nationally representative sample of 8,000 women and 8,000 men, asked about their experiences as victims of various forms of violence including intimate partner violence. Researchers found that women living with female intimate partners experience less intimate-partner violence than women living with male intimate partners. Nearly 25 percent of surveyed women said they were raped and/or physically assaulted by their male partner. Slightly more than 11 percent of the women who lived with a woman reported being raped, physically assaulted, and/or stalked by their female intimate partner. On the other hand, men living with male intimate partners reported more violence than men who lived with female intimate partners. Approximately 15 percent of the men who have lived with a male intimate partner reported being raped, physically assaulted, and/or stalked by a male partner while 7.7 percent of men who lived with women reported such violence by their female partner. The patterns and differences in experiences of violence in heterosexual, gay, and lesbian relationships need to be carefully examined (and the experiences of transgender persons need to be included) if our motive is to develop the best understandings, interventions, and prevention strategies. If we view all relationship violence as the same, we run the risk of treating all cases of relationship violence as equivalent and interchangeable when that does not seem to be the case (Ristock, 2002).

Although many of the tactics used in abusive same-sex relationships are the same as those used in abusive heterosexual relationships, there are some specific abusive behaviours that reflect the larger context of homophobia, biphobia, transphobia, and heterosexism surrounding LGBTQ relationships. These behaviours include threats to reveal the sexual or gender identity of a partner to one's boss, landlord, or a family member; threats to jeopardize custody of children because of a person's sexual or gender identity; threats to jeopardize immigration because of sexual orientation; and/or threats to reveal the HIV/AIDS status of a partner.

Several small studies have been conducted that show the need to consider the specific contexts in which people experience relationship violence. (It is important to note that the exclusive emphasis on a gender-based analysis of violence can obscure the differing contexts surrounding heterosexual violence as well.) Such research explores the impact of contexts such as one or both partners dealing with a stigmatized illness such as HIV/AIDS; the effects of alcohol and drug use; social isolation in rural communities; experiences of dislocation as recent immigrants; and experiencing the combined effects of racism, classism, and violence. Although these differing contexts are not exhaustive and may overlap with one another, they reveal the ways that violence is connected to structural factors in the social context that create and sustain inequalities and disadvantages.

Perhaps the most significant impact of a larger context of homophobia, biphobia, transphobia, and heterosexism is in the barriers that they create for accessing support. For example, it can be very difficult for LGBTQ persons to tell family members, coworkers, and neighbours what is happening if they are in an abusive relationship because of the fear that the violence will be seen as evidence that their sexual identity or gender identity is unhealthy. Several studies have reported on the many barriers LGBTQ people experience when trying to access support services for victims of violence, such as perceived or actual homophobia (Scherzer, 1998), transphobia, and racism (Kanuha, 1990; Waldron, 1996). These studies comment on the inability of most services to fully respond to same-sex partner violence because of mainstream heterosexual approaches and assumptions (Ristock, 1994; Russo, 1999). For example, a gay or bisexual man presenting at a hospital with physical injuries is less likely to be asked about domestic violence than a woman who presents with physical injuries (Island and Letellier, 1991). Or as one woman said so profoundly about not even seeking support: "I feel like I can't talk about it, I mean how many therapists/social service providers are going to understand queer, s/m, abuse, intersexed, interracial [all features of her abusive relationship]—It's too complicated, there is too much explaining that I'd have to do" (Ristock, 2005).

ILLNESS AND AGING

In traditional societies, compulsory heterosexual family structures fulfilled the role of caring for aging or ill parents. Most people became parents and then grandparents; if they became unable to live independently, it was commonplace for their adult children to provide for them. Typically a married daughter would take in her aged parents, or an unmarried daughter would move in with her aged parents to look after them. More recently, a system of nursing homes and independent-living complexes has developed to take the place of family support. More recently still, the health of aging people is such that many can provide for themselves in their homes well beyond the age at which an earlier generation might have needed to be looked after by others.

In many ways the issues of aging LGBTQ people are, of course, the same issues all aging people face: inability to shop and do laundry; increasing health problems and decreasing mobility; outliving one's contemporaries and becoming the oldest people around. All of these are compounded for LGBTQ people, most of whom do not have children to look out for them. Many LGBTQ couples' nightmare is that they will end up in a straight nursing home, either together with their partner but unable to share a room, or worse, alone, surrounded by homophobic and transphobic residents and staff. Brotman et al. (2003) report that the "legitimate fears that gay and lesbian seniors have about the homophobia and heterosexism they face in seeking health and social services prevent many of them from receiving the care and support that they need" (p. 7).

The baby-boom generation of people born between 1946 and 1964 were the first to come out of the closet in large numbers and the oldest of them are now facing a future of life as an elderly person living outside the heterosexual culture that is still dominant. For many, "the notions of senior housing or assisted living revive memories of the ostracism and prejudice they faced in high school. In fact, some worry old age may mean again struggling to pass as heterosexual."[8] The worries are many: will staff recognize their partners as having legal rights to oversee medical care or visit them in hospital? Will their partner's birth family interfere if one of them becomes disabled? Canada's same-sex legal equality means that the situation for aging LGBTQ people here is vastly better than in other countries such as the United States, but homophobia and transphobia continue to be the norm in many cultural spaces, and these are compounded by racism, classism, and other interlocking oppressions for many LGBTQ people: for example, "If you're HIV, gay and black, it's like a triple threat. And then on top of that, you can often add class discrimination."[9]

Many LGBTQ people have organized their own support systems for aging. These range from informal circles of friends who agree to look out for each other by advocating for their medical needs and arranging for support services, to legally empowered steering committees that fundraise to build LGBTQ complexes and oversee their management. The latter of course are expensive and access is limited to financially advantaged people. Some organizations offer cultural competence training on LGBTQ issues to seniors' facility staff. All are dedicated to the goal of preventing LGBTQ people—in all their diversity, not just the white, middle-class ones who blend in well—from having to withdraw into the closet when they age:

> If a place says it's 'inclusive,' does that mean it's inclusive for a person who's gay but doesn't make anyone nervous about it, or that it's inclusive for a gay man who crosses his leg, waves his wrist and tells campy stories at the dinner table in the cafeteria?[10]

As daunting as it is to contemplate having to stare down homophobic and transphobic discrimination in one's old age, baby boomers are probably well equipped to do it. Many have participated in LGBTQ rights activism from the 1960s onward. They demonstrated strong organizing and advocacy to push for humane and effective medical treatment through the AIDS crisis, and cared for sick and dying people in the absence of state support. And they are old enough to remember what high school was like and determined not to relive the experience.

CONCLUSION

LGBTQ people face the family issues everyone faces: dating, marriage, divorce, parenting, separation by aging and illness. However, each of these issues is inflected by the continuing backdrop of homophobic and heteronormative discourse in which the legitimacy of LGBTQ families is still treated as open to debate. Although it has been over 40 years since homosexuality was decriminalized in this country and the LGBTQ rights movement started gaining ground, if we look to the history of other rights movements such as the Black civil rights movement in the United States, we should expect the struggle to go on for many years more. The discourses of homophobia and transphobia, like that of racism, are social constructs that have proven quite malleable, but they are deeply rooted in the structures of identity of people in some pockets of society and therefore profoundly resistant to change. While LGBTQ families live their lives in the context of those discourses, they are also caught up in the LGBTQ movement's struggle between striving for the assimilation of the most "normal" LGBTQ families into mainstream society, and striving to integrate LGBTQ families in their true gender and ethnic diversity.

While the struggle continues to integrate all families in all their diversity into Canadian society, LGBTQ people might hope that the efficacy of law proves to be closer to Plato's assessment than to Thoreau's. The famous philosopher, writing in the context of ancient Greece's own struggles between democratic ideals and systems of privilege and oppression, observed that laws can teach as well as enforce: "Laws are partly framed for the sake of good men [sic], in order to instruct them how they may live on friendly terms with one another, and partly for the sake of those who refuse to be instructed" (360 BCE). Situated as we are in a time of conflicting social interests, LGBTQ Canadians have fought hard for to be included in federal and provincial law, both for its symbolic legitimizing effect and for its protective force against those who "refuse to be instructed" that LGBTQ rights are human rights.

Summary

- Legal equality has been largely achieved for LGB families in Canada (though not for transgender families).

- However, there is ongoing conflict between socially conservative and socially progressive discourses about LGBTQ families and relationships.

- Within the LGBTQ population, discourses of assimilation and integration are in tension.

- LGBTQ people's personal lives are conducted in the context of these public discourses.

- Although the situation is improving, LGBTQ partners, parents, and children continue to experience social prejudice and discrimination, as do children with LGBTQ parents.

Notes

1. Stacey Beldom provided research assistance invaluable to the development of this chapter in the form of an extensive literature search and annotated bibliography.

2. Martin, N. (2004, Dec 10). "Ruling a Testament to Canada's 'Cadillac' Human Rights Laws." *Winnipeg Free Press* (MB), 08281785, p. A4.

3. Stefanson, Sarah. (2008, Fall). "Why Did Native People in Alternative Sexual Roles Feel They Had to Create a New Term to Describe Themselves? Sense and Sensuality—Two-Spirit: Alternative Sexuality in Native Culture. *Cahoots Magazine*. Retrieved from http://www.cahoots magazine.com.

4. Taylor, C.G., Peter, T., Schachter, K., Paquin, S., Beldom, S., Gross, Z., & McMinn, TL. (2009). *Youth Speak Up About Homophobia and Transphobia: The First National Climate Survey on Homophobia and Transphobia in Canadian Schools: Phase 1 Report.* Toronto ON: Egale Canada Human Rights Trust.

5. Taylor, C.G., Peter, T., Schachter, K., Paquin, S., Beldom, S., Gross, Z., & McMinn, TL. (2009). *Youth Speak Up About Homophobia and Transphobia: The First National Climate Survey on Homophobia and Transphobia in Canadian Schools: Phase 1*

Report. Toronto ON: Egale Canada Human Rights Trust. [Climate Survey data Q54 Record 1375]

6. Taylor, C.G., Peter, T., Schachter, K., Paquin, S., Beldom, S., Gross, Z., & McMinn, TL. (2009). *Youth Speak Up About Homophobia and Transphobia: The First National Climate Survey on Homophobia and Transphobia in Canadian Schools: Phase 1 Report*. Toronto ON: Egale Canada Human Rights Trust. [Climate Survey data Q54 Record 1356]

7. Taylor, C.G., Peter, T., Schachter, K., Paquin, S., Beldom, S., Gross, Z., & McMinn, TL. (2009). *Youth Speak Up About Homophobia and Transphobia: The First National Climate Survey on Homophobia and Transphobia in Canadian Schools: Phase 1 Report*. Toronto ON: Egale Canada Human Rights Trust. [Climate Survey data Q54 Record 139]

8. Reproduced with permission of BALTIMORE SUN COMPANY, from "Gay Boomers Are Wary of Homophobic Retirement Care," by Linell Smith, *The Baltimore Sun*, April 6, 2007; permission conveyed through Copyright Clearance Center, Inc.

9. Ibid.

10. Ibid.

Critical Thinking Questions

1. Discuss the ways in which same-sex rights are family rights. Why do the debates persist over same-sex marriage and parenting rights? Why is legal change alone insufficient to achieve social legitimacy for LGBTQ people?

2. Why might some LGBTQ people/families wish to assimilate while others wish to stress differences and diversity? What are some of the tensions between assimilationist and anti-assimilationist discourses?

3. Think of some examples of the ways heterosexuality is assumed and reinforced within family structures. How might we work to disrupt the enforcement of "compulsory heterosexuality"?

Websites

EGALE
http://www.egale.ca
> EGALE (Equal Rights for Gays and Lesbians Everywhere) seeks to advance equality and justice for lesbian, gay, bisexual, and trans-identified people and their families. It posts current material about LGBT issues in Canada including the recent report on Homophobic Bullying in Schools.

Supporting Our Youth
http://www.soytoronto.org
> Supporting Our Youth is a program of the Sherbourne Health Centre in Toronto that is dedicated to improving the quality of life for lesbian, gay,

bisexual, transsexual, and transgender youth. Supporting Our Youth has an active webpage with videos and links to many resources. The organization takes an anti-oppression stance and offers a range of programs including one for Black queer youth, and a newcomer/immigrant program.

Family Pride Canada

http://www.uwo.ca/pridelib/family/index.html

Family Pride Canada is a national online resource centre for queer people and their families.

Suggested Readings

Mary Boeneke (Ed). 2003. *Trans Forming Families: Real Stories about Transgendered Loved Ones.* Hardy, VA: Oak Knoll Press.

This anthology is filled with personal accounts by trans persons, and friends and family members of trans persons. The volume includes sections on raising gender-variant children, parents learning from adult trans children, couples reinventing their relationships within a new gender paradigm, the experiences of trans persons as parents, and a few articles by therapists who work with transgenders. The collection presents a very diversified range of experiences.

David Rayside. 2008. *Queer Inclusions, Continental Divisions.* Toronto: University of Toronto Press.

Rayside explores the politics of sexual diversity in Canada and the United States by analyzing three contentious areas—relationship recognition, parenting, and schooling. He enters long-standing debates over Canadian–American contrasts while paying close attention to regional differences. Rayside offers an important analysis of change over time in the public recognition of sexual minorities. He considers media, legal, and social science accounts of developments in Canada and the United States. He shows that Canada has made significant gains in relationship recognition and parenting while the United States has, surprisingly, made more substantial changes to the schooling system than those instituted by Canada.

Rachel Epstein (Ed). 2009. *Who's Your Daddy?: And Other Writings on Queer Parenting.* Toronto: Sumach Press.

This collection of 40 essays offers narrative and academic voices from Canada, the United States, Australia, and England on issues of queer parenting. These include butches raising sons; queer youth as parents; trans experiences in fertility clinics; race relations in the family, heteronormativity in queer families' kids' books; and reflections on the meanings of biology and "queer" parenting. The book moves away from the position of trying to show queer families as "normal" and instead offers a more honest and exploration of the diversity that exists within "queer" families.

References

Alberta. 2009. Bill 44: *Human Rights, Citizenship, and Multiculturalism Amendment Act*, 2009. http://www.assembly.ab.ca/bills/2009/pdf/bill-044.pdf (accessed April 4, 2010).

Althusser, L. 1971. "Ideological State Apparatuses." *Lenin and Philosophy* (pp. 127–186). Trans. B. Brewster. London: New Left Books.

Anderssen, Erin. 2008, April 12. "A Skeleton That's Still in the Closet: Domestic Violence Is More Widespread Among Same-Sex Couples Than Straights." *The Globe and Mail*, p. F1.

Armstrong, J. 2004, June 12. "The Body Within." *The Globe and Mail*, pp. F1, F6.

Brill, S.A. and R. Pepper. 2008. *The Transgender Child: A Handbook for Families and Professionals*. San Francisco: Cleis Press.

Brotman, S., W. Ryan, and E. Meyer. 2003. *The Health and Social Service Needs of Gay and Lesbian Seniors and Their Families in Canada*. Montreal: McGill School of Social Work.

Canfield-Lenfest, M. 2008. *Kids of Trans Resource Guide*. San Francisco: Colage. http://www.colage.org (accessed April 4, 2010).

CBC News Online. 2004, September 14. Same-sex Divorce. http://www.cbc.ca/news/background/samesexrights/samesexdivorce.html (accessed April 4, 2010).

Coontz, S. 2000. *The Way We Never Were: American Families and the Nostalgia Trap*. New York: Perseus.

D'Augelli, A.R., S.L. Hershberger, and N.W. Pilkington. 1998. "Lesbian, Gay, and Bisexual Youth and Their Families: Disclosure of Sexual Orientation and Its Consequences." *American Journal of Orthopsychiatry*, 68(3): 361–371.

Eldridge, V., L. Mack, and E. Swank. 2006. "Explaining Comfort with Homosexuality in Rural America." *Journal of Homosexuality*, 51(2), 39–56.

Epstein, Rachel (Ed.). 2009. *Who's Your Daddy?: And Other Writings on Queer Parenting*. Toronto: Sumach Press.

Fone, B. 2000. *Homophobia: A History*. New York: Henry Holt.

Foucault, M. 1986. "On the Genealogy of Ethics: An Overview of Work in Progress." In P. Rabinow (Ed.), *The Foucault Reader* (pp. 340–372). Harmondsworth: Peregrine.

Fumia, D. 2007. "'I Do' Belong in Canada: Same Sex Relationship and Marriage." In D. Cheal (Ed.), *New Canadian Families* (pp. 177–194). Toronto: Oxford University Press.

Goldberg, A.E. 2007. "Talking About Family: Disclosure Practices of Adults Raised by Lesbian, Gay, and Bisexual Parents." *Journal of Family Issues*, 28(1): 100–131.

Grossman, A., A. D'Augelli, T. Howell, and S. Hubbard. 2005. "Parents' Reactions to Transgender Youths' Gender Nonconforming Expression and Identity." *Journal of Gay & Lesbian Social Services*, 18(1), 3–16.

Herek, G. and M. Gonzalez-Rivera. 2006. "Attitudes toward Homosexuality among US Residents of Mexican Descent." *Journal of Sex Research*, 43(2), 122–135.

Hershberger, S. and A. D'Augelli. 1995. "The Impact of Victimization on the Mental Health and Suicidality of Lesbian, Gay and Bisexual Youths." *Developmental Psychology*, 31, 65–78.

Hicks, S. 2005. "Queer Geneologies: Tales of Conformity and Rebellion amongst Lesbian and Gay Foster Carers and Adopters." *Qualitative Social Work*, 4(3), 293–308.

Hillier, L. and L. Harrison. 2007. "Building Realities Less Limited than Their Own: Young People Practising Same-Sex Attraction on the Internet." *Sexualities*, 10(1), 82–100.

Holley, L.C., N.C. Larson, M. Adelman, and J. Trevino. 2008. "Attitudes among University Undergraduates toward LGB and Five Ethnic/Racial Groups." *Journal of LGBT Youth*, 5(1), 79–101.

Ingram, M. 1987. *Church Courts, Sex and Marriage in England, 1570–1640*. Cambridge, UK: Cambridge University Press.

Island, D. and P. Letellier. 1991. *Men Who Beat the Men Who Love Them: Battered Gay Men and Domestic Violence*. New York: Haworth Press.

Jacobs, S., T. Wesley, and S. Lang. 1997. *Two-Spirit People: Native American Gender Identity, Sexuality, and Spirituality*. Urbana: University of Illinois Press.

James, S.E. 2002. "Clinical Themes in Gay- and Lesbian-parented Adoptive Families." *Clinical Child Psychology and Psychiatry*, 7(3), 475–486.

Kanuha, V. 1990. "Compounding the Triple Jeopardy: Battering in Lesbian of Color Relationships." *Women and Therapy*, 9: 169–184.

Kinsman, G. 1996. *The Regulation of Desire: Homo and Hetero Sexualities*. 2nd ed. Montreal: Black Rose Books.

Kuvulanka, K.A. and A. Goldberg. 2009. "'Second Generation' Voices: Queer Youth with Lesbian/Bisexual Mothers." *Journal of Youth & Adolescence*, 38(7): 904–919.

Lewis, G. 2003. "Black-White Differences in Attitudes toward Homosexuality and Gay Rights." *Public Opinion Quarterly*, 67: 59–78.

Lindsay, J., A. Perlesz, R. Brown, R. McNair, D. de Vaus, and M. Pitts. 2006. "Stigma or Respect: Lesbian-parented Families Negotiating School Settings." *Sociology*, 40(6), 1059–1077.

Lynch, J.M. 2000. "Considerations of Family and Gender Composition." *Journal of Homosexuality*, 40(2): 81–95.

Martin, N. 2004, Dec 10. "Ruling a Testament to Canada's 'Cadillac' Human Rights Laws." *Winnipeg Free Press* (MB), p. A4.

McHoul, A. and W. Grace. 1993. *A Foucault Primer: Discourse, Power, and the Subject*. Melbourne: Melbourne University Press.

Miller, R., D. Forte, B. Wilson, and G. Greene. 2006. "Protecting Sexual Minority Youth from Research Risks: Conflicting Perspectives." *American Journal of Community Psychology*, 37: 341–348.

Morrison, L. and J. L'Heareux. 2001. "Suicide and Gay/Lesbian/Bisexual Youth: Implications for Clinicians." *Journal of Adolescence*, 24: 39–49.

Morrow, D. 2004. "Social Work Practice with Gay, Lesbian, Bisexual, and Transgender Adolescents." *Families in Society*, 85(1): 91–99.

Newman, F. and G. Muzzonigro. 1993. "The Effects of Traditional Family Values on the Coming Out Process of Gay Male Adolescents." *Adolescence*, 28(109): 213–226.

Olson, L., W. Cadge, and J. Harrison. 2006. "Religion and Public Opinion about Same-sex Marriage." *Social Science Quarterly*, 87(2): 340–360.

Pelka, S. 2009. "Sharing Motherhood: Maternal Jealousy among Lesbian Co-mothers." *Journal of Homosexuality*, 56(2): 195–217.

Peplau, L.A. and X. Spalding. 2003. "The Close Relationships of Lesbians, Gay Men and Bisexuals." In L. Garnets and D. Kimmel (Eds.), *Psychological Perspectives on Lesbian, Gay, and Bisexual Experiences* (pp. 449–474). New York: Columbia University Press.

PFLAG Canada. 2009. "Learn about PFLAG Canada." http://www.pflagcanada.ca/en/index-e.asp (accessed April 4, 2010).

Plato. 360 BCE. *Laws*. Part 11. Trans. B. Jowett. Atheneum Reading Room. http://evans-experientialism.freewebspace.com/plato_laws11.htm (accessed April 4, 2010).

Rayside, D. 2008. *Queer Inclusions, Continental Divisions*. Toronto: University of Toronto Press.

Ristock, J. 2002. *No More Secrets:Violence in Lesbian Relationships*. New York: Routledge.

Ristock, J. 2005. "Relationship Violence in Lesbian/Gay/Bisexual/Transgender/Queer [LGBTQ] Communities: Moving beyond a Gender-based Framework." *Violence Against Women Online Resources*. http://www.mincava.umn.edu/documents/lgbtqviolence/lgbtqviolence.html (accessed April 4, 2010).

Rivers, M. 2003. "Shock and Confusion with Love." In M. Boenke (Ed.), *Trans forming families: Real Stories about Transgendered Loved Ones*, 2nd ed. (pp. 59–60). Hardy, VA: Oak Knoll Press.

Rosario, M., M. Rotheram-Borus, and H. Reid. 1996. "Gay-related Stress and Its Correlates among Gay and Bisexual Male Adolescents of Predominately Black and Hispanic Background." *Journal of Community Psychology*, 24: 136–159.

Rose, N.E. 2003. "The Family Lecture." *Journal of Lesbian Studies*, 6(3): 235–241.

Rose, S.M. and D. Zand. 2002. "Lesbian Dating and Courtship from Young Adulthood to Midlife." *Journal of Lesbian Studies*, 6(1): 85–109.

Russo, A. 1999. "Lesbian Organizing Against Lesbian Battering." In B. Leventhal and S. E. Lundy (Eds.), *Same-Sex Domestic Violence: Strategies for Change* (pp. 83–96). Thousand Oaks, CA: Sage.

Saewyc, E., C. Poon, N. Wang, Y. Homma, A. Smith, and the McCreary Centre Society. 2007. *Not Yet Equal: The Health of Lesbian, Gay, and Bisexual Youth in BC*. Vancouver, BC: McCreary Centre Society.

Saltzburg, S. 2004. "Learning That an Adolescent Child Is Gay or Lesbian: The Parent Experience." *Social Work*, 49(1): 109–119.

Scherzer, T. 1998. "Domestic Violence in Lesbian Relationships: Findings of the Lesbian Relationships Research Project." *Journal of Lesbian Studies*, 2(1): 29–47.

Schulte, L. and J. Battle. 2004. "The Relative Importance of Ethnicity and Religion in Predicting Attitudes towards Gays and Lesbians." *Journal of Homosexuality*, 47(2): 127–142.

Smith, L. 2007a, April 1. "Gay Boomers, Who Fought Discrimination and Confronted AIDS, Face a New Fight as They Grow Old." Baltimoresun.com (accessed April 27, 2010).

Smith, L. 2007b, April 6. "Gay Boomers Are Wary of Homophobic Retirement Care." BaltimoreSun.com (accessed April 4, 2010).

Sollors, W. (Ed.). 2000. *Interracialism: Black-White Intermarriage in American History, Literature, and Law*. New York: Oxford.

Somerville, M. 2003, April 29. "The Case against 'Same-sex Marriage.' A Brief Submitted to the Standing Committee on Justice and Human Rights, April 29, 2003." Montreal: McGill University.

Statistics Canada. 2008. "2006 Census Information on Same-sex Common-law and Married Couples." http://www12.statcan.ca/census-recensement/2006/ref/info/same_sex-meme_sexe-eng.cfm (accessed April 4, 2010).

Stefanson, S. 2008, Fall. "Why Did Native People in Alternative Sexual Roles Feel They Had to Create a New Term to Describe Themselves? Sense and Sensuality—Two-Spirit: Alternative Sexuality in Native Culture." *Cahoots Magazine*. http://www.cahoots magazine.com (accessed April 26, 2010).

Stoutenborough, J., D. Haider-Markel, and M. Allen. 2006. "Reassessing the Impact of Supreme Court Decisions on Public Opinion: Gay Civil Rights Cases." *Political Research Quarterly*, 59(3), 419–433.

Taylor, C.G. 2008. "Counterproductive Effects of Parental Consent in Research Involving LGBTTIQ Youth: International Research Ethics and a Study of a Transgender and Two-Spirit Community in Canada." *Journal of LGBT Youth*, 5(3): 34–56.

Taylor, C. and T. Peter. 2010. "Left Behind: Sexual and Gender Minority Students in Canadian High Schools in the New Millennium." In T. Morrison, M. Morrison, D.T. McDermott, and M.A. Carrigan (Eds.), *Sexual Minority Research in the New Millennium*. Hauppauge, NY: Nova Science.

Taylor, C.G., T. Peter, K. Schachter, S. Paquin, S. Beldom, Z. Gross, and T.L. McMinn. 2009. *Youth Speak Up about Homophobia and Transphobia: The First National Climate Survey on Homophobia and Transphobia in Canadian Schools: Phase 1 Report*. Toronto: Egale Canada Human Rights Trust.

Teague, J. 1992. "Issues Relating to the Treatment of Adolescent Lesbians and Homosexuals." *Journal of Mental Health Counseling*, 14, 422–439.

Thoreau, H.D. 1849. "Civil Disobedience." [Originally published as "Resistance to Civil Government"]. *The Thoreau Reader*. http://thoreau.eserver.org/civil1.html (accessed April 4, 2010).

Tjaden, P., N. Thoennes, and C.J. Allison. 1999. "Comparing Violence over the Life Span in Samples of Same-Sex and Opposite-Sex Cohabitants." *Violence and Victims*, (14) 4: 413–425.

Waldron, C.M. 1996. "Lesbians of Color and the Domestic Violence Movement." In C. Renzetti and C. H. Miley (Eds.), *Violence in Gay and Lesbian Domestic Partnerships* (pp. 43–52). New York: Harrington Park Press.

Weeks, J., B. Heaphy, and C. Donovan. 2001. *Same Sex Intimacies: Families of Choice and Other Experiments*. London: Routledge.

White, T. and R. Ettner. 2004. "Disclosure, Risks and Protective Factors for Children Whose Parents Are Undergoing a Gender Transition." *Journal of Gay & Lesbian Psychotherapy*, 8(1/2): 29–145.

Wilson, A. 1996. "How We Find Ourselves: Identity Development and Two-Spirit People." *Harvard Educational Review*, 66(2): 303–317.

Wilson, B. and R. Miller. 2002. "Strategies for Coping with Sexual Orientation Among African American Men Who Have Sex with Men." *Journal of Black Psychology*, 28: 371–391.

Chapter 6

Families in Tough Times: The Impact of Economic Crises on Canadian Families

Ann Duffy

". . . the global financial system is experiencing its most severe crisis[1] since the 1930s" (Bank of Canada, December 2008).[2]

LEARNING OBJECTIVES

In this chapter, you will learn that:

1. the personal realities of Canadian families intersect with the shifting patterns of the Canadian economy,

2. economic crises on regional, national, or global levels directly affect many aspects of family life, including family formation, family roles, family conflict and even family size,

3. larger economic realities affect Canadian families throughout the family life cycle and that evidence of these outcomes is apparent when examining the impact of the 2008 recession on families in Welland, Ontario,

4. the economic crises that affect our personal and familial lives are part of the larger trends in Canadian social history and in the development of contemporary capitalism,

5. today, the impact of economic changes on families and personal lives has a distinct global dimension.

INTRODUCTION

The history of modern **capitalism** has been punctuated with a series of economic "crises"—most recently, in the early 1970s, early 1980s,[3] early 1990s, early 2000 (the dot-com collapse) and, of course, starting in the fall of 2008, "The Great Recession."[4] In many of these events, hundreds of thousands of Canadians lost their jobs, official unemployment rates[5] pushed into or at least toward double-digit territory, and recovery took a number of years (Stanford, 2008). Most Canadians alive today have lived through several of these economic downturns and, in most instances their families, whether poor, working-class, or middle-class, were affected by them. Not surprisingly, actual or feared unemployment, financial worries and stress managing family finances are always likely to affect numerous Canadians, particularly those who are most economically vulnerable. Increases in stress and worries among family members may be tracked to family dysfunction or even violence and family breakdown—all originally emanating from these intensifying economic pressures. Understanding our families—in terms of structures and content—means paying attention to this ongoing ebb and flow of economic well-being. Even among the most stable couples, widespread unemployment or **underemployment** along with fears of financial insecurity is likely to have a strong dampening effect on family formation and child bearing, on family happiness and overall familial well-being.

The impact of this series of economic crises on Canadian families cannot be fully appreciated unless the upheavals are located in the larger historical context of long-term trends toward the "**new economy**" and new forms of capitalism (Henwood, 2003; Stiglitz, 2010). Alongside the long history of fluctuating good and tough times, Canadians are also in the midst of a far-ranging re-organization of their economic and employment life. The old forms of work—male-dominated resource extraction and manufacturing jobs—are being steadily supplanted by service-sector work. Traditional manufacturing jobs, such as working in the local steel plant or auto factory peaked in Canada in 2002 and since that time, 772,400 of these jobs have been eliminated or eroded[6] (Campbell, 2009, p. 33). Predictably, in this same process the "permanent" 40-hour week/8-hour day has been widely displaced by contract, shift, part-time, short-term, and other forms of **precarious or marginal employment** that are commonplace in service-sector work (Fox and Sugiman, 2006; Vosko, 2000). Ironically, it is precisely these nonstandard work schedules that are associated with worse family functioning, more depressive symptoms, less effective parenting, and a strain on the well-being of both parents and children (Strazdins et al., 2006; see also Lewchuk, Clarke, and Wolff, 2008).

Predictably, alongside this growth of service-sector work, there has been an important growth since the mid-1970s in the proportion of low-paid workers in the labour force. Much of the service employment that is being generated in the "new economy" is relatively low-wage work such as call centre work, retail sales positions, and so on. In 1976, only about one in five of full-year, full-time workers earned less than two-thirds of the median annual earnings; by 2004, the numbers had grown to one in four and this is, of course, prior to the 2008 crisis (LaRochelle-Cote and Dionne, 2009). Ironically, for many families, the increased labour force participation of family members, notably women, has not translated into significant increases in family earnings. In part, this is likely the result of the loss of well-paid manufacturing work—work that frequently included overtime work at high rates of pay. Today, despite their increased time in the paid labour force, many families have experienced an erosion of their financial situation as household debt has mushroomed over the past several decades. A variety of factors including pressures from the consumer market, increased educational costs, and postponed employment for many youth have meant that numerous families are today mired in heavy debt while facing an uncertain economy.

In the course of these economic changes, the so-called traditional 1950s family—with a stay-at-home wife and bread-winner husband—has been all but expunged. Increased economic pressures, particularly skyrocketing housing costs, have meant that the typical family has had to expand its financial base by deploying wives and also teenagers into the paid labour force if it wants to simply maintain its standard of living. Indeed, by 2007, 85 percent of Canadian two-parent families had at least two earners in the household (Vanier Institute of the Family, February 2010). In fact, throughout history and around the globe today, single-earner families (despite a dramatic rise in lone-parent-mother-headed families) have been an anomaly and families have typically had to rely on the income earned by a variety of family members (including children and youth). It was only for a relatively few years in the course of the 1950s to 1970s—during the so-called **Golden Age of Capitalism**—that the majority of the population in the industrialized North was able to maintain a comfortable lifestyle on the income earned by one male wage earner (Rollings-Magnusson, 2009; Stanford, 2008).

These changes in the economy echo directly through family lives. As a result of more and more family members holding jobs in the emergent service economy, families have confronted increased time stress and longer hours at work (Gordon, 2009, p. E7). By 2008 three-quarters of couples with dependent children were growing up in dual-earner families (up from one-third in 1976) and the single-earner-husband family declined to 21 percent of Canadian families (Marshall, 2009, p. 7). Although the deployment of two or more family members has allowed individual family members to avoid longer and longer personal work weeks indeed, the average time spent by individual Canadians at the job decreased recently (Usalcas, 2008) the family as a unit is spending significantly more time at paid work. In 1976 a husband and wife would average a combined 58 hours per week in the labour force; by 2008 work responsibilities had increased to 65 hours per week (LaRochelle-Cote, Gougeon, and Pinard, 2009). This increase means that together husbands and wives are contributing almost one full work day more to paid employment each week in 2008 than they were in 1976 (Marshall, 2009, p. 6).

Pulled by the demands of their paid employment and pushed by pressing economic needs, families often face a dearth of hours in the day. The average Canadian household with children was devoting almost 200 more hours a year to paid work in 2004 than it did in 1996 and, ironically, some of those families devoting long hours (50 hours a week or more) to paid employment—because their employment is minimum or low wage or unpredictable—are not producing greater economic rewards for their families despite these long hours of work (Yalnizyan, 2007, p. 21; Gordon, 2009, p. E7). Long hours at minimum or near minimum wage may still result in a family income near the poverty line.[7] Despite the well-documented relationship indicating that children benefit from living in families with reasonable and stable economic resources as well as time to spend with parents and siblings, it seems that many families are experiencing the worst of both worlds—less time and inadequate financial resources (Phipps and Lethbridge, 2006; Turcotte, 2007).

The new economy may also create a dearth of family time through pressures to relocate to more economically active (typically urban) centres. As discussed below, young people may be forced by economic needs to permanently move away from their extended families into urban centres to pursue careers, and other families may need to relocate to more economically active areas of the country. Many men and some women, for example, leave their East Coast families for months at a time in order to take high-paying jobs in the Alberta tar sands or to work on oil-drilling rigs in the North Atlantic. The impact on husband–wife as well as parent–child relationships and the increased pressures on the "single"' parent (the so-called "oil patch widows") left behind are likely erosive of family well-being (Agrell, 2008, p. L1).

Alongside these major shifts—the decline in well-paid manufacturing and resource-extraction jobs, the growth in service-sector[8] employment, the standardization of the multi-earner family and increases in time and economic pressures on families—there is another key ingredient emerging in the "new economy." Since the 1970s there has been a marked erosion of the Canadian **social safety net** and this fact is having a dramatic impact on many families over the course of the current recession. With the rise of neoliberalism and governmental acceptance of privatization, many of the agencies and government departments that provided assistance and support to families—particularly, those struggling with economic issues and their fall-out—have been downsized or eliminated (Ilcan, 2009; see Luxton and Corman in this text). Even Employment Insurance (EI), an employee-funded program designed to help workers weather periods of unemployment, has dramatically reduced its coverage while increasing its requirements.[9]

In 1989, 83.0 percent of unemployed workers received regular EI benefits but by 1995 the figure dropped to 49.7 percent. Put succinctly, workers who do receive EI are required to work longer for payments that are smaller and last for shorter periods (Burman, 1997, pp. 196–197). While, in response to the recent economic upheaval, the federal government introduced initiatives to extend the length of EI payments for displaced workers, many of the criticisms of the program persist. For example, in early 2009 a Toronto worker who was laid off needed to have accumulated 630 hours of paid employment to qualify to receive a maximum of 17 weeks of EI and, under recent changes, the same worker would need 560 hours of paid work and would receive 25 weeks of benefits. Despite these small improvements, the duration of benefits is often inadequate in terms of locating new employment in the midst of high unemployment rates. Further, qualification differences (reflecting regional variations in unemployment) across the country have been "toned down." However, this does little to address the needs of the almost 40 percent of Canadian workers who are nonstandard (part-time, temporary, or short-term) workers and who will struggle to accumulate sufficient hours to qualify or for the numerous industrial workers whose jobs are lost forever. EI–supported retraining programs have often been overwhelmed by applicants, many of whom do not manage to meet program qualifications (Goar, 2010, p A23). Currently, EI eligibility requirements mean about 60 percent of jobless workers no longer qualify and, of course, self-employed,[10] part-time, and contract workers are not even covered by the plan (Goar, 2009, p. 21; Arsenault and Sharpe, 2009, pp. 27–28). In addition, concerns persist that the two-week waiting period for claimants may put an unfair burden on the economically marginal, that the benefit period is too short and that the actual payments are too low[11] to meet the needs of many workers. Finally, the requirement that long-term workers first deplete their severance package[12] before qualifying for EI is seen by many as unnecessarily cruel treatment.

For those who do not qualify for EI or run out of EI supports, social assistance (welfare) has also become increasingly stringent and stingy while retaining its social stigma. In a number of provinces, social welfare payments have been significantly reduced and qualifications have increased. For example, welfare recipients are now allowed very little in the way of personal assets if they are to qualify for assistance; in many instances they are expected to engage in workfare ("community participation") to compensate for their state support (Hunter and Miazdyck-Shield, 2006; Broad and Hunter, 2010). While social welfare rates have never been generous, the current regime virtually guarantees that many of the unemployed will end up impoverished (Arsenault and Sharpe, 2009, p. 28) and severely hampered in their efforts to pull themselves out of poverty.[13]

These contradictory pressures on family members—to work to support the family while having less time to devote to these relationships and facing very uncertain economic times along with an inadequate social support system—are key to understanding the struggles of many contemporary Canadian families.

The theoretical viewpoint that will be used to examine these struggles is **feminist political economy**. Put simply, this approach advocates prioritizing the economic and power structures in society as key ingredients in social relationships and realities. As noted author Eli Zaretsky explained in 1986, understanding the emergence of modern individuals and their families requires an examination of the ways in which capitalism has developed over the past three centuries. For example, in many respects, the modern individual working for pay and living in a downtown condo is a product of structural economic changes in which more communal, family-based patterns of work/life were steadily outmoded. Today, living in a period of ascendant international capitalism has direct consequences for how we live our lives and how we conceptualize those lives.

For example, the mass consumerism embedded in the modern capitalist economic arrangements means that individual Canadians frequently turn to some form of consumption (of products or services) to meet their needs for meaning or human connection. The enormous popularity of computers, the Internet, Facebook, and Twitter speak directly to these links between consumption, personal lives, and human relationships in contemporary advanced capitalist economies.

The capitalist economy in which we now live is clearly driven by its traditional imperative of profitability—companies and corporations sell goods and services at more than the costs of production in order to satisfy their needs for profit. As Karl Marx pointed out, individual workers sell their labour to produce these goods and services—the salesperson, the taxi driver, and the industrial worker are all selling their employer their labour, which is in turn sold (as a service or commodity) at a higher rate to the consumer and thus generates a profit.[14] Clearly, in this arrangement it is the owners of the corporations who are setting the tune and garnering the majority of assets. Social agents who seek to control or confront corporations—such as organized labour or governmental agencies—in recent years have had relatively little success in confining or directing the actions of corporations. Indeed, as discussed below, the recession of 2008 may figure as a crisis in the unabated frenzy of international financial capitalists (banks and related institutions) to garner more and more profits at greater and greater risks.

Political economy as a theoretical perspective implies that we pay particular attention to the specific historical organization of the economy (today, global capitalism), our relationship to the economy (for example, paid employee or retiree), and to those individuals who control the economy (notably, corporate owners and directors). Feminist political economy urges us to attend to the specific ways in which gender (and related intersecting patterns of inequality, including persons living with disability, age, race/ethnicity, immigrant and Aboriginal status, sexual orientation, and social class) play a pivotal role in that women, persons with disabilities, the young and old, visible minorities along with immigrants and Aboriginals are all more likely to be exploited and oppressed within the current economic and power relationships while at the same time they play key roles in the maintenance of that economic system (see Luxton and Corman in this book; Luxton, 2006; Hiroko, 2008; Folbre, 2001).

THE UPHEAVAL OF 2008

At the turn of the century, many economists were envisioning uninterrupted growth and stability. As noted MIT economist Rudi Dornbusch stated in 1998, "The U.S. economy likely will not see a recession for years to come. We don't want one, we don't need one, and, as we have the tools to keep the current expansion going, we won't have one. This expansion will run forever" (as cited in Henwood, 2003, p. 3)[15] This optimism, shared by many mainstream economists, was, of course, ill-founded. Within the decade, global economies would be racked by crisis and uncounted workers would lose their employment.

During the fall of 2008, newspaper headlines were rife with frightening warnings of economic upheaval—even collapse. Social commentators ruminated about the prospects for a new "great"' **depression** as the financial mainstays of Canada's chief trading partner staggered under unanticipated pressures. Unbelievably, esteemed Wall Street investment firms collapsed and banks folded or turned to federal bailouts to weather the storm. On September 13, 2008, the fourth-largest U.S. investment bank, the venerable 158-year-old Lehman Brothers, was forced to file the biggest bankruptcy in U.S. history (*Toronto Star*, September 9, 2009, p. B4). By the fall of 2009, 80 banking institutions had been closed by U.S. regulators (*Toronto Star*, August 22, 2009, p. B7). The Canadian economy also reeled as the Toronto Stock Exchange between June 2005 and February 2009[16] saw a 45 percent point drop in value from its peak (Arsenault and Sharpe, 2009, p. 17).

Major employers throughout the United States and Canada slashed their workforces. The auto industry, notably General Motors and Chrysler, teetered on the brink of bankruptcy and the jobs of tens of thousands of North Americans hung in the balance. From October 2008 to July 2009, 410,000 jobs disappeared, the largest decline since the 1991–92 economic crisis. Official unemployment numbers pressed into double digits and unemployment figures that included discouraged workers (those who were no longer actively looking for work), workers on recall, and **involuntary part-time workers** reached almost 12 percent by the summer of 2009 (Sauve, 2010, pp. 6, 7). From October 2008 to October 2009, the number of Canadians collecting Employment Insurance (EI) grew from 500,000 to 809,000 (*Toronto Star*, January 26, 2010, p. B2). While in late 2009 the rates began to decline, there were still more than three-quarters of a million Canadians relying on EI (Acharya-Tom Yew, 2009a, p. B3). By the beginning of 2010 the Canadian unemployment rate hovered around 8.4 percent with unknown numbers of discouraged workers not included in these numbers (*The Daily*, January 8, 2010, pp. 2–8).

In the United States, the economic picture remained grimmer, with more than 10 percent of workers officially listed as unemployed in 2009 and an estimated 1.7 million workers who had opted out of the labour force (Willis and Schlisserman, 2010). From April 2008 to August 2009, the U.S. unemployment rate almost doubled from 5.0 to 9.7. In March 2010, it remained at this elevated level (U.S. Bureau of Labor Statistics, 2010). Even those fortunate U.S. workers who succeeded in finding employment spent an average of 29.1 weeks locating work—the longest time since records began in 1948 (Willis and Schlisserman, 2010). Analysts estimate that 8.4 million jobs were eliminated from the U.S. economy during The Great Recession and, despite improvements in early 2010, it was clear a deep job crisis remained (*Toronto Star* February 6, 2010, p. B7). Predictably, loss of employment strongly intersected with home foreclosures as the U.S. housing bubble burst in 2009 and 2010, and an estimated 5.8 million homes went into foreclosure (*New York Post*, January 31, 2010).

As the "bad news" accumulated, both Canadian and U.S. governments reacted by investing huge funds to provide bailouts for restructured auto companies and deploying tens of millions of dollars of "stimulus"' money to communities across North America. By the fall of 2009, newspaper accounts were increasingly rosy as commentators suggested the worst had past and that an economic upswing was on the horizon.[17] Yet at the same time, Canadian analysts were forecasting a $50 billion addition to the federal deficit and ongoing deficits for at least the next four years, adding $100 billion to the country's debt. By early 2010, Canada's national debt had increased to $520,705,000,000[18] ($15,338.03 per Canadian)[19] but national debt for Canada's principal trading partner, the United States, had surpassed $12,878,705,000,000 ($41,784.24 per American) (http://www.debtclock.ca; http://www.brillig.com/debt_clock.ca). Not only was the Canadian auto-sector bailout costly (to the tune of $3.2 billion), but also general declines in economic activities very quickly translated into reduced tax revenues and growing unemployment rates meant greater expenditures on the jobless. In the first quarter of 2009, Employment Insurance premium payouts jumped 47 percent from the preceding year (Beltrame, 2009, p. B3; Acharya-Tom Yew, 2009c, p. B3). Financial analysts predicted that by the time the economy regained its composure, $420 billion ($2007) would have been lost in foregone production (Arsenault and Sharpe, 2009, p. 15).

While by early 2010 the Canadian economy might be better off than that of the United States and it may not be headed for the mass unemployment and lengthy breadlines of the 1920s, this is a significant economic bump. It's likely, following the experience of the 1990s recession, employment rates and personal incomes will not rebound for several years—indeed, in the 1990s recession unemployment did not return to its pre-recession rate for almost eight years. The Organisation for Economic Cooperation and Development (OECD)[20] predicts that unemployment in Canada has not yet peaked and will reach toward 10 percent in 2010. Young people 15 to 24 years of age (with an unemployment rate of 16.3 percent in 2009) are expected to be particularly hard hit (Marlow, 2009b, p. B4). Diana Petramala, an economist for T.D. Canada Trust suggests that employment gains in the next several years will be "muted" (CBC *News*, October 9, 2009). And, of course, many workers in resource extraction and manufacturing will never see their jobs return and can reasonably anticipate that their future work may be less well paid and benefited. At the same time, the continued weaknesses in the U.S. economy does not bode well for the Canadian economy and the ballooning Canadian (and U.S.) deficit is very likely to serve as justification for social policy initiatives designed to continue the erosion of social services (including health care) while also further downloading the costs of such services onto individual Canadians and their families. In the midst of the "economic crisis," cutbacks to services along with wage restraints and challenges to social entitlements are likely to be mobilized (Klein, 2007).[21] Indeed, the federal budget of 2010 reflected precisely these policy responses.

Absent from this synopsis of events is the impact on the day-to-day lives of hundreds of thousands of Canadians, an impact that continues to reverberate despite media accounts of a seemingly rosier future. Indeed, when asked, many Canadians have been very clear about the continuing negative effects on their lives. A Pollara poll conducted in December 2009 found that 60 percent of Canadians felt the recession had a negative impact on their family and, of this group, 25 percent felt that the negative impact was major. One in four of those surveyed believed it was somewhat or very likely that someone in their household would lose their job in the next 12 months (as cited in Sauve, 2010, p. 6). Similarly, despite media optimism in the early months of 2010, a Royal Bank of Canada survey reported that 30 percent of Ontarians and 25 percent of Canadians indicate that a member of their household is worried about losing their job or is being laid off. Although improved, 47 percent of Canadians surveyed described the Canadian economy as bad (Acharya-Tom Yew, 2010, p. B5).

Furthermore, for many families, the Great Recession was another blow in a long series of setbacks that date to the 1970s for the current generation and, of course, are an endemic feature of modern capitalism (Stanford, 2008). In the past three decades, for example, there has been a series of economic crises. In the 1980s, unemployment rates hit levels not seen since the Great Depression, interest rates edged beyond 18 percent, and mortgage payments became unmanageable for many families, especially the numerous families who have been directly impacted by the closure of mills, factories, and processing plants across the country. Similarly in 1991 and 1992, 356,000 jobs were lost and the losses were not made up until 1995 (Lochhead and Tipper, 2009, p. 2). In 2001 the so-called dot-com collapse saw many families' investments and pension plans decimated. Indeed, almost imperceptibly, numerous families have been battered by repeated economic crises that have threatened their well-being and financial stability. While these crises have not all mirrored the social and economic collapse of the 1930s, the economic upheaval is very real for many Canadian families—poor, middle-class, and even those who are relatively well off.

ECONOMIC CRISIS AND THE FAMILY LIFE COURSE

In the course of the most recent "crisis," evidence of social turmoil became increasingly apparent in the manufacturing and resource extraction centres across Ontario. Windsor, Oshawa, Hamilton, St. Catharines, and other major cities all roiled as they faced further dramatic reductions in employment and,

frequently, plant closures. For example, St. Catharines, once a hub of auto manufacturing, suffered the steepest job cuts of any Canadian community between
December 2008 and June 2009 as the number of unemployed people soared
by 40 percent. In Ontario, where in 2002 1.1 million workers were employed
in factories, the manufacturing workforce dropped to 778,000 (Scofield,
2009, p. A4). In these battered communities, it is easy to discern the impact on
families as welfare rates escalate along with family breakdown and reports of
family violence. In Niagara, which lost 7,000 manufacturing jobs between
2005 and 2009, between December 2008 and January 2009, 17,000 people
were added to the welfare case load and welfare applications for the first three
months of 2009 were up 25 percent from 2008. Through 2009, the caseload
increased by another 20 percent. As other laid-off workers exhaust their EI
benefits, these figures are predicted to rise still further (Forsyth, 2010, p. 19;
Niagara This Week, 2009, pp. 15, 18).

This is a stark contrast to the 1950s and 60s when young men (and, more
recently, women) could walk out of high school and hope to obtain a fairly
secure job with good wages and benefits in one of many unionized plants or
mills. Today the overwhelming majority of those jobs have vanished while
those that remain are held by workers in their 50s and 60s whose seniority
still guarantees their place at work. Young Canadians who lack postsecondary
credentials have few good job prospects and face the probability of marginalized, part-time, and contract work in the service sector of the economy. They
are often working as salespeople, servers, call centre workers, and caregivers;
necessity means they are frequently working several jobs at the same time or
combining their employment with educational and training efforts. The combined lack of time and money are hardly a promising formula for family formation and do not bode well in terms of family harmony and well-being for
those families that youth do create. In this social context, it is far from surprising that the fastest-growing household type in Canada is the single-person
household and that the number of unattached individuals 18 to 64 years old is
up 50 percent since 1990 (Sauve, 2009, p. 5).

These interrelated changes in the economy and family date back to the
1970s and, of course, beyond. From the 1970s onward, employment in
Canada shifted increasingly away from resource extraction and manufacturing
while service-sector jobs flourished. Increasingly, the traditional male breadwinner family gave way to the **dual-earner family** as more and more
wives/mothers entered the paid labour force. Further, wives have not only
moved into the paid labour force, but also consistently increased their average
work hours (while husbands' average work time has decreased). Of families
with at least one employed parent, the share of families with two parents
working full-time, full year increased from 15 percent in 1980 to 32 percent
in 2005 and was almost identical to the proportion of families where one parent was employed full-time, full year and the other was partially employed.
Meanwhile, the so-called traditional family where one parent was employed

and the other was not declined to about 11 percent of families (LaRochelle-Cote, Gougeon, and Pinard, 2009, p. 8). By this point, women were contributing 45.3 percent of total family employment hours. Significantly, in 2009, for the first time women surpassed men in terms of their proportion of the paid labour force (Marshall, 2009).

Not surprisingly, more earners and more hours of paid work translate into less family time. Between 1986 and 2005, the average time spent with family on a typical working day decreased from 4.2 hours per day to 3.4 hours (Vanier Institute, March 2009a). Predictably, decreased family time is related to increased stress. In dual-earner families where both partners are employed full-time and there are preschool children at home, more than one in three (38 percent) of mothers and almost one-quarter (24 percent) of fathers report **"severe time-crunch stress."** Severe time crunch means that respondents answered yes to questions such as "I feel that I just don't have time for fun anymore." As a direct result of the increased numbers of dual-earner families, more Canadian families are living with stress and its repercussions. Not surprisingly, high time stress is, in turn, related to decreased satisfaction with work–life balance, to a diminished sense of well-being, and to negative physical and psychological health consequences (Marshall, 2009, p. 10).

Viewed from a historical perspective, more and more Canadian parents are spending time in the paid labour force, even when they have young children at home, and a sizeable minority of these parents report they are severely time-stressed by this arrangement. However, only a minority of dual-earner couples, even when they have young children at home, indicate they would prefer fewer hours and less pay. Presumably, despite the hectic pace, it does not seem financially feasible to reduce working hours (Marshall, 2009, pp. 5, 7, 10). Or, as suggested by others, the second earner (along with other strategies such as **moonlighting**), are seen by families as a necessary form of family insurance against job loss during recurrent periods of economic upheaval (Sauve, 2009, p. 8).

Recessions underscore the financial and time pressures experienced in the family. As in most recessions, many families will at the very least lose financial ground as men and women's working hours are reduced. In all likelihood, the majority of families will experience concerns about their current or future economic well-being. After all, both service-sector employers and manufacturing plants often trim scheduled work in the face of reduced demand for either services or product. When a manufacturing plant closes down, the local restaurant may shorten its hours in the hopes of staying open. Indeed, hours worked actually decreased faster than number of jobs from January 2008 to May 2009 (Arsenault and Sharpe, 2009, p. 21). Even public-sector workers in permanent positions, somewhat protected from the immediate upsurge in job loss, will likely face wage restraints and/or reduced hours as municipal, provincial, and federal government agencies struggle to combat growing budget deficits (Robertson, McKenna, and McFarland, 2010, pp. F1, F6, F7).

Of course, actual job loss is particularly disastrous for families. As Henrietta Ross of the Ontario Association of Credit Counsellors comments, "Double income families will become single income families but with a double income debt load" (as cited in Sauve, 2009, p. 7). As recounted in a recent documentary film by Laura Sky and Cathy Crowe (*Home Safe Toronto*), the consequences are varied if uniformly negative. In the film, one man loses his job in Windsor only to be laid off again from his new job in Brampton. His wife must work up to 70 hours a week at a doughnut shop to keep the family afloat and yet they have already been threatened with eviction (Walkom, 2009, p. A23). Of course, the loss or reduction of work has implications far beyond financial.

In some instances, loss of work may produce some beneficial effects on time pressures in the family. A U.S. study of a self-employed, middle-class, childless couple who both lost much of their contract work as a result of the crash of the high-tech bubble in April 2000 reported that the couple started spending more time together as they joined in efforts to find new clients. There were financial pressures—cutting back on weekly restaurant meals, shopping binges, and the use of housecleaners—but there was also time for them to indulge in a modest holiday, pottery lessons, trips to the opera, and times with friends. Not surprisingly, once business picked up their busy and separate lives went back to "normal." While it is useful to emphasize, as discussed in more detail below, in spite of the diversity and complexity of outcomes in periods of economic crisis, it is clear that those who are well-educated, financially well off, and childless are buffered from many of the negative outcomes. Interestingly, even this relatively privileged couple were not unaffected by the upheaval and even as the economy rebounded remained "more doubtful now about their prospects" for a wealthy retirement (Montgomery, 2008, p. 55).

However, the overwhelming message from the extensive literature on unemployment is that job loss carries heavy personal costs—the sense of social isolation, exclusion, stigmatization, and frustration—that may have significant short- and long-term impacts on individuals and their families (Burman, 1988, 1997). In the current recession between October 2008 and April 2009, 406,100 full-time jobs were lost and 43,600 part-time jobs were added to the Canadian labour market (Arsenault and Sharpe, 2009, pp. 20–21). Even if the impact on family income is taken out of the picture, a period of unemployment can "scar" an individual[22] (Arsenault and Sharpe, 2009, p. 20). Once (if) new work is found, the unemployed often continue to struggle with concerns about personal security, worth, and trust. Clearly, such personal pressures inevitably impact on the nature and quality of family relations.

Not only is it difficult to construct and maintain a family—particularly when times are tough—it is increasingly likely that young adults will need to delay marriage and parenthood as well as will have to turn to their family of origin to access support—in the form of both housing and financial resources.

A generation or two previously, when young men graduated from high school and/or decided they were ready for paid work, they could hope to secure well-paid resource extraction and manufacturing jobs. These jobs were sufficiently well paid that it was possible to marry and have children all while supporting the household (including owning a home and having many middle-class conveniences) on one salary (Luxton, 1980). With the loss of jobs in both these sectors due to global competition and increased use of technology (particularly robotization), not only were the number of the **"good" jobs** reduced, but also they increasingly went to the older, experienced workers who had been displaced from other workplaces or were advantaged by **seniority rights**. Where once young men were the norm in factories and mines, today it is not uncommon to find a workforce heavily represented by men in their 50s. In place of manufacturing and resource-extraction jobs have come increasing numbers of service-sector jobs—today, making up about 70 percent of the labour market. In particular, retail and wholesale trade is one of the fastest-growing employment sectors.

It is, of course, precisely the well-paid, benefited, secure, and unionized jobs in the goods-producing sector that have been in decline and have been hard hit in the current recession. Although they represent only 23.5 percent of total employment, job losses in this sector account for almost 90 percent of employment losses (Arsenault and Sharpe, 2009, p. 23). In place are often retail jobs—where workers earn an average of $14 an hour (below the Canadian average of $19.50). Indeed, in 2008, retail sector work officially topped manufacturing as the largest employment sector in Canada. In total, there are 1.8 million retail workers and 1.2 manufacturing workers and, of course, the recession has intensified the trend away from manufacturing jobs (Lewenza, 2009, p. A21). The jobs that are flourishing tend to be part-time, insecure, nonunionized, and poorly paid. Indeed, the current recession, with its glut of workers desperate for work, has allowed some retail employers to press for a reduction in the quality of work. In a recent labour conflict, Zellers, owned by U.S. private equity firm NRDC Equity Partners, asked for $16,000 a year in wage cuts, elimination of severance pay entitlements, and the conversion of more jobs to temporary employment (Lewenza, 2009, p. A21).

Today, young people, especially those without extensive educational credentials, are likely to secure employment only in this relatively low-wage service sector of the economy. For many, working in fast-food outlets, retail stores, and so on is how they first enter the labour market. This early experience, despite its low- or minimum-wage constraints, allows them to contribute, perhaps by covering their personal clothing and entertainment costs, to the family coffers. These McJobs also allow them to shoulder some of the rising costs of postsecondary education. However, the typical service-sector work available to youth is not sufficient to support a family. Despite long hours and even **multiple job holding**,[23] they are unlikely to be able to secure a family wage. Young couples in this situation who do marry and have children are, as a result, much more likely to form families that struggle with poverty and economic insecurity even when they are both participating in the paid labour force.

These difficulties for youth were simply magnified when the economy fell into recession. In July 2009 unemployment among students aged 15 to 24 rose to 21 percent, surpassing all previous levels. Not surprisingly, hard-pressed employers had very little to offer in the way of summer jobs and many youth faced carrying increased educational debt once they entered the labour market on a full-time basis (*CAUT Bulletin*, 2009, pp. A1, A6).

Given this economically pressured scenario, basic steps toward family formation may appear very problematic for numerous Canadian young people. The simple act of buying a home may be difficult since by 2009 average house prices were about $340,000 while average incomes for dual-earner families with children were $81,400 (in constant 2007$) (Sauve, 2010, p. 28). The Canadian Payroll Association survey found that two in three young (18 to 34) first-time home buyers "would be pinched if their pay cheque was delayed by even one week" (as cited in Sauve, 2010, pp. 12–13).

In this context, it is to be expected that increasing numbers of young Canadians continue to live at home as adults or return to their parents' home after a brief sojourn into the costly housing market. These patterns do not preclude significant intimate relationships among young people but increasingly these relationships are common law, do not produce offspring, and do not result in a long-term relationship (see Box 6.1). Meanwhile, the family dynamics in the family of origin are changing. Parents of adult children retain their parental responsibilities long past the previously typical "launch"[24] period and adult children must accept some measure of dependency and control despite their age. The outcomes on individual families are, not surprisingly, mixed. Some parents report that they enjoy the continued presence of their children (Mandell, Wilson, and Duffy, 2008) while others complain about the lack of privacy and continued obligations in their senior years. Certainly some cultural backgrounds are more receptive to adult children continuing to live in the home. However, there is clearly the potential here for familial conflict and unrest, and it's likely that family resources—size of home, total family income, and so on—strongly influence the individual family's ability to cope with any resultant stresses and strains.

BOX 6.1   LOOKING FOR LOVE IN THE MIDST OF A RECESSION

Not surprisingly, when individuals find themselves unemployed, their prospects for "finding someone special" often decline dramatically. Unemployment becomes a stigma that must be carefully managed. According to sociologist and relationship expert Pepper Schwartz, men are careful to avoid revealing that they are unemployed and side-step the issue by explaining they are "on a sabbatical" from work. Such ruses do not negate the problems associated with the costs of dating and "cheap" dates may simply put a potential partner off (Scott, 2009, p. L2). While much of this

(continued)

(*continued*)

discourse focuses on unemployed men's difficulties dating, it is likely that women who are out of work similarly struggle to make a positive impression when searching for a new relationship.

If adults do form a relationship and consider children, it is likely their decisions about child rearing are impacted by economic insecurities. Most Canadians are well aware that the birth rate has dropped considerably since the post-war period. Indeed, the decline in the birth rate is one of the most dramatic changes in Canadian family life in the past five decades. In 1959 there were 116 births per 1,000 women aged 15 to 49 years; by 2002, the rate had dropped to 57 births (Lindsay and Almey, 2006, p. 41). In just 30 years between 1971 and 2001 the numbers of families with children living at home dropped by slightly more than 10 percent while the numbers of families without children at home increased by a comparable amount. Further, the average number of children living at home per family dropped from 1.8 to 1.1 (Lindsay and Almey, 2006, p. 52). While social scientists would be quick to point out the multiple relevant causal factors, especially the baby boomers and the aging of the Canadian population, it is interesting to note that there is a "significant gap between the number of children Canadians say they want to have compared to the number they actually have." In 2006, women (and men) indicated they wanted roughly 2 children (women 2.2 and men 2.1); however, they actually had 1.6 children (Vanier Institute of the Family, February 2009b). Although various factors may enter into the decision to have children, research does suggest that economic factors are likely to play a significant role. Indeed, recent research in Central and Eastern Europe also reveals that various social and economic factors, such as the lack of part-time work options along with inadequate child care options may result in postponed and reduced child rearing (Haskova, 2007). Finally, common sense clearly supports the conclusion that couples will be more inclined, when possible, to postpone child bearing (perhaps indefinitely) if their economic and employment situation appears troubled and uncertain.

THE DIFFERENTIAL IMPACT OF ECONOMIC CRISIS

As evident above, the recent spate of economic crises and the 2008–09 upheaval can be seen to have affected family members throughout the life course—from children cared for by grandparents to parents postponing family formation to seniors struggling with economic insecurities (see Boxes 6.2 and 6.3). However, as much as recessions and depressions impact all family members, they tend to have a differential impact across the Canadian population. A trip in 2009 to Bloor Street in Toronto or through Stanley Park in Vancouver may, aside from the occasional homeless panhandler, leave the impression that affluence and conspicuous consumption are the norm in Canadian society. Yet, at the same time, throughout Canada food banks are pleading for contributions and welfare rolls are skyrocketing. Clearly, economic hard times are not shared equally across the population—lone parents (especially single mothers), children living in poor families, visible minorities, recent immigrants, persons with work-limiting disabilities and Aboriginals living off-reserve continue to bear the brunt of economic hardships (Sauve, 2009, p. 21).

Unfortunately, given the 18-month time lag in the collection of data on low-income patterns, it will be at least "two more years before the crisis is reflected in poverty statistics" (Arsenault and Sharpe, 2009, p. 25). Indeed, the

BOX 6.2   THE HIGH COST OF MOTHERHOOD

Amazingly, the recession of 2008 triggered a dramatic upsurge in the numbers of pregnant women being fired across Ontario. Despite 50 years of Ontario Human Rights Code legislation that bars such discrimination, Ontario's Human Rights Legal Support Centre received a dramatic increase in complaints as employers in all sectors of the economy told pregnant women there would not be a job waiting for them on their return or refused to be tied down to specific return-to-work dates. Since women need 600 hours of work in the 52 weeks prior to applying for maternity leave benefits, loss of employment may jeopardize their benefits. However, not only is a complaint to the Human Rights Commission a lengthy process, but also employers may rationalize their dismissal by suggesting the worker's efforts were shoddy or there is no longer enough work available (Pigg, 2009, p. A1). Needless to say, fear of such economic penalties may cause women to reconsider plans to become pregnant.

Potential parents are certainly cognizant of the costs associated with child bearing and rearing. They know, for example, that women with children are likely to experience a "child penalty" or "motherhood earnings gap." Currently, Canadian women with children earn 12 percent less than those without children, and this gap increases with the number of children (Zhang, 2009, p. 11). Further, child rearing by itself is a costly proposition. The Vanier Institute estimated in 1999 that from newborn to age 18, average child-rearing costs were approximately $160,000 (McCloskey, 1999). More recent U.S. research incorporates the intervening impacts of age and number of children along with family structure (single- or two-parent family). This research still concludes that married-couple, middle-income families will be spending over $200,000 (USD) to raise a single child from birth to age 17 (Folbre, 2008, p. 74). It is likely that economic factors contextualize the decision to have children and that this impact is intensified in especially periods of economic upheaval.

In sum, a wide variety of research suggests that child-bearing decisions are strongly influenced by unemployment and economic uncertainty (Crompton and Keown, 2009, p. 48). Similarly, once the children are born, patterns of employment, inadequate family finances, and economic insecurities (along with inadequate social services) may alter the ways in which those children are cared for. Indeed, whether or not parents will take leave and how long is directly influenced by their financial situation. More than 40 percent of new parents in 2006 could not take maternity leave because their financial situation did not allow it and 81 percent of those parents who did take leave indicated they would have stayed at home longer if they could have afforded it (Beaupre and Cloutier, 2007).

The difficulties that new families currently face in the employment market may also figure as an important ingredient in the upsurge in the numbers of grandparents who are assuming, formally or informally, parental responsibilities for their grandchildren. Even in an intact young family, fathers and mothers employed in the service sector are likely to not earn adequate funds to allow for paid childcare services in a licensed centre (McKinley, 2010). Part-time, shift, and on-call work, all of which is common in the new fields of employment, all lend themselves to reliance on grandparents for all or some of the childcare needs. Young, one-parent families are in even more dire straits in regards to both income and consistent time schedules and, once again, one or several grandparents may find themselves providing considerable childcare.[25] Even work–travel requirements—relocating to another province in pursuit of work, a lengthy and unpredictable commute to work, or out-of-town work-related travel—may all result in reliance on grandparents for childcare. Finally, there may be direct financial

(continued)

(continued)

consequences for the parents of adult children. A recent survey found that 60 percent of seniors are providing an average of $3,675 per year to their adult children and 25 percent of these seniors are finding this an economic burden. At the same time, a minority of these sandwich-generation boomers are also spending an average of $6,000 on their aged parents. Not surprisingly, being caught in the middle exacts a financial toll in terms of reduced consumption, cancelled travel, and fewer retirement savings and, in turn, contributes to increased reports of stress (Trichur, 2010a, pp. B1, B2).

In some instances, grandparents are even required to take over parental responsibilities for their adult children. Economic hard times and the lack of future prospects likely contribute to various personal difficulties—alcohol and drug addiction, mental health issues—that often render young parents unable to provide adequate care for their children and result in permanent or short-term custody being awarded to grandparents. In sum, particularly those living on the front lines of the economic crisis may find that their familial roles—as parent, child, grandparent—stray far from traditional social expectations.

Of course, economic pressures may not only expand the familial roles of Canadian seniors, but also jeopardize their financial well-being. At present, the majority of Canadian workers (66 percent) lack a workplace pension and nearly one-third of all Canadian families lack any pension savings (Whittington, 2010, p. A6). However, even the fortunate minority of older Canadians who are pensioned saw their investments fall in value by 20 percent or more through the fall and spring of 2009 (Lochhead and Tipper, 2009, p. 1; Yakabuski, 2009). The investment of pension funds in the stock market necessarily meant that the dramatic loss of value in the stocks was mirrored in the decline of the value of pensions. In particularly dire circumstances, some Canadians watched as their former employers entered bankruptcy and the value of their pensions dropped precipitously. One female retiree interviewed by the *Toronto Star*, said that after 30 years as a customer service representative at Nortel Networks Corp. and two years of retirement, she now was faced with a serious erosion of her pension benefits. For this pensioner, the impact of the recession was absolutely a family issue. She explicitly connected her pension to the financial support of her husband (who did not have a pension of his own) and her adult children, "I was counting on that pension to keep us going—and the kids. ... This will seriously impact our family" (Marlow, 2009a, pp. B1, B2).

After the fall of 2008, many senior Canadians in their 50s and early 60s who had not yet retired needed to re-evaluate their ability to sustain retirement and many of those in their 60s and older who had already retired needed to "tighten" their belt or look for supplemental income from some form of paid employment. At least as significant as these developments was the growing sense of insecurity about pensions. In 2009 the Supreme Court of Canada ruled that companies were allowed to move monies from a defined benefit plan (an increasingly uncommon pension plan that guaranteed pensions at a specific level of benefit) to cover their obligations under a newer defined contribution plan (an increasingly common pension plan in which the company guarantees only to contribute a specific level of funds to an employee's pension plan and in no way guarantees a specific pay-out in the event of retirement). This decision along with the decision to allow companies to use pension money to pay themselves for "reasonable" pension administration costs, concerned many labour advocates who argued that there needs to be a summit of provincial premiers to develop government legislation that protects workers' pension rights and ensures that Canadians do not

(continued)

have to face retirement with no or inadequate pensions (*Toronto Star,* August 3, 2009, p. B2). Most recently, in early 2010, even the once "gold standard" pensions earned by members of the federal civil service—pensions that are not only relatively generous and secure but also inflation protected—have been identified as possible targets for federal deficit reduction (Whittington, 2010, p. A6).

It takes very little imagination to sketch out the implications of inadequate or insecure pensions for older Canadian families. From 1990 to 2007, bankruptcies among Canadians 55 and older increased by 541 percent and recent estimates suggest that one in seven men and one in five women 65 and over lives in poverty. Visions of "Freedom Fifty-Five" travel and leisure, especially for middle-class seniors, are being supplanted by economic worries and even forced re-entry into the labour market. Ironically, the poorest seniors are buffered from some of this economic pressure since it is the wealthiest 80 percent of Canadian households who experience a drop in their annual income when they reach age 65 (Prince, 2009, p. 6).

Many fast-food restaurants and giant retailers are happy to provide low-wage, **unbenefited work** to senior servers, cooks, and greeters and many other employers embrace the economic benefits of hiring a senior who will be working part-time, on contract, and/or as a consultant. While much of this work for seniors may be far from the retirement previously envisioned, searching for and securing some form of paid work may become increasingly the norm in segments of Canadian senior families. In 2005, prior to the pension fund meltdown of 2008, 17 percent of retirees returned to paid work after their first retirement and almost half (48 percent) of these returnees cited financial considerations as their reason for returning to work (Statistics Canada, 2006, p. 6). Without income, having and retaining a family home, participating in many family events, assisting family members, and so on may be impossible. Fulfilling familial roles—caring for a spouse with dementia or providing homecare to a grandchild—may all hinge on some measure of economic security and resources. For example, owning a car may make the difference between being able to consistently access community resources (such as caregiver support) or not. Predictably, the inability to fulfil familial roles may translate into profound unhappiness and stress within families.

BOX 6.3   INCREASED PRESSURES ON GRANDPARENTS IN "TOUGH TIMES"

In a recent letter to "Ellie," an advice columnist featured in the *Toronto Star*, a grandparent lamented, "Whatever happened to the so-called 'freedom' of retirement years?" She or he goes on to say that part-time work is now a necessity in order to keep afloat financially, but at the same time there are onerous "grandparent duties" to be juggled. Since their adult children married much later than they did and then quickly had children (before it was too late), the "children" are now in their mid-30s managing two careers and an enormous mortgage. Grandma and grandpa are needed for babysitting, for pick up from day care, for co-signing loans, and for just general ongoing family support. The letter writer concludes, "I'm exhausted! And, not getting to the travel and tranquility I'd expected." (*Toronto Star,* September 17, 2009, p. L3). Such frustration can certainly lead to resentment and poison familial relationships.

most recent (2007) statistics convey the lowest level of poverty since the beginning of the series in 1976. However, since it is clear from past research that poverty and unemployment rates parallel one another, it is reasonable to assume that the current economic upheaval will have a dramatic and prolonged impact on the economically marginal. Analysts estimate that poverty rates are already hovering around 12 percent and research indicates food bank use increased 18 percent from March 2008 to March 2009. Given that it took 18 years for the poverty rates to crawl out of the trough created by the recession of the early 1990s, the legacy of the Great Recession may echo for many years (Sauve, 2010, pp. 18, 19).

Of course, poverty itself is not randomly distributed amongst the population; specific segments of the population are particularly susceptible to low income and will likely be hard pressed in today's "bad times." In Toronto, for example, poverty rates among racialized groups increased by 360 percent between 1980 and 2000, while they declined 28 percent among the nonracialized population (Galabuzi, 2007, p. A17). Not surprisingly, it is the racialized segment of Toronto's population that is criticized for its excess of lone-parent families and unruly children and youth. Families cut off from economic resources do not tend to fare well. After all, simply having a job "is a source of livelihood, identity and sense of belonging" (Galabuzi, 2007, p. A17). Not having a job, facing discrimination in the pursuit of employment or having access only to jobs that are inadequately compensated and insecure jeopardizes the foundation of society, "Hope lives in the belief that there can be real opportunity for [youth] in the future, and parents participating fully in the lives of their children, instead of being away at multiple jobs at all hours of the day just to make ends meet" (Galabuzi, 2007, p. A17).

Children and youth who are growing up in economically marginalized home—among lone parents, immigrant, **visible-minority** or Aboriginal parents and in low-income families—are clearly likely to feel the stress of being marginalized in our consumer society. Currently (2006) 760,000 children under 18 years of age (11.3 percent of all Canadian children) live below the Statistics Canada low-income cut-offs. A whopping 40 percent of these children are living in a lone-mother family (Statistics Canada, 2008). Predictably, such families are particularly subject to economic fluctuations. By definition, they typically have fewer economic resources and, unlike couple-based families, are completely reliant on the efforts of one parent—a parent who as a woman is subject to the gender bias of the employment market. In this context, it's not surprising that lone-parent families (the majority of which are woman-headed) shoulder one of the heaviest debt burdens ($28.32 per $100) of any family type in Canada. They are surpassed only by "young" two-parent families (headed by someone under 35) who stagger with $39.40 worth of debt for every $100 of assets (up 17.2 percent between 1999 and 2005) (Statistics Canada, 2006, pp. 5, 6).

These families are the ones most likely to be tormented with an immediate economic shortfall when the economy hits a bump—they are the ones who will find themselves caught between paying the rent and feeding the children. Currently 13 percent of Canadian households with children under 6 years of age confront food insecurity. In the current economic upheaval, while inflation has been low (about 1 percent), food prices have been an anomaly, growing by 10 percent between March 2008 and 2009. As a result, poor families are faced with the necessity of stretching their already overextended food budget (Lochhead and Tipper, 2009, p. 1).

Clearly, the groups identified above are also more likely to number among the "official" poor—they receive low incomes and/or are completely reliant on government transfer payments, including social welfare. However, it is not just poor families that are suffering in economic upheavals. Analysts are remarking on a growing divergence in the Canadian class structure. Put simply, the rich are getting richer and the rest of us are losing ground.[26] In 2004, the average earnings of the richest 10 percent of Canada's families raising children were 82 times that earned by the poorest 10 percent (Yalnizyan, 2007, p. 3). In 2005, the wealthiest one-fifth (quintile) of Canadians owned 69.2 percent of the total net worth of all Canadians; the remaining four-fifths shared the remaining 30 percent. While the poor's (lowest quintile) proportion of total wealth remained the same from 1999 to 2005, the middle quintiles (2, 3, and 4) all experienced some erosion in their net worth (Statistics Canada, 2006, pp. 5, 6, 9). Other data suggest that from 1990 to 2007 all but the richest fifth of Canadian families have seen their percentage share of after-transfer and after-income-tax incomes decrease—particularly, the lower middle and middle fifth, while the wealthiest fifth experienced a 2.5 percentage point increase so that they now earn 39.7 percent of the total incomes generated by all families in the economy. The remaining four-fifths of Canadian families share approximately 60 percent of yearly incomes (Sauve, 2010, p. 19; Yalnizyan, 2007).

This differential impact on the middle and lower classes was reinforced through the recessions of the 1980s and 1990s, with the wealthiest two quintiles experiencing only a 3.0 and 5.1 percent drop in average market income while the lowest and second lowest quintiles experienced 37.8 and 71.4 percent decreases respectively. While mitigated somewhat by Canada's[27] progressive transfer payments and taxation, it remains clear that even when considering after-tax income, it was the lower and middle quintiles that tended to experience the largest declines between 1980 and 1983 and 1989 and 1992. Since "there is no reason to believe that the current recession will be different in terms of the distributional impact of income losses," it seems likely that the gap between the well-to-do and other Canadians will widen and the lower and middle classes will be particularly hard hit (Arsenault and Sharpe, 2009, p. 14).[28]

Evidence of the unpleasant economic pressures confronting many middle-class families are suggested by recently revealed patterns of growing family indebtedness. The median debt load for family units rose 38 percent between 1999 and 2005 and families shouldered larger mortgages (reflecting increased housing costs), greater credit card and instalment debt (up 58 percent between 1999 and 2005), and dramatically larger line-of-credit debt (Statistics Canada, 2006, pp. 5, 6, 9). Put simply, Canadians on average have been spending more and saving less. For the past 20 years household debt has been increasing annually by 4.7 percent (CGA, 2009, p. 5). Between 1990 and 2006, average household incomes rose by only 11.6 percent while spending increased by 24.4 percent. By the end of 2008, average Canadian household savings were 3 percent of disposable income, down from 13 percent in 1990; in the United States annual savings dropped from 7 percent to 1 percent in the same time period (Lochhead and Tipper, 2009, p. 3; Sauve, 2009, p. 10).

While the wealthiest one-fifth of families likely remains insulated from these patterns, growing numbers of Canadian families are faced with increased economic insecurity—unable to respond when confronted by an unexpected expense or any loss of paid work hours. After all, it is not the poor who are taking out mortgages, getting credit cards, or opening lines of credit—it is typically the middle classes; in periods of economic recession, loss of employment now weighs heavily on those families in the debt-ridden middle. Not surprisingly, many families have embraced savings and between 2008 and 2009 there was a 50 percent increase in family savings. However, numerous families are still mired in debt and between 2008 and 2009 bankruptcies increased by 26 percent, while mortgage delinquencies were up by 50 percent and credit card delinquencies grew by 40 percent (Sauve, 2010, pp. 10, 11).

This pattern of increased financial insecurity is also reflected in a recent survey of family finances by the Canadian Payroll Association. Fifty-nine percent of Canadians indicated they would be in financial trouble if their paycheque was delayed by one week. Not surprisingly, 72 percent of lone parents answered that this delay would have a serious impact. Further, half of Canadians are able to save only 5 percent of their income for retirement, although 10 percent is recommended. Suggestions that these Canadians should cut back and find ways to economize often ignore the time/income pressures experienced in middle- and lower-income families. Likely reflecting the recessionary times, one-third of Canadians surveyed said they were trying to save more money than a year ago but had been unable to do so and another 42 percent are not even trying to save extra money. As one woman commented, she could economize by making home-made meals every day but, given when she gets home from work, this would mean that dinner would always be late and her baby's bedtime schedule would be negatively impacted (Boesveld, 2009, p. L4; Acharya-Tom Yew, 2009b, p. B1). Many families frantically and precariously juggle their finances so that they can somehow manage time for their partners, personal time, and time for their children. The net result, however, may be growing debt and living paycheque to paycheque.

The reasons behind this financial insecurity and increased indebtedness (total average household debt is now equal to a record 140 percent of disposable household income and could be up to 160 percent by the end of 2012) likely has many roots, including the pervasiveness of consumer culture (Sauve, 2010, p. 13). However, it is not the case that Canadian families are spending and not working. As noted, more family members are employed and many are working longer hours. However, this intensification of families' involvement in paid employment does not match the significant jumps in educational and health care insurance premium expenditures. Between 2000 and 2009, out-of-pocket expenditures for medical care and health services increased by 81 percent (Sauve, 2010, p. 22). Average undergraduate tuition in Canada increased by 165.1 percent from 1991/92 to 2007/08 and this increase is dwarfed by the increases in the costs of enrolling in professional programs such as engineering, law, and dentistry (CAUT Almanac, 2008–2009, p. 38). While medical care is a necessity and postsecondary education may seem a wise investment for a family, these kinds of dramatic increased costs necessarily cut into the family budget. Further, the wages of hourly paid and salaried employees (controlling for inflation) are at basically the same level in 2008 as they were in the mid-1990s and the median "real earnings of Canadians barely increased" from 1980 to 2005 (Lochhead and Tipper, 2009, p. 2; Sauve, 2009, p. 9). Finally, some responsibility must rest with the financial institutions, retailers, and even the government that have encouraged middle-class Canadians to live beyond their means and to save the economy by spending.

As retailers and financial institutions proffer low-interest loans or mortgages and defer interest payments on purchases for one or two years, consumers may easily become overextended. In the event of unemployment, reduced hours, or short and long-term layoffs, the consequences for family lives may be harsh. Yet the current recession has meant exactly this kind of crisis for Canadians working in manufacturing and resource sectors and for those who are self-employed. Abruptly, the good times are a thing of the past and many families are left scrambling to pay their bills or just keep up with payments. For example, the extraordinary high rates of youth unemployment throughout the summer of 2009 mean many families may now need to help shoulder tuition and living expenses while young people are also burdened by ever more debt (Javed, 2009, p. G12).

The impact cuts a wide swath. While poorer families (those with incomes under $30,000) are twice as likely to "struggle to keep their personal debt under control," almost one-third (31 percent) of those who are relatively affluent (those with incomes of more than $100,000) are in the same boat (Sauve, 2009). Periods of economic upheaval simply underscore their fragility. As the executive director of a nonprofit credit counselling service recently commented,

"People are looking for help. It's a high-stress time for them. Some are getting calls four and five times a day. They're getting threats from collection agencies and they don't know where to turn" (quoted by Acharya-Tom Yew, 2009d, p. B1). Not "Happy Days" indeed.

Learning[29] from other Periods of Economic Upheaval

There have been numerous examinations by social analysts of the impact of economic hard times on families. No era resonates more profoundly with these researchers than the Great Depression. This decade of economic decline, from 1929 to 1939, has become the principle standard against which other periods of economic upheaval are measured. And doubtless this was a period of Canadian history that blighted the lives of hundreds of thousands of Canadians and resonated for generations. At the height of the crisis, one in two wage earners in Canada were receiving some kind of relief and one in five Canadians (one in three in Montreal and other big cities) were dependent on charity and public relief. Although the average yearly income was less than $500.00 a year, the official poverty line for a family of four was twice this amount—in other words, the average Canadian family was impoverished. Families patched and repatched clothing and scraped by on the cheapest foods until empty cupboards and their children's hunger forced them to face the humiliation of going to the local public relief office. In Montreal in 1933 a family of four whom inspectors deemed "destitute" would receive a weekly relief voucher for $4.58. In that harsh economic climate, it is not surprising that visible minorities and recent immigrants, traditional social scapegoats, were much more likely to figure among the economically deprived and socially marginalized. For example, Chinese in Saskatoon in 1933 were denied public relief and were reduced to scavenging from back alleys for bones and kitchen waste (Berton, 1990, p. 184). At the same time (in an interesting parallel to current economic realities), anyone who was lucky enough to have a steady job and/or a secure financial situation might be living quite well, since the cost of living actually decreased over this time period (Berton, 1990, pp. 9, 13, 15, 507). In short, the social realities of the Great Depression were sharply divided along racial and social class lines.

The down-trodden and marginalized quickly gained the attention of social analysts in this period. There was concern that high rates of unemployment amongst men would result in a loss of authority and power for men in their families and, as a result, an erosion of patterns of family and public order. There was, for example, ample evidence that many men, unable to support themselves or their families, had become transients—in 1932 an estimated 100,000 men were "riding the rails" in search of employment and cities were coping with increasing numbers of homeless "girls" as well as men (Berton, 1990, p. 137). In the context of increasing political unrest, fears of rising Bolshevism, and unstable municipal governments, there was concern that the basic fabric of society, including families, was self-destructing. As Pierre Berton observes in his definitive discussion of Canada's Great Depression, "In other circumstances, they [transients] might have stayed put, married early and settled down. Now they were off on what used to be called 'the open road'" (1990, p. 148).

Popular media attempted to counter the pessimistic view held by a "great many people" that "marriage is . . . a hopeless adventure" with stories of young lovers who marry and rise above their impoverishment. However, the realities were much harsher. Marriage for many Canadians was hard to manage given inadequate and uncertain employment. Having children meant the loss of employment for the wife and intensified deprivations. Families were routinely forced to move from one site to another in the search for affordable accommodation; in the absence of public health care, illness or disease among family members might easily result in unbearable burdens on the family—including homelessness. The short- or long-term outcomes might be the official or unofficial breakdown of the family as husbands left to find work elsewhere and wives returned to their parental home (Berton, 1990, p. 184).

Not surprisingly, in this context social activists quickly identified birth control as an important response to family troubles. Alvin Kaufman, a well-to-do Kitchener manufacturer, realized that many of his laid-off workers had large families and could not survive on public relief. In common with many birth-control advocates of the time, he was also concerned that the poorer classes were reproducing at an alarming rate and threatened to overwhelm the "better people" at the top. He offered his employees the choice between sterilization or fitted diaphragms and received a stunningly positive response. As a result, he launched a birth-control crusade that included pioneering clinics in Hamilton, Windsor, and Toronto and a coast-to-coast system for distribution of jelly, nozzles, and condoms. Predictably, these efforts ignited a firestorm of controversy and sharp criticism from various religious organizations. Ultimately, birth-control would not be officially legalized until the 1960s but public attitudes towards it softened and birth control devices became more easily available (Berton, 1990, pp. 367–375). In short, the Depression and the unsupportable economic burden large families put on breadwinners contributed to not only reduced family sizes but also a reframing of the relationship between parent and child. As "unwanted" children became increasingly uncommon, fathers and, in particular, mothers would experience profound changes in their parental roles.

Of course, talk of birth control and shifting roles for mothers spurred concern from some conservative analysts that the basic family structure was under attack. Predictably, for example, in impoverished families where women were able to locate employment or some form of paid activities and increase their role in the economic support of the family, they did indeed strengthen their overall position in the family. However, while working wives might have improved their family status, they did not in most instances become a "dominant partner" and husbands, at best, helped out with household and child care responsibilities rather than taking them over. Even if the wife did not shoulder new economic responsibilities, an unemployed husband might mean a shift in family authority patterns—particularly when his role was based on his provider role more than "love and respect." If the pre-Depression family was strongly patriarchal and the man's familial position was directly linked to his provider role, loss of employment might disrupt the husband's traditional prerogatives. In sum, the impact of husband's unemployment was complex and depended, among many things, on his attitude toward his family, his own morale, his ongoing relationship with his wife, and his willingness to help family members out. While changes occurred as a result of the loss of the provider role, other factors such as the wife's willingness to respect her husband and her husband's emotional connection with family members might mitigate any profound upheaval in husband–wife and parents–children relationships (Wandersee, 1981, pp. 107–109).

Other research suggests that well-organized families, despite dramatic effects from the Depression, remained well organized while disorganized families only deteriorated through the course of the economic upheaval. Well-organized families were defined in this research as uniting in family objectives and ideals, subordinating personal ambitions for family goals, locating satisfaction of personal interests within the family group and an acceptance of assigned and complementary roles. In many ways, this is the iconic "traditional" family (as eulogized in The Godfather and numerous other films): father dominated in economic matters, mother dominated in the household, and together they controlled the children. Even if the mother was compelled by economic conditions to take over paid employment obligations, the basic structure was not disrupted and family roles simply adapted to the new circumstances. In short, analysts suggest that families that functioned well prior to the Depression continued to do so despite the dramatic decline in their standard of living and a readjustment of their familial roles. If the woman was forced to take employment in response to her husband's loss of work, it was seen as a temporary solution while the traditional male-headed family pattern remained (Wandersee, 1981, pp. 109–110).

However, clearly not all family members were equally impacted and some might find the economic upheaval particularly difficult to manage. Men who lost their employment were particularly troubled since they lost their family provider role, their prestige (in and out of the family), and their daily routines. To the degree to which men responded negatively or rigidly to these changes, the Depression-era family might experience considerable stress and the family might suffer as a consequence. Case histories from the Depression era suggest that men (often foreign-born or first-generation immigrants) who insisted on maintaining a rigid patriarchal system might find their actual loss of power when their wife was employed intolerable and, as a result, they might withdraw from the family or even desert it.

According to the research of C. Wight Bakke, this outcome might flow from a multi-stage process. In the first stage, the husband's unemployment necessitates the family's economic decline. In the next stage, if the woman gains employment, the woman starts to assume greater responsibility for the management and distribution of income, while also maintaining her role in domestic chores. In this context, discouraged at his lack of success in seeking work, the husband withdraws from parental responsibilities, leaving this to his wife. In the third stage, while still shouldering her traditional domestic role, the wife takes over management and planning for the family. The husband remains only the titular head of the family and is, in effect, absent from the power relationships within the family. Older children may enter the labour force and their economic input allows them to challenge the mother's authority. By this point, the family is, according to Bakke, seriously disorganized— especially since there is no clear leadership. The mother's authority will not be supported by the community and her economic contribution to the family is likely much lower than that previously earned by her husband or currently by her sons (and possibly her daughters). Further, as long as the husband remains in the home, most wives are unwilling to usurp his token authority and, if the husband abandons the family, adult children may challenge the woman's leadership role (Wandersee, 1981, pp. 111–112).

This diverse research, much of it working from the traditional premise that all families will have "leaders," suggests that the Great Depression took a clear toll of families—leading to stress, tension and, likely, violence. In terms of long-term implications, analysts suggest that the role of employed women in Depression-Era families—although it was far from liberating for the women involved—set the stage for families in the 1950s and 60s (particularly working-class families) to accept the possibility of wives working outside the home. Indeed, the events of the 1920s—the movement of women into the workforce and the declining birth rate, both functioned to broaden women's horizons and improve their independence within marriage. However, the prevailing ideologies about marriage and motherhood as the only source of happiness for women retained much of their strength. And the increase in the numbers of young men during the Depression forced by their economic circumstances to postpone marriage meant that there were decreased opportunities for women to find a husband and familial happiness. At the same time, decreased familial resources meant it was less likely that higher education for daughters would win parental support (Wandersee, 1981, p. 115).

The images of families fraught with tensions as their traditional roles— husband, wife, even child—are caught up in dramatic social change are far from uniformly negative. As noted above, to some degree the stage was set for a more companionate family in which men and women shared more equally in family responsibilities and in which women were assured more independence. Other commentators argued that during the Depression the family assumed greater importance as family members looked for their entertainment in the home, listening to the radio, and through dint of necessity working together on labour-extensive household work required by a lower standard of living (Wandersee, 1981, p. 115). As so artfully captured by the 1970s television show The Waltons, the more idealized Depression-era family was marked by intense family interactions and loyalties, shared hardships providing the basis for mutual respect and support. In many respects, this is the image of the family "as a haven in a heartless world" that gained such notoriety in sociology 30 years later.

However, even this more pleasant image of family lives necessitates trends that might be questioned by contemporary Canadian families. In The Waltons, for example, grandma, ma, and the girls take on the domestic tasks while the grandpa, pa, and the boys are off doing the physical, outside work. Children of both sexes are expected to grow up quickly so that they can contribute to the family's need for domestic and paid work, but it is particularly young women whose lives are constrained by the centrality of marriage, the family, and domestic duties (Wandersee, 1981, p. 116). The challenge to gendered families posed by the "roaring twenties'' with its flappers and suffragists was pushed into the background by the sheer necessities of the 1930s and the prospects for women's emancipation within families and in the larger society did not resume its momentum until the 1960s.

The period from the 1960s to the present has been far from tranquil. In the mid-1970s the Japanese economy was buffeted by a sharp downturn as a result of oil price increases and structural changes. Here once again there are interesting links between economic crises and changes in familial lives and gender roles. Although throughout the postwar era Japanese society was premised on a traditional male-income earner, female-housewife family, the economic upheaval was reflected in the emergence of new family forms as the total fertility rate decreased from 2.1 in 1970 to 1.29 in 2004, the marriage rate plummeted from 10 in 1970 to 5.9 in 2003, and divorce increased from below 1 percent to 2.25 percent during the same period. As Takeda Hiroko concludes, "By the time that the economic downturn had been unequivocally acknowledged in the mid-1990s, changing families both in terms of forms and ideas had become an established fact" (2008, p. 199). In the new millennium, fewer Japanese tend to form families and if they do so the commitment comes later in life. Family formation is no longer seen as a social imperative and there has been growing concern about the "individualization of the family" as exemplified by the "parasitic singles"—those single Japanese in their 20s and 30s who continue to live at home (Hiroko, 2008).

In Canada, the early 1980s were marked by another economic bump. In 1981 the global economy headed into its most serious recession since the great Depression. Almost a half million long-term Canadian workers lost their jobs between 1981 and 1984, and the unemployment rate pushed into double digits. Plant closures accounted for almost half of these losses (Picot and Wannell, 1988, p. 6). In 1985 14 percent of men aged 25 to 44 did not have jobs (up from 9 percent in 1975) (Lindsay, 1987, p. 13). In Hamilton, Ontario, 25 percent of manufacturing jobs were eliminated and many other workers were confronted with pay cuts, greater work insecurity, and more unpredictable schedules (Luxton and Corman, 2001).

The lived realities of this period are, once again, embedded in these statistics. Meg Luxton and June Corman's widely acclaimed examination of Hamilton steelworkers' lives during and after this period, reveals some of these experiences. One stay-at-home woman, for example, who was married with three children under 10, lives through six months of strike in 1981 without any income. When the strike is resolved, her husband is laid off. Faced with no savings and a mortgage to pay, the family rents out their home and moves into a two-room basement flat. The woman's comment, "It was hell" clearly sums up the impact on family relationships (Luxton and Corman, 2001, p. 56).

This period of economic instability also helped to ensure that more and more Canadian families would deploy two wage earners so that periods of reduced income could be somewhat more manageable. One Stelco wife whose husband was laid off in the early 1980s found that they had to rely not only on her income but also handouts from her mother to simply make ends meet. A survey of 234 steelworkers who experienced indefinite lay-offs in the early 1980s found that 83 percent of their partners had paid employment for part or all of the lay-off period. A full 50 percent of women who had formerly been full-time homemakers entered the paid labour force and only 17 percent of women whose partners were on indefinite lay-off continued as full-time homemakers (Luxton and Corman, 2001, pp. 135–136). Necessarily, this movement of women into paid employment contributed to the ongoing renegotiation of family roles—a process rife with possibilities for conflict and frustration.

Even decisions about numbers of children in the family were increasingly conditioned by the family's financial needs and the pressures to have a two-earner family. Women in Luxton and Corman's study reveal that even though they might have wanted more children, couples decided to stop at one or two in order to manage the woman's paid employment and its implications for home life (2001, p. 143).

Finally, the crisis of the early 1980s, while pushing many women into paid work, also ensured that the gains that a few women had made in terms of gaining access to the well-paid, unionized jobs at Stelco[30] and in other industrial settings were eroded. The gains between January 1978 and January 1980 when the number of women in Ontario manufacturing increased by 24 percent were almost completely eliminated by the economic depression and lay-offs in the early 80s (Luxton and Corman, 2001, p. 125). As one woman commented, "'Women are the shock troops for capitalism. We have to absorb all the ups and downs of capitalist profit-making, and when times are hard, women get hit the hardest'" (quoted in Luxton and Corman, 2001, p. 150). The loss of these gains is particularly significant in light of the growing numbers of Canadian families that are female-headed, lone-parent families (currently exceeding 1 million families) (Statistics Canada, 2009).

WELLAND, ONTARIO: A CASE STUDY[31]

Norene Pupo, June Corman, and I are currently researching the impact of economic upheaval on workers and their communities in Welland, Ontario. As part of this research, we have recently completed 54 in-depth interviews with unionized and nonunionized workers from a plant that is relocating to Mexico. While the full analysis of this data will not be available for several years, it is possible to identify several of the outstanding themes, particularly as they apply to workers' families.

Welland provides a stark example of the impact of deindustrialization on families and communities. No doubt, there are hundreds of other towns that might also be targeted. Certainly in Ontario, Hamilton, Windsor, Oshawa, Smith Falls, and others have been shaken by the closure of key manufacturing plants and substantial job losses. Across Canada, not only manufacturing but also resources extraction employment has been subject to dramatic turbulence. For example, the forestry and fishing industries have been "on the ropes" on both the West and East coasts, and throughout the interior of British Columbia many forestry towns struggle to survive.

In this national context, Welland is both typical and, appropriately, individual. Founded in the late 1700s as a transportation hub that combines water (the Seaway), rail, and road alternatives as well as proximity to the U.S. market, the small city (currently 50,000) thrived in the 1960s and 70s as its manufacturing sector flourished. The 1980s recession brought decline but it was with the turn of the century that the economic news became unrelentingly negative for many Welland residents. One after another, local manufacturers— Heninges, Atlas Steel, Stelpipe—closed and/or laid off workers. In December 2008, after an apparently successful negotiation of a new contract, a major U.S.–based manufacturer abruptly announced that it was closing its Welland plant, relocating the plant work to Mexico, and concentrating its efforts at its U.S.–based plants. This was the demise of the last large manufacturing plant in the city and meant the loss of 800 unionized and nonunionized jobs. While smaller manufacturers clung to life and local politicians touted the emergence of new, small manufacturing sites, it was clearly the end of an era.

When we talked with displaced workers from this plant, it was clear that family relations immediately and then persistently figured in their concerns. Spouses were typically the first to be told when news of the closure was announced at the plant; husbands and wives worried about the impact on their spouses as dual-earner families often devolved to single-earner families, at least in the short run. Almost all the interviewees lived in dual-earner families. Men and women spoke touchingly about the strength and support their partners had provided and yet they also worried about the hidden costs of the pressures and fears generated by an uncertain economic future and the sudden necessity to become the major breadwinner. In many instances, the employed partner, typically female, needed to work more hours in order to try to meet the family's financial needs, and many combined several part-time jobs.

While it was clear that the marriages and common-law unions at the base of these families were far from perfect, they were generally valued. Only a small fraction of individuals took this abrupt change in their working lives as an opportunity to re-evaluate and then leave their partners. Similarly, the opportunity to leave behind meddlesome in-laws or a claustrophobic "small town" mentality barely surfaced in the interviews. When the going got tough, it was indeed the immediate family, the extended family, and then friends who were there with emotional and financial support.

Some families were particularly in need of precisely this support system. Workers with young children were especially concerned about their future financial well-being and many indicated they were already having to "cut back" on family activities. In a society premised so heavily on cash expenditures for children—to pay for extracurricular activities at school, to purchase fashionable goods, to celebrate holidays and special events—it is not surprising that these parents were frustrated and worried at having to "deprive" their children of a middle-class[32] lifestyle. In divorced or separated families, workers expressed concerns about losing contact with their noncustodial children if they were forced to search for work outside the area. Similarly, workers worried about not being there for their aging parents (many had parents and other extended family members residing in the Niagara area) if they too were forced to move their family in the search for employment.

While this may seem an inevitable cost of the contemporary capitalist economy, it is a bitter pill for many individuals who grew up in the Welland area. This is an array of communities where family roots often run back through several generations, where large immigrant families conveyed an extended family-like atmosphere in neighbourhoods; where family members often lived on the same street and celebrated family events together in the ethnic halls that dot the city; and where fathers, brothers, brother-in-laws, and cousins often worked side by side in the town's factories. Despite their hopes that their children would be able to continue to live in Niagara, many parents realize they may have to accept that this is now an unrealistic dream.

With unemployment rates in the Niagara region rising into double digits (10.5 percent) by the summer of 2009, the competition for even "'bad'" jobs is intense (Brownlee, 2009, p. 10). A recent job fair at a newly opened hardware chain store attracted a lineup of hundreds of hopeful job applicants. As elsewhere in Canada, call centres have emerged as one of the new employers but they are particularly mobile and quick to uproot in search of cheaper labour costs and, as a result, the employment they offer is not only often tedious and poorly paid but also unreliable.

Other job seekers are turning to the growing demand for personal support workers in the burgeoning retirement communities in the Niagara peninsula but this work, with its physical and emotional demands and relatively low pay, is far from a satisfactory replacement for the industrial jobs that have disappeared.

Given the absolute dearth of well-paid manufacturing jobs in the area, many workers clearly feel torn between maintaining family ties and finding work comparable to their previous employment. While often willing to commute an hour or more into the periphery of the Greater Toronto Area, many realize that locating work might in fact compel them to uproot their families and disrupt extended-family relations. While the clear majority state they want to stay in the area, at the same time they want to provide their children with the lifestyle and opportunities that are afforded only by better-paying work. Not surprisingly, hope and fear, frustration and worry compete in their narratives about themselves and their families.

As the support systems that sustain and maintain many individuals and their families are stressed and eroded by these developments, family dysfunctions may become increasingly apparent. Admittedly, although the links between economic crises and family violence are complex, it is revealing that agency workers in Welland do suggest that plant closures, job loss, reduced income, and empty food banks are absolutely correlated with increased reports of spousal violence (Fox et al., 2002). The Director of Women's Place South Niagara reports that crisis calls to the two local shelters were up more than 20 percent between December 2008 and September 2009 and the overwhelming majority of these calls concerned domestic violence (see Box 6.4). In the same time period, there had been a 38 percent increase in the number of women placed in secure housing (Brownlee, 2009, p. 10).

BOX 6.4   LINKING FAMILY VIOLENCE AND ECONOMIC STRESS

Other locales hard hit by the economic crisis also suggest a link between economic upheaval and domestic violence. In Massachusetts, between January 9 and February 3, 2010, at least five women were killed in domestic violence and two others were severely wounded in a total of six incidents. According to women's advocates, "an unforgiving economy ... has intensified family disputes, inflamed some men's abusive tendencies, and left some women more reluctant to leave violent relationships (Schworm and Guilfoil, 2010). A survey of 600 domestic violence shelters located across the United States found that 75 percent reported an increase in the number of women seeking assistance between September 2008 and May 2009 and about the same percentage explained this increase in terms of financial issues (Schworm and Guilfoil, 2010).

WORLDWIDE IMPACT OF ECONOMIC CRISES

The recession that began in 2009 has had implications far beyond Canada and the United States. From a global perspective, this downturn was the worst since the Great Depression of the 1930s (Arsenault and Sharpe, 2009, p. 6). Although some optimism returned in 2009 and 2010, unemployment remained a significant issue throughout the developed world. The European Commission, for example, predicted in 2009 that the jobless rate would increase to 11.5 percent by 2010—a 10-year high (*Toronto Star*, August 29, 2009, p. B3). Young people (15 to 24) were particularly hard hit throughout North America and Europe. Although youth unemployment in Canada was well into double digits by 2009 (11.6 percent), European analysts were sufficiently alarmed at their unprecedented rates to talk of a "lost generation." In the United Kingdom almost one in seven (about 1 million British youth) was unemployed but this was surpassed by France (18.1 percent) and Italy (21.3 percent).

The United Nations estimates that 40 percent of the unemployed are young people—despite the fact they comprise only 25 percent of the world's working population. Further, the work they do obtain is often "informal, insecure and low-wage" (Olive, 2009, p. A17). Not surprisingly, periods of unemployment at this point in life jeopardize both education and long-term work prospects. High rates of un- and underemployment are, in turn, likely to be reflected in the full range of familial concerns noted above—postponed and reduced family formation, reduced numbers of children, increased return of adult children to a parental home, increased reliance on teens and children in the family to contribute in terms of either paid wages to the family or through the provision of unpaid domestic work, increased numbers of singles/unattached households, and decreased ability to provide support for those family members who are aging.

Families in the developing world have also been transformed by economic upheavals. From 1981 to 1986 the world economy struggled through what was then the most severe and prolonged recession since the 1930s. Much of the developing world was impacted by a global debt crisis. While the 1950s, 60s, and the beginning of the 70s had been characterized by economic growth in many national economies, in the early 1970s the price of oil began to steadily rise and many countries borrowed heavily so that they could keep their oil-reliant economies functioning. However, in 1978–79 another sharp increase in oil prices triggered a worldwide recession.

Developing countries soon found that the prices for the commodities they exported were falling dramatically while at the same time growing trade protectionism by industrialized economies translated into dramatically increased costs for imports. Many developing countries were caught in a perfect storm. Unable to earn as much from their exports while at the same time facing rising import costs and interest rates that had surged to an unmanageable 18 to 20 percent, many countries faced economic catastrophe. When developing countries turned to the only lender that would still lend to them—the International Monetary Fund (IMF)—they were required to accept draconian debt provisions that necessitated a neoliberal approach to public policy. So-called structural adjustment plans required by the IMF as conditions for credit translated into severe cutbacks in government expenditures, in credit creation, and in subsidies. Predictably, provisions for health and education along with support for the poor were decimated (Vickers, 1991).

Developing countries reeled. Through the 1980s, real wages fell by 40 percent in Mexico and 75 percent in Ghana. Throughout many countries in South and Central America, unemployment rates soared into the double digits with 25 percent of Jamaicans, 16 percent of Chileans, and 11 percent of Peruvians being officially listed as unemployed in the 1980s. The economic crisis, the dramatic decline in commodity prices for developing countries' exports, and their enormous indebtedness meant that the flow of money was reversed. Instead of aid flowing to the South, the repayment of interest and loans meant that there was a net transfer of capital from the impoverished South to the industrialized North. The poor were becoming poorer and the impact on family life was visceral. Many families in developing countries were compelled to work longer and harder to simply survive and, despite these efforts, the poor struggled with inadequate food, clothing, and shelter.

Today, in many developing countries the legacy of economic crises persists. Globally, many workers continue to navigate a precarious economy, one that may translate into not only hazardous, unhealthy working conditions but also pressures to work long hours for meagre wages. Unprotected by unions or (enforced) employment standards legislation, workers in Vietnam and Mexico may be docked three days' pay for every day off and in Russia workers report having to work two hours for every hour missed. In many developing countries the work day may reach 15 hours and last 6 or 7 days a week. Noncompliant workers may find themselves docked pay or fired. In this context, many parents often must leave very young children alone or in the care of another child, placing the children at high risk for not only injuries from household accidents but also malnutrition and school failure. When a child is sick, parents may be forced to choose between leaving the child alone, risking their job by staying home, or pulling another child out of school to provide care. Girls are often taken out of school in order to provide supervision, thereby ensuring a cycle of poor education and inadequate employment (Heymann, 2006).

The vast slums surrounding many major cities in developing countries continue to speak to these realities. Starvation-level incomes, absent or inadequate educational facilities, scant medical services, and inadequate government support translate into the veritable destruction of families. The World Bank estimates that between 2009 and 2015 up to 2.8 million additional children may die and 46 million more people will be trapped living on less than $1.25 a day if the global financial crisis persists (as cited in Ward, 2009, p. IN5). Children sicken and die, family members migrate into urban centres or emigrate to other countries in a search for work, and those parents as well as the children fortunate enough to find paid work need to spend most hours of the day engaged in earning a living (Vickers, 1991).

The often ongoing economic crises in developing countries have also triggered extensive emigration in search of economic opportunities. Men and women from Mexico, the Philippines, the Caribbean, and Eastern

Europe frequently must leave their families and, legally or illegally, seek employment in the United States, Canada, and Western Europe. Often absent for months, if not years, their only option for supporting their families is to be absent from them. In short, the economic crises of the 20th and 21st centuries have had a profoundly different impact on families in developing economies. In extreme instances, economic recessions have resulted in the death of family members from starvation, malnutrition, and disease, and even those families that survive may be undermined by long hours of work or forced migration.

In many areas around the globe, the bad news continues. Recent news reports on India suggest that the pressures of the move into the "new" economy have triggered an alarming increase in suicides. The credit-based economy, for example, has left numerous farmers insolvent as the world economy has soured. In Vidarbha, a cotton-growing area, 2,050 farmers killed themselves in 2009 and 1,240 committed suicide in 2008. Ironically, suicide has become the only mechanism for these men to fulfil their family obligations. Since widows and their families often receive compensation from the government, suicide offers a way out of overwhelming debt. As a result, increasing numbers of rural Indian families are headed by widows who struggle to support their families (Westhead, 2009, p. A15).

CONCLUSION

Already, by the early months of 2010, there was a tendency, often expressed in the mass media, to become more hopeful about the future trajectory of the economy. Corporations were posting profits and bankers were once again being criticized for their hefty bonus packages. However, some analysts are suggesting we are far from out of the woods. Joseph Stiglitz, winner of the Nobel Prize in Economics, is calling for "deep and fundamental changes" in our economic and political system. He concludes, "We have created an ersatz capitalism with unclear rules—but with a predictable outcome: future crises . . ." (2010, p. 296). His words echo more radical assessments that the Great Recession is a systemic crisis for capitalism that can be resolved only through a major restructuring of the system (Kotz, 2009, p. 306; Smith, 2010).

Certainly, for many families in Canada and for many communities, the crisis continues to reverberate. Unemployment figures remain high and the fragile improvements in economic stability appear to have been achieved primarily by government-sponsored stimulus spending and a growing deficit. These contradictory good news/bad news assessments of reality likely speak, at least in part, to a growing bifurcation in the country between those who are bruised by the recurrent economic crises—especially the working class, women, immigrants, low-wage workers, seniors—and those whose economic position buffers them from economic shocks (Townson, 2009).

Nationally and internationally,[33] the well-to-do minority are less impacted and, therefore, often retain the resources needed to facilitate family life. While the inevitable shocks of living—death, disease, disability, and so on—cannot be avoided, in a market economy many of the problems of family life can be addressed by consumption—purchasing the services of nannies, therapists, private schools, tutors—or by taking a break from the pressures of family life and relationships with a vacation, family cottage, or posh summer camp.

For the majority of Canadians—the 80 percent who are not wealthy—these options are frequently out of reach. When economic crises add new dimensions to the routine pressures of family life, the resultant stress, unhappiness, and frustration may be overwhelming. The spin-offs—including family breakdown, psychological and physical health problems, increases in family violence, and dysfunction—are managed as well as limited economic resources and a shredded social support system allow or are all too often simply endured. In this context, it is perhaps telling that increasing numbers of Canadians are never marrying,[34] are living on their own, are not having children or having fewer children than they desire.

Summary

- Family lives in Canada have been directly impacted by a variety of economic increases, including the Great Recession of 2008.

- Economic crises have occurred regularly in recent decades and are embedded in dramatic changes in the economy and the labour market.

- Economic crises impact families throughout the life course, from youth and family formation to seniors and grandparenting.

- Past economic crises, notably the Great Depression, underscore the significance of economic upheavals for families.

- Research in Welland, Ontario, reveals the ways in which the recession of 2008 directly impacted displaced workers.

- Economic crises have a worldwide impact.

Notes

1. A recession is technically defined as two consecutive quarters (in a year) that are marked by the absence of economic growth. Economic growth is usually gauged in terms of the Gross Domestic Product (GDP). The GDP is the value of all the goods and services that are produced for money in the economy in the course of a year. Notably, the GDP excludes the value of work that is not performed for money, such as the millions of hours Canadians devote to the care of children and seniors in the home.

2. This item is cited in Sauve, 2010: 4. See Bank of Canada, 2008.

3. These periods of crisis have been far from minor. The 1981–82 recession recorded the highest jobless rate since the Great Depression (11 percent) (Burman, 1997, p.195).

4. The precise timing of these crises depends upon the signposts identified. The Standard and Poors and Toronto Stock Exchange investment return index indicates that significant economic downturns occurred in 1974, 1982, 1990, 2002, and 2009 (Andex Chart, 2009).

5. By early 2010, the official unemployment rate was improving, and 43,000 jobs were added to the labour force in January, 2010. However, as analysts are quick to point out, the official rate must be carefully scrutinized. Not only does it not include those who have given up on the search for work (the disillusioned worker), it counts everyone working part-time as employed, regardless of their rate of pay, benefit level, or their desire for full-time work. Further, the official statistics include as "employed" those 180,000 Canadians who are working short work weeks as part of the EI Work Sharing arrangements estab-lished in a variety of settings. Lastly, much of the recent growth in full-time work has been in the public sector. As the federal government has made clear its intention to reduce the federal deficit by cutting public-sector employment, these wins may be short term (Lewenza, 2010: A13).

6. Some industrial workplaces, for example, have introduced a tiered wage system in which new hires earn appreciably less per hour than more senior members of the workforce.

7. The minimum wage in Ontario is currently $10.25 per hour. An individ-ual working 40 hours a week for 50 weeks a year would earn only $20,500. With both parents working such jobs, a dual-earner family would earn $41,000 a year—slightly above the Statistics Canada low-income cut-off for a family of four living in an urban area (see note below).

8. Service-sector employment, as noted by many contemporary analysts, is often not only poorly compensated (in terms of both wages, benefits, and work security) but it is frequently precarious—often organized as nonunionized, part-time, contract, and other nonstandard work arrange-ments (Cranford, Vosko, and Zukewich, 2006).

9. In response to social protest, the federal government increased the length, but not the amount, of coverage of employment insurance for many workers impacted by the 2008 recession.

10. The federal government has recently introduced legislation that would allow the self-employed to "buy in" to the Employment Insurance pro-gram. Given the economic pressures that are commonplace among the

self-employed, it is not evident that this approach will resolve the coverage gap. In 2009, 950,000 Canadian women were self-employed in Canada and numbers were expected to increase (Trichur, 2010b, p. B5).

11. EI payments are approximately $400 a week and are subject to taxation.

12. Of course, many workers do not receive severance packages. PMP Manufacturing, a Vaughan, Ontario–based American auto parts manufacturing company closed shop without providing severance packages to its workers (many of whom had worked for the company for a decade or more) (Fiorito, 2010, p. GT2)

13. In Canada, there is no official definition of poverty. Instead, government statistics on poverty are based on Statistics Canada's Low Income Cut-offs (LICOs). LICOs use data from the Survey of Household Spending. They are calculated for seven different family sizes (from single individual to a family of seven or more) and for five community sizes (from rural to an urban area with more than 500,000 inhabitants). The LICO income threshold represents the level at which families are expected to spend 20% more than the average family on food, shelter, and clothing. For a family of four living in Toronto in 2006, the LICO was $33,216.

14. Public-sector workers are technically not working for a profit but the same economic logic often exists in contemporary public sector work—pressure to keep wages low and productivity (efficiency) high.

15. In a well-publicized event, Queen Elizabeth's economic advisors apologized to her for failing to predict the recession of 2008.

16. While there are a variety of elements in an economic downturn, including increased jobless rates, declines in the stock market and so on, the recession of 2008 appears to have hit its depths in the late fall of 2008.

17. As Nobel Prize–winning economist Joseph Stiglitz points out, these rosy forecasts may be the result of inadequate measures of economic and social well-being. The Gross Domestic Product (GDP) has long been used to indicate economic growth. However, these measures may be inconsistent with citizens' own experiences. Efforts are now afoot to provide better measures of what is going on in our complex society. As Stiglitz concludes, "Such reforms will help us direct our efforts (and resources) in ways that lead to improvement in both [the economy and society]" (2009: A15).

18. This is up from $91,000,000 in 1980/81.

19. The per Canadian figure includes all men, women, and children included in the current Canadian population.

20. The OECD is an international organization founded in 1961 and now composed of 30 member states, including Canada. Its official purpose is to help governments address economic, social, and governance challenges. To this end, it is an important source of research information.

21. The federal Canadian budget of spring 2010 indeed followed this script.

22. As noted by Charles and James (2003), for both men and women, the significance of paid work and the priority given to home and work are affected by experiences of job insecurity, changing domestic arrangements, and life-cycle stage.

23. Currently, almost one-quarter of Canadians are working more than one job.

24. The problematic relationship between older parents and their adult children was skewered in the recent film, *Failure to Launch*. Like much humour, there is a serious subtext. Older parents may find their marriage and their privacy compromised by the ongoing presence of adult children.

25. Patterns of childcare clearly influence a child's experience of childhood and their relationship with family members. Currently, since Canada lacks a national childcare program and since licensed childcare centres are (outside Quebec) often too costly or inaccessible for many families, parents rely most commonly on unlicensed child care in the home of the child care provider. Such informal, neighbourhood care clearly lends itself to unpredictable outcomes in terms of quality and reliability of care, consistency of care, and so on (see McKinley, 2010).

26. This is not to say that the wealthy avoided the recession. The number of millionaires worldwide shrank by 17.8 percent. However, there was still a significant minority of individuals (3.5 percent of the United States population are millionaires) who were extremely well off compared to their fellow citizens (*Toronto Star*, September 16, 2009, p. B2).

27. The United States is characterized by a much sharper economic divide. Despite the recession of 2008, the number of affluent U.S. households (defined as those with net assets of $500,000 or more) increased from 7.8 million in 2008 to 12.7 million in 2009 (*Toronto Star*, March 10, 2010, p. B6).

28. Interestingly, Rudd and Root suggest that the sacrifices around family life that they uncovered with their research in a mid-western U.S. manufacturing plant are a result of "the more extreme forms of social inequality in the United States today" (2008, p. 82). Faced with deep fears of losing their footing in this sharp class hierarchy, male and female workers were prepared to subordinate family needs to the necessity of keeping their jobs.

29. Drawing on the experiences of the 1930s may not be far-fetched. Although in Canada the unemployment rate in 1930 doubled from 8.7 percent to 15.9 percent, the jobless rate was calculated differently at the time. Government unemployment statistics now exclude workers who have given up looking for work, are on leave, are on strike, are working part-time, or are enrolled in job-training programs. If differences in these calculations are

eliminated, the jobless rate in 2009 would be 16.3 percent—slightly higher than 1930. Further, as in the recessions of 1991 and 2001, recovery in employment took several years to achieve (McKenna, 2009, p. B10)

30. Campaigns were waged in Hamilton and elsewhere to get women "Back into Stelco." Reflecting on the fact that women had worked in industrial jobs during World War II, activists effectively mobilized to get women hired once again into these well-paid, unionized jobs. These gains were basically eliminated as manufacturing jobs were decimated throughout the 1980s and 90s.

31. This research was made possible through the generous support of a Social Sciences and Humanities Research Council SRG grant.

32. Although industrial workers, many enjoyed relatively high wage rates and above-average family incomes.

33. According to the United Nations, the 500 richest people in the world earn more than the 416 million poorest people (cited in Ward, 2009, p. IN5).

34. In the United States 35 percent of men and 28 percent of women 15 and older have never married (USA Today, 2009, p.1A.)

Critical Thinking Questions

1. What are the immediate as well as the long-term economic outcomes of an economic crisis and in what ways might they impact families? In your answer consider both the external structures of families and the inner realities.

2. Family gender roles have been particularly affected by economic crises. What are the ways in which gender roles have been impacted by the economic crises discussed by Berton, Wandersee, and Luxton?

3. Drawing on your own family and friends, what was the impact of the Great Recession on your family and the families in your community? Do you think there will be long-term consequences and did you learn specific strategies to minimize the impact of economic crises on your family?

4. Why are some families more vulnerable to economic crises than others, and how is this likely to change in the next several decades?

5. Why have recent economic crises been particularly hard on Canadian youth and what are the implications for Canadian families?

Websites

Canadian Centre for Policy Alternatives
http://www.policyalternatives.ca
     This is an independent, nonprofit research organization that promotes research on economic and social policy issues from a progressive point of view.

National Council of Welfare
http://www.ncwcnbes.net
> This is an arm's-length advisory body to the Federal Minister of Human Resources and Skills Development on matters of concern to low-income Canadians. This resource provides up-to-date information on poverty and welfare rates across Canada.

Make Poverty History
http://www.makepovertyhistory.org
> This site is the world's largest civil society and poverty alliance and is a helpful resource on global poverty rates.

Economics for Everyone
http://www.economicsforeveryone.com
> This site was created by Jim Stanford, economist for the Canadian Auto Workers union and economics columnist for *The Globe and Mail*. Here you will find information and resources on the Canadian economy.

Canadian Council on Social Development
http://www.ccsd.ca/home.htm
> This nongovernment, not-for-profit organization was founded in 1920 and seeks to develop and promote social policies inspired by social justice, equality, and the empowerment of individuals and communities. Here you will find research reports on the current Canadian economy and its impact on Canadians and their communities.

Suggested Readings

Pierre Berton. 1990. *The Great Depression: 1929–1939.* Toronto: Anchor Canada.
> This social history is the definitive study of the impact of the economic turmoil of the 1930s on Canadian society, including Canadian families.

Meg Luxton and June Corman. 2001. *Getting by in Hard Times: Gendered Labour at Home and on the Job.* Toronto: University of Toronto Press.
> Luxton and Corman's study of Hamilton steelworker families has quickly become a classic in the field. Their work reveals the ways in which women and men negotiated their changing work and domestic roles as the steel industry was significantly dismantled and numerous industrial jobs disappeared.

Patrick Burman. 1988. *Killing Time, Losing Ground: Experiences of Unemployment.* Toronto: Thompson Educational Publishing.
> This is a riveting account of the toll that unemployment takes on Canadians and their families. Drawing extensively on in-depth interviews, the author provides keen insight into the direct and indirect outcomes of losing a job.

References

Acharya-Tom Yew, Madhavi. 2009a. "Bankruptcies Skyrocket in March." *Toronto Star*, May 13, p. B1.

Acharya-Tom Yew, Madhavi. 2009b. "Jobless Claims Fall for First Time in 11 Months." *Toronto Star*, September 29, p. B3.

Acharya-Tom Yew, Madhavi. 2009c. "Most Canadian Workers Living Close to the Abyss." *Toronto Star*, September 14, p. B1.

Acharya-Tom Yew, Madhavi. 2009d. "Number Receiving Jobless Benefits Rises 5.1% in June." *Toronto Star*, August 26, p. B3.

Acharya-Tom Yew, Madhavi. 2010. "Workers Still Afraid of Job Loss." *Toronto Star*, March 2, p. B5.

Agrell, Siri. 2008. "Oil Industry Takes Its Toll on Domestic Life." *The Globe and Mail*, January 22, pp. L1, L2.

Andex Chart. 2009. http://www.andexcharts.com (accessed April 6, 2010).

Arsenault, Jean-Francois and Andrew Sharpe. 2009, June. *The Economic Crisis through the Lens of Economic Wellbeing: Special Report. Centre for the Study of Living Standards/Institute of Wellbeing.* http://www.ciw.ca/en/TheCanadianIndexOfWellbeing.aspx (accessed April 6, 2010).

Bank of Canada. 2008. "Financial System Review" (December). http://www .bankofcanada.ca/en/fsr/2008/fsr_1208.pdf (accessed April 6, 2010).

Beaupre, Pascale and Elisabeth Cloutier. 2007. *Navigating Family Transitions: Evidence from the General Social Survey, 2006. General Social Survey, Cycle 20: Family Transitions Survey.* Statistics Canada Catalogue no. 89-625-XIE-No. 002. Ottawa: Minister of Industry. http://www.statcan.gc.ca/pub/89-625-x/89-625-x2007002-eng.pdf (accessed April 6, 2010).

Beltrame, Julian. 2009. "Recession Takes Toll on Ottawa's Finances." *Toronto Star*, August 22, p. B3.

Berton, Pierre. 1990. *The Great Depression: 1929–1939.* Toronto: Anchor Canada.

Boesveld, Sarah. 2009. "Living Hand to Mouth: It's Not Just a Recession Thing." *The Globe and Mail*, September 15, p. L1, L4.

Broad, Dave and Garson Hunter. 2010. "Work, Welfare and the New Economy: The Commodification of Everything." In N. Pupo and M. Thomas (Eds.), *Interrogating the New Economy: Restructuring Work in the 21st Century* (pp. 21–42). Toronto: Garamond/UTP.

Brownlee, Alison. 2009. "Recession Linked to Increased Abuse." *Niagara This Week*, September 17, p. 10. 51.

Burman, Patrick. 1988. *Killing Time, Losing Ground: Experiences of Unemployment.* Toronto: Thompson Educational Publishing.

Burman, Patrick. 1997. "Changes in the Patterns of Unemployment: The New Realities of Joblessness." In Ann Duffy, Daniel Glenday, and Norene Pupo (Eds.), *Good Jobs, Bad Jobs, No Jobs: The Transformation of Work in the 21st Century* (pp. 190–216). Toronto: Harcourt Brace.

Campbell, Bruce. 2009. "Economic Downturn Is Already as Bad as in the Early 1930s." *CCPA Monitor*, Vol. 16, No. 3 (July/August), pp. 19, 30–34.

CAUT Almanac (Canadian Association of University Teachers) 2008–2009. Ottawa, Ontario.

CAUT Bulletin. 2009. "A Bleak Outlook for Students." 56 (7) (September): A1, A6.

CBC News October 9, 2009. "Future Employment Gains Are Likely to Be Considerably More Muted." http://www.cbc.ca/canada/story/2009/10/09/unemployment-rate-jobless-statistics-labour.html (accessed April 22, 2010).

CGA-Canada (Certified General Accountants Association of Canada). 2009. "Weighing In on Household Debt and Consumption in Canada." *Transition*, 39(2): 5.

Charles, Nickie and Emma James. 2003. "Gender and Work Orientations in Conditions of Job Insecurity." *British Journal of Sociology*, 54(2) (June): 239–257.

Cranford, Cynthia J., Leah F. Vosko, and Nancy Zukewich. 2006. "The Gender of Precarious Employment in Canada." In Vivian Shalla (Ed.), *Working in a Global Era: Canadian Perspectives* (pp. 99–119) Toronto: Canadian Scholars' Press.

Crompton, Susan and Leslie-Anne Keown. 2009. "Do Parental Benefits Influence Fertility Decisions?" *Canadian Social Trends*, October 27: 45–52.

Fiorito, Joe. 2010. "Get Your Diploma, Give Up Your EI Benefits." *Toronto Star*, February 22, p. GT2.

Folbre, Nancy. 2001. *The Invisible Heart: Economic and Family Values.* New York: Free Press.

Folbre, Nancy. 2008. *Valuing Children: Rethinking the Economics of the Family.* Cambridge, MA: Harvard University Press.

Forsyth, Paul. 2010. "Welfare Caseload Continues to Rise in Niagara." *Niagara This Week*, January 28, p. 19.

Fox, Bonnie and Pamela Sugiman. 2006. "Flexible Work, Flexible Workers: The Restructuring of Clerical Work in a Large Telecommunications Company." In Vivian Shalla (Ed.), *Working in a Global Era: Canadian Perspectives* (pp. 74–95). Toronto: Canadian Scholars' Press.

Fox, Greer Litton, Michael L. Benson, Alfred A. DeMaris, and Judy Van Wyk. 2002. "Economic Distress and Intimate Violence: Testing Family Stress and Resource Theories." *Journal of Marriage and the Family* (August) 64: 793–807.

Galabuzi, Grace-Edward. 2007. "Toward a Decade of Hope and Prosperity." *Toronto Star*, July 8, p. A17.

Goar, Carol. 2009. "Lots of Creative Thinking on EI—None in Ottawa." *Toronto Star*, September 11, p. A21.

Goar, Carol. 2010. "EI's Problems Forgotten, Not Fixed." *Toronto Star*, February 3, p. A23.

Gordon, Andrea. 2009. "Parents' Long Hours Don't Pay Off." *Toronto Star*, August 26, p. E7.

Haskova, Hana. 2007. "Fertility Decline, the Postponement of Childbearing and the Increase in Childlessness in Central and Eastern Europe: A Gender Equity Approach." In Rosemary Crompton, Suzan Lewis, and Clare Lyonette (Eds.), *Women, Men, Work and Family in Europe* (pp. 76–85). London: Palgrave Macmillan.

Henwood, Doug. 2003. *After the New Economy*. New York: The New Press.

Heymann, Jody. 2006. *Forgotten Families: Ending the Growing Crisis Confronting Children and Working Parents in the Global Economy*. New York: Oxford University Press.

Hiroko, Takeda. 2008. "The Political Economy of Familial Relations: The Japanese State and Families in a Changing Political Economy." *Asian Journal of Political Science* 16 (2) (August): 196–214. http://www.TradingEconomics.com 2010, January 31 (accessed April 6, 2010).

http://brillig.com/debt_clock (accessed April 22, 2010).

http://www.debtclock.ca (accessed April 22, 2010).

Hunter, Garson and Dionne Miazdyck-Shield. 2006. "From Welfare to Workface: Public Policy for the New Economy." In D. Broad and W. Antony (Eds.), *Capitalism Rebooted* (pp. 108–127). Halifax: Fernwood Publishing.

Ilcan, Suzan. 2009. "Privatizing Responsibility: Private Sector Reform under Neoliberal Government." *Canadian Review of Sociology*, 46(3) (August), pp. 207–234.

Javed, Noor. 2009. "No Jobs Means Big Loans for Students." *Toronto Star*, September 5, p. G12.

Klein, Naomi. 2007. *The Shock Doctrine: The Rise of Disaster Capitalism*. Toronto: Alfred A Knopf Canada.

Kotz, David M. 2009. "The Financial and Economic Crisis of 2008: A Systemic Crisis of Neoliberal Capitalism." *Review of Radical Political Economics*, 41, p. 305–317.

LaRochelle-Cote, Sebastien and Claude Dionne. 2009. "International Differences in Low-Paid Work." *Perspectives on Labour and Income* (June): 5–13.

LaRochelle-Cote, Sebastien, Philippe Gougeon, and Dominique Pinard. 2009. "Changes in Parental Work Time and Earnings." *Perspectives on Labour and Income* (October): 5–16.

Lewchuck, Wayne, Marlea Clarke, and Alice de Wolff. 2008. "Working without Commitments: Precarious Employment and Health." *Work, Employment and Society*, 22(3): 387–406.

Lewenza, Ken. 2009. "Retail Workers Deserve a Better Deal." *Toronto Star*, September 6, p. A21.

Lewenza, Ken. 2010. "Rising Employment Number Masks Devastated Job Market." *Toronto Star*, February 8, p. A13.

Lindsay, Colin. 1987. "The Decline in Employment among Men Aged 55–64, 1975–1985." *Canadian Social Trends* (Spring): 12–15.

Lindsay, Colin and Marcia Almey. 2006. "Family Status." *Women in Canada: A Gender-based Statistical Report* (pp. 33–52). Statistics Canada Catalogue # 89-503-XPE. Ottawa: Minister of Industry.

Lochhead, Clarence and Jennie Tipper. 2009. "What's Up with Household Debt?" *Transition* 39 (2): 1–4.

Luxton, Meg. 1980. *More than a Labour of Love: Three Generations of Women's Work in the Home.* Toronto: Women's Press.

Luxton, Meg. 2006. "Feminist Political Economy in Canada and the Politics of Social Reproduction." In Kate Bezanson and Meg Luxton (Eds.), *Social Reproduction: Feminist Political Economy Challenges Neo-Liberalism* (pp. 11–44). Montreal: McGill-Queen's University Press.

Luxton, Meg and June Corman. 2001. *Getting by in Hard Times: Gendered Labour at Home and on the Job.* Toronto: University of Toronto Press.

Mandell, Nancy, Susannah Wilson, and Ann Duffy. 2008. *Connection, Compromise and Control: Canadian Women Discuss Midlife.* Toronto: Oxford University Press.

Marlow, Iain. 2009a. "Unemployment Is 'Bottomline' of Crisis." *Toronto Star*, September 17, p. B4.

Marlow, Iain. 2009b. "Pensions Protest Pay Loss As 'Corpse Is Being Cut Up.'" *Toronto Star*, October 8, p. B1, B2.

Marshall, Katherine. 2009. "The Family Work Week." *Perspectives on Labour and Income* (April): 5–13.

McCloskey, Donna. 1999. "The Cost of Raising a Child." *Transition Magazine* 29(2) (Summer).http://www.vifamily.ca/library/transition/292/292.html#3 (accessed April 22, 2010).

McKenna, Barrie. 2009. "Jobless Conditions Have Ominous 1930s Overtones." *The Globe and Mail*, September 15, p. B10.

McKinley, Renee. 2010. "Childcare Policies in Ontario." M.A. Thesis, M.A. in Critical Sociology. Brock University.

Montgomery, Alesia F. 2008. "Kitchen Conferences and Garage Cubicles: The Merger of Home and Work in a 24-7 Global Economy." In Elizabeth Rudd and Lara Descartes (Eds.), *The Changing Landscape of Work and Family in the American Middle Class* (pp. 41–59). Lanham: Lexington Books.

New York Post. 2010, January 31. "Foreclosure Move Tossed." http://www.NYPOST.com (accessed April 22, 2010).

Niagara This Week. 2009. "Applications for Welfare, Subsidized Housing Soar," June 19, p. 15, 18.

Olive, D. 2009. "Young People Have Been Hardest Hit." *Toronto Star*, August 30, p. A1, A17.

Phipps, Shelley and Lynn Lethbridge. 2006. *Income and the Outcomes of Children*. Statistics Canada Catalogue No. 11F0019MIE—No. 281. Analytical Studies Branch Research Paper Series.

Picot, G. and T. Wannell. 1988. "Job Displacement." *Canadian Social Trends* (Spring): 6–11.

Pigg, Susan. 2009. "Employers Fire Mothers-to-be." *Toronto Star*, April 24, p. A1. A2.

Prince, Michael J. 2009. "Retirement (in)Security for Canadians." *Transition* 39(2): 6.

Robertson, Grant, Barrie Mckenna, and Janet McFarland. 2010. "'We See Nothing But Doom and Gloom.'" *The Globe and Mail*. March 13: F1, F6, F7.

Rollings-Magnusson, Sandra. 2009. *Heavy Burdens on Small Shoulders: The Labour of Pioneer Children on the Canadian Prairies*. Edmonton: The University of Alberta Press.

Rudd, Elizabeth and Lawrence Root. 2008. "We Pass the Baby Off at the Factory Gates: Work and Family in the Manufacturing Midwest." In Elizabeth Rudd and Lara Descartes (Eds.), *The Changing Landscape of Work and Family in the American Middle Class* (pp. 61–85). Lanham: Lexington Books.

Sauve, Roger. 2009. *The Current State of Canadian Family Finances—2008 Report*. Ottawa: Vanier Institute of the Family. http://www.vifamily.ca/library/cft/famfin08.pdf (accessed April 6, 2010).

Sauve, Roger. 2010. *The Current State of Canadian Family Finances—2009 Report*. Ottawa: Vanier Institute of the Family. http://www.vifamily.ca/library/cft/famfin09.pdf (accessed April 6, 2010).

Schworm, Peter and John M. Guilfoil. 2010. "Rising Economic Stress Cited in Domestic Violence Increase." *The Boston Globe*, February 3. http://www.boston.com (accessed April 22, 2010).

Scofield, Heather. 2009. "Six Slices of the Job Market." *Toronto Star*, June 6, p. A4.

Scott, Megan K. 2009. "Finding Romance in a Cold Economy." *The Globe and Mail*, June 8, p. L2.

Smith, Murray E.G. 2010. *Global Capitalism in Crisis: Karl Marx and the Decay of the Profit System*. Halifax: Fernwood Publishing.

Stanford, Jim. 2008. *Economics for Everyone: A Short Guide to the Economics of Capitalism*. Halifax: Fernwood Publishing.

Statistics Canada. 2006. *The Wealth of Canadians: An Overview of the Results of the Survey of Financial Security 2005*. Ottawa: Minister of Industry. Catalogue no. 13F0026MIE.

Statistics Canada. 2008. "Income of Canadians 2006." *The Daily*, May 5: 2–5.

Statistics Canada. 2009. *Canadian Year Book 2009*. Ottawa: Minister of Industry.

Statistics Canada. 2010. "Labour Force Survey December 2009." *The Daily*, January 8: 2-8.

Stiglitz, Joseph. 2009. "Lies, Damned Lies and GDP Statistics." *Toronto Star*, September 13, p. A15.

Stiglitz, Joseph. 2010. *Freefall: America, Free Markets and the Sinking of the World Economy.* New York: W.W. Norton & Company.

Strazdins, Lyndall, Mark S. Clements, Rosemary J. Korda, Dorothy H. Broom, and Rennie M. D'Souza. 2006. "Unsociable Work? Nonstandard Work Schedules, Family Relationships, and Children's Well-being." *Journal of Marriage and the Family* 68 (May): 396–410.

Toronto Star. 2009. "Balance Your Time and Enjoy Your Retirement," September 17, p. L3.

Toronto Star. 2009. "Europeans Upbeat About Economic Outlook," August 29, p. B3.

Toronto Star. 2009. "Lehman 'Villain' Feels 'Dumped On,'" September 9, p. B4.

Toronto Star. 2009. "More U.S. Banks Seized by Regulators," August 22, p. B7.

Toronto Star. 2009. "Pension Alarm Sounded," August 3, p. B2.

Toronto Star. 2009. "World's Wealthiest Get Poorer," September 16, p. B2.

Toronto Star. 2010. "Extend Jobless Benefits, CLC Urges," January 26, p. B2.

Toronto Star. 2010. "Jobless Rate Hits 5-Month Low But Payrolls Drop," February 6, p. B7.

Toronto Star. 2010. "Millionaires' Ranks Rise," March 10, p. B6.

Townson, Monica. 2009. "Women: Poorest of the Poor." *Toronto Star,* September 5, p. IN6.

Trichur, Rita. 2010a. "Caught in Boomer Sandwich." *Toronto Star,* January 6, p. B1.

Trichur, Rita. 2010b. "Women Self-Employed Numbers Growing." *Toronto Star,* February 23, p. B5.

Turcotte, Martin. 2007. "Time Spent with Family During a Typical Workday, 1986 to 2005." *Canadian Social Trends* (Summer): 2–11.

Usalcas, Jeannine. 2008. "Hours Polarization Revisited." *Perspectives on Labour and Income.* (March): 5–14.

U.S. Bureau of Labor Statistics. "Unemployment Rate," March 2010. http://data .bls.gov/cgi-bin/surveymost (accessed April 22, 2010).

USA Today. 2009. "USA Today Snapshots," October 12, p. 1A.

Vanier Institute of the Family. 2009a. "As work time increases . . . family time falls." *Fascinating Families,* March, Issue no. 14. http://www.vifamily.ca/families/ff14.pdf (accessed April 22, 2010).

Vanier Institute of the Family. 2009b. "Fertility Intentions: If, When and How Many?" *Fascinating Families,* February, Issue no. 13. http://www.vifamily.ca/families/ ff13.pdf (accessed April 22, 2010).

Vanier Institute of the Family. 2010. "Two Incomes the Norm . . . and the Necessity." *Fascinating Families,* February (25). http://www.vifamily.ca/families/ff25.pdf (accessed April 22, 2010).

Vickers, Jeanne. 1991. *Women and the World Economic Crisis.* London: Zed Books.

Vosko, Leah F. 2000. *Temporary Work: The Gendered Rise of a Precarious Employment Relationship.* Toronto: University of Toronto Press.

Walkom, Thomas. 2009. "Gravy Train Doesn't Stop Here Anymore." *Toronto Star,* October 7, p. A23.

Wandersee, Winifred D. 1981. *Women's Work and Family Values: 1920–1940.* Cambridge, MA: Harvard University Press.

Ward, Olivia. 2009. "The Crash's Real Victims: The Destitute." *Toronto Star,* April 18, p. IN5.

Westhead, Rick. 2009. "Farmer Suicides Blight India." *Toronto Star,* September 1, p. A15.

Whittington, Les. 2010. "Tories Target Civil Service Pensions." *Toronto Star,* February 20, p. A6.

Willis, Bob and Courtney Schlisserman. 2010. "Shrinking U.S. Labor Force Keeps Unemployment Rate from Rising." *BusinessWeek.* January 8. http://www.BusinessWeek.com (accessed April 6, 2010).

Yakabuski, Konrad. 2009. "Retirement Lost." *The Globe and Mail,* October 24, p. B1, B4.

Yalnizyan, Armine. 2007. *The Rich and the Rest of Us.* Ottawa: Canadian Centre for Policy Alternatives.

Zaretsky, Eli. 1986. *Capitalism, the Family and Personal Life.* New York: Harper & Row Publishers.

Zhang, Xuelin. 2009. "Earnings of Women With and Without Children." *Perspectives on Labour and Income* (March): pp. 5–13.

Chapter 7

Families at Work: Individual versus Collective Strategies for Making a Living

Meg Luxton and June Corman

LEARNING OBJECTIVES

In this chapter, you will learn that:[1]

1. family survival depends on two labours, but income-generating work and domestic labour are contradictory,

2. women's and men's responsibilities for income-generating and domestic labour change, often setting couples against one another,

3. in countries with a capitalist democracy, such as Canada, the conflicts caused by work–family conflicts are also the responsibility of the state and employers,

4. appropriate state-based policies include quality, affordable childcare and eldercare; more statutory holidays and longer and better-paid parental leaves,

5. family-friendly work arrangements include flex-time, topping up parental leave payments, and leaves associated with emergencies, compassion, and illness,

6. neoliberal policies, which advocate individualism, have dramatically increased the wealth of a very few people and had a negative impact on the majority of families,

7. policies develop out of the negotiations, contestations, and struggles of different groups and reflect the concerns and interests of those who mobilize to put them forward.

INTRODUCTION[2]

In 1953, the school superintendent walked up to Rita Tagseth as she hung diapers on the line. He offered her a teaching position. Rita was excited because her husband's income was barely enough to provide for a family of four. Yet she was already busy looking after two children. She knew the offer was unusual. Few married women, much less mothers, had employment in the 1950s. Managing both jobs would be a challenge (Study 1, 1985).

By 2010, mothers who had paid employment still faced many of the challenges confronted by Rita Tagseth and her family. Maternity and **parental leaves** gave some relief after giving birth to those who were eligible for them but the absence of a nationwide, quality, affordable child-care program left many parents scrambling. Cooking, cleaning, and household maintenance have to be fitted in around employment schedules.

Families depend for their survival on two kinds of labour—the activities involved in making a living, such as running a business, farming, fishing, or earning a wage or salary, and the activities involved in running the home and caring for the people who live there. While the two labours sustain individual families, they also are key aspects of **social reproduction**—the activities required to ensure the day-to-day and generational reproduction of the population. In contemporary capitalist societies like Canada, the organization of **income-generating work** on the one hand and **domestic labour**, and especially caregiving, on the other, has resulted in a situation where the demands of one are contradictory to the demands of the other. The state partially regulates the conflicts between the two spheres (for example, through the provision of education and health care) while also shaping the context in which both operate. As a result, throughout the past century, the problems posed by those contradictions have led to struggles between, for example, women and men, employees and employers, and citizens and their governments—struggles that have generated profound social changes in the way families work.

Here we examine families at work, arguing that, while every family is unique, and while families make a living in a wide variety of ways, there are some key trends that have been common to the way most families have worked in Canada since the late 19th century. We illustrate our argument with aggregate statistics and examples from four case studies:

1. The Saskatchewan Rural School Teachers Project

2. The Hamilton Steelworkers Project

3. The Caregiving Among Family, Friends, Neighbours, and Community Project

4. Ensuring Social Reproduction: A Longitudinal Study of Households in Social Policy in Three Ontario Centres (see Appendix A at the end of this chapter for details)[3]

Together, these studies look at families between the years 1910 and 2010, in rural farming communities, a small community in central Ontario, an industrial city, a region of small cities and towns with a mixed economy, and economically diverse Toronto.

At the start of the 20th century, most families were **heterosexual and nuclear** and based on a sharp sex/gender division of labour. Men of all classes, as husbands and fathers, typically engaged in income-generating work, either by producing for the market (for example, by farming or fishing), by running businesses, or by working for wages. Most women, as wives and mothers, devoted themselves to running their homes and caring for their families. The higher and more secure the man's income relative to household costs, the easier it was for the family to conform to that idealized sex/gender division of labour. Where family incomes were more precarious, women were under pressure to take up income-generating work. At the same time, that division of labour left married women vulnerable to economic dependence on their husbands and restricted their capacities to participate in social, political, and economic life.

Throughout the 20th century, this family form was a site of contestation in struggles that undermined the dominance of the heterosexual nuclear family. Gays, lesbians, and transpeople fought for legal and social recognition of same-sex marriages and for the right to have and adopt children. Waves of immigrants and refugees lobbied for recognition of other family and household forms, usually based on wider groups of kin (Hathaway, 1994a; 1994b). At the same time, many continue to have significant familial obligations in their home countries (Arat-Koc, 2006). Changing demographic patterns mean that as family size gets smaller, and more seniors live longer, more frail seniors do not have children to look after them. More people live alone; there are more lone parent/child households. In the early 21st century, family and household forms are more diverse and varied.

At the same time, women entered the paid labour market in growing numbers. As they struggled with the demands of their paid employment and their family responsibilities, they challenged the prevailing sex/gender division of labour both in the home and in the labour force (Luxton and Corman, 2001, pp.58–60). Men are under greater pressure to be more involved in domestic labour while women have fought for and won access to jobs traditionally reserved for men (such as steelworkers, police, and political leaders). Same-sex couples challenge prevailing sex/gender divisions of labour in the home. These changes have had significant implications for the ways in which families make a living.

In free market economies, cycles of prosperity and recession affect the number and kinds of income-generating jobs available. The state plays an important role in shaping how these cycles are experienced by the people most directly affected. In the postwar boom of the 1940s and 1950s, the thousands of men returning from military service in the war were provided with education, health care, cheap mortgages, and other government supports, and relatively well paid jobs for men were widely available; the growth of government services in the 1960s provided many women with relatively secure and well-paid jobs. Many families were able to increase their standard of living as a result of government intervention. In contrast, the economic depression of the 1930s, the recession of the 1980s and the financial crisis beginning in 2008 all resulted in massive job losses, making it harder for many families to get by (Braedley and Luxton, 2010b). The neoliberal policies of the Canadian state in the 2000s offered little support. For example, despite massive layoffs and job losses, restricted availability of employment insurance left many people unprotected.

Struggles over the extent to which the well-being of individuals is a private family matter or a collective social responsibility have generated changing patterns of state and workplace provision of social services. For example, when governments wanted married women in the paid labour force during the war of 1939–1945 they provided childcare services and produced propaganda insisting that childcare was good for children. However, in an effort to get married women out of the labour force in the postwar period, they closed the nurseries and produced propaganda claiming maternal care was best for children (Prentice et al., 1988, pp. 298–99, 305–06). Continuing debates about whether the provision of social services is best done by governments, by the not-for-profit sector, or through the market have significantly altered the legal and policy contexts in both governments and workplaces. For example, in the 1980s, the existing Keynesian welfare state policies were challenged by neoliberal advocates who argued that individuals and families, not governments, should bear responsibility for the livelihoods and well-being of the population. Neoliberal governments cut social services, reduced or eliminated income supports for those who needed it (for example, reducing welfare payments and restricting employment insurance payments), and imposed more costs on individuals (for example, by increasing university and college tuition) (Braedley and Luxton, 2010). As a result, in the early 21st century, families that depend on income-generating work and domestic labour face the same challenges of trying to resolve the tensions between the two, but in the context of an economic crisis where the support systems offer little protection from the vagaries of the market.

INCOME-GENERATING WORK

Men's Work

Men as husbands and fathers have typically assumed primary responsibility for earning the income that supports their families. The type of job they can get, its earnings and benefits, its hours and vacations, the flexibilities it permits workers, and the way it energizes or exhausts them, all affect not only the kind of living men can provide for their families but also the ways in which they can participate in family life. Wealthy men can obviously provide high standards of living for their families. The systemic discriminations working-class men, men of colour, Aboriginal men, immigrant men, and men with disabilities confront in the labour force have profound effects, limiting the livelihoods they can provide and the family life possible for them, sometimes even making family life impossible.

The expectation that men are responsible for family financial security imposes a compulsion on those men who are, or want to be, husbands and fathers to find and keep a source of income and job security, tying them to the job even when it is personally unrewarding, detrimental to their health, or demeaning. Ironically, this economic imperative to support their families reduces the possibility of their active involvement in domestic labour. Whether they run businesses, farm or fish, or work for pay, the occupations typically available to men have been organized on the assumption that while men are on the job they are freed from their domestic responsibilities and most families organize their domestic divisions of labour to accommodate the demands of men's jobs. Their financial contribution discharges their major obligation to their family, simultaneously justifying their lack of involvement in domestic labour and entitling them to its benefits.

Women's Work

Women have increasingly become involved in earning an income in ways that have taken them away from the home, particularly through participation in the labour force. In 1901, only 14 percent of all women were in the formal labour force, making up just 13 percent of the total labour force. Many women, and particularly married women, increasingly moved into the paid labour force so that by February 2009, 62 percent of women between 15 and 65 years old (compared to 73 percent of men) were in the formal labour force, making up almost half of the total labour force (Statistics Canada, 2009a).

These overall patterns obscure the significant differences among women, especially the ways in which race and class privilege and discrimination differentiate women's lives. Bourgeois women, most of whom also enjoy race privilege as whites, command sufficient wealth to hire other people to do their domestic labour, including paying nannies or boarding schools for childcare (Duffy, 1986).

The work patterns of women in other classes and minority groups reveal the centrality of the competing demands of paid employment and domestic labour. In the early 20th century, women's attachment to the labour force was largely precluded by marriage, and labour force limitations strongly reinforced prevailing sexual divisions of labour by creating economic incentives for women to marry. Women were limited to specific occupations that typically reflected the kinds of work that women were expected to do in the home. A woman who "chose" to teach explained: "Another reason for choosing teaching was the fact that when I completed High School in 1939–40, there were not many choices career wise for women: teacher, nurse, or housewife" (Study 1, 1985).

Women's wages were typically much lower than men's, rarely high enough to support a woman on her own and inadequate to support children (Fox, 1980). Women of racial and ethnic groups faced racial discrimination, a fundamental component of Canadian Aboriginal and immigration policies, and of labour force employment practices. Racism meant that both family formation and income security were more precarious. Aboriginal women had few opportunities for paid work even as their access to the land and its resources was restricted (Campbell, 1973; Statistics Canada, 2008a). Black and immigrant women were forced into the lowest-paid and least secure jobs and typically had higher than average rates of labour force participation, making it harder for them to devote time to domestic activities and caregiving for their families (Brand, 1983; Bristow et al., 1994). Sometimes legal restrictions prohibited some immigrants, such as domestic workers, from having families (Bakan and Stasiulis, 1997).

These patterns of discrimination continued into the early 21st century. A 2007 study revealed that immigrant women who arrived in Canada between 2001 and 2006 had more difficulties finding jobs than Canadian-born women, despite having higher education (Statistics Canada, 2007). If the participation rates of immigrant women and Canadian-born women had been the same, there would have been 200,000 more women in the labour force (Statistics Canada, 2006f).

Married women not in the formal labour force developed various strategies to contribute to their families' economies. In family enterprises—from farms to corner stores—wives often worked alongside their husbands, but such activities were seen as part of their commitment to the marriage, rather than a career choice. Some contributed additional income by extending their domestic labour in their own homes—taking in boarders, or doing laundry or sewing, for example (Bradbury, 1985) (Box 7.1).

BOX 7.1   FARM FAMILIES MAKE THE TRANSITION

Driving around the grain fields gave 75-year-old Eddie lots of time to reflect. His son certainly works a lot differently than he had. When Eddie was 35, he had spent the summer bumping up and down on the tractor seat, exposed to the sun, cultivating the fields day in and day out. When he finished for the day, he was too hot and tired to do much of anything but put his feet up and watch television. In contrast, his son, Ted, drives a large air-conditioned tractor that seems to finish the work in no time. Ted's not so beat at the end of the day. Good thing too because his wife often can't be home. Ted cooks meals, vacuums, and minds the kids.

Eddie had never had the time or energy for those jobs. But of course, his wife had worked on the farm too. She had minded the children while she grew vegetables, made preserves, canned chickens, sewed the clothes, cooked the meals, and cleaned the house. Ted's wife doesn't have time for a garden, chickens, and sewing. With her paycheque she can buy all those goods and more. Her paycheque is pretty handy now that grain prices are so low. Besides, she enjoys socializing at the office and, truth be known, Ted really enjoys his time with the children.

As households increasingly needed more cash, particularly with the dramatic increase in the costs associated with property taxes, housing, and heating, it became harder for people to meet their needs by intensifying their labour at home. Changing standards of living meant that many basic household goods and services such as heating had to be purchased (Connelly, 1978,

p. 54). Increasingly, items such as clothing or baked goods that had formerly been produced at home could be bought as finished goods more cheaply than the raw materials for home production. As compulsory schooling kept children out of paid labour, their capacity to contribute to household earnings declined and their prolonged economic dependency increased their parents' expenses. As a result, the importance of women's income steadily increased throughout the 20th century for both urban and rural women. A woman who taught off and on for 25 years between 1946 and 1983 commented:

> I don't think I intended a lifetime career of teaching. It was generally understood that your teaching career ended with marriage. In fact, prior to 1951, I never met any married women teachers. I started teaching in 1946, married in 1953 and stayed home for 5 years. Economic pressures plus poor living accommodations prompted a return to teaching in 1958 for 25 years (Study 1, 1985).

Many women also wanted paid employment, both to secure their own financial independence from their husbands and to provide them with the interest and status accorded paid work. A career teacher explained: "I planned a lifelong career, but did stop for about 11 years to raise three children until the youngest was of school age. Even then, when there was not a teacher available I filled in for weeks or months at a time. I enjoyed teaching and found it rewarding and challenging" (Study 1, 1985). As individuals, through women's organizations, and through the labour movement, women organized and fought for access to education, to jobs, and to better pay and working conditions. However, the growing involvement of married women in the paid labour force generated considerable opposition and created problems for women and their families.

The belief that men should be income earners making a "family wage" sufficient to support a wife and children was so deeply entrenched in the early 20th century that even when employers preferred to hire women, they often felt compelled to defend their practices (Parr, 1990). Employed women were subject to discrimination that was justified in terms of nuclear family male income-earner ideologies (Sangster, 1995, p. 107). The assumption that women would be homemakers permeated socialization practices and educational systems, with the consequences that, until recently, women were discouraged from obtaining the educational or training credentials that would enable them to qualify for many jobs (Gaskell, McLaren, and Novogrodsky, 1989).

Women's difficulties both in obtaining the education and training necessary to apply for paid work and in getting hired kept married women out of the paid labour force in large numbers. This position was reinforced by hiring practices that prevented married women from holding paid work and by state regulations that either explicitly prevented them from holding civil service jobs or more generally made such employment difficult. For example, as late as 1946, many urban school boards, including those in Saskatoon and Winnipeg, refused to hire married women as teachers, only changing their policies when the severe shortage of male teachers forced the issue (Corman, 2002, pp. 78–79). The assumption that women should and would have husbands to support them was used to justify both the limited range of occupations open to them and their lower wages.

Despite such barriers, during the second half of the 20th century there was an increasing trend for married women to combine responsibility for domestic labour with paid employment (Duffy and Pupo, 1989). The proportion of women with young children in the labour force increased rapidly. By 2006, two-thirds (66.1 percent) of mothers with at least one child under two years were in the labour force; 82 percent of mothers whose youngest child was 6 to 14 were in the labour force (Statistics Canada, 2008b). Women gradually expanded the range of occupations open to them and challenged existing pay differentials. But in 2006, women were still primarily located in "women's occupations"; 67% of all employed women were working in one of teaching, nursing, and related health occupations, clerical or other administrative positions, or sales and service occupations. This compared with just 30% of employed men (Statistics Canada, 2006a). Even when women were working for pay full-year and full-time, they earned only 72 percent of what men earned (Statistics Canada, 2006b). Working full-year, full-time, married women earned only 71 percent of what married men earned (Marshall, 2009). And the real gap was much greater because so many women, especially wives and mothers, had part-time or part-year employment (Statistics Canada, 2006c). Aboriginal and visible-minority women earned even less than white women. As a result, it continues to be difficult for most women to support themselves and their children without a partner. There remains an economic compulsion for women to marry.

Family Finances

By the early 21st century, while some families continued to rely on farming, fishing, or other family businesses, the majority of adults depended on paid employment (Statistics Canada, 2009a). The majority of two-parent families depended on the earnings of both adults. By 1992, on average, families needed at least 77 weeks of paid employment to meet the basic standard of living for the year. If a man was earning for 52 weeks, someone had to work for pay for at least an additional 25 weeks over the year (Vanier Institute of the Family, 1997). In 2003, 38.4 percent of female-headed lone-parent households were low income (Statistics Canada, 2006a). In 2005, 18 percent of families raising children with one income were low income; only 3 percent of dual-earner families with children were low income. If these women had not been employed, this number would have increased significantly (Sauve, 2006).

At the same time, as more and more families depended on both adults participating in the labour force, paid employment for most workers became less compatible with family life (Duffy, Mandell, and Pupo, 1989). The relative decline in earnings that had pushed more married women into the labour force was accompanied by a growing insecurity as many workers faced layoffs, more and more jobs became precarious, access to social security provisions such as Employment Insurance was increasingly restricted, and more jobs demanded shift work, irregular hours, or longer hours from their employees. The demands of paid employment were eroding workers' time and energy for family life without providing any significant financial recompense (Duffy, this volume).

DOMESTIC LABOUR

Unlike paid employment, domestic labour is unregulated, unpaid, and often so taken for granted that, despite its vital importance in reproducing daily life, it is often not recognized as work. As the awkward term "domestic labour" indicates, there is no everyday word for unpaid work in the home. It refers to all the activities that maintain the household and the people who live in it, transforming earnings into commodities and services, shopping, cooking, cleaning, laundry, and caring for children and adults while also ensuring that income earners can continue working to earn the money needed to sustain the household. In the 1990s, in response to feminist demands that it be recognized as an important economic contribution, various statistical and economic agencies began to explore ways of calculating its contribution to the economy. The United Nations reported that internationally in 1995, the monetary value of unpaid labour was $16 trillion—$11 trillion produced by women (UNDP, 1995, chapter 4).

As part of such initiatives, Statistics Canada conducted studies to investigate what domestic labour was done in Canadian households, who typically did the work, and how much time it took. It found that, since 1960, women have continued to do about two-thirds of all unpaid work in Canada; women do more domestic labour than men, even as teenagers (Statistics Canada, 2000, p. 97). Women who were employed did more than their male partners; in fact, men living with employed women did less than men whose wives were not employed. The 2006 Census reported that women were 2.4 times more likely than men to spend more than 30 hours a week looking after children without pay, 2.6 times more likely to spend more than 30 hours a week on unpaid housework, and 1.9 times more likely to spend 10 or more hours on unpaid caregiving to seniors (Statistics Canada, 2006e).

Statistics Canada evaluated the 1992 value of domestic labour performed in Canada by calculating the replacement costs, that is, how much workers in the paid labour force doing the same work are paid.[4] It concluded that the value of household work was $285 billion, equal to 41 percent of the GDP and 60 percent of personal disposable income. Comparing women's and men's contributions, Statistics Canada concluded that the domestic labour done by women was worth almost $17,000 per year and that done by men worth about $13,000 (Chandler, 1994). Since then there have been no national studies to permit updates, but domestic labour continues to make a major (though still unrecognized) contribution to Canada's economy. Domestic labour not only takes up enormous amounts of time and energy and contributes extensively to the national economy, but also plays a critical role in ensuring the well-being of the population (Luxton and Corman, 2001, p. 181).

Domestic labour includes all those activities required to maintain a home and care for the people who live in it. It involves at least four distinct types of work: housework, household maintenance, managing household economics, and caregiving. In contrast to paid employment, where the divisions of labour and the hours of work are clearly (and usually contractually) known, domestic labour is task-oriented and the tasks involved can vary in the amount of time they take each time they are done and in the frequency with which they are done. The skills required for domestic labour and the amount done on a regular basis in any particular household vary enormously and have changed significantly throughout the century (Parr, 1995). They depend on a complex interaction of factors such as the number and ages of the people living in the house; the amount of time, energy, and money they have available; the size and condition of the house; the type of household machinery available such as vacuums, washing machines, dryers, and microwave ovens; the personal preferences and standards of the people who live there, and even natural events such as snowfall or how quickly the grass grows.

The caregiving aspects of domestic labour are even more complex. The assumption that family members love each other and that love is expressed through ongoing, mutual expressions of care makes it harder to see the labour aspects of caregiving because the demands of caregiving as a labour process are often obscured by discourses of romantic love, parental dedication, and family devotion. A woman trying to explain what looking after her husband and children meant to her revealed the tensions and ambiguities between loving and caring about others and looking after or caring for them: "That's what family is about; it's about caring for your husband and your kids. If you get married and have kids, then you have to care for them. After all, you love them, naturally you would look after them. And I do love them. I want to care for them." She went on to express her frustration with the demands such caring imposed on her: "I feel pulled in all directions at once. I want to be more attentive, more loving, and I want to scream" (Study 2, 1984).

Caregiving is most clearly understood as work when it involves looking after those who cannot look after themselves—especially children or those who are ill or elderly or who have special needs. But even the most loving marriage requires considerable emotional work to sustain it. The type of work, its intensity, and how the caregiver experiences it all depend on the quality of the relationship at the time: the experience of comforting someone who is vomiting is very different if the person has the flu or is drunk. Caregiving is also shaped by the degree of dependence and the nature of the care needed: raising a child involves different dynamics than nurturing an elderly person who is dying.

A man described how he came to appreciate the complexity of domestic labour and how difficult it was for him to learn how to do it well:

> Thirty years I was married and my wife did all the household stuff—cooking, cleaning, shopping. She kept our home nice and it was always so easy. There was always good food in the fridge, nice meals, a tidy house. I never gave it any thought—just took it for granted. After she left, I assumed it was all easy, what she did and that I could manage just as well as she could. Well, was I in for a shock! Nothing was easy and I had to learn everything (Study 3, 2001).

His new appreciation of the knowledge, skill, and work involved in running a home also reveals how often women's domestic labour is invisible, not only to economists estimating the value of work done in a national and international economy, but also to family members who are its direct beneficiaries.

Women's Work

In the early 20th century, the dominant assumption was that, as wives and mothers, women were responsible for running the home and caring for family members (Strong-Boag, 1986). These activities were often described as "a **labour of love**" and equated with "natural" feminine behaviour, obscuring the recognition that they also involved work. The assumption that domestic labour was "women's work" both justified men's resistance to doing it and posed difficulties for those men who did it. A women in her 40s described her father:

> He was used to my mother doing everything at home. He never did anything inside the home. When he moved in with me, it was the same thing. He would sit in his chair and call out when he wanted something, a drink, the paper, his other shoes, it didn't matter what. At the dinner table, it was the same thing. He'd announce 'More potatoes' and expect me to serve him. And he was shocked when I didn't jump (Study 3, 2001).

The widespread claim about the importance of being a wife and mother and caring for the family encouraged many women to opt for being at home full-time. While working full-time at home offered many women great satisfaction, its low status, endless demands, social isolation, and lack of pay reveal the contradiction between the rhetoric of its importance and the actual lack of social respect shown to women who do it. Similarly, the limited number of jobs available to women in the formal labour force and the lack of conveniences to meet the demands of domestic labour reinforced the tendency for women to be homemakers. Throughout the 20th century, as more and more married women took on paid employment, and as the spread of feminist ideas undermined beliefs in fixed sex/gender divisions of labour, the easy association of domestic labour and women became more problematic. The more involved they were in paid employment, the less time and energy women had for domestic labour. At the same time, a growing acceptance of principles of gender equality forced women and men to confront existing divisions of labour and ask whether they were fair and why they should continue, especially when women were also contributing to family incomes.

While housework and other household tasks were gradually recognized as work that could be done by a variety of people without challenging fundamental family values, women as mothers, wives, and daughters continued to be providers of caregiving in general and most specifically of childcare. A woman described what this meant in her life in 2001:

> My husband and [two] kids (aged 24 and 27) are great about doing their share of housework. They cook and clean. My husband made a chore chart and we all take turns and I think they do it all as well as I do. No problems there. But they still expect me to, kind of, I can't describe it. They expect me to notice what they are feeling, ask them about it, give them emotional support. And none of them ever think I need that too. Mom's the strong one who makes sure everyone else feels okay (Study 3).

Women's responsibility for caregiving has a direct impact on their ability to make a living. As Zhang notes "the earnings of women with children fall below those of women without children" and the gap generally widens as the number of children increases (Zhang, 2009, pp. 5–6).

As mothers' free labour disappeared, parents had to find other ways of providing childcare. For example, in 2003 about 54 percent of children aged 6 months to 5 years had some nonparental care, up from 42 percent in 1995 (Bushnik, 2006). As more and more young children were cared for by people other than just their parents, questions about what kind of childcare arrangements were or should be available, who should bear the costs, and what arrangements were best for children, families, and society as a whole became hotly debated. Conservatives insist that mothers should stay home to care for their own children, a strategy that keeps women out of the labour force (Richards, 1997, Teghtsoonian, 1993). The women's movement calls for a national program that would provide free, top-quality, nonprofit childcare for all, arguing that collective care was ideal for children, a strategy that requires significant government support and investment (Cameron and Pike, 1972; Friendly, Beach, Fern, and Turiano, 2007). Neoliberals argue that parents should make whatever arrangements suit them individually and that if mothers choose to work for pay, then the individual family is responsible for finding and paying for alternative care (Bezanson and Luxton, 2006), a strategy that leaves childcare up to individual parents.

However, few men earn enough to support a wife and children, and households are vulnerable if the men lose their jobs. Even family farms and independent fishers increasingly rely on women's earnings (Binkley, 2002, p. 151; Kubik and Moore, 2001, p. 8). Women who remain out of the labour force are vulnerable, just a death or divorce away from poverty and unlikely to have a secure income in their old age; many single, widowed, or divorced women over 65 are poor (Statistics Canada, 2009c).

At the same time, centre-based childcare is hard to find as governments have, for the most part, refused to develop either a national childcare policy or a system of affordable and high-quality childcare centres (Statistics Canada, 2006d). After years of promises by various federal governments to institute a national childcare policy and fund centres, in 2004 the Liberals under Paul Martin proposed a program to ensure that children would have access to high-quality, government-regulated spaces at affordable cost to parents. In 2005 bilateral agreements between the federal and provincial and territorial governments were implemented. However, in January 2006 a new federal Conservative government under Stephen Harper cancelled those agreements, arguing instead that governments should leave childcare arrangements up to parents. The government provided instead a Universal Child Care Benefit, which paid $100 per month to parents of all children aged 0 to 6 years. Parents interviewed for the household and social policy study said that while every little bit of money helps, the UCCB money could not pay for childcare. A women with four children said she and her spouse found the $200 they received "handy," but said they spent it paying for taxes and diapers. She explained: "But, if you're thinking of it for childcare . . . the cheapest we found is $35 a day plus you have to take your lunch for each. So that doesn't cover it" (Bezanson, 2010, p. 103).

In 2006, due to the lack of regulated childcare centres in Canada, only 17.2 percent of children between 0 and 12 years of age had access to such centres (Friendly, Beach, Ferns, and Turiano, 2007). Regulated childcare was also expensive. In 2008, regulated childcare cost about $9,000 or more. For example, in 2009, the Rosalind Blauer Child Care Centre at Brock University in St. Catharines, Ontario, charged $211 a week for infants and $181 a week for toddlers.[5] Care in large urban centres is even more expensive. Most centre-based child care is privately operated on a not-for-profit basis (79 percent); 21 percent is for-profit (Friendly, Beach, Ferns and Turiano, 2007). Given the lack of spaces and the costs, most children were cared for by unlicensed providers (de Wolff, 2003, p. 10; Cleveland et al., 2008). The availability of quality, affordable childcare increases women's access to the labour force. When Quebec introduced a $5 per day universal care system in 1997, the number of mothers in the labour force increased. By 2003, 43 percent of all children under 12 in Quebec were in child care (Statistics Canada, 2006g). In provinces such as Alberta and Saskatchewan, which had fewer childcare places, fewer mothers were in the labour force (Statistics Canada, 2006f).

Even when they have excellent childcare arrangements for young children or when the children as teenagers no longer require full-time care, parenting still takes up many hours each week and requires extensive care, attention, and skill.

Childcare is not the only responsibility. Many adults also have to provide care for dependent adults with disabilities or for frail seniors. Sometimes they have to combine multiple caregiving responsibilities with their other work. The consequences can be hard on the care provider:

> When I have to choose between my mother and my daughter. That's the worst thing for me. And ah so I'm not so often in that situation now but I have been a lot in the past. Um with my daughter older now it's better and working part time makes it easier but it's still this massive juggling, it's just always this massive juggling act, you know? (Study 4).

Typically, women still do more domestic labour, especially caregiving, than men, logging on average two hours more than men each day (Lindsay, 2009).

Men's Work

While domestic labour has been overwhelmingly "women's work," men have always been involved in certain aspects such as household maintenance, car repairs, grass cutting, and snow removal. Many men have played an active role in their children's lives, even if they did not take responsibility for primary care. As women were increasingly unable to do, and more and more unwilling to accept responsibility for, all the domestic labour in their households, men were under pressure to take on greater responsibility for a wider range of household work.

Several factors impede men's participation in domestic labour. Some men resist, defending their privileges. Some women actively discourage men's involvement, claiming domestic labour as their particular sphere of control. Most men's paid jobs are organized on the assumption that men are freed from domestic responsibilities when they are at work. A man contrasted his experiences at work (as a senior partner in a large office) with his wife's (as a bank teller) as they both struggled to care for a seriously ill child:

> Well her workplace is highly regulated, specified times for holidays, specific leaves, what have you. But they were terrific. Her manager said she should take whatever time she needs, keep track of the hours off and she can make them up later, any time in the next three years. I'm a partner, one of the bosses, but my partners were adamant I couldn't take time off. I did take two days and they called a meeting and chewed me out. One of them even told me: 'It's your wife's responsibility. Leave it to her' (Study 3, 2000).

A woman described how her husband's job in a major steel plant precluded his involvement in childcare even in an emergency: "Once I was in hospital and both our kids got sick. He tried to get time off work to stay with them, but his foreman said he had no time coming so if he didn't come in, he would be suspended or fired" (Study 2, 1994).

Gender ideologies about what is appropriate for women and men mean few boys learn the skills of domesticity and many men are subject to ridicule if they admit doing such work. A 26-year-old man described the first months after he and his female partner started living together:

> We agreed we would do things together. That's fair. I think men should do their share of the housework. But suddenly we were having fights and I realized, I didn't know what to do. I'd never cooked or cleaned up. My mother had always done all that stuff. She taught my sisters but not me. But my girlfriend expected me to know stuff and slowly we came to see that I didn't even know what I didn't know! I had to learn everything. My girlfriend is still mad at me even though she knows I'm trying (Study 3, 2001).

Another described his family's reaction when he decided to stay home to look after their three young children:

> They went nuts. The whole lot of them were up in arms, telling me I was [a] fool to give up my job (but they never criticized my wife when she did it), that I was setting a terrible example for my son (he's three for heaven's sake). My uncle told me I was a wimp (Study 2, 2000).

The demands of their paid work combined with the assumptions that childcare is women's work mean that many men do not know their children very well and are unsure of how to care for them. These gender differences mean that parental labour is not neutral; one parent cannot simply substitute for the other, because parents develop different levels of skill (Luxton and Corman, 2001, p. 198). As children learn that their mothers are likely to be more responsive, they themselves become active agents in reproducing gender-specific patterns of parenting. When a father of two preschoolers got laid off, he and his wife cancelled the babysitter and he stayed home with the children:

> At first it was awful. They kept telling me 'mummy does it this way' and as soon she came in the door they were all over her wanting her, not me. There would be great tears at bedtime when I tried to give them a bath or read their story. They always wanted mummy. I think they are more used to me now but they still prefer her to me anytime (Study 3, 2000).

Even when men do domestic labour, their participation is often qualified. Men are frequently described as babysitting when they do childcare, implying that they are helping out rather than fulfilling a parental obligation. A 32-year-old man, employed full-time and whose wife was also employed full-time, described his involvement with his 3-year-old son:

> I am very involved with my son. I'd say we share caring for him. Well, she stayed home with him for the first year so I didn't do much then. I'd get up at night with him if she was really exhausted but, you know, I had to go to work the next day, so most nights she took care of him. Since she went back to work, he goes to a sitter. I take him every day and pick him up every evening unless I have to work late. So I am very involved. And on weekends, I sometimes take him to the park. I really like that (Study 3, 2000).

He explained that his wife got the child up every morning and put the child to bed each night. He had never changed a diaper and had never refused to work late because he had childcare responsibilities. His wife had to be ready to pick the child up any evening he decided to work late even though the journey added an extra hour to her travel time. His insistence that he was very involved and shared caregiving was undermined by his description of his own ability to choose when he provided care, a choice predicated on his confidence that his wife would always be there if he wasn't.

However, such gender patterns are under pressure and subject to change. In 1994, a steelworker described how such attitudes had changed over two generations: "I'm thirty-five and there's quite a few guys in my age bracket, say from forty down and then, the forty above. And it's like two different species . . . there might be six guys around the lunch table, and for three, there's no problem changing diapers" (Study 2, 1994).

Even when men actively want to share domestic labour, the imperatives of their financial obligations are difficult to overcome. Parents of newborn babies often plan to share parenting equally but the circumstances they find themselves in make it difficult. Economically it makes sense for the lower-income earner, usually the woman, to take a leave and care for the baby. The resulting drop in income puts pressure on the man to work longer hours if possible (Fox, 2006). Men who try to change the way their paid work is organized to make it more accommodating to domestic labour often confront ridicule and criticisms that they are not serious about their careers. In 2001, a new father described the reactions of his coworkers when he announced his plan to take parental leave: "Most of them thought I was nuts. They said I would get way behind, that I was hurting my chances for promotion. One guy got pissed off and yelled at me that he would have to do more work to cover for me and that wasn't fair. Only one guy, who has a little kid too, said he wished me well" (Study 3, 2000).

The 2006 Census indicated that men were more involved than in earlier years in both housework and caregiving (Statistics Canada, 2006e). However, a wide array of studies from Canada and internationally indicate that men's involvement in domestic labour remains more discretionary and less time consuming than women's and that the overall responsibility for its planning and execution remain largely in the hands of women. And even if men actually do half of all domestic labour in their households, the problem remains that the demands of paid employment and unpaid domestic labour are incompatible. In that context, individual families develop a range of coping strategies (McMahon, 1999; Bakker and Silvey, 2008).

FAMILY STRATEGIES

Most families try to manage the competing demands on them by attempting to ensure that enough domestic labour gets done, especially childcare, while at the same time, family members earn enough to provide an adequate standard of living. Few people succeed in finding jobs that pay well, with regular hours and the flexibility to take time off for family responsibilities. In fact, the trend since the 1980s has been for more and more employment to be low paid and precarious, with few benefits, irregular hours, and little recognition of workers' family responsibilities (Vosko, 2000). Constrained by the larger economy and the availability of services, individual families have a variety of options available. On the one hand, they can try to either increase their earnings so that they can buy more services or they can attempt to limit their hours of paid work so they have more time available at home. On the other hand, they can try to increase the available domestic labour by increasing the involvement of men and children while also reducing the domestic labour done. All of these strategies are problematic. Even if all household members cooperate, there is not enough time available, especially for satisfactory caregiving. For the most part, women assume responsibilities for handling the tensions associated with efforts to combine paid employment with caregiving.

The higher a family's income, the more they can purchase goods and services to make their lives easier and more comfortable. Almost all the tasks involved in domestic labour can be bought, from prepared foods and dog walking to childcare and eldercare. However, people often have difficulties ensuring satisfactory care, even when they can afford it.

For people with fewer financial resources, the possibilities are more limited. The most readily available option draws men and children into domestic labour. But efforts to get men and children more involved often create tensions over what work has to be done, who should do it, and to whose standards. These efforts also often end up making more work for women, who are often responsible for assessing options, developing strategies, and implementing them. While increased sharing of domestic labour reduces some of the workload on women, it does so by increasing pressures on men and children, who are often already under pressure to work harder on the job and at school.

In many households women (and sometimes men) adapt their labour force participation to the demands of their household responsibilities. They take part-time employment, get jobs closer to home, work at home, or take time off to be at home. For example, in 2009, 21 percent of women aged 25 and over in the work force worked fewer than 30 hours a week at their main job as compared with just 10 percent of men. More than one in five women said they worked part-time because of personal or family reasons as compared with 2 percent of men (Statistics Canada, 2009b). The long-term economic consequences of such strategies have contributed to women's higher poverty rates. In some households, parents try to coordinate their schedules, working alternating shifts, so that one of them is at home with the children all the time. Such strategies depend on their workplaces accommodating their choice of shifts and often limit their chances for promotion or to move to a better job. While that approach assures childcare, the adults rarely have time together. Each ends up working a double shift, so neither has much time left to be together or for anything else.

Another option involves cutting back on domestic labour by lowering standards and leaving undone as much as possible. Up to a point such cuts may have a limited impact on standards of living. More subtle dynamics may also be at work as some men respond to the pressures on them by spending money to offset their own labour and as the economics of purchasing goods and services is made more possible by the increased income available from the woman's earnings.

However, especially when the cuts affect caregiving, the tradeoffs may be costly, creating stress and anxiety. Parents with few other options may be forced to leave their children unattended, trusted to care for themselves before and after school. But even when children are clearly old enough to be on their own, parents may worry that a lack of supervision may permit the children to "get into trouble." A mother described her concerns about the impact of her absence on her 16-year-old son and 12-year-old daughter:

> She is such a good girl, so reliable. I trust her completely but I worry because I think she takes on too much. She doesn't want to worry me so she would never tell me if she was scared to be alone or if anything unpleasant happened to her. She tries to protect me. My son is another story. He is such a difficult one, I worry about him all the time. I suspect he is smoking, and even drinking when I am not there, and maybe worse. I phone them every afternoon around four when they should be home. If they don't answer, I get ballistic but even when they do, I still worry. I don't think I really have my mind on work from the end of school til I get home (Study 3, 1999).

In the absence of state support, such as childcare, after-school programs, support for people with disabilities, and eldercare, the responsibility for providing care falls to their immediate families, and typically to women, no matter what burden that imposes. But individual families do not have the capacity to absorb unlimited demands on their resources. A woman with a toddler and a seriously ill teenager and elderly mother was having difficulty coping when her father-in-law became ill. "Then the doctor phones to announce that I have to move my husband's father into our house because he needs—get this—full-time care. I lost it. I was totally hysterical." She had a nervous breakdown. Several years later she noted: "If they had just given me a little help when I first needed it, we would have been okay. Instead, all of us needed lots of help for a long time and it cost the system so much more" (Study 3, 2000).

While people may grumble about the specific way their paid work and family responsibilities conflict, and may develop strategies for coping, it is difficult for individuals to envision how things might be arranged differently and to organize for such changes. A woman who had worked as a steelworker and who had been active in the feminist movement offered this insight. She explained that in workplaces, the combination of collective action and institutional practices supported women who were trying to change sexist behaviours and offered men ways to change without humiliating them:

> In the union, we could say: "There's discrimination going on here" and there were lots of other women and some men who would agree and who would help us try to change it. And there were policies and laws and stuff. And years of the women's movement. So you could go to some guy who was being a real pain and say, "Hey man, you can't do this and here's why." And if he didn't change, you had lots of ways of dealing with him, like other guys would talk to him, or he could be charged or whatever. And you could always make him feel like it wasn't him that was a jerk, even if he was. You could say, "This is how things are done here. Like it or lump it" (Study 2, 1996).

She contrasted that with the dynamics in private family relations:

> But in the home, it's his home, it's his wife. What's she going to say? She can't just say it's not OK for men to sit around while their wives do all the work because society doesn't work that way any more. She doesn't have any union to say we have policies that men have to do their share of the housework or legislation that says she has a right to pay

equity in the home if she wants to go shopping. No. Instead it's like her saying, 'I don't like who you are any more.' She has to be really mad before she'll go that far. And he sure won't find that easy to hear (Study 2, 1996).

Her insight, that efforts to change things at the level of individual families easily pits women and men against each other, underscores her argument that the most effective ways to make paid employment and family responsibilities more compatible lies in collective actions aimed at improving workplace and state policies and services.

STATE AND WORKPLACE POLICIES

State and workplace policies (such as minimum wage rates, employment insurance, parental and care leaves, health and safety standards, welfare eligibility and rates, pensions, health care, and child care provision), create the context in which people make a living and care for each other. Unlike some European countries, none of the provinces of Canada, except for Quebec, have explicit family policy; rather, they have an array of policies and practices that affect families either directly or implicitly in at least three distinct areas: family formation, such as marriage, divorce, reproduction, adoption, custody and child support; family income, such as minimum wage and employment insurance, taxes, child and leave benefits; and family services, such as subsidized housing, family-related leaves, adult dependant care, home care and health services, childcare, and child protection (Baker, 2006) (Box 7.2). In contrast to the federal government and other provinces, since the 1980s, Quebec has focused explicitly on family policy, from massive state support for childcare to housing and labour market policies such as unpaid family-responsibility leave up to five days a year (Le Bourdais and Marcil-Gratton, 1994; Cameron, 2006; Friendly, Beach, Ferns, and Turiano, 2007).

BOX 7.2   STATE SUPPORT FOR EMPLOYEES WITH FAMILY RESPONSIBILITIES

1. Quality, affordable, and available childcare and eldercare
2. Longer and higher-paid parental leave
3. State-legislated provisions for family-responsibility leave
4. More paid vacations and statutory holidays and mandatory paid sick days
5. Quality health-care programs that provide care in the hospital and in the home
6. National program for extended health, pharmacare, dental, and vision insurance
7. A well-funded education system that does not rely on parental support for children's learning or school-based fundraising
8. Expanded definitions of families and spouses
9. Employment equity programs

Such policies develop out of the negotiations, contestations, and struggles of different groups. Throughout the 20th century in Canada, groups representing the interests of wealthy elites and corporate capitalism have argued for free market policies such as lower taxes, limited regulations on how businesses operate, and greater restrictions on the organizing efforts of unions. They also tended to oppose the expansion of social programs. In contrast, many people, through labour unions, the women's movement, antiracist coalitions, and other social justice groups organized to improve their lives, winning, for example, pensions to support retired workers, a universal old age pension, and health care for everyone. Workers struggled, and won the right to unionize and over the years successfully negotiated better working conditions, pay rates, and benefits. These accomplishments continue to be contested and under neoliberal governments have been seriously eroded as the advocates of free markets have imposed their perspective on the policy climate. As Vivian Shalla (2007, p. 24) notes: ". . . the structures, relations, and ideologies that define paid and unpaid work under contemporary capitalism are outcomes of human agency and thus changeable, notwithstanding their appearance of solidity and immutability."

In Canada, the mix of federal, provincial, territorial, and municipal policies (with their often competing allocation of powers) combined with those in different workplaces produces a hodge-podge of policies. For example, there are two distinct types of benefits available: employment-based and citizen-based. Each of these can be either universal or targeted. Where policies are universal, recipients are entitled to them and they foster greater equality among the population. In contrast, targeted policies subject recipients to bureaucratic scrutiny and foster inequalities.

Benefits based on employment include some government-legislated programs such as Employment Insurance, Workers' Compensation, and Canada Pension Plan required for all employees covered by the legislation. Others are employer-specific as some workplaces, especially where unionized workers have won contract provisions, also have policies that complement or extend state policies such as additional paid and unpaid leaves, and various additional health, drug, and dental plans (Box 7.3). Paid for out of payroll deductions and employer contributions, these are typically available only to full-time, long-term employees of large enterprises. While employees' spouses and children are often also covered, part-time, temporary employees rarely are and employees in small enterprises or self-employed people typically are not. According to a federal study, two-thirds of firms do not have formal policies such as part-time work options, flexible work hours, and childcare or eldercare services. One-third of firms have flex-time schedules but provision of other policies is almost nonexistent (Beauchesne, 2003).

Citizen-based benefits are available to those who meet the regulated criteria and, reflecting assumptions about familial self-reliance and male income earners, were typically designed to supplement family obligations and to provide minimal support when family support was not available. Paid for out of

BOX 7.3   EMPLOYER SUPPORT FOR EMPLOYEES WITH FAMILY RESPONSIBILITIES

1. Workplace childcare
2. Assistance with the care of sick children
3. Facilities for seniors or family members with disabilities
4. Opportunities for part-time work, job-sharing, and flextime
5. Extended paid parental leave
6. "Top-up" of employment benefits during parental leave
7. Family-responsibility leaves
8. Paid sick leave
9. No overtime in situations where members are laid off
10. Limited mandatory overtime

general tax revenue, these include the two major universal programs for health care and education, as well as social assistance, child benefits, Old Age Security, and Guaranteed Income Supplements. Typically, the latter offer minimal support, are often punitive in their implementation, and rarely work to help the recipients develop long-term strategies for improved standards of living (Bezanson et al.,2003; O'Connor, Orloff, and Shaver, 1999).

Other workplace initiatives recognizing employees' caregiving responsibilities include a variety of alternative working arrangements such as flextime or personal and bereavement leaves (Skrypnek and Fast, 1996; de Wolff, 2003). A woman whose husband was hospitalized for three weeks said that her employer allowed her to have one week paid "emergency" leave and two weeks unpaid leave. She was deeply grateful and made full use of both: "It was so wonderful. I could just stay at the hospital and not have to even think about work. My company was really good to me" (Study 3, 2000). However, her husband's illness lasted more than the time allowed her. She had to go back to work just when he was sent home, still too ill to care for himself. Like so many others in her situation, she found that existing policies are insufficient. "I was in a state of panic for weeks. It was so difficult. I went to work, but how could I concentrate? I was frantic with worry about what was happening at home" (Study 3, 2000). As her experience shows, such policies offer important, but seriously limited support. They are also available to only some workers. Most people have access to few such supports.

Maternity and parental leaves are illustrative. Such leaves are vital, so that women can have babies, and parents can look after new children without the risk of losing their jobs while being assured of a sufficient income (White, 1993). Responding to demands for better parental leaves, in 2003, federal government policy granted those eligible 17 weeks of maternity leave for a woman giving birth and 37 weeks of parental leave for parents of a newborn or adopted child. The possibility of men's involvement in domestic labour was recognized in policy when the new parental leaves permitted both men and women to stay home with a new child. However, the benefit was so low, at 55 percent of insurable earnings to a ceiling of $423 a week, that few parents could afford to take it and the eligibility criteria excluded many parents (Friendly, Beach, Ferns, and Turiano 2007). Some unions won victories requiring their employer to pay "top-ups" from the government's 55 percent of insurable income to 95 percent. Only 20 percent of employees, however, received a financial top-up from their employers in 2001 (Harding, 2003).

The absence of a cohesive national family policy is consistent with the dominant frameworks shaping both government and business policies: families are, and should be, private, self-sufficient units in which the family group assures the well-being of all its members. Government regulations and policies typically reflect that orientation while responding to pressures generated when families are not and cannot be self-reliant, and, to a lesser extent, when inequalities within families make some members, particularly women and children, more vulnerable.

In the 1950s and 1960s, Canada, like many OECD countries, developed a welfare state that offered a few programs that modified the individual-responsibility model. Based on the assumption that "the well-being of the economy depends on the well-being of the people in it," governments regulated the capitalist market and taxed capital to provide some basic security and social services (Cohen, 1997, p. 5). In particular, government services provided a range of caregiving intended to supplement family care. However, the assumptions underlying the Canadian welfare state were that the prevailing and appropriate family was heterosexual, nuclear, and based on a division of labour in which men were income earners and women were full-time homemakers, and most of the government's policies reinforced such relations (McKeen and Porter, 2003, p. 110).

Since the early 1980s, governments in Canada, inspired and supported by most business organizations and pressure from the United States as a result of international trade agreements, increasingly rejected earlier orientations toward a welfare state, adopting instead neoliberal policies that tend to minimize interventions in the marketplace and to reduce state spending on social services (OECD, 1981). These policies reasserted claims that individuals and families must bear more of the costs of social reproduction themselves (Allahar and Cote, 1998; Braedley and Luxton, 2010a). The prevailing ideology of **neoliberalism** replaced the philosophy of the welfare state with a belief that "social and economic well-being for people is subordinate to the well-being of the corporate sector" (Cohen, 1997, p. 5). Justified by arguments about competitiveness and fiscal restraint, "efficiencies" in the public and private sectors were often actually a transfer of costs to the domestic sector where they were hidden by the invisibility of domestic labour.

Increasingly, the majority of families, and particularly women, were compelled to absorb the costs of cuts to schools, hospitals, and social service agencies, or do without the caregiving and related services altogether.

CONCLUSION

The way families are able to make a living, and the standard of living they can achieve, depends on the interactions of many forces: social and cultural values about family and gender relations, economic cycles, job markets, state and workplace policies, consumer goods markets, rates of unionization, and a range of other domestic and international patterns.

Since the 1980s, the cumulative effect of neoliberal changes in the way work is organized has had a profound impact on families. A small privileged elite has experienced increased wealth that reduces the constraints on their family life. For the majority of people in Canada, the demands of both paid employment and domestic labour have increased without securing greater possibilities for family life. One of the clearest indications that families aren't working well is that women are delaying childbirth and having fewer children. In 1968, the average age of women at the birth of their first child was 23 years. By 1997 it was 26.8 (Statistics Canada, 2000, p. 35) and by 2007, George (2007) reported that it was 31 years. In 1959 there were 116 births per thousand women aged 15 to 49 years. In 1970 this rate had dropped to 71 births per thousand women and by 1997 it was down to 44 births per thousand women, a decrease of 23 percent since 1990 (Statistics Canada, 2002, p. 34). By 1996 woman on average were having only 1.8 children, fewer than the 2.1 that is required to ensure population replacement (Dumas and Belanger, 1997, p. 41). By 2005 women on average were having 1.5 children, one of the lowest birth rates in the world (Friendly, Beach, Ferns, and Turiano, 2007).

Expressed popularly as the problem of balancing work and family, the conflicts, at one level, are problems of scheduling, of arranging alternative care for dependants, of the fatigue of the double day. But the conflicting demands of work and family are more than that. At a deeper level, family households embody the contradictions between the process of producing and sustaining people and the process of profit maximization for enterprises and shareholders. The conflict between, on the one hand, employers trying to reduce labour costs to maximize profits and governments eliminating services to cut taxes and, on the other hand, workers struggling to ensure their livelihoods through higher wages, benefits, and services, means that social reproduction for the majority is in conflict with the process of capital accumulation and profit maximization. At stake is the way the costs of social reproduction of the population as a whole are met in a capitalist society: to what extent are the responsibilities and costs borne by individuals and by employers or provided by the state with the costs spread across all taxpayers? The costs of social reproduction are reduced for the business sector to the extent that families and households absorb them and bear the costs themselves. Conversely, the more that working people are able to insist on collective responsibility for social reproduction, funded either by employers directly or by personal and corporate taxes, the higher their standards of living and the less profit individual capitalists can appropriate for themselves. Either side—labour or capital—can only win concessions. This contradiction, systemic to a free market economy, cannot be resolved.

Consigning the responsibility of producing and sustaining daily life to individual households has implications beyond the costs and accumulations of tensions and stress for family members. As Barrett and McIntosh (1982, p. 78) have argued, the nuclear family takes so much time and energy that participants have little left over for building and sustaining strong friendship networks or community organizations, or to organize collectively through protest movements. Wherever people have the opportunity to come together, pool information, and develop shared analyses, they have the possibility of generating strategies for change. In their workplaces and unions, in community groups and in political movements such as the women's movement, and in single-issue groups, people have formulated demands and put them on the political agenda. Women, in particular, through the labour movement and the women's movement, have called for a range of policies intended to make it easier for recipients to manage their lives and caring responsibilities (de Wolff, 2003). Both women and men need these structural supports because resolving the contractions between paid employment and family life is not a women's issue but a social issue.

Any measures that ensure greater economic security for the majority of people, such as an adequate income or decent prices for crops and fish, control over hours, improved minimum-wage legislation, employment insurance, pay equity, old-age pensions, higher pay rates, and benefits, all provide the recipients with a better standard of living—the basic prerequisite for personal and family life. A range of other services such as long-term and home care for people with disabilities or chronic illnesses, or those who are elderly, as well as childcare and education, directly affect the demands that domestic labour makes on individual households. For example, although Canada as a whole has one of the lowest birth rates in the world, when Quebec introduced its child care policy and a monthly child benefit, the birth rate increased; there were 10,000 more babies born in 2006 than in 2002 (George, 2007).

The more public services available, the easier it is for individuals to manage. The more such services are universal, the greater equality is fostered. The struggle over the extent to which governments and employers will assume responsibility for resolving the tensions between paid work and family life is still a major political challenge in the 21st century. The ways in which those responsibilities are distributed significantly affect whether or not people can actually form families, and shape the kinds of families and the lives they lead.

Summary

- Domestic labour is often taken for granted as women's work.

- Although domestic labour, especially childcare, is said to be important, it is accorded low status.

- Family-based strategies alone cannot resolve the underlying contradictions between participating in both income-generating work and maintaining a household.

- Both the state and employers have responsibilities for addressing these conflicts.

- Policies develop out of the negotiations, contestations, and struggles of different groups and reflect the concerns and interests of those who mobilize to put them forward.

- Neoliberalism, the current political agenda informing most government policies, promotes free market profit making, reduces state funding of social services, and holds individuals and their families responsible for their own livelihoods.

- Both women and men need these structural supports because resolving the contractions between paid employment and family life is not a women's issue but a social issue.

Notes

1. Luxton and Corman prefer not to assume what the students will learn but rather they take responsibility for the arguments presented in the chapter.

2. We thank Bonnie Fox, Ester Reiter, Viola Bartel, Ann Duffy, and Nancy Mandell for their comments on an earlier version.

3. Whenever we have quoted from one of the four case studies, we have indicated which study (Study 1, 2, 3, or 4 and the date of the interview).

4. For a critique of Statistics Canada's approach that argues it seriously underestimates the time involved and value of the labour, see Luxton, 1997, pp. 431–439.

5. Interview by June Corman with the coordinator of the Rosalind Blauer Child Care Centre, Brock University, St. Catharines, Ontario, April 28, 2009.

Critical Thinking Questions

1. What conditions set up women as responsible for domestic labour?

2. What conditions impede men's participation in domestic labour?

3. Why are state and employer policies a more appropriate response than simply leaving individual families to cope with these tensions?

Websites

Labour Force Historic Review
http://www.chass.utoronto.ca/datalib/codebooks/dsp/lfhr2002.htm
> This website contains information on participation in the labour force for women and men over the last century from the document "Labour Force Historical Review."

York University: Gender and Work
http://www.genderwork.ca
> Drawing on statistics and published papers, this website contains valuable information on paid and unpaid labour in Canada.

Human Resources and Skills Development Canada
http://www.hrsdc.gc.ca/eng/lp/spila/wlb/11programs_policies_practices.shtml
> This website contains reports on work-life including a study of caring provisions in major collective agreements in Canada.

Childcare Resource and Research Unit
http://www.childcarecanada.org
> This website reports on policy research relating to early childhood education and care, and family policy.

Suggested Readings

Marion Binkely. 2002. *Set Adrift: Fishing Families.* Toronto: University of Toronto Press.
> Women married to men who work in the coastal and deep-sea fishery provide labour necessary both to support their husband's ability to earn an income and to organize their households on a daily basis.

Alice de Wolff. 2003. *Bargaining for a Better Life.* Toronto: Ontario Federation of Labour.
> This informative document outlines a workplace checklist for creating work–life balance. It proposes that employees have more control over their work, enhanced paid and unpaid leaves, and workplace services for children and seniors.

Barbara Ehrenreich. 2001. *Nickel and Dimed: On (Not) Getting By in America.* New York: Metropolitan Books.
> Drawing on her own experiences and her observations as a minimum wage worker, the author analyzed the strategies of minimum wage earners to make ends meet. The benefits of minimum wages and the associated lack of benefits and pensions to the American capitalist economy involve great sacrifices for the workers and their families.

Meg Luxton and June Corman. 2001. *Getting By in Hard Times: Gendered Labour at Home and On the Job.* Toronto: University of Toronto Press.

Based on working-class households in Hamilton, Ontario, the book charts how families make a living by combining paid employment and unpaid domestic labour and the impact of economic restructuring on their lives.

Statistics Canada. 2005. *Women in Canada: A Gender-based Statistical Report, 2005.* Catalogue no. 89-503-XPE Ottawa: Minister of Industry.

This book provides an overview of Statistics Canada's data on women.

References

Allahar, Anton and James Cote. 1998. *Richer and Poorer: The Structure of Inequality in Canada.* Toronto: Lorimer and Co.

Arat-Koc, Sedef. 2006. *"Whose Social Reproduction? Transnational Motherhood and Challenges to Feminist Political Economy."* In Kate Bezanson and Meg Luxton (Eds.), *Special Reproduction: Feminist Political Economy Challenges Neo-liberalism* (pp. 75–92). Montreal & Kingston: McGill-Queen's University Press.

Bakan, Abigail and Daiva Stasiulis. 1997. *Not One of the Family: Foreign Domestic Workers in Canada.* Toronto: University of Toronto Press.

Baker, Maureen. 2006. *Restructuring Family Policies: Convergences and Divergences.* Toronto: University of Toronto Press.

Bakker, Isabella and Rachel Silvey (Eds.). 2008. *Beyond States and Markets: The Challenges of Social Reproduction.* London and New York: Routledge.

Barrett, Michelle and Mary McIntosh. 1982. *The Anti-Social Family.* London: Verso.

Beauchesne, Eric. 2003. "Many Firms Don't Help Balance Work and Family." *The Leader Post,* July 7, p. 4.

Bezanson, Kate. 2010. "Child Care Delivered through the Mailbox: Social Reproduction, Choice and Neoliberalism in a Theo-Conservative Canada." In Susan Braedley and Meg Luxton (Eds.), *Neoliberalism and Everyday Life* (pp. 90–112). Montreal & Kingston: McGill-Queen's University Press.

Bezanson, Kate and Meg Luxton. 2006. *Social Reproduction: Feminist Political Economy Challenges Neoliberalism.* Montreal & Kingston: McGill-Queen's University Press.

Bezanson, Kate, Anne O'Connell, and Sheila Neysmith. 2005. *Telling Tales: Living the Halifax Effects of Policy Change.* Halifax, NS: Fernwood.

Binkley, Marian. 2002. *Set Adrift: Fishing Families.* Toronto: University of Toronto Press.

Bradbury, Bettina. 1985. "The Home as Workplace." In Paul Craven (Ed.), *Labouring Lives: Work and Workers in Nineteenth Century Ontario* (pp. 412–478). Toronto: University of Toronto Press.

Braedley, Susan and Meg Luxton (Eds.). 2010a. *Neoliberalism and Everyday Life.* Montreal and Kingston: McGill-Queen's University Press.

Braedley, Susan and Meg Luxton. 2010b. "Competing Philosophies: Neoliberalism and the Challenges of Everyday Life." In Susan Braedley and Meg Luxton (Eds.), *Neoliberalism and Everyday Life* (pp. 3–21). Montreal and Kingston: McGill-Queen's University Press.

Brand, Dionne. 1983. "A Working Paper on Black Women Toronto: Gender, Race and Class." *Fireweed*, 16: 149–55.

Bristow, Peggy, Dionne Brand, Linda Carty, Afua P. Cooper, Sylvia Hamilton, and Adrienne Shadd. 1994. *"We're Rooted Here and They Can't Pull Us Up": Essays in African Canadian Women's History.* Toronto: University of Toronto Press.

Bushnik, Tracey. 2006. "Child Care in Canada." Statistics Canada cat. no. 89-599-MIE2006003.

Cameron, Barbara. 2006. "Social Reproduction and Canadian Federalism." In Kate Bezanson and Meg Luxton (Eds.), *Social Reproduction: Feminist Political Economy Challenges Neo-Liberalism* (pp. 45–74). Montreal-Kingston: McGill-Queen's University Press.

Cameron, Barbara and Cathy Pike. 1972. "Collective Child Care in a Class Society." Discussion Collective #6. *Women Unite.* Toronto: The Canadian Women's Educational Press.

Campbell, Maria. 1973. *Halfbreed.* Toronto: McClelland and Stewart.

Chandler, William. 1994. "The Value of Household Work in Canada, 1992." *Canadian Economic Observer.* Statistics Canada. Cat. No. 11-010 (April), 3.1–3.9.

Cleveland, Gordon, Barry Forer, Douglas Hyatt, Christa Japel, and Michael Krashinsky. 2008. "New Evidence about Child Care in Canada: Use Patterns, Affordability and Quality." http://www.irpp.org/choices/archive/vol14no12.pdf (accessed April 27, 2010).

Cohen, Marjorie. 1997. "What Women Should Know About Economic Fundamentalism." *Atlantis: A Women's Studies Journal* (21/2): 4–15.

Connelly, Patricia. 1978. *Last Hired, First Fired Women and the Canadian Work Force.* Toronto: The Women's Press.

Corman, June. 2002. "Returning to the Classroom: Married Women Fill the Void for Teachers in Saskatchewan." *Atlantic: A Women's Studies Journal* 27(1): 77–86.

De Wolff, Alice. 2003. *Bargaining for Work and Life.* Toronto: Canadian Labour Congress, Ontario Coalition for Better Child Care, Ontario Federation of Labour, and the Feminist Political Economy Network, Graduate Program in Women's Studies, York University.

Duffy, Ann. 1986. "Reformulating Power for Women." *CRSA* 23(1): 22–46.

Duffy, Ann, Nancy Mandell, and Norene Pupo. 1989. *Few Choices: Women, Work and Family.* Toronto: Garamond Press.

Duffy, Ann and Norene Pupo. 1989. *Part-Time Paradox: Connecting Gender, Work and Family.* Toronto: McClelland and Stewart.

Dumas, Jean and Alain Belanger. 1997. *Report on the Demographic Situation in Canada 1996*. Ottawa, Statistics Canada, cat. no. 91-209.

Friendly, Martha, Jane Beach, Carolyn Ferns, and Michelle Turiano. 2007. *Early Childhood Education and Care in Canada 2006*. Childcare Resource and Research Unit Toronto.

Fox, Bonnie (Ed.). 1980. *Hidden in the Household: Women's Domestic Labour under Capitalism*. Toronto: Women's Educational Press.

Fox, Bonnie. 2006. "Motherhood as a Class Act: The Many Ways in Which 'Intensive Mothering' Is Entangled with Social Class." In Kate Bezanson and Meg Luxton (Eds.), *Social Reproduction: Feminist Political Economy Challenges Neo-Liberalism* (pp. 231–262). Montreal and Kingston: McGill-Queen's University Press.

Gaskell, Jane, Arlene McLaren, and Myra Novogrodsky. 1989. *Claiming an Education: Feminism and Canadian Society*. Toronto: Our Schools/Ourselves Education Foundation.

George, Lianne. 2007. "Making Moms: Can We Feed the Need to Breed?" *Maclean's* (May 28) http://www.macleans.ca/article.jsp?content=20070528_105313_105313 (accessed April 6, 2010).

Harding, Katherine. 2003. "Few Employers Are Topping Up Parental Benefits." *The Globe and Mail*, April 23, p. C3.

Hathaway, Jim. 1994a. *Report of the National Consultation on Family Class Immigration Convened by the Department of Citizenship and Immigration*. Toronto: Government of Canada and Refugee Law Research Unit, Centre for Refugee Studies, York University.

————. 1994b. *Towards a Conceptualized System of Family Class Immigration Convened by the Department of Citizenship and Immigration*. Toronto: Government of Canada and Refugee Law Research Unit, Centre for Refugee Studies, York University.

Kubik, Wendee and Robert J. Moore. 2001. *Women's Diverse Roles in the Farm Economy and the Consequences for Their Health, Well-being and Quality of Life*. University of Regina, Campion College.

Le Bourdais, Celine and Nicole Marcil-Gratton. 1994. "Quebec's Pro-active Approach to Family Policy: Thinking and Acting Family." In Maureen Baker (Ed.), *Canada's Changing Families: Challenges to Public Policy* (pp. 103–116). Ottawa: Vanier Institute of the Family.

Lindsay, Colin. 2009. "Are Women Spending More Time Than Men on Unpaid Domestic Labour?" *The General Social Survey Matter of Fact #9* Statistics Canada catalogue no. 89-630-X. http://www.statcan.gc.ca/pub/89-630-x/2008001/article/10705-eng.pdf (accessed April 10, 2010).

Luxton, Meg. 1997. "Women, the United Nations and the Politics of Unpaid Work." *Women's Studies International Forum* (special issue on "The Home") 20(3): 431–439.

Luxton, Meg and June Corman. 2001. *Getting By in Hard Times: Gendered Labour at Home and on the Job*. Toronto: University of Toronto Press.

Marshall, Katherine. 2009. "The Family Work Week," *Perspectives*. Statistics Canada cat.no.75-001-X.

McKeen, Wendy and Ann Porter. 2003. "Politics and Transformation: Welfare State Restructuring in Canada." In Wallace Clement and Leah Vosko, (Eds.), *Changing Canada Political Economy as Transformation* (pp. 109–134). Montreal and Kingston: McGill-Queen's University Press.

McMahon, Anthony. 1999. *Taking Care of Men: Sexual Politics in the Public Mind.* Cambridge, UK: Cambridge University Press.

O'Connor, Julia, Ann Shola Orloff, and Sheila Shaver. 1999. *States, Markets, Families: Gender, Liberalism and Social Policy in Australia, Canada, Great Britain and the United States.* Cambridge, UK: Cambridge University Press.

OECD. 1981. *The Welfare State in Crisis.* Paris: OECD.

Parr, Joy. 1990. *The Gender of Breadwinners: Women, Men and Change in Two Industrial Towns, 1880–1950.* Toronto: University of Toronto Press.

———. 1995. "Shopping for a Good Stove; A Parable about Gender, Design and the Market." In Joy Parr (Ed.), *A Diversity of Women: Ontario, 1945–1980* (pp. 75–97). Toronto: University of Toronto Press.

Prentice, Alison, Paula Bourne, Gail Cuthbert Brandt, Beth Light, Wendy Mitchinson, and Naomi Black. 1988. *Canadian Women: A History.* Toronto: Harcourt, Brace.

Richards, John. 1997. *Retooling the Welfare State.* Toronto: CD Howe.

Sangster, Joan. 1995. *Earning Respect: The Lives of Working Women in Small-Town Ontario, 1920–1960.* Toronto: University of Toronto Press.

Sauve, Roger. 2006. *The Current State of Canadian Family Finances 2006 Report.* Ottawa: Vanier Institute of the Family http://www.vifamily.ca/library/cft/state06.html#wow (accessed April 6, 2010).

Shalla, Vivian. 2007. "Theoretical Reflections on Work." In Vivian Shalla and Wallace Clement (Eds.), *Work in Tumultuous Times—Critical Perspectives* (pp. 3–29). Montreal and Kingston: McGill-Queen's University Press.

Skrypnek, Berna and Janet Fast. 1996. "Work and Family Policy in Canada: Family Needs, Collective Solutions." *Journal of Family Issues* 17(6): 793–812.

Statistics Canada. 2000. "Women in Canada 2000: A Gender-Based Statistical Report." Ottawa: Industry Canada.

———. 2002. *Historic Labour Force Review.* Ottawa: Ministry of Industry, Science and Technology.

———. 2006a. "Women in Canada: Work Chapter Updates." http://www.statcan .gc.ca/pub/89f0133x/89f0133x2006000-eng.htm#10 (accessed April 6, 2010).

———. 2006b. "Employment Income Groups. http://www12.statcan.gc.ca/census-recensement/2006/dp-pd/tbt/Lp-eng.cfm?lang=e&apath=3&detail=0&dim= 0&fl=a&frce=0&gc=0&gid=0&gk=0&grp=1&pid=0&prid=0&ptype=88971, 97154&s=0&showall=0&sub=811&temporal=2006&theme=81&vid=0&vnamee= &vnamef (accessed April 28, 2010).

————. 2006c. *Women in Canada: A Gender-Based Statistical Report*, 5th ed. Ottawa: Ministry of Industry.

————. 2006d. *Child Care in Canada*. Catalogue no. 89-599-MIE2006003 Ottawa: Ministry of Industry.

————. 2006e. "General Social Survey: Paid and Unpaid Work." *The Daily* (July 19). http://www.statcan.gc.ca/daily-quotidien/060719/dq060719b-eng.htm (accessed April 28, 2010).

————. 2006f. "Study: Changing Patterns of Women in the Canadian Labour Force." *The Daily* (June 15).

————. 2006g. "Study: Changing Patterns of Women in the Canadian Labour Force." *The Daily* (June 15). http://www.statcan.gc.ca/daily-quotidien/060615/dq060615c-eng.htm (accessed April 10, 2010).

————. 2007. "Study: Canada's Immigrant Labour Market." *The Daily* (September 10) http://www.statcan.gc.ca/daily-quotidien/070910/dq070910a-eng.htm (accessed April 6, 2010).

————. 2008a. "Aboriginal Peoples Living Off-reserve and the Labour Market." *The Daily* (December 15). http://www.statcan.gc.ca/daily-quotidien/081215/dq081215a-eng.htm (accessed April 6, 2010).

————. 2008b "Labour Force Activity." Catalogue no. 97-559-XCB2006017. Ottawa: Statistics Canada.

————. 2009a. "Latest Release from the Labour Force Survey." *The Daily* (March 13). http://www.statcan.gc.ca/subjects-sujects/labour-travail/lfs-epa/lfs-epa (accessed April 10, 2010).

————. 2009b. "Table 1: Labour Force Characteristics by Age and Sex." *The Daily* (April 9). http://www.statcan.gc.ca/subjects-sujets/labour-travail/lfs-epa/t090409al-eng.htm.

————. 2009c. "Table 202-0802: Persons in Low Income, Annual." CANSIM tables from E-STAT. http://www4.hrsdc.gc.ca/.3ndic.1t.4r@-eng.jsp?iid=23 (accessed April 10, 2010).

Strong-Boag, Veronica. 1986. "Pulling in Double Harness or Hauling a Double Load: Women, Work and Feminism on the Canadian Prairies." *Journal of Canadian Studies* 21(3): 35–52.

Teghtsoonian, Katherine. 1993. "A Neo-Conservative Ideology and Opposition to Federal Regulation of Child Care Services in Canada and the United States." *Canadian Journal of Political Science* 16(1): 97–122.

United Nations Development Programme. 1995. *Human Development Report*. New York and Oxford: Oxford University Press, chapter 4.

Vanier Institute of the Family. 1997. *From the Kitchen Table to the Boardroom*. Ottawa: Vanier Institute of the Family.

Vosko, Leah. 2000. *Temporary Work: The Gendered Rise of a Precarious Employment Relationship.* Toronto: University of Toronto Press.

White, Julie. 1993. *Sisters and Solidarity: Women and Unions in Canada.* Toronto: Thompson Educational Publishing.

Zhang, Xuelin. 2009. "Earnings of Women with and without Children." *Perspectives* (March) Statistics Canada.

Appendix A

This chapter reports on the findings from four case studies conducted by the authors:

1. The Saskatchewan Rural School Teachers Project (June Corman)
   Based on 250 firsthand accounts, collected by Irene Poelzer and June Corman, this project explores the lives of women who began teaching in Saskatchewan between 1910 and 1955.

2. The Hamilton Steelworkers Project (June Corman, David Livingstone, Meg Luxton, and Wally Seccombe with Belinda Leach)
   Between 1983 and 1996 the project conducted four surveys, five different sets of open-ended in-depth interviews, and one time budget study. This included interviews with 196 steelworkers (2 women and 194 men) who were members of Local 1005 employed by Stelco at Hilton Works in Hamilton, Ontario; 187 people (2 men and 185 women) who were partners with one of the steelworkers interviewed; 34 (22 men and 12 women) steelworkers who had been laid off by Stelco; 26 women who were involved in the campaign to get women hired at Stelco or who were hired as a result of the campaign; and 798 randomly selected people from the Hamilton area. Subsequently, follow-up interviews were conducted with a total of 103 participants. For details of this project, see Luxton and Corman, 2001, pp. 267–70 "Appendix A Data Collection Strategies."

3. The Caregiving Among Family, Friends, Neighbours, and Community Project (Meg Luxton)
   A total of 137 in-depth interviews were conducted in Toronto, Ontario, between January 1999 and January 2002 with 97 women and 40 men. The interviews investigated what is involved in negotiating informal caregiving among family, friends, neighbours, and communities.

4. Ensuring Social Reproduction: A Longitudinal Study of Households and Social Policy in Three Ontario Centres (Kate Bezanson and Meg Luxton)
   About 100 in-depth interviews were conducted in three Ontario centres between 2006 and 2010. The interviews investigated the impact of social policy on how people manage the competing demands of income earning and domestic responsibilities.

Chapter 8

Marriage-Go-Around: Divorce and Remarriage in Canada

Aysan Sev'er

LEARNING OBJECTIVES

In this chapter, you will learn that:

1. divorce is an increasingly common phenomenon in Canadian family life,

2. legal changes in 1968 and 1985 liberalized divorce, making it easier to obtain,

3. different theoretical perspectives offer explanations for the reasons for, and consequences of, divorce on partners and children,

4. personal, social, economic, and cultural factors explain why certain groups of people are more likely to divorce than others,

5. upon divorce, women's family income drops while men's increases,

6. child support payments remain a pressing issue for children of divorce,

7. rising remarriage rates lead to an increase in blended families.

The great French philosopher Michel de Montaigne once said, "Marriage is like a cage; one sees the birds outside desperate to get in, and those inside equally desperate to get out" (Great Quotes, *Marriage*). In de Montaigne's words, this chapter is an analysis of those who (willingly or unwillingly) "got out" and others who "got in" again. Divorce is the dissolution of a marriage, and the termination of the legal duties and responsibilities of that marriage between two people. In Canada, finalization of divorce requires the formal sanction of a legal authority to dissolve the marital union. Once completed, divorce cancels the marital status of the parties, allowing each to marry another, if they so choose. Thus, marriages can be dissolved by divorce or death of one or both of the partners. Moreover, divorce is different than annulment. In divorce, a legally existing marital union is dissolved, whereas in annulment, the marriage is declared null and void (as if it never happened).

HISTORY OF DIVORCE

All major religions, in their own ways, have advocated for the continuation of marriages. In Matthew's words: "What therefore God hath joined together, let not man put asunder" (The Bible, 19:6). In Roman Catholicism, this protectionism has reached an all-out ban against divorces, which continues to the current times. In Islam and in Judaism, although there have been provisions for marital dissolution, they have been granted under extraordinary conditions, and even then, only grudgingly permitted. Moreover, the divorce process is usually gendered, where men have more rights than women. For example, under Islamic Law (**Shari'a**), it was sufficient for a man to repeat three times "*Talak*" (I divorce you) to his wife in front of at least three (male) witnesses. Although women were also permitted to seek divorce (*Khula*), the procedure in the latter case required the return of marital gifts. Although it was not absolutely necessary, wives often had to have a more definitive ground for divorce (Naser, 2005). In more traditional practices of Judaism, and regardless of the civil laws that govern the process, religious divorce can take place only when the wife receives a certificate (get) from the husband. Some men made it either difficult or impossible for their wives to obtain the "get" that would set them free (Katz and Lavee, 2005). In Sanskrit-driven Hinduism (the laws of Manu), not only is marriage seen as a lifelong process, but even the lives of widows who have survived their husbands' death are subdued in many ways (Puri, 1998).

So there is lots of moral cajoling embedded in societies against "asunder." The prohibitions of most religious teachings may still ring true for a number of their devoted followers, in different parts of the world. They may also survive in ethnic and cultural enclaves of the Canadian multicultural mosaic. Nevertheless, in most of the industrialized societies—including Canada—dissolutions of marriages have been increasingly removed from religious realms into the domain of secularized, civil laws. In modern societies, civil laws apply to all, and are less likely to discriminate on the basis of class, minority, or gender status. Moreover, attitudes toward divorce and perceptions of divorcees have become more tolerant. In the current chapter, we will trace the key points in this transition.

Divorce in Canada

With a few exceptions[1] highly industrialized societies have high divorce rates (Ambert, 2005; Statistics Canada, 2005; United Nations, 2005). However, until the late 1960s, Canada had one of the lowest rates of divorce among all industrialized nations. Using the crude divorce rate as number of divorces/100,000 population, in early 1920s, the rate of divorce in Canada was around five. Between 1925 and 1965, this rate rose from 5.9 to 45.7 (Sev'er, 1992). This exceptionally low prevalence did not mean that Canadian couples were uniquely happy and satisfied with their marriages. More accurately, the low rates reflected the difficulty of obtaining a divorce, the lack of standardization of the divorce process among the provinces and territories, the necessity to travel to Ottawa to receive a Parliamentary resolution, costs incurred in travel and legal wrangling to straighten out the provincial expectations and federal requirements, and the heavy religio-cultural pressures against divorce in provinces such as Quebec (Sev'er, 1992). To achieve uniformity among the provinces and to bring the legal system in line with the changing norms about marriage dissolution, the federal government enacted first the 1968 and then the 1985 *Divorce Acts*.

In order to put an end to the discrepancies among regions/provinces, and in sync with the liberalization of attitudes toward divorce, the Canadian government introduced the **Divorce Act, 1968.** The strengths of the act were numerous: (1) it constituted a step forward to releasing couples who were locked in unhappy marriages, (2) it established federal uniformity across provinces/territories, (3) and it established divorce as a secular process (and indirectly reduced religious hegemony on marriage dissolution). Table 8.1 provides divorce rates for Canada for selected years. It is not surprising that only one year after the introduction of the *Divorce Act*, 1968, divorce rates in Canada rose to 124.2/100,000 and have continued to rise until 1987 (362.3/100,000), which is considered the peak year (Sev'er, 1992; Ambert, 2005). However, the

Table 8. 1   **CANADIAN DIVORCE RATES (PER 100,000 POPULATION) BY SELECTED YEARS**

1921	6.4
1941	21.4
1961	36.0
1968	54.8
1969*	**124.2**
1981	271.8
1985	253.6
1986**	**298.8**
1987***	**362.3**
1990	295.8
1995	262.2
1997	224.8
2000	228.4
2002	223.0
2003	224.0
2004***	**0379/1000 marriages**

The table is compiled from different Statistics Canada publication summaries.

* Shows the immediate rise after the *Divorce Act*, 1968

**Shows the immediate rise after the *Divorce Act*, 1985

***Shows the peak year in divorce rates in Canada

****Note that the denominator in this estimate is different, and it is derived from the latest available divorce information available (Statistics Canada, 2008c).

Divorce Act, 1968 was only a partial liberation in divorce laws, since the basic premise of 'fault' was retained. Under the *Divorce Act*, 1968, people seeking marriage dissolution could do so for various "marital offences" ranging from adultery, bigamy, sodomy, bestiality, and rape to homosexual acts of their partners. People could also seek marriage dissolution for mental or physical cruelty. One way or another, the petitioner had to "prove" that his or her partner was guilty of the alleged acts (thus, the "fault" principle). The more liberalized portion of the *Divorce Act*, 1968 allowed a "marriage breakdown" category, for living apart for not less than three years, or for desertion for not less than five years. Although the required waiting period for the no-fault option was quite substantial, more than 30 percent of the couples used the "marriage breakdown" rather than "marital offence" category as the grounds for divorce (Sev'er, 1992; Richardson, 2001).

In 1985 (although the act came into effect in 1986), Canadian divorce law went through a final liberalization. Although three items from the "marital offence" categories were retained (adultery and physical or mental cruelty), the *Divorce Act*, 1985 now classifies the grounds for divorce as "marital breakdown." So, in the new act, the clear message is the secular, social-contract nature of marriages as opposed to their moral "sacredness" or religious "indissolubility." Moreover, the waiting period has been substantially reduced, where either member of the couple can get a legal divorce on the grounds of separation for not less than one year. In cases where both parties agree (mutual consent), couples can now get their divorce papers without having to go through long and tedious petitioning before the courts (Richardson, 2001). In 2004, 94.5 percent of the 69,608 divorces granted in Canada used the no-fault grounds (separation for not less than one year) (Statistics Canada, 2008b).

The *Divorce Act*, 1985 also ushered in other important changes. The first is the replacement of the "alimony" or "maintenance" concepts with the egalitarian version of "support." However, under the rubric of egalitarianism, this change may have inadvertently brought some hardship for women. We will have an opportunity to discuss in detail this hardship in the section about economic consequences of divorce. It is important to keep in mind that the economic hardship is greater for "displaced homemakers" who are women who have lived their adult lives in traditional, male-bread-winner type families (Coontz, 2000). Although there have been numerous gender-sensitive rulings in this regard, the fact remains that women are now in the position to prove to the court that they have contributed to their families/family property/family business in substantial ways (albeit not monetarily) in order to receive extended periods of support. Given the general social invisibility of housework and childcare, this may place women under a complicated burden of proof obligation.

The third major change the *Divorce Act*, 1985 introduced is the explicit emphasis on "the best interest of the child" in custody decisions. It also replaced the "custody" term with "parental responsibility"; however, "custody" is still widely used in the divorce literature. In the applications of the earlier legislation

(*Divorce Act*, 1968), the "tender-years" ideology was prevalent, deriving from the gender-based sentiments that young children need maternal care. In the *Divorce Act*, 1985 there is an overt recognition that the best interest of the child may be difficult to establish (see Box 8.1).

BOX 8.1   AN IMPORTANT SUPREME COURT DECISION: "THE BEST INTEREST OF THE CHILD"

On September 28, 2001, the Supreme Court of Canada released its decision in the custody case between Kimberly Van de Perre and Theodore and Valerie Edwards. This decision is notable for upholding the "best interest of the child," even under the complicating issues surrounding race.

Trial Court: In 1996, Ms. Perre (Caucasian/Canadian) had an affair with Mr. Edwards (African/American) who was a professional basketball player. At the time of the affair, Mr. Edwards was married, and was the father of twin daughters. After Elijah was born in 1997, Ms. Perre started custody proceedings, and sought child support from Mr. Edwards. After a lengthy hearing, the judge awarded sole custody to Ms. Perre, and ample visitation rights to Mr. Edwards.

Court of Appeal: Mr. Edwards contested the Trial Court decision. In this case, the Court of Appeal accepted Mrs. Edwards (African/American) as a "joint" appellant in seeking custody of Elijah. The Edwards were successful in their appeal, and Elijah was placed under their care.

Supreme Court: The Supreme Court upheld that custody decisions are to be made on the best interests of the child. It acknowledged that the decisions made by the Trial Judge are dependent on the specific facts in an individual case—facts to which the Court of Appeal does not have access. Moreover, in custody cases, the Supreme Court argued that finality is both a social interest and important to the parties and the child. In this case, Elijah's not being certain about where his home was, because of the Court of Appeal's intervention, was found to be problematic. The Supreme Court also rejected the decision to involve Mrs. Edwards in the appeal, given the fact that Elijah already had two biological parents willing to parent. In terms of the Appeal Court's suggestion that the Edwards would provide a stable home for Elijah, the Supreme Court supported the Trial Judge's position that Mr. Edwards' marriage might not be that stable, and if he engaged in a different affair, this might hurt Elijah. Moreover, the Supreme Court held that a custody decision can be made only on the parental qualities of the biological parents, not on how good a wife the appellant has. Most importantly, the Supreme Court stated

> Race can be a factor in determining the best interests of the child because it is connected to the culture, identity and emotional well-being of the child . . . Nevertheless, it is generally understood that biracial children should be encouraged to positively identify with both racial heritages. . . . notwithstanding the role that race may play in custody determinations, it appears that the Trial Judge noted that this issue was not determinative and that, in this case, Elijah would be in a more stable and loving environment if custody was granted to [his mother]."

Thus, the Supreme Court rejected the Appellant Court's decision, and restored sole custody to Ms. Perre. (Summarized from "Important Supreme Court Custody Decision," 2001. A docudrama on this case with pseudo-names was aired on Canadian CTV on April 5, 2009, under the title of "Playing for Keeps.")

The parental responsibilities and the best interest of the child provisions of *Divorce Act*, 1985 was later clarified with Bill C-22 (Department of Justice, 2003). Bill C-22 translates as Child Centered Family Justice Strategy. It has ushered in many clarifications on the best interest of the child, including nonadversarial dispute resolution strategies. Bill C-22 also brings a tougher stance on child support payments, including suspension of driver's licences, garnering unemployment benefits, lottery winnings, and if all fails, jail sentences for noncomplying parents (mostly fathers). The amendment now includes consultation with the child about his or her preferences—to the best of his or her capability—and provisions for assuring greater safety of the child, in cases where there is the potential for violence. The augmentation of *Divorce Act*, 1985 has somewhat reduced the traditional female sole-custody decisions, and increased the joint-custody decisions (Gorlick, 2005). For example, in 2004, out of the 31,764 custody decisions, mothers received custody in 14,309 cases, and there were 14,773 joint-custody decisions (Statistics Canada, 2008a). However, the perusal of statistics from parental responsibility decisions reveals that in excess of 80 percent of cases, mothers still retain *physical custody of their children*, followed at a considerable distance by fathers (12 percent) (Ambert, 2005; Statistics Canada, 2008a). In a small number of cases where neither biological parent is seen as fit or available, the custody goes to third parties (grandparents, aunts, older siblings), or it goes to the state. For example, in 2004, in 124 cases, custody was granted to third parties (Statistics Canada, 2008a).

STATISTICAL INFORMATION ON DIVORCES IN CANADA

Divorces can be measured crudely (number of divorces/1,000 or 100,000 population). This is a crude measure because divorce is often (but not exclusively) a young-adult and middle-aged phenomenon. All members of the population are not similarly at risk for divorce (for example, children, never-married, very old). Therefore, sometimes studies on divorce use the rate of divorces/per marriages/per year. However, these rates also have problems, since shorter duration marriages are more likely to end in divorce than longer-duration marriages. Thus, students should keep in mind that although measures of divorce have shortcomings (Ambert, 2005), they still provide valuable information for comparison.

In 2003, there were 147,391 marriages in Canada (Statistics Canada, 2007). The crude marriage rate per 1,000 population was 4.7. Most of these marriages took place in the most populous provinces (Ontario, Quebec, British Columbia, and Alberta, in that order). In the same year, there were 70,828 divorces in Canada. Quebec, Alberta, British Columbia, and Ontario (in that order), had the highest rates. It is interesting to note that prior to 1968, Quebec had the lowest rates of divorce in Canada, but currently, it has the highest rate of all provinces (Ambert, 2005). The Atlantic Provinces and one of the Territories (Nunavut) had the lowest rates (Statistics Canada, 2006b).

From the provided statistical information, it can be calculated that divorces in a given year constitute about 48 percent of marriages in the same year. However, this is a misleading calculation, and the 48 percent rate does not apply to all types of marriage dissolutions. Divorce rates substantially vary on the basis of region, duration of marriages, first versus subsequent marriages, and so on. The probability of a marriage to end in divorce before the couples celebrate their 30th anniversary is a better measure, and this rate is 37.9 percent in Canada as reported in the last row of Table 8.1 (Ambert, 2005; 2006; Statistics Canada, 2008c).

Nevertheless, divorce statistics seriously underrepresent marital dissolution. Divorce statistics are calculated only on "legal" marriages, and thus omit the breakdown in long-term, common-law relationships. Given the fact that common-law living, both pre-marriage and postdivorce, have been on a sharp rise (Gorlick, 2005; Statistics Canada, 2006a) and now constitute about 14 percent of all coupled living, the dissolution in these relationships is a form of divorce that escapes detection in national statistics. In addition, until 2005, same-sex relationships were not considered a legal form of marriage, so their dissolution was also omitted from the official divorce statistics. If break-up in all forms of long-term relationships are taken into account, the dissolution rates would be sharply higher than the officially reported divorce rates.

THEORETICAL APPROACHES TO UNDERSTANDING DIVORCE

There are no theories that are specifically developed to understand divorce. Instead, social scholars borrow the relevant concepts from existing theories in related areas to understand the causes and consequences of divorce. Within this context, it is worthy to mention exchange views, general conflict views, and feminist theories.

Exchange Theory

The exchange theory's approach to human relations parallels microeconomic models (Thibaut and Kelly, 1959). The exchange theory falls under the interactionist paradigm, and looks at stability versus dissolution in relationships at the micro level. It is suggested that people make rational choices and stay in relationships where the benefits of the relationship surpass its costs. In marriages, benefits and costs can be monetary, but also can include other valued symbolic dimensions (status, presence of children, beliefs in nondissolubility of marriages, and presence or absence of alternatives). According to social exchange, people also consider the cost of getting out of relationships (monetary such as lawyer's fees, support payments, but also nonmonetary, such as losing touch with children, loss of intimacy, and sexual access). It is argued that "the principle of least interest" will predict those who see the smallest benefit in continuation of relationships, and will become the most likely to break off relationships (Nelson, 2010, p. 285). The more dependent one is in a relationship—economically, socially, or emotionally—the more vulnerable he or (most likely) she will be in that relationship.

Conflict Theories

General conflict theories are macro-level theories. Macro theories search for the causes and consequences of social phenomena within structural and cultural dynamics, rather than in personal or interactional realms. Marxist versions of conflict theories start from the assumption that social life is determined by the material conditions that sustain that life. In other words, the mode of production in a given society will determine the social, political, legal, and intellectual life in that society. In that sense, Marx has introduced a highly critical analysis of the excessively materialistic, highly industrialized societies. His followers have shown how the capitalistic mode of production strains family life (Engels, 1993; Seccombe, 1975). It is argued that the mass production in factories removed labour from homes and farms, thus making the production of materials by families obsolete. For the satisfaction of their needs (food, clothing, shelter), families became increasingly dependent on the market. Wages for work in factories became the means to buy commodities. However, since factories became more partial to male labour over time, other members of the family (especially women and children) became dependent on the wages of men. The long hours necessary to earn wages, and the repetitiveness of work, diminished the time and energy that are necessary for the preservation of intimate lives.

Capitalism has had an additional negative impact on families. The mechanization that has reduced the production process to its most rudimentary forms has led to the deskilling of jobs, and made workers easily replaceable in the production process. The cyclical booms in capitalism are accompanied with unchecked spending, followed by economic busts that come with uncertainty and job loss. Even at the boom times, women are poorly paid, so that they constitute an exploitable labour force (McMullin, 2004). During economic downturns, the stress in family lives erodes trust and interdependency, and creates hostilities that are not easily reconcilable. Violence against women and children also shows a rise during times of economic unrest (Sev'er, 2002a). It is also interesting to note that although divorce rates experience a lull in major economic busts (possibly due to people's reluctance to make major changes during unpredictable times), they peak shortly after economic recovery (Sev'er, 1992). The economic busts are also particularly hard on families who are already separated and divorced. The level of difficulties may hit female lone parents the hardest, since the sole responsibility for their children may have already strained their engagement with gainful employment, and may have made them dependent on part-time work (Duffy and Pupo, 1992). The possible downturn in the economic circumstances of the estranged partner may also diminish the predictability of support payments, and play havoc with the lone parent's budget.

Feminist Political Economy

Political economy goes beyond the mostly unidimensional economic determinism of Marx. In political economy, the concern is with the clusters of institutions and social relations that form the social, political, and economic systems (Armstrong and Armstrong, 1984; 2002), and how these systems impact different populations. Political economy takes into account how variations of opportunity in employment, wages, housing, education, and health care, coupled with how differential legal and political policies, expose populations to differential outcomes. Feminist political economy adds the lens of gender, and argues that political, economic, and ideological features of a society are not only integrally linked, but also gendered (Armstrong and Armstrong, 1984; 2002). For example, through feminist political economy, how societal values and ideas about women and men translate into inequalities of power, influence, and access to resources can be analyzed.

It is also argued that social and political ideologies influence public policy and the distribution of economic resources. Thus, political economy also encompasses a materialistic dimension. For example, through the application of the feminist political economy views, we can understand the clusters of disadvantages female lone parents face after divorce. The disadvantages could be in terms of lowered income, reduced opportunities of work, poorer housing, lack of access to education, and greater dependence on health care, as well as legal hurdles in accessing support or public assistance. Through feminist political economy, we can better understand the difficulties minority women, non-white women and/or immigrant women may face as lone parents (Calliste, 2000); in addition to limited income, they may face discrimination in housing and work situations. Rather than making their lives more predictable, government policies such as taxing support payments may further increase the pressures on their lives.

Other Feminist Approaches

Liberal Feminism   Although there are many variations of feminist theories, most converge on the inequalities between men and women. Liberal feminism is mostly interested in the creation of a just and compassionate society. Like other liberal discourses, liberal feminism aims at creating equal opportunities for men and women to ensure that members of a society fulfil their individual potential. In Canada, the liberal feminist agenda is intimately interwoven with the recommendations of the Royal Commission on the Status of Women in 1970. In 1973, the establishment of the National Action Committee on the Status of Women continued to provide a collective voice for women's needs and concerns. Thus, liberal feminists worked toward employment equity, pay equity, parental leave, subsidized day care and affordable housing issues. Most of the liberalization of the Canadian divorce laws discussed above were due to the concerted efforts of the liberal feminist movement (Calixte, Johnson and Motapanyane, 2010). Nevertheless, liberal feminists seek social change within the existing system, specifically through liberalized laws, without demanding a rapturous change in structural factors that continue to generate these inequalities (such as race, class, gender, sexual orientation). However, it is difficult to analyze the multiplexity of disadvantages in women's, racialized women's or **lone mothers'** lives through simplified notions of equality.

Socialist Feminism Socialist feminists attempt to address inequalities both in the public and the private spheres of life. At the public dimension, socialist feminists focus on inequalities in work conditions, wages, benefits, opportunities for promotion, presence of chilly climates, and sexual harassment issues. In the private sphere, the focus of socialist feminist theories has been on persistent inequalities in the division of labour in housework, childcare, and eldercare. The focus has been on the double burden most women have to carry, since men's contribution to house or childcare has not kept up with the sharp increase of women's paid labour force participation. When women do not work for pay, but dedicate their lives to their homes, families and children, their contributions will be less than adequately appreciated or visible. Thus, one way or another, the inequalities in the home and in the workplace will find a way to seep into family lives, and in time, will generate misunderstandings, tensions, and more overt types of conflict (Hartmann, 1981; Hochschild, 1997; Hochschild and Machung, 1990).

Socialist feminists have also introduced the "feminization of poverty" concept to highlight the much higher likelihood of women to be poor (Calixte, Johnson, and Motapanyane, 2010). In general, women's segregated work, lower pay, transient labour-force participation, invisibility of contribution to care for families, children, and the elderly all combine to produce gendered distribution of poverty. Women are also likely to experience a substantial loss in their standard of living after a divorce.

What theory one chooses will determine how one sees the causes and consequences of divorce. Interactionist theories like the exchange theory will focus on personal and intimate dimensions, whereas macro theories will address the societal, structural, legal, and political contexts. Feminist theories will always remind us about the importance of gender and differential power, and women's vulnerabilities in class, race, and gender systems.

CORRELATES OF DIVORCE

Divorces are due to a combination of factors, some macro-, others micro level, which accumulate across time in a marriage (Ambert, 2005; 2006). Each divorce is as unique as the couple who seeks it. Therefore, it is better to talk about correlates of divorce, rather than the more definitive-sounding "causes." Social research over the years has identified some factors that closely correlate with divorces. The order of importance of these factors will depend on the theoretical position that is utilized; however, it is still possible to summarize these factors under personal, social, ideological, and structural levels.

Personal Correlates

The personal reasons for divorce may relate to addictions such as alcohol, drugs, or gambling; presence of psychological/physical/sexual violence; adultery; impotence; and/or parental incest. In light of the exchange theory, the presence of any one or a collection of these factors may make it too costly for one (or both) of the partners to stay in the marriage. Although we often talk about personal factors as if they occur on their own, sociologists often underscore the importance of social conditions that sometimes reduce the probability, but at other times exacerbate the divorce outcomes.

Social Correlates

The most hazardous social correlate is the inverse relationship between divorce and age: the younger the couple at marriage, the higher the probability of divorce (Ambert, 2005; Statistics Canada, 2006a). However, there may be a slight erosion in the protective nature of mature ages, since dissolution of marriages of older couples with long-term marriages are also on the rise (Wu and Penning, 1997). Common-law living before marriage, existence of parental divorces, and existence of nontraditional age differences (older women, much younger men) are also found to be risk factors (Hall and Zhao, 1995; Statistics Canada, 2006a). Higher levels of education (of both men and women), presence of young children (the larger the number, the lower the probability), and the duration of marriage (the longer, the more robust) are found to be protective factors, whereas low income, low education, mixed-race or mixed-faith marriages are risk factors for divorce (Hall and Zhao, 1995).

In Canada, especially among the younger, urban, and highly educated populations, mixed-race and mixed faith couples are on the rise. However, mixed-couples still form only about 3 percent of all couples (Milan and Hamm, 2004). The propensity to form mixed-marriages widely varies from group to group; Japanese and Latin Americans are the most likely, and South Asians and Chinese are the least likely (Milan and Hamm, 2004). In terms of faith, Protestants are the most likely to marry other faith groups, whereas Sikhs, Muslims, and Hindus are the least likely to intermarry (Statistics Canada, 2006c).

The fact that their numbers are increasing does not assure total acceptance of mixed couples. Although some of the social taboos may have been broken, mixed-race or mixed-faith families may still experience added pressures (social costs) from their social surroundings, and each other's kin (LaRose, 2008). They may also experience overt forms of racism and discrimination (Calliste, 2000). These social processes may explain the higher rates of divorce among mixed-couples (Statistics Canada, 2006a). Interestingly, availability (or perceived availability) of alternatives is also a social correlate of divorce. In ethnic enclaves of the Canadian mosaic where remarriages or common-law living is not tolerated, people will be less eager to end an existing marriage, and risk life-long singlehood.

Ideological Correlates

Ideological correlates of marital dissolution include ideas about women's rights, egalitarian ideals, importance of "individuality" and "self-fulfillment," the level of general liberalism and secularism in a society (versus the power of religious doctrines about indissolubility of marriages). In Canada, it is not surprising that the first round of liberalization of divorce laws (1968) more or less coincided with the second wave of feminism in late 1960s and 1970s. It is also due to increased liberalization and secularization that Quebec's divorce rates changed from the lowest in the country to the highest.

Increased individuation and the erosion of communities have also reduced family ties that once provided social and economic support for families. Individuals are expected to be much more self-reliant than in the past. Neoliberal governments have exploited the heightened individuation norms by reducing or retrenching social safety networks (Noce, 2005). Therefore, there are close links between ideologies and structural constraints.

Structural Correlates

Structural factors involve liberal divorce laws (versus strict and punitive ones). Structural factors may also include paid work availability for women, and women's participation in the labour force, at the macro levels (Ambert, 2005). Other opportunities (versus constraints) are availability and enforcement of governmental policies in support payments (especially for children), availability of universal childcare and affordable housing, liveable wages above poverty lines, and/or existence of welfare, disability or unemployment benefits. In traditional societies where women's labour-force participation is not allowed, where there are not many social safety networks for women and their children, where women and the children they bear are totally dependent on male providers, divorce rates are minimal. In Canada, like in most other industrialized nations, there are fewer structural constraints to prevent women and men from seeking divorces. Still, as we will see in the economic consequences of divorce, there are macro-level constraints on especially low-income, **lone-parent** women's lives, which can be resolved only through family-friendly policies and equity-based legislation.

So many correlates of divorce should not lead readers to the conclusion that if any one or a set of these factors are present, couples will immediately seek divorce. On the contrary, marital satisfaction research shows that some couples choose to stay together, despite falling under multiple risk factors for divorce. Others may have a low tolerance for adversity in their marriage, and may have alternatives to make a divorce decision more readily. So divorce, marriage breakdown, and dissatisfaction in marriages are not always identical processes. However, in countries where divorce laws permit no-fault uncoupling (Canada, since 1985); where social-safety networks exist (such as childcare, housing geared to income, welfare); and where equality, individuality, and self-fulfilment are part of highly valued social ideals, divorce rates will be high.

GENERAL AND GENDERED CONSEQUENCES OF DIVORCE

Economic Consequences and Debunking Myths

There are many, sometimes contradictory, myths that surround divorce. One of the widely held myths is that "men are taken to the cleaners by their ex-wives." This myth is fuelled by many vested-interest groups such as men who relentlessly lament about division of family property during divorce settlement and child-support payments after settlement; conservative politicians and policy makers who are determined to preserve male privileges to keep women in place; conservative media that runs after sensationalized divorce cases; and even standup comedians who milk the topic for their jokes. Mickey Rooney, a severely height-challenged American comedian is quoted as saying, "A lot of people have asked me how short I am. Since my last divorce, I think I am about $100,000 short" (Great Quotes, *Divorce*). To some degree, a few publicity-seeking socialites/celebrities have also contributed to the myth. After a long-fought 1992 divorce, Ivana Trump is quoted as saying, "Don't get mad, get everything" (cited in Lewis, 2005). She received a $25 million-dollar settlement from what appeared to be the bottomless pit of Trump assets. Most recently, Heather Mills, after a bitter and much-publicized divorce, received the equivalent of $48.7 million from former Beatle Paul McCartney (Kreps, 2008). Mills also negotiated a $70,000/year child support, and all school and nanny expenses for their 4-year-old daughter.

However, celebrity divorces also work in opposite ways. For example, Kevin Federline's divorce from Britney Spears made him a rich man. He settled for assets worth more than $13.5 million, and $25,000 a month in child support for each of the couple's two children until they reach 18. He will also get his share of the couple's Malibu mansion ("Kevin Federline Divorce Settlement," 2007). Ending her marriage to filmmaker Guy Ritchie cost Madonna more than CDN$90 million. This is deemed to be "one of the largest payouts ever in a divorce settlement" ("Madonna, Ritchie Divorce Settlement," 2008).

However, students of sociology should be extremely cautious about making generalizations from a few "juicy" celebrity divorces, media pundits, or disgruntled ex-husbands. The following are the sobering facts about Canadian women's and children's postdivorce experiences:

* Since the enactment of the *Divorce Act*, 1985, the concept of alimony has been abolished, and divorced spouses are expected to be self-sufficient or reach self-sufficiency within a designated period of time. Women are no longer automatically entitled to "maintenance" (under the 1968 *Divorce Act*). Instead, both men and women are entitled to seek spousal support, and only for a designated period of time (usually, one year). Prolonged support requires proof of the economic handicaps a spouse may have experienced during his or her marriage. Although these provisions appear egalitarian, they nevertheless ignore the fact that marriages are not egalitarian unions. Historically, and especially during

child-bearing and rearing years, women still disproportionally sacrifice personal time, energy, and leisure. There are also indirect costs for women such as lost wages, lost accumulation of wealth, and lost benefits/pensions. Yet, only in rare cases do these sacrifices translate into postdivorce support payments, now called "rehabilitative alimony." As the term implies, even when awarded, this is not a permanent arrangement, and few women receive such settlements (Coontz, 2000; Rogerson, 2002).

• In uncontested cases, and despite the new emphasis on the "best interest of the child" ideology embedded in the *Divorce Act*, 1985, a very high percentage of divorced women still end up being the custodians of their children. In Canada, only about 10–12 percent of children of divorce reside with their fathers, and most of these are older children (Ambert, 2005). For example, in 2004, out of the 31,764 custodies awarded, only 2,558 fathers received sole custody (Statistics Canada, 2008a). So, gendered court decisions in allocation of custody, and their economic implications, still remain as concerns. Although child-support payments seem to have received some legislative attention in Canada (Bill C-22), most men still pay only a small fraction of what it takes to raise a child, and a large proportion default a year after separation. Almost all men stop child support payments before their children reach legal age and/or self-sufficiency (Finnie and Sweetman, 2003). Thus female lone parents are much more likely to be poor, and much more likely to receive welfare (Ambert, 2006; Women and Poverty, ND).

• Almost without exception, divorce studies suggest that women and their children experience a major economic downturn after divorce (Statistics Canada, 2009a, 2009b). It is estimated that approximately 52 percent of women raising families by themselves are poor (Ambert, 2006; Income and Poverty Gaps, 2004; Women and Poverty, ND. For example, in 2006, although the median income of couple families was $70,400, the median income of lone-parent families was only $33,000. It should be kept in mind that female lone parents still have to bear the costs of childcare, housing, clothing, food, schooling etc., which are often shared in two-parent households. Although Statistics Canada (2009b) did not differentiate between female versus male-headed lone-parent family incomes, other research suggests that 80–85 percent of lone-parent families are headed by women (Ambert, 2005, 2006; Richardson, 2001).

Even more disturbing are the following:

• Although median income of couple families between 2002 and 2006 has gone up more than $9,000, median income of lone-parent families has gone up less than $5,000 (calculated from Statistics Canada, 2009a, 2009b).

- Whereas 46.3 percent of lone-parent families live on $30,000 or less per year, only 5 percent of couple families do so. Ten percent of all lone-parent families survive on $10,000 or less; no couple families in Canada live in such a low income bracket (calculated from Statistics Canada, 2009a, 2009b).

- Finnie and Sweetman (2003), in their longitudinal analysis, also observe that women are poorer than men and spend more years in poverty than men, and 17.5 percent of the consistently poor are lone-parent mothers.

- In line with the clusters of disadvantages suggested by the feminist political economy views, the economic constraints often force women with younger children to drop out of workforce/school, or seek temporary employment and/or social assistance (Ambert, 2006; Gorlick, 2005; Rotermann, 2007; Women and Poverty, ND). There is a parallel downward slide in the standard of living, and often women and their children have to find cheaper accommodation in less desirable locations (Ambert, 2006; Sev'er, 1992; 2002a). Children often have to change friends and schools, and drop out of extracurricular activities that might cost money (McLanahan, 1997). In Canada, more than 1 million children live in poverty, mainly because their mothers are poor (Women and Poverty, ND).

- Many men experience a rise in their personal disposable income and in their standard of living after divorce (Finnie and Sweetman, 2003; Galarneau and Sturrock, 1997). Analyzing the National Health Survey data from over 12,000 couples, of which over a thousand had gone through a divorce over the study period (1995–2005), Rotermann (2007) found that 29 percent of men reported an increase in their income over a two-year period after divorce, whereas 43 percent of the women reported a decrease in their income. In an earlier ground-breaking study, Weitzman (1985) found that women experience a 73 percent postdivorce decline in their standard of living, whereas men experience a 42 percent increase. Gadalla (2009) also echoes some of the persistent inequalities. In a longitudinal study, Gadalla found that women's income was only 80 percent of that of men's, one year after divorce, and has risen to only 85 percent of men's income even five years after divorce. What is important to note is that Gadalla's (2009) sample included only employed men and women. Many divorced women are either not in the paid labour force or are transiently related to it due to their increased responsibilities as lone parents (Gorlick, 2005).

OTHER CONSEQUENCES OF DIVORCE

As serious as the economic outcomes for women are, consequences of divorce go beyond a socioeconomic downturn, and involve issues about litigation, emotional costs, violence, and consequences for children.

Litigation

The fact that Canadian divorce laws have moved toward a no-fault approxima-tion (*Divorce Act*, 1985) means that divorce in uncontested cases is much easier to obtain. In contested cases, however, the division of property, support, and custody issues may be both monetarily and emotionally draining for men as well as women. For women, the legal process may be frightening, and costs of litigation may be unbearable, especially at a time when their standard of living is at a decline. Lawyers and judges may be insensitive to or totally dismissive of the more personal trauma involed in divorce. In addition, the liberalized *Divorce Act* (*Divorce Act*, 1985) may have inadvertently created more difficulties for women who have been in traditional marriages. These women may be locked in prolonged litigation to convince the courts about their specific needs, which may not be well served under the "self-sufficiency" expectation of the *Divorce Act*, 1985.

Emotional Costs

Although the traditional stigma of divorce/divorcees has substantially declined over the years, there is no doubt that North American social life still favours couples (Gerstel, 1990). Thus, both divorced women and men may experience a period of social marginalization and isolation (Rotermann, 2007). Friends and kin may take sides, apportioning blame to the wife or husband. It is likely that the blame process will work against women more than men. The public–private divide in married life often has relegated the latter as the women's domain. Despite major gains in women's paid employ-ment, expectations about the division of labour have not been balanced (Guendozi, 2006; Baker, 2006). Regardless of what may have initiated the divorce, the social criticism of a wife as "failing to keep her family together" may be harsher than the evaluation of a husband's contribution to the breakup. The inequality in attributions of blame may even be true in cases of blameworthiness (i.e., male violence). Children, especially older children, may add their own voices to the chorus of blame, and/or may get trapped in split loyalties toward their newly estranged parents (Sev'er, 1992; Wallerstein, 2003).

Numerous studies look at postdivorce depression as an index of emotional cost. After a controlled pre/post divorce study, Rotermann (2007) reports that depression in separated or divorced people is four times more common than in their still-married counterparts. Moreover, depression in men was more common than depression in women. After controlling for the financial and support network changes divorced people experience, the gendered effects of divorce on depression were attenuated, but not totally eliminated. This may partially explain why divorced men are more likely to remarry than divorced women, as we discuss in the remarriage section.

Postdivorce Violence

In Canada, about one in three marital relationships are violent. In most cases, the perpetrators of violence are men, and targets are women and children (Sev'er, 2002b; 2002c). Even when children are not directly targeted, a large proportion do get indirectly victimized through witnessing violence against their mothers (Sev'er, 2002b; 2002c). However, unlike other personal relationships, the end of an intimate relationship/marriage does not necessarily signal an end to violence. As a matter of fact, relationships that were not previously violent may turn violent, or pre-existing violence may escalate during separations and divorces (Sev'er, 2002c). In the worst cases, women (and sometimes children) are killed by their estranged husbands (Sev'er, 1997; Sev'er, Dawson, and Johnson, 2004). This pattern shows that some women are at high risk for victimization after divorce, and explains why some women are afraid to terminate their (violent) marriages.

Children

According to the 2006 Canadian Census (Statistics Canada, 2006c), of the 7,494,965 children who live in a family setting, 19.8 percent live with a lone parent (16.2 percent with female lone parents). Of course, a fraction of the lone-parent families are due to the death of a partner, and a few are due to lone-parent adoptions/pregnancies. However, the most substantial reason for female lone-parenthood is divorce (Ambert, 2006).

Most data on children of divorce are generated from clinical samples, since well-adjusted children (from intact or from lone-parent families) rarely are asked to participate in studies. Thus, some studies have found dire and irreversible negative effects of divorce on children (Cherlin, 2004). Other studies suggest caution in making pessimistic generalizations (Hetherington and Kelly, 2002; Kelly and Emery, 2003; Kerr and Michalski, 2007; Strohschein, 2005).

The nature of effects on children of divorce are also quite varied. If nothing else, most children feel weak, insecure, and impotent in relation to their parental strife. Many may feel abandoned by one or both parents, as living conditions and social relations change around them (Wallerstein, 2003). Earlier studies report a host of somatic and psychosomatic ailments such as asthma, bed-wetting, anxiety attacks, tantrums, nightmares, and depression in preschool children (Amato and Keith, 1991; Kalter, 1977). More recent studies underscore adjustment problems in children, such as hyperactivity, decline in school performance, difficulties in intimate relationships, and trust issues (Kerr and Michalski, 2007; Sun and Li, 2001; Wallerstein, 2003).

Hetherington and Kelly (2002) have also observed adjustment problems in children of divorce, but argue that these problems are temporary. By the end of the elementary-school years, they claim that children from divorced and intact families become more or less the same.

During and post high school years, correlations between parental divorce and increased substance abuse, promiscuity, and criminality have been observed. Higher propensity for (adult) children's divorces are also reported (Ambert, 2006). Children of female lone parents may also have lower educational levels and may have children sooner. What is noted is that female and male children may react differently. Whereas males may externalize their anger and frustration (act out), females may internalize their angst (depression) (Furstenberg and Cherlin, 2001). Some researchers also caution us about "sleeper" effects, where children appear to be fine at the time of or following parental divorce, but start manifesting problems as they mature (Wallerstein, 2003). Nevertheless, Furstenberg and Cherlin (2001), wisely caution us that not all children get caught up in destructive cycles after the breakup of their parents' marriages.

There is the additional need to decipher how many of the problems observed in children of divorce are due to divorce and how many are produced or exacerbated by the circumstances that surround divorce. A longitudinal study of 2,819 children between 1994 and 1998 provides some answers (Strohschein, 2005). Children whose parents stayed together during the study period were compared with those whose parental marriages ended in divorce.

Strohschein found that there were *already existing* differences at the beginning of the study. The children whose parents eventually separated were already manifesting higher levels of anxiety, depression, and antisocial behaviour than those whose parents' marriage stayed intact (Strohschein, 2005). So attributing negative outcomes to divorce will be misleading without a careful analysis of what factors, in which ways, and under what circumstances are related to negative outcomes.

- Stability of living conditions is important for children. Thus, children who do not experience a significant economic downturn (along with their mothers) are likely to do better than their counterparts who get catapulted to the margins of poverty after parental divorce (Ambert, 2006; Women and Poverty, ND; Strohschein, 2005). Poverty is correlated not only with mental and physical health, but also with school performance and criminality (National Crime Prevention, 1995).

- Children who are able to sustain stable and loving relationships with both their custodial and noncustodial parent may fare better than their counterparts who are caught between bitter conflicts, custodial battles, and parental manipulation. However, as Wallerstein (2003) cautions us, forcing children to spend time with noncustodial parents who are dismissive, noncaring, and even abusive may further hurt the emotional well-being of children.

- Children who might have seen their parents' relationship as stable and loving may experience a harder time dealing with the divorce than children who have witnessed long and relentless strife between their parents (Amato and Booth, 1997; Wallerstein, 2003). This dimension is also very much related to how much open and honest communication has taken place between the parent(s) and the child about the imminence of divorce. In families where there have been ongoing threats, violence, and other serious manifestations of conflict, divorce may signal relief rather than mourning. On the other hand, the temporary relief may not assure long-term adjustment, since the effects of witnessing conflict and violence will also take its toll on the adjustment prospects (Sev'er, 2002a; 2002c).

In some of my earlier work, I have argued that although parental divorce may be emotionally and economically difficult for many children, the detrimental effects may even be worse in continuing to live in homes where there is blatant mistrust, lack of caring, ongoing subjugation and violence, and/or addiction problems (Sev'er, 1992; Sev'er and Pirie, 1991a; 1991b). After two decades, I still stand behind this assertion. The comparison group for adjustment of children from divorced/separated families should be children from intact but highly dysfunctional families. In the latter comparison, parental divorce may still be favourable to growing up in an unpredictable and destructive social environment. Recent results reported by Strohschein (2005) provide some support for this position. After divorce, there was indeed a reduction in the antisocial behaviour of children originally from intact but conflictual families.

POSTDIVORCE REMARRIAGE

Great 18th-century British philosopher Dr. Samuel Johnson once said that "remarriage is the triumph of hope over experience" (Bartlett's Familiar Quotations, 1980). There is a kernel of truth in these words when we examine the increased risk for redivorce among the remarried. Remarriage is the marriage of two people where one or both were married before. In remarriages, the dissolution of the previous marriage could have been due to the death of a partner, or due to divorce. In this chapter, our focus is on postdivorce remarriages, which often lead to the creation of **step families**.

Statistics Canada defines step families as "a family in which at least one of the children in the household is from a previous relationship of one of the parents" (GSS, 2002). Considering all step families in 2001, Statistics Canada reports the prevalence of four types as: only "his" children (10 percent), only "her" children (50 percent), **blended family** with no children in common (8 percent), and blended family with children in common (32 percent) (GSS, 2002). Blended families are defined as containing "children of both spouses from one or more previous unions or one or more children from the current union and one or more children from previous unions" (GSS, 2002, p. 8). In 1995, step families constituted only 10 percent of all families in Canada, but that proportion has risen to 12 percent (ibid).

Until 2005, only heterosexual marriages were considered legal in Canada, so the term "remarriage" applied to heterosexual divorcees who were legally married before. Since the legalization of same-sex marriages in 2005, the remarriage term/process now equally applies to same-sex couples where one or both were previously married. In the future, Statistics Canada will also report on marriage and remarriage trends among same-sex couples, information that has been lacking from official statistics so far.

A large proportion of divorcees, but not all, do indeed remarry. For example, in the General Social Survey (GSS, 2002), 89 percent of the marriages in the year of the survey (2001) were between never-before married people. The remaining 11 percent contained at least one previously married partner (GSS, 2002; Wu and Schimmele, 2005). According to Statistics Canada (2008b), this proportion has risen to over 16 percent for both men and women. So remarriage is common, but by no means universal. In fact, most divorcees seem to prefer common-law or serial common-law relationships after a divorce (Wu and Schimmele, 2005). A few remarry their ex-partners (see Box 8.2).

BOX 8.2   EMINEM REMARRIES EX-WIFE IN MICHIGAN

Eminem, the superstar rapper, remarried his high school sweetheart, a month after the announcement that they were getting back together. News helicopters hovered overhead, and paparazzi congregated outside Meadow Brook Hall as Eminem and Kim Mathers arrived in a limousine, and were whisked inside the 110-room mansion. Eminem's first marriage to Kim Mathers had ended after two-plus years of marriage in 2001, after an ugly legal fight that included a custody battle over their young daughter. Eminem, 33, and Kim Mathers, 30, reconciled in late 2004, and got back together in matrimony in 2006. The pair were "teenage sweethearts," while growing up in the suburbs along Detroit's northern border. (Summarized from TMZ, 2006).

In the earlier sociological literature, remarriage was conceptualized as another form of marriage. More recent literature focuses on differences, rather than similarities. The following list highlights some of the differences between first versus remarriages, while also underscoring gendered observations.

- The mean age at first marriage for men and women in Canada is around 28 and 30 respectively (Statistics Canada, 2007). The second and subsequent marriages occur at mid- or late adulthood (Wu and Schimmele, 2005). Moreover, the age difference between remarrying men and women jumps up to 9–10 years. This is partially due to older (and presumably more established) men's desire for younger wives, and younger women's willingness to marry older men. In the remarriage market, this age gradient puts divorced women (older) in iniquitous competition with much younger, and possibly never married, women.

- More divorced men than divorced women enter a remarriage (Wu and Schimmele, 2005). This pattern may be an outcome of many different reasons that are also gendered:
  - Like the age gradient, the socioeconomic gradient may be at work (men's tendency to marry women who are slightly lower on the socioeconomic scale, which is hypergamy for women and hypogamy for men). In remarriages, this traditional tendency may be exaggerated. This means that while accomplished, educated divorced men can easily find a new mate, accomplished, highly educated, financially independent divorced women will likely remain on their own. One recent alternative to this pattern is what Jessie Bernard (1972) calls "cream-of-the-crop" women picking from "the-bottom-of-the-barrel" men. However, there may still be a social reaction against nontraditional choices women make (Sev'er, 1992).
  - To parallel the hyperactivation of age and socioeconomic gradients, second and subsequent marriages are also more heterogeneous in ethnicity, faith, and race. This increased diversity may reflect a heightened acceptance of differences among remarrying couples. This pattern may also reflect the reduced influence of kin/family on the choices of older divorcees (as opposed to younger adults in first marriages). However, mixed remarriages, like mixed marriages, have a higher probability of breakup (Statistics Canada, 2006a).
  - The gendered skew in custody decisions is clearly reflected in remarriages (GSS, 2002). Findings show that only 10 percent of stepfamilies have "his," but 50 percent have "her" children alone, while an additional 8 percent have children from previous marriages of both partners. So, obviously, women with depended children do remarry. However, multiple children from earlier marriage(s) may act as a hindrance to women's remarriage prospects; not too many men are eager to raise someone else's children. For men, however, the number of children they have from a previous marriage will not diminish their desirability, since it is highly likely that their children will reside with their ex-wives.
- On average, first marriages last 12–14 years in Canada (Ambert, 2005). Second and subsequent marriages are more prone to dissolution, and more prone to dissolution after a shorter duration than first marriages. For example, one in five remarried Canadians had already left their spouse within an average of 7.5 years (Statistics Canada, 2006a).
- On average, satisfaction in second marriages is reported to be higher than in first marriages (Bibby, 2005). Maybe this is because the remarried couples are older at remarriage than their first-time counterparts. Maybe the remarried couples may be slightly more established in their lives, and thus a little more resilient to economic or family pressures. Yet it is worth

noting the incongruence between the higher reported satisfaction and higher risk for divorce in subsequent marriages. Maybe having already gone through a divorce before makes these couples more prepared to end a relationship if it does not meet their expectations (Statistics Canada, 2006a).

- Compared to first marriages, there is a potential for multiplicity and complexity of relationships in subsequent marriages (Eichler, 1997). Ex-wives, ex-husbands, children from the prior marriages of either or both partners, mutual children of the couple, presence of an older set and newer set of grandparents/kin, and a complex lineage of in-laws can exhaust the remarried couple. Of course, the blended families will also be more vulnerable to the lingering tensions from previous marriages, especially if earlier divorce/custody battles have been toxic.

- Children in blended families report less support from parents, and more conflict with parents (Nilan, 2000). However, it cannot be assumed that the presence of step-children is the reason that remarriages have a higher risk for dissolution. When other variables are controlled for, presence of children is not associated with the dissolution of remarriages (Statistics Canada, 2006a).

CONCLUSION

In this chapter, we saw that divorces and remarriages are already common occurrences in Canada, and separated, divorced, or remarried parents and their children are part of the diverse family forms people live in. We also debunked some common myths that surround divorce. One myth was that men suffer from the excessive economic demands of their ex-wives. The other myth was that divorce is unconditionally bad for children. In the sociological literature, there are only a few researchers who see divorce as a social and/or personal failure and as the source of many social ills (Popenoe, 1993; 2008). These excessive positions may appeal to right-wing politicians and ultra-orthodox social groups, but do not lead to constructive insights. Fortunately, most family scholars provide more realistic analyses of divorce and remarriage. Indeed, coupled intimacies within heterosexual or same-sex marriages, remarriages, common-law relationships, mixed-marriages, and serial marriages[2] do provide choices for adults and many benefits to children who live and grow in those relationships. In addition, the literature shows us what factors are correlated with the stability of marriages, and what other factors are related to heightened risks of marriage dissolution (such as youth, low socioeconomic status, and prior cohabitation). Even when many positive correlates like higher education, higher income, and later marriages come together, there is no guarantee that the couple will stay together "till death [does them] part." On the other hand, some couples stay together despite all odds and many negative experiences. So, at best, we can discuss probabilities, not unconditional predictions.

In Canada, life expectancy of both men and women has made substantial gains. Women and men now can look forward to a life that spans into the early 80s. It is increasingly unlikely that a decision a young couple makes at the age of 25 will still be the most appropriate/desirable choice for them throughout the next 50 to 60 years of their life. Longevity, combined with the other risk factors we discussed, signals high divorce rates, give or take small fluctuations across the decades. Baby boomers who are approaching their retirement years may indeed push the ages of divorce and remarriage into much later years in life (Wu and Schimmele, 2007). Thus, the most constructive way to address divorce and remarriage is to avoid instigations of moral panics or social blame games. Instead, societies must work toward the creation of personal, social, and structural mechanisms to reduce the negative effects of divorce, especially on women and children. Divorce is not the end of the North American Family, as some claim. Divorce is one of many alternatives available in the diversity of family forms.

We noted that higher education and income often serve as protective mechanisms against marriage breakdown. This may be because educated men and women often avoid very early marriages. Early marriages carry one of the highest risks for marriage dissolution. It is also possibly that educated women will have higher self-confidence and a better prospect in the paid-labour market. These acquired qualities may elevate their bargaining power in their marriages. Even when their marriages disseminate, educated/working women and their children may fair better than their lower socioeconomic status and less well prepared counterparts.

Conflict theories, including feminist political economy views, also inform us that intimate relationships are firmly grounded in social and structural contexts. It is important to understand the link between what is considered to be personal troubles and the social inequalities that fuel them. The perfect example to this link is the propensity of so many women and their children to face a downward slide in their standard of living after divorce. Rather than a personal trouble, these clustering and gendering of disadvantages show existing cracks at the social, economic, legal, and political levels. Despite the overall affluence in Canada, we still live in a society that has systemic inequalities in distribution of opportunities and resources. We still have not achieved pay equity, equal pay for work of equal value, equality in benefits, and equality in promotions for working men and women. We still have major earning differences between immigrant and nonimmigrant groups, especially if the immigrants are from the non-Western parts of the world. The imbalances between how much men and women contribute to home and childcare still disproportionally tax women's time and opportunities. So although divorces and effects of divorces may appear as personal troubles, they are very much cradled in social and structural apportioning of opportunities and government policies that do not ameliorate class, race, gender-based disadvantages.

So, rather than discussing whether divorce is bad for women and children, it will be much more fruitful to ask what needs to be done to support families and children, regardless of the family type they live in (Eichler, 1997). Liveable wages; generous social, health, and parental benefits; and availability of skills training or continuing education will go a long way for individuals, parents, or lone parents to live meaningful and productive lives. Regardless of one's station in life, help with childcare through quality, geared-to-income programs and access to safe and affordable housing are important for all families, especially lone mothers. It is a disgrace to all Canadians that more than 1 million of our children are still living below the poverty line. Most of these are the children of lone mothers (Statistics Canada, 2006a; 2006b). Child credits and subsidies, tax credits, and other transfer payments must fill the poverty gap for all Canadians, again, regardless of which type of family they live in. Divorces, remarriages, and lone parents will remain as part of the diverse topography of family life in which people live and children are raised. The challenge is to remove the structural barriers that lock some of these families in perpetual disadvantage.

In cases of violence toward estranged partners, the social justice system must also kick into action to protect lone mothers and their children. Enshrining "the best interest of the child" in legislation is positive but not sufficient unless it is backed by enforcement of rules and regulations. Although Bill-C22 (Department of Justice, 2003) has gone a long way in protecting the rights of children, support payments in divorce cases are still low, and many payments are still in arrears. Without the provision of nutritious food, warm clothes, and a safe place to call home, "the best interest of the child" will be only rhetoric. Without the chance to attend good schools and participate in mind/body enhancing extra-curricular activities, and without protection from postdivorce violence against their mothers or themselves, "the best interest of the child" will be an unfulfilled social promise. Whether married, remarried, or single, whether men or women, all citizens of an affluent society like Canada have a stake in the true best interest of children, in whichever type of family they live in.

Summary

- Domestic labour is often taken for granted as women's work.

- Although domestic labour, especially childcare, is said to be important, it is accorded low status.

- Family-based strategies alone cannot resolve the underlying contradictions between participating in both income-generating work and maintaining a household.

Notes

1. Traditionally, Italy's, Japan's and Ireland's divorce rates were low, even though they were industrialized societies. Even in these traditional exceptions, the divorce rates are now on the rise (Sev'er, 1992).

2. The marriage, divorce, and remarriage cycles (including possibly redivorce, and additional marriages) create serial marriages.

Critical Thinking Questions

1. What are the differences between micro and macro approaches toward the analyses of divorce? In terms of the economic outcomes of divorce for women, which approach do you think is better? Why?

2. After the steep climb in Canadian divorce rates after the 1968 Divorce Act, some people argued that liberal divorce laws caused high rates of marital dissolution. Do you agree or disagree with such an assertion? Why?

3. What measures do you think are crucial to cushion the possible negative effects of divorce on children? Discuss what parents, society, and laws can do to ameliorate negative effects.

4. In which ways do you think the states can assure the well-being of families? Discuss.

Websites

Women and Poverty Factsheet (Canadian Research Institute for the Advancement of Women)
http://www.criaw-icref.ca/WomenAndPoverty
> *Women and Poverty* combines reasons and outcomes of poverty for women (and their children). The website combines statistical, media, and social scientific research summaries. Divorce is evaluated among the primary reasons behind poverty for women.

Divorce: Facts, Causes and Consequences (The Vanier Institute of the Family)
http://www.vifamily.ca/library/cft/divorce_05.pdf
> *Divorce: Facts, Causes and Consequences* is a recent series of publications by the Vanier Institute of the Family. It is written by Anne-Marie Ambert, who is a leading Canadian scholar on the area of divorce. In this publication, Ambert discusses the causes and consequences of divorce. She also clarifies what statistical numbers mean, and how accurate or misleading they can be.

The Daily—Statistics Canada
http://www.statcan.gc.ca/daily-quotidien/070117/dq070117a-eng.htm
> *The Daily* is a Statistics Canada series that publish on a variety of subjects on the Canadian society (from heads of cattle to all sorts of demographic findings). I refer students to the marriage and divorce sections at the link above.

The Department of Justice Canada
http://laws.justice.gc.ca/en/D-3.4/index.html
> This site includes the complete version of Canada's 1985 *Divorce Act*.

Suggested Readings

A-M. Ambert. 2006. *One-Parent Families: Characteristics, Causes, Consequences and Issues.* Ottawa: Vanier Institute of the Family.

> One-parent families are on the rise in Canada, and there is also a slight shift from almost exclusively female-headed forms to some occurrence of male-headed forms. However, in this work, Ambert rightly underscores the economic and social difficulties that continue to disproportionately affect female-headed families and the children who live with their mothers.

A. Ambert. 2005. *Divorce: Facts, Causes and Consequences,* 2nd ed. Ottawa: Vanier Institute of the Family.

> Anne-Marie Ambert's work on divorce is one of a few pillars of Canadian divorce literature. Her careful analysis of causes and consequences of divorce bring into focus the complexity of the divorce process. Especially in terms of the consequences, Ambert uses a gender-sensitive focus.

Vanier Institute of the Family. 2004. *Profiling Canadian Families III.* Ottawa: VIF.

> Vanier Institute of the Family has been in the business of studying Canadian families over many decades. As such, its work also allows the study of trends and across-time changes that are occurring in family life in Canada.

Statistics Canada. 2002. *Changing Conjugal Life in Canada.* General Social Survey (GSS-Cycle 15). Cat. 89-576-XIE.

> This document contains one of the most comprehensive statistical information about changes occurring in marriage or marriage-like unions in Canada.

References

Amato, P. and A. Booth. 1997. *A Generation at Risk: Growing up in an Era of Family Upheaval.* Cambridge, MA: Harvard University Press.

Amato, P. and B. Keith. 1991. "Parental Divorce and the Well-being of Children: A Meta-Analysis." *Psychological Bulletin,* 110: 26–46.

Ambert, A. 2005. *Divorce: Facts, Causes and Consequences,* 2nd ed. Ottawa: Vanier Institute of the Family.

Ambert, A-M. 2006. *One-parent Families: Characteristics, Causes, Consequences and Issues.* Ottawa: Vanier Institute of the Family.

Armstrong, P. and H. Armstrong. 1984. *The Double Ghetto,* revised ed. Toronto: McClelland and Stewart.

Armstrong, P. and H. Armstrong. 2002. *Thinking It Through: Women, Work and Caring in the New Millennium.* Halifax, Canada: Canadian Institutes of Health Research. Nova Scotia Advisory Council on the Status of Women and Atlantic Centre of Excellence for Women's Health.

Baker, M. 2006. *Choices and Constraints in Family Life.* Toronto: Oxford.

Bartlett's Familiar Quotations. 1980. 125th Anniversary Edition. E.M. Beck (Ed.). New York: Little Brown.

Bernard, J. 1972. The Future of the Family. New York: Bantam.

Bibby, R.A. 2005. Future Families Project: A Survey of Canadian Hopes and Dreams. Ottawa: Vanier Institute of the Family.

Calliste, A. 2000. "Black Families in Canada: Exploring the Interconnections of Race, Class and Gender." In M. Lynn (Ed.), Voices: Essays on Canadian Families (pp. 199–220). Toronto: Thomson Nelson.

Calixte, S.L.L., J.L. Johnson, and J.M. Motapanyane. 2010. "Liberal, Socialist and Radical Feminism." In N. Mandell (Ed.), Feminist Issues (5th ed.) (pp. 1–39). Toronto: Pearson.

Cherlin, A.J. 2004. "The Deinstitutionalization of American Marriage." Journal of Marriage and Family 66: 848–861.

Coontz, S. 2000. "Marriage: Then and Now," Phi Kappi Phi Journal 80: 10–15.

Department of Justice. 2003. Family Justice Newsletter (spring). pp. 1–4. http://canada.justice.gc.ca/en/ps/pad/news/052003.html (accessed March 2009).

Duffy, A. and N. Pupo. 1992. Part-Time Paradox. Toronto: McClelland & Stewart.

Eichler, M. 1997. Family Shifts: Families, Policies and Gender Equality. Toronto: Oxford.

Engels, F. 1993 [1942]. The Origin of the Family, Private Property and the State. New York: International.

Finnie, R. and A. Sweetman. 2003. "Poverty Dynamics: Empirical Evidence for Canada." Canadian Journal of Economics, 36: 291–325.

Furstenberg, F.F. and A.J. Cherlin. 2001. "Children's Adjustment to Divorce." In B. Fox (Ed.), Family Patterns, Gender Relations, 2nd ed. (pp. 491–499). Toronto: Oxford.

Gadalla, T.M. 2009. "Impact of Marital Dissolution on Men's and Women's Incomes: A Longitudinal Study." Journal of Divorce & Remarriage 50(1): 55–65.

Galarneau, D. and J. Sturrock. 1997 (Summer). "Family Income after Separation." Perspectives, pp. 18–28. (Statistics Canada Catalogue No. 75-001-XPE).

Gerstel, N. 1990. "Divorce and Stigma." In C. Carlson (Ed.), Perspectives on the Family: History, Class and Feminism. (pp. 460–478). Thousand Oaks, CA: Wadsworth.

Gorlick, C.A. 2005. "Divorce: Options Available, Constraints Forced, Pathways Taken." In N. Mandell and A. Duffy (Eds.), Canadian Families: Diversity, Conflict and Change. Toronto: Thompson.

Great Quotes. Divorce. http://www.great-quotes.com/cgi-bin/viewquotes.cgi:? (accessed April, 2009, keyword "divorce").

Great Quotes. Marriage. http://www.great-quotes.com/cgi-bin/viewquotes.cgi:? (accessed April 2009, keyword "marriage").

GSS. 2002. Statistics Canada. *General Social Survey. Changing Conjugal Life in Canada.* Cat. 89-576-XIE. http://dsp-psd.tpsgc.gc.ca/Collection/Statcan/89-576-X/89-576-XIE2001001.pdf (accessed April 12, 2010).

Guendozi, J. 2006. "'The Guilt Thing': Balancing Domestic and Professional Roles." *Journal of Marriage and the Family,* 68: 901–909.

Hall, D.R. and J.Z. Zhao. 1995. "Cohabitation and Divorce in Canada: Testing the Selectivity Hypothesis." *Journal of Marriage and the Family,* 57, 421–427.

Hartmann, H. 1981. "The Unhappy Marriage of Marxism and Feminism: Towards a More Progressive Union." In L. Sargent (Ed.), *Women and Revolution* (pp. 1–41). Boston: South End.

Hetherington, E.M. and J. Kelly. 2002. *For Better or for Worse: Divorce Reconsidered.* New York: W.W. Norton.

Hochschild, A.R. 1997. *Time Bind:When Work Becomes Home and Home Becomes Work.* New York: Metropolitan.

Hochschild, A.R. and A. Machung. 1990. *The Second Shift.* New York: Avon.

"Important Supreme Court Custody Decision Handed Down." 2001. Ontario Women's Justice Network. http://www.owjn.org/index.php?option=com_content&view=article&id=147&Itemid=67#facts (accessed April 12, 2010).

"Income and Poverty Gaps between Women and Men Persist." 2004. Womennet.ca. http://www.womennet.ca/news.php?show&1587 (accessed March 2009).

Kalter, K. 1977. "Children of Divorce in an Outpatient Psychiatric Population." *American Journal of Orthopsychiatry,* 47, 40–51.

Katz, R. and Y. Lavee. 2005. "Families in Israel." In B.N. Adams and J. Trost (Eds.), *Handbook of World Families* (pp. 486–506). Thousand Oaks, California: Sage.

Kelly, J.B. and R.E. Emery. 2003. "Children's Adjustment Following Divorce: Risk and Resilience Perspectives." *Family Relations,* 52, 352–362.

Kerr, D. and J.H. Michalski. 2007. "Family Structure and Children's Hyperactivity Problems: A Longitudinal Analysis. "*The Canadian Journal of Sociology,* 32(1), 85–112.

"Kevin Federline Divorce Settlement: Britney Spears Pays Up." 2007. http://gossip.elliottback.com/kevin-federline-divorce-settlement-britney-spears-pays-up (accessed March 2009).

Kreps, D. 2008. "Paul McCartney Divorce Settlement: $48.7 Million." *Rolling Stone Magazine* (March 17). http://www.rollingstone.com/rockdaily/index.php/2008/03/17/paul-mccartney-divorce-settlement-487-million/ (accessed April 12, 2010).

LaRose, L. 2008. "Mixed-Race Taboo Drops Away: Canadian Interracial Marriages on the Rise, But Some Barriers Remain." *CBC News.* http://www.cbc.ca/news/background/census/mixed-marriages.html (accessed March 2009).

Lewis, J. 2005. "Profile: Ivana Trump." *Money Week* (December 12). http://www.moneyweek.com/news-and-charts/profile-ivana-trump.aspx (accessed March 2009).

"Madonna, Richie Divorce Settlement to Surpass $90 Mil." 2008. *CBC News.* http://www.cbc.ca/arts/media/story/2008/12/15/madonna-ritchie-finance .html?ref=rss (accessed April 12, 2010).

McLanahan, S. 1997. "Parent Absence or Poverty? Which Matters More?" In. G.J. Duncan and J. Brooks-Green (Eds.), *Consequences of Growing Up Poor* (pp. 33–48). New York: Russel-Sage.

McMullin, J.A. 2004. *Understanding Social Inequality.* Toronto: Oxford.

Milan, A. and B. Hamm. 2004. "Mixed Unions." *Canadian Social Trends.* Ottawa: Statistics Canada Cat. 11-008.

Naser, A.F. 2005. "Kuwait's Families." In B.N. Adams and J. Trost (Eds.), *Handbook of World Families* (pp. 507–535). Thousand Oaks, California: Sage.

National Crime Prevention Council of Canada. 1995. *Offender Profiles.* Ottawa: NCPC.

Nelson, A. 2010. *Gender in Canada,* 4th ed. Toronto: Pearson.

Nilan, A. 2000. *One Hundred Years of Families; Canadian Social Trends.* Ottawa. Statistics Canada.

Noce, M.L. 2005. "Support Networks and Welfare State Restructuring: The Experiences of 40 Ontario Households." Unpublished Ph.D. Thesis, University of Toronto, Department of Sociology and Equity Studies.

Popenoe, D. 1993. "American Family Decline, 1960–1990: A Review and Appraisal." *Journal of Marriage and the Family,* 55: 527–555.

Popenoe, D. 2008. *War Over the Family.* New Brunswick, N.J.: Transaction Publishers.

Puri, D. 1998. "Gift of a Daughter: Change and Continuity in Marriage Patterns." Unpublished PhD. Thesis, University of Toronto, Sociology.

Richardson, C.J. 2001. "Divorce and Remarriage." In M. Baker (Ed.), *Families: Changing Trends in Canada,* 4th ed. (pp. 206–237). Toronto. McGraw-Hill.

Rogerson, C. 2002. "Developing Spousal Support Guidelines in Canada: Beginning the Discussion." Department of Justice Canada. http://www.canada.justice.ca/en/ dept/pub/spousal (accessed March 2009).

Rotermann, M. 2007. "Marital Breakdown and Subsequent Depression." *Health Report,* 18(2): 33–44.

Seccombe, W. 1975. "Domestic Labour: Reply to Critics." *New Left Review,* 94: 85–96.

Sev'er, A. 1992. *Women and Divorce in Canada: A Sociological Analysis.* Toronto: Canadian Scholars' Press.

Sev'er, A. 1997. "Recent or Imminent Separation and Intimate Violence Against Women: A Conceptual Overview and Some Canadian Examples." *Violence Against Women,* 3(6): 566–589.

Sev'er, A. 2002a. "Flight of Abused Women, Plight of Canadian Shelters: Another Road to Homelessness." *Journal of Social Distress and the Homeless,* 11(4): 307–323.

Sev'er, A. 2002b. "Too Close to Home, Too Toxic for Children: Mental Health Consequences of Witnessing Violence against Mothers." *Women's Health and Urban Life*, 1(1): 4–23.

Sev'er, A. 2002c. *Fleeing the House of Horrors: Women Who have Left Their Abusive Partners*. Toronto: University of Toronto Press.

Sev'er, A., M. Dawson, and H. Johnson. 2004. "Lethal and Non-lethal Violence against Women by Intimate Partners: Trends and Prospects in the US, UK and Canada." *Violence Against Women*, 10(6): 563–577.

Sev'er, A. and M. Pirie. 1991a. "Factors That Enhance or Curtail the Social Functioning of Female Single-Parents." *Family and Conciliation Courts Review* 29(3): 318–337.

Sev'er, A. and M. Pirie. 1991b. "More than Making It: An Analysis of Factors That Enhance the Social Functioning of Female Single-Parents." *Family Perspective*, 25(2): 83–96.

Statistics Canada. 2005 (March 9). *The Daily*. Marriages and Divorces. http://www.statcan .ca/daily-quotidien/050309/dq050309b-eng.htm (accessed April, 2010).

Statistics Canada. 2006a. *Till Death Do Us Part? The Risk of First and Second Marriage Dissolution*. By W. Clark and S. Crompton. http://www.statcan.gc.ca/pub/11-088-x/2006001/ 9198-eng.htm (accessed March 2009).

Statistics Canada. 2006b (March 22). *Divorces by Province and Territory*. http://www40 .statcan.gc.ca/101/cst01/famil02-eng.htm (accessed March 2009).

Statistics Canada. 2006c (October 3). *The Daily*. http://www.statcan.gc.ca/daily- quotidien/061003/dq061003/dq061003b-eng.htm (accessed March 2009).

Statistics Canada. 2007 (January 17). *Marriages*. http://www.statcan.gc.ca/daily- quotidien/070117/dq070117a-eng.htm (accessed March 2009).

Statistics Canada. 2008a. CANSIM Table 101-6512. *Number of Dependents in Divorces Involving Custody Orders by Party to Whom Custody Was Granted, Canada, Provinces and Territories*.: http://estat .statcan.gc.ca/cgi-win/CNSMCGI.EXE?Lang=E&amp (accessed June 2009).

Statistics Canada. 2008b. CANSIM Table 101-6503. *Divorces by Marital Status of Husband, and Wife Just Prior to Marriage, Canada, Provinces and Territories*. http://estat.statcan.gc.ca/ cgi-win/CNSMCGI.EXE?Lang=E&amp (accessed June 2009).

Statistics Canada. 2008c. CANSIM Table 101-6511. 30 and 50 Year Total Divorce Rates per 1000 Marriages Canada. http://cansim2.statcan.gc.ca/cgi-win/CNSMCGI.PGM (accessed March 2009).

Statistics Canada. 2009a. *Family Income by Family Type—Couple Families*. http://www40 .statcan.gc.ca/101/famil106a-eng.htm (accessed March 2009).

Statistics Canada. 2009b. *Family Income by Family Type—Lone-Parent Families*. http://www40 .statcan.gc.ca/101/famil106b-eng.htm (accessed March 2009).

Strohschein, L. 2005. "Parental Divorce and Child Mental Health Trajectories." *Journal of Marriage and the Family*, 67(5): 1286–1300.

Sun, Y. and Y. Li. 2001. "Marital Disruption, Parental Investment and Children's Academic Achievement." *Journal of Family Issues*, 22: 27–62.

Thibaut, J.W. and H.H. Kelley. 1959. *The Social Psychology of Groups*. New York: Wiley.

TMZ. 2006. *Eminem Remarries Ex-wife in Michigan*. http://www.tmz.com/2006/01/15eminem-remarried-ex-wife-in-michigan (accessed March 2009).

Wallerstein, J.S. 2003. "Children of Divorce: A Society in Search of Policy." In M.A. Mason, A. Skolnick, and S.D. Sugarman (Eds.), *All Our Families: New Policies for a New Century*, 2nd ed (pp. 66–96). New York: Oxford.

United Nations. 2005. *Demographic Yearbook*. New York: UN.

Weitzman, L. 1985. *The Divorce Revolution: The Unexpected Social and Economic Consequences for Women and Children in America*. New York: Free Press.

Women and Poverty. ND. Fact sheets (3rd Ed.). CRIAW. http://www.criaw-icref.ca/factSheets/Women%20and%20Poverty/PovertyFactsheete.htm (accessed March 2009).

Wu, Z. and M.J. Penning. 1997. "Marital Instability after Midlife." *Journal of Family Issues*, 18: 459–478.

Wu, Z. and C.M. Schimmele. 2005. "Re-partnering after 1st Union Disruption." *Journal of Marriage and Family*, 67(1): 27–36.

Wu, Z. and C.M. Schimmele. 2007. "Uncoupling in Late Life." *Generations*, 31(3): 41–47.

Part 3
Confronting Challenges and Change

Chapter 9

Violence in Canadian Families across the Life Course

Mavis Morton

LEARNING OBJECTIVES

In this chapter, you will learn that:

1. violence within families is a common social phenomenon where there is a disjuncture between the common perception of fear of victimization and reality of violence in families,

2. violence within families has prolonged and extensive negative impacts on victims as well as perpetrators and society overall,

3. the term "family violence" is a sweeping concept that does not address the unique features and/or societal context so crucial to understanding the varieties of abuse, neglect, maltreatment, and physical violence that children and adults experience in their intimate relationships through the course of their lives,

4. an individual's "social location" and, in particular, the specific intersection of gender, age, class, race/ethnicity, sexual orientation, ability, and immigrant status are crucial lenses through which we can deepen our understanding of and policy response to violence in families,

5. gender is a particularly vital characteristic in understanding familial violence especially in patriarchal societies.

INTRODUCTION

Violent crime conjures up visions of guns, gangs, and grow-ops. While this kind of violence is sure to be headline news, almost half the criminal violence reported to police is in fact committed by a family member (Department of Justice, 2009).[1] That physical victimization is as likely to be caused by a family member[2] as by a stranger is in direct contrast to our impression of criminality represented in the media, popular culture or even our parents' warnings about strangers! In fact, contrary to much of the frequently provided safe-keeping advice that Canadians receive (from police, friends, families, and spouses), they are more likely to be victimized by those same friends and families, than they are by the strangers they are being warned about. This distance between our fears of stranger perpetrators and the reality of victimization, particularly in familial relationships, speaks to our misunderstanding of both crime (its perpetrators and victims) and family relations. These faulty social perceptions divert our attention and vital societal resources away from some of the more destructive elements in familial and spousal relationships.

Our illusions about the actual experiences of violence that occur across the lifespan (including violence against children, spouses, and older adults) are based in large part on the way in which our beliefs about "families" are socially constructed. Over the past half century, researchers have clearly sub-stantiated the prevalence and magnitude of abuse and violence occurring in our Canadian families. Nonetheless, the dominant familial ideology (Barrett and McIntosh, 1982) continues to characterize families as places of stability, refuge, and safety while eulogizing (and lamenting) the increasing scarcity of the traditional heterosexual patriarchal nuclear family.

There now exists a vast literature documenting both the historical para-meters and current patterns of family violence. Prior to the advent of the modern women's movement in the 1960s, familial violence elicited relatively little academic attention. Since that time, attention to this issue has increased dramatically. Entire journals are now devoted to specialized aspects of familial violence such as child abuse (notably, *Child Abuse and Neglect: The International Journal* and *Child Maltreatment*). Books related to the subject are increasingly common and popular, including not only a myriad of personal accounts of victimization but also scholarly treatises on the roots of such violence. Indeed now, it is difficult to adequately survey the vast literature that has appeared under the rubric "family violence." Here, I will explore only a few dimensions of family violence through lens of feminist theory. Specifically, I will identify a number of the key features and implications of (1) child abuse, (2) violence against women in intimate relations, and (3) abuse of older adults (primarily focusing on the abuse of older women). I will invite the reader, to extend your learning by attending to the wide variety of important features of family violence (sibling violence, child-to-parent violence, teen abuse, the general abuse of older adults, to name a few) that goes beyond the scope of this chapter.

DEFINING VIOLENCE IN FAMILIES ACROSS THE LIFESPAN

The Department of Justice Canada defines "family violence" as including many different forms of violence and/or abuse that may be experienced across one's life span by those sharing a familial relationship (2009). As is clear below, the field is understood as fluid and dynamic:

> Family violence includes many different forms of abuse, mistreatment or neglect that adults or children may experience in their intimate, family or dependent relationships.

The definition of family violence continues to evolve as the nature and extent of violence within intimate relationships and families becomes better understood (Department of Justice Canada, 2009).

The evolving nature of what we define as "family violence" and the language we use to refer to it are not only products of learning more about the kinds and prevalence of violence occurring in intimate relationships (such as sibling violence, child-to-parent violence), but also results in efforts to understand, explain, and prevent such violence.

VIOLENCE, ABUSE, AND NEGLECT AGAINST CHILDREN AND YOUTH

There is growing support for the suggestion that different types of family violence (from childhood to older age) share similar explanations and causes as well as common risk factors and prevention strategies (Walsh et al. 2007, p. 491). There is also growing evidence that one form of violence occurring in a family may be a strong predictor of other simultaneous and/or subsequent forms in that same setting (Appel and Holden, 1998, in Walsh et al., 2007, p. 491). Knowledge about these different, yet seemingly interconnected, forms of intrafamilial violence and abuse across the lifespan is useful in understanding and preventing current and future violence. Clearly from this vantage point, child abuse may be approached as a first step in a life-long and intergenerational pattern of victimization.

As pointed out in the introduction, violent acts against children and youth tend to be perpetrated by people known to the victims. Eighty percent or more "of maltreatment [of youth and children] is perpetrated by parents or parental guardians, apart from sexual abuse, which is mostly perpetrated by acquaintances or other relatives" (Gilbert et al., 2009, p. 69).

For every 100,000 young persons, 334 were victims of physical or sexual violence by a friend or an acquaintance, 187 experienced violence by a family member, and 101 were victimized by a stranger, according to 2005 police-reported data (Statistics Canada, 2008b).

In 2003, 59 Canadian children under the age of eighteen were killed; the majority, 31 of these children, were killed by a family member (Statistics Canada, 2005).

While we have clear documentation of violent crimes reported to the police, statistics on violence against children and youth (that is handled outside the criminal justice system) is more difficult to obtain. One of the only sources of nationwide Canadian data on child abuse and neglect comes from the Canadian Incidence Study (CSI) of Reported Child Abuse and Neglect, which provides nationwide estimates. Commencing in 1998, CIS data have been collected every five years directly from child welfare workers/agencies in Canada about children and their families investigated because of reported child maltreatment (Trocmé et al., 2005). Although the 2008 research is underway, the most recent numbers available come from the 2003 cycle. The CIS classifies

22 different forms of maltreatment. The data collected in this survey are based on the definition of maltreatment as a "harm" or "substantial risk of harm" standard, which includes situations where children have been already harmed. It also refers to situations where children are considered to have been at substantial risk of harm (Trocmé et al., 2003, p. 1430). The inclusion of "substantial risk of harm" reflects the clinical and legislative definitions and practices used in many Canadian jurisdictions (for example section 37(2) of the Child and Family Services Act of Ontario, 1990) around "exposure to" or "witnessing domestic violence."

The 2003 CIS report estimated that the child welfare system substantiated over 31,000 incidents of **physical** maltreatment (Trocmé et al., 2005). Close to half of the child investigations that were conducted (47 percent of 217,319 cases) in Canada (excluding Quebec) were substantiated cases of child maltreatment (Trocmé et al., 2005). "Substantiated cases" refer to those instances where there is a balance of evidence to indicate that abuse or neglect occurred (Trocmé et al., 2003, p. 1430). It is significant to note that the 2003 study identified an increase in child maltreatment of 125 percent (from 9.64 cases per 1,000 children in 1998 to 21.71 cases per 1,000 in 2003) (Trocmé et al., 2005). Some analysts suggest this increase is mostly attributable to improved reporting and investigation procedures as well as changes in policy (rather than actual increases in maltreatment). In particular, legislation increasingly designates "exposure to domestic violence" as putting a child at risk of emotional abuse and therefore in "need of protection," which may, in turn, result in child welfare interventions.

As was the case in the first CIS cycle in 1998, **neglect** remains the most common form of maltreatment in Canada (Trocmé et al., 2003, p. 1). Nearly one-third (30%) of all cases in which maltreatment was substantiated through a child welfare investigation involved neglect[3] as the primary category of maltreatment (Trocmé et al., 2003, p. 2). This totals an estimated 30,366 neglect investigations at a rate of 6.38 cases of substantiated maltreatment per 1,000 children (Trocmé et al., 2003, p.1). Since the definition of neglect includes the caregiver's failure to provide for or protect their children physically, emotionally, medically and so on, many instances are a direct consequence of poverty and inadequate social support services rather than malevolence.

One indicator of this relationship to poverty is the large numbers of Canadian children relying on food from foodbanks. The Daily Bread Foodbank's Who's Hungry 2009: Key Findings indicate that "over one third of food bank clients are children" (Daily Bread Foodbank, 2009). This certainly suggests that much of this "parental" neglect may have societal roots that goes well beyond the traditional target of moral and legal opprobrium (neglectful adults who more or less "willingly" neglect their children).

Significantly, exposure to domestic violence was the second most common form of substantiated maltreatment, followed closely by physical abuse (Trocmé et al., 2003, p. 1). When compared to the first CIS cycle in 1998, the 2003 cycle showed a 259 percent increase in the rate of investigated exposure to domestic violence, with substantiated cases increasing from

1.72 cases per 1,000 children in 1998 to 6.17 in 2003 (Trocmé et al., 2005). We have seen that child welfare policy and legislation have increasingly reflected the view that children who are exposed to domestic violence are at risk of emotional and physical harm and therefore are in need of protection. This emergent interpretation of "emotional harm" has increased the pressure on police and child welfare agencies to intervene in situations of domestic violence and has resulted in these higher recorded maltreatment incidence rates.

In recent years, child welfare agencies have been subject to considerable criticism from abused women, women's advocates, and equality-seeking women's organizations, for disproportionately holding abused women responsible for the violence to which they and their children have been subjected. The primary question for many is "Why doesn't she leave?!" (Morton, 1996). This focus has diverted attention and resources away from understanding the basis of their victimization as well as using this knowledge to support and protect abused women and their children. The blame that has been directed against individual mothers, who may at times be unable to provide for their children or prevent them from witnessing parental violence, is evidence of a persistent individualistic, as opposed to sociological, approach to violence against women. This approach sees individuals as separate from and wholly responsible for the social conditions in which they live. Developing social policy responses out of this world view constrains us to responding to social problems as though they were individual troubles and therefore does nothing to address the larger social, political and legal context in which individuals are located. Reducing social and political problems like domestic violence and poverty to the problems of individuals rather than systemic societal failures may only undermine our ability to address them.

The prevalence and impact of children's exposure to domestic violence through their life course is increasingly well documented. Despite numerous methodological problems when examining children's exposure to this violence, researchers have been able to arrive at increasingly solid evidence (see Holt, Buckley, and Whelan, 2008 for a detailed description of these problems). Current data suggest that high percentages of children in Canada and the United States have some experience with witnessing domestic violence. Drawing on this research, McDonald et al., (2006) suggest that each year in these two countries upward of 15 million children see, hear, intervene in, and/or cope with the aftermath of domestic violence. With a combined population of around 350 million, this represents approximately 4 percent of the entire population and at least 12 to 16 percent of the combined population of Canadian and American children (aged 0 to 16 years of age) (McDonald, et al., 2006). Research in Canada estimates

- where there is spousal violence, children have seen violence or threats in 37 percent of these households.

- about 70 percent of children who witnessed spousal violence saw or heard assaults against their mothers.

- about one-half of women who took their children to shelters in Canada did so to protect their children from witnessing the abuse of their mother; 39 percent did so to protect the child from psychological abuse, 18 percent from physical abuse, and 5 percent from sexual abuse (Baker and Jaffe, 2007, p. 9).

Before highlighting what the research tells us about the **impact** on children exposed to violence in their homes, the following list provides some insight into *how* children are "exposed" to this violence.

How children are "exposed" to woman abuse:

- seeing a mother assaulted or demeaned
- hearing loud conflict and violence
- seeing the aftermath (e.g., injuries)
- learning about what happened to a mother
- being used by an abusive parent as part of the abuse
- seeing a father abuse his new partner when they visit him on weekends
- being denied what is owed them for child support (Cunningham and Baker, 2007).

A variety of evidence suggests that growing up in an abusive home environment can seriously jeopardize the developmental progress and personal ability of children (Holt, Buckley, and Whelan 2008, p. 807). In a comprehensive literature review, Holt et al. note that the cumulative effects can significantly contribute intergenerationally to children's own involvement in adult violence (2008, p. 807). See Box 9.1.

BOX 9.1   THE IMPACTS OF CHILDREN'S EXPOSURE TO ABUSE

- Watching, hearing, or learning later of a mother being abused by her partner threatens young people's sense of stability and security.
- Children and adolescents may experience increased emotional and behavioural difficulties.
- Some young people display traumatic stress reactions (e.g., flashbacks, nightmares, intensified startle reactions, constant worry about possible danger).
- Children and adolescents living with domestic violence are at increased risk of experiencing physical injury or childhood abuse (e.g., physical, emotional).
- The abuser may use children and adolescents as a control tactic against adult victims.
- Children and adolescents may experience strong mixed feelings toward their violent parent; affection exists along with feelings of resentment and disappointment.
- Young people may imitate and learn the attitudes and behaviours modeled when woman abuse occurs in the home.
- Exposure to violence may desensitize children and adolescents to aggressive behaviour. When desensitization occurs, aggression becomes part of the "norm" and is less likely to signal concern to young people (Baker and Jaffe, 2007).

CHILD ABUSE—FIFTY YEARS OF ADVANCES AND QUESTIONS

The history of academic research on child abuse is a relatively short one. Only in the past half-century have researchers carefully examined the multiple harms experienced by children within their families. It was in 1979 that several decades of organizing efforts culminated in the United Nations' International Year of the Child. This event signaled a wake-up call to the devastation and poor condition of children in many parts of the world (Korbin, 2003). Change in this field has unfolded at a dramatic pace: "(f)ollowing the cornerstone article on child abuse and neglect in the United States (Kempe et al. 1962), the First International Congress on Child Abuse and Neglect held in Geneva in 1976, and the founding of the International Society for the Prevention of Child Abuse and Neglect, attention also focused on abused and neglected children around the world (Donnelly 2002)" (as cited in Korbin, 2003, p. 432).

As child abuse and neglect came to public and professional attention, questions were increasingly posed about conceptualizations of this behaviour and its causes. Anthropologist Jill Korbin categorizes violence toward children as occurring at three levels. These are (1) individually (as in child maltreatment), (2) collectively (in culturally sanctioned rites or disciplinary practices), or (3) structurally (as a result of poverty, inequality, lack of opportunity, and so on). Violence directed at children occurs across these three levels and often at multiple levels. For instance, individual maltreatment is frequently associated with structural violence (poverty).[4]

Korbin argues that a cross-cultural and international perspective is best able to address the multiple parameters of child maltreatment. Using this framework, she explains the ways in which societal abuse and neglect of children (or the structural violence of poverty), including inadequate health care and lack of educational and employment opportunities are all conditions that may impact and contribute to the incidence of individually perpetrated child abuse and neglect (2003, p.434). We must remember, for instance, that the most common form of "child abuse" identified in Canada is "neglect" (Trocmé et al., 2003, p. 41). This abuse is often a direct result of the inadequate resources and supports available to parents and their communities—for example, inadequate welfare payments, low-paying jobs, inadequate access to subsidized housing, lack of accessible and affordable childcare, and so on. Not only are analysts identifying the societal, cultural, and individual levels of child abuse, but also there is increasing attention to its global manifestation. While reports of child maltreatment, date back to ancient civilizations, only recently have we begun documenting the global magnitude and impact of violence against children. According to the *World Report on Violence Against Children: An End to Violence Against Children*, violence against children "occurs in every country in the world in a variety of forms and settings and is often deeply rooted in cultural, economic, and social practices" (Pinheiro, 2006, p. 6).

Macro Approaches to Child Maltreatment: Poverty as Child Abuse

While "neglect" is defined in the CIS as "failing to provide for or protect children," all provincial and territorial statutes include "neglect" or some reference to acts or omissions, such as "failure to supervise or protect," as grounds for investigating maltreatment. For instance, the Ontario Children's Aid Society (OCAS) (2008) defines neglect as a caregiver failing to provide basic needs such as adequate food, sleep, safety, supervision, clothing, or medical treatment. Based on some 30 years of research, researchers are increasingly aware that failing to provide the basic needs for one's child/children is explained more as a result of poverty, isolation, and lack of support than it is by some kind of personal shortcoming or pathology.

The 2009 *Report Card on Child and Family Poverty in Canada: 1989–2009* reminds us that 1 in 10 children in Canada still live in poverty and 1 in 4 children in Aboriginal communities grow up in poverty (see Figure 9.1). The incapacity to provide basic needs should not be surprising while living under persistent social and economic inequality (Campaign 2000).

Although many factors influence the healthy development of children and the ability of parents and caregivers to provide for and protect their children, we know that certain risk factors strongly correlate with abuse and neglect. One of the most relevant correlates is poverty. Children in families with greater material resources enjoy more secure living conditions and attachments (Gupta, de Whit, and MacKeown, 2007). While neglect and abuse occurs in families from all social classes, the fact remains that being economically disadvantaged does place children at greater risk of being abused and neglected (Faulkner and Faulkner, 2004, p. 104). It also may place parents at greater risk of being identified by state agencies, such as the Children's Aid Society and the

Figure 9.1   **CHILD POVERTY RATES FOR SELECT SOCIAL GROUPS IN CANADA: CHILDREN 0–14 YEARS, 1996–2006**

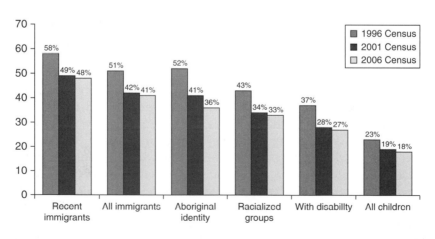

Source: Campaign 2000. *2009 Report Card on Child and Family Poverty in Canada: 1989–2009.* © 2009 Family Service Toronto. Online: http://www.campaign2000.ca/reportCards/national/2009EnglishC2000NationalReportCard.pdf.

police, which can in turn result in increased reporting of child abuse and neglect. Conversely, advantaged families who are having difficulty "dealing with" their children will have access to a much broader range of services and supports (and privacy) simply by token of their ability to pay for them. So, not only are advantaged families less likely to be subject to neglectful aspects of child abuse, they are less likely to be identified as responsible for it.

Predictably, poverty is identified in the CIS (2003) as a relevant risk factor for abuse and neglect. For instance, the 2003 cycle found that "almost a quarter (24%) of households depended on social assistance or other benefits as their major source of income, 13% of households lived in public housing, 9% were considered to be living in unsafe conditions . . ." (Trocmé et al., 2003, p. 6). It also found that "43 percent involved children who lived in a family led by a lone parent (39% by a female parent and 4% by a male parent)" (Trocmé et al., 2003, p. 6). As explained in the 2009 *Report Card on Child and Family Poverty in Canada*, approximately one out of three mother-led lone-parent families live in poverty and therefore face many obstacles and challenges that help to explain why they may not be able to provide for their children and meet the legal standard that defines inadequately providing for their children.

> Lone mothers face the challenge of being the sole provider while also having to find adequate child care and secure housing, often at astronomical costs. They struggle to balance education or training, community service and/or paid work with family responsibilities. Women earn approximately 71 percent of what men earn for full-time, year-round work, and are more likely to be found in low wage work. The result is often insufficient time and money to provide what they know their children need and want (Campaign 2000, p. 2).

Levels of poverty in Canada are higher for families headed by lone female parents, immigrant and visible-minority families, families with disabled children, and Aboriginal families (Gupta, de Whit, and MacKeown, 2007, p. 667). Part of understanding and explaining the dire economic and social conditions in which certain populations of Canadian families find themselves is to identify Canada's failure in addressing the insecurity of income, employment, housing, childcare, and food (Raphael et al., 2008). The gradual dismantling since the early 1990s of the Canadian welfare state has been extensively documented (Morrow, Hankivsky, and Varcoe, 2004). The implementation of neoliberal policies has led to more passive public policy that does not see poverty and related problems as primarily social problems. Rather, it sees them as atomized personal failures. Today, a kind of "fiscalized" social policy where the state of the economy trumps all other concerns has come to dominate public discourse (Morrow, Havensky, and Varcoe, 2004). One of the results is not only a climate in which discrimination against poor and marginalized Canadians has intensified but, their relative poverty has increased (i.e. the relative difference between legal policy makers and those subject to their laws and policies) and there is a corresponding poverty of imagination for developing effective social policies. It is this social context that structures contemporary experiences of violence against children. In particular, social structural influences (such as poverty and restricted educational opportunities), historical influences (such as histories of forced slavery and migration), and systematic oppression must all be considered when studying the rates at which different groups experience family violence and their willingness to seek help for it (West, 2005, in Malley-Morrison and Hines, 2007, p. 947).

> The hardships these families face include labor market entry problems, discrimination (Statistics Canada, 2003), high rates of poverty, single parents (Campaign, 2000, 2006), physical and mental health problems, lack of access to adequate housing (Mitchell, 2005), living in disadvantaged neighbourhoods, and social isolation (Hou and Picot, 2004). Problems of this kind can often put the parents under considerable stress and have an adverse impact on family relationships and child care (Mitchell, 2005) (in Lavergne, Dufour, Trocmé, Larrivee, 2008, p. 60).

UNDERSTANDING ABORIGINAL CHILD WELFARE

As noted previously, Canadian Aboriginal families are particularly at risk for reports of child maltreatment and neglect. The disproportionate rate of child abuse in native communities can only be understood when located in terms of both history and current social context and policies. In particular, attention must be directed to the racist treatment of Aboriginal people through Canadian policies and, in particular, the tactics that were used to suppress Aboriginal nations through the mistreatment of Aboriginal children (for example, the creation of residential schools that resulted in both cultural oppression and poverty). As the Royal Commission on Aboriginal Peoples (1996) noted, "Assimilation policies have done great damage, leaving a legacy of brokenness affecting Aboriginal individuals, families and communities (Bennett and Blackstock, 2002, p. 9). The residential school experience and ensuing individual, familial and community devastation is one example of the impact systematic racism has on Aboriginal communities and families. There is clearly a direct link to Aboriginal over-representation in reports of child neglect. This federal government's ill-advised and poorly monitored assimilation policy not only denied several generations of Aboriginal children the opportunity to learn the traditions of their peoples but also disrupted the intergenerational relationships so important to cultural integration and pride. In addition, many of these Aboriginal children experienced direct physical, sexual and emotional abuse at the hands of their religious educators. Inevitably, many of these children became parents and, predictably, replicated what they had "learned."

> The European cleric's ways of raising children—absolute obedience reinforced by shame, whipping and harsh denial—infiltrated and contaminated the traditional Aboriginal childrearing traditions of modeling behaviour and never hitting a child (Fournier and Crey, 1997, pp. 62–63 as cited in Bennett and Blackstock, 2002, p. 9).

Recognizing the failure of the residential school system, child welfare agencies (as of the 1960s) replaced residential schools as the preferred system of care for Aboriginal children (Armitage, 1995, in Bennett and Blackstock,

2002, p. 21). Instead, many agencies relied on adoption and foster parenting, often into non-Aboriginal families, to provide care for Aboriginal children. The children who were apprehended into "care" as a result of the new policy were the offspring of parents who had attended residential schools and who were often ill equipped to care for their children—particularly in the severe conditions of poverty that characterized many Aboriginal communities. Here, poverty and anti-Aboriginal policies directly lead to children being taken away from their parents under the prevailing definition of "neglect."

> Finding a grandmother caring for several small children in a home without a flush toilet, refrigerator or running water was enough to spur a worker to seize the children and take them into care . . . (85–86) (in Bennet and Blackstock, 2002, p. 22).

These ongoing experiences of forced assimilation, colonialism, and racism by Aboriginal children, families, and communities have created acute suffering, pain, and loss of identity that continues to impact the level of alcohol and drug use, suicides, incarceration, severe poverty, and disarray of many Aboriginal communities (Bennett and Blackstock, 2002, p. 24). One of these continuing impacts is the overrepresentation of Aboriginal children in reports to child welfare.

Using the CIS-2003, children of Aboriginal heritage were compared with non-Aboriginal children. Findings indicate that Aboriginal families have less stable housing, less dependable sources of income, higher rates of maltreatment as a child, higher rates of alcohol and drug abuse, and are more often reported to child welfare based on issues of child neglect versus physical or sexual abuse. "Over half (56%) of all substantiated Aboriginal child investigations involved neglect as the primary category of maltreatment, an estimated 6,833 neglect investigations (17.06 child investigations per 1,000 children)" (Trocmé et al. 2006, p. 5).

CHILD ABUSE IN IMMIGRANT FAMILIES

Aboriginal children and families are an important Canadian example of the effects that racism, sexism, and other forms of oppression have on the forms of abuse that members of marginalized groups experience (Malley-Morrison and Hines, 2007, p. 947). They are also an important reflection on the response of the state to specific patterns of abuse, neglect, and violence. However, Aboriginal people do not stand alone in this devastating intersection of racism, sexism, and oppression. There is a growing awareness of the oppressive conditions facing immigrant families in Canada. Recent research suggests that immigrant families may be at particular risk for disrupted parent–child relations and intensified intergenerational conflict (Maiter, Alaggia, and Trocmé, 2004, p. 310). For example, recently immigrated families are more likely to experience intergenerational conflicts especially in cases where the children identify more with the host country and, as a result, challenge the more traditional standards and values of their parents.

A recent Canadian example is the death of sixteen-year-old Aqsa Parvez (Fatah, 2008). Natasha Fatah, a producer for CBC Radio's current affairs show *As it Happens* found that family, friends, and associates said that the teen had been having arguments with her father because he allegedly wanted her to wear a traditional hijab and she wanted to be more Western. "She kinda wanted to go a different way from the way her family wanted her to go," said one friend (Fatah, 2008). Allegedly, the Mississauga teen died a day after being strangled by her father. Her 57-year-old father was charged with murder and her 26-year-old brother was charged with obstructing police Footnote: On June 15th, Aqsa's father and brother pleaded guilty to second degree murder and both received life sentences. http://www.cbc.ca/canada/toronto/story/2010/06/15/parvez-guilty-plea.html (Fatah, 2008). This kind of violence has sparked discussion and debate about the tensions between the accommodation of cultural differences and the respect for women's fundamental human rights (Bilge, 2006). Recently, these same tensions between cultural traditions, women's rights to self determination, provision of public services, liberal democratic views of criminal justice and the rights of the accused to face their accusers (and look them in the eye) are now manifest in a rapidly expanding public and international debate. Discussions about whether women should be forced or not forced to wear the burqa or niqab in certain countries are making headlines. For instance, France is considering legislation which would ban wearing a face-covering veil in 'public places'. http://www.globalissues.org/news/2010/05/23/5708. Sirma Bilge calls for a readjustment of the multicultural lens by taking into account intra-group and inter-group power relations shaped not only by cultural differences but also by social processes that are themselves shaped by racialization, gender, and class domination (2006, p. 173).

Bilge argues against a kind of "cultural defence," which she suggests has come to be seen as a way of condoning male violence against women and children in minority groups. This has become a real paradox for feminists who are committed to intersectionality and recognize that using "culture talk" in law can work toward women's equality by challenging laws and state responses that do not reflect minority women's experiences. On the other hand, culture can also conflict with women's equality since ". . . culture often props up stifling gender roles" (Deckha, 2004, p. 15). For example, in some minority cultures, deference to cultural practices that try to maintain extreme control over dependent daughters such as veiling, child marriage, arranged marriages, and so on may be detrimental to women/girls and result in further conflict and violence in families. Social policy must navigate a difficult course that does not excuse such actions as simply "cultural differences" while also recognizing that criminalization must recognize the cultural roots of such practices.

Child discipline patterns may be another example of these cultural influences in child-rearing. The use of physical abuse in visible-minority families appears to be closely associated with disciplinary methods and child-rearing practices different from those advocated by the majority culture (Maiter,

Alaggia, and Trocmé, 2004). Some analysts suggest that parenting behaviour develops within a cultural belief system that either encourages or discourages physical punishment of children (Durrant, Rose-Krasnor, and Broberg, 2003). In many countries and cultures, physical punishment is a common experience of childhood. Twenty years ago, it was estimated that up to 88 percent of Canadian parents and more than 90 percent of American parents used physical punishment (Straus, 1991). However, physical punishment is not universally practiced and, in many developed countries, has become increasingly uncommon. In a study of 90 societies, Levinson (1989) found it to be present in 74 percent of families. (Durrant, Rose-Krasnor, and Broberg, 2003, p. 586).

Although child-rearing practices may be differently defined in various immigrant communities in Canada, Western-based conceptions of child abuse and neglect have been privileged and have led to a cataloguing of "harms" that children may experience in a range of cultural contexts as "abuse" rather than corrective punishment by parents. And yet many Western child-rearing practices would also be viewed as abusive from the vantage points of other cultures (Korbin, 2003, p. 435). A well known example of this is the culturally specific practices around babies and sleep. In Western countries, including Canada and the United States, child-rearing experts commonly endorse the requirement that young children sleep on their own. Parents are advised to physically shut their children in their bedroom despite their tears, fears, and wailing entreaties. While parents are instructed to briefly re-enter the bedroom to reassure the child, they are advised to leave again and keep the door shut (Ferber, 1985). The prevailing theory is that eventually the child will be acclimatized to sleeping alone, develop some fledgling self-reliance in calming him- or herself, and parents will regain the privacy of their bedroom. Another important but inevitable milestone will be crossed. In other cultures (and likely throughout most of human history), families have slept together. Efforts to isolate a child would be seen as both unnecessary and cruel:

> Isolation for sleep at night, for example, is widely regarded cross-culturally as detrimental to children, yet it is the ideal practice in middle-class families in the United States (Korbin, 2003, p. 435).

Similar comments might be made about breast feeding. In contemporary developed economies, breast feeding beyond six months is seen as aberrant, even bizarre and subject to social comment and contempt. Yet in other cultures, there is no great rush to put an end to this feeding activity that is comforting to both mother and child. Finally, it is also worth noting that although conceptions of child abuse in North America and Western Europe have had a focus on physical violence, in some societies verbal violence toward children is regarded as much more serious than physical violence (Korbin, 2003, p. 435). These culturally relative definitions of child neglect and abuse indicate that there is some Eurocentrism at work in attributing child abuse to "backward" cultures. Of course, such monochromatic approaches are also counterproductive in developing effective social policy.

Viewed in this context, the overrepresentation of children from visible-minority groups (especially black and Latinos) in child welfare records remains a question that is open to debate. Structural issues (such as poverty and/or stress from unemployment or underemployment) could account for this overrepresentation, since these families often lack access to support systems that protect other children from entry into the child welfare system (Maiter, Alaggia, and Trocmé, 2004). Alternatively, or perhaps in addition, this overrepresentation may reflect negative stereotypes—shared by child welfare workers and the general public—about certain minority groups and their tendency to have more punitive attitudes about child rearing (Maiter, Alaggia, and Trocmé, 2004, p. 310). This may result in immigrant families being more vulnerable to intervention by child protection and police and in turn may put more pressure on parents and family members to "control" their kids in an effort not to be targeted by the state. Whether higher rates of child maltreatment cases in minority and poor populations reflect actual abuse or biased responses is still a controversial question even though research does suggest that children from poor and minority families are more vulnerable to receiving the label of "abused" than children from more affluent and majority households (Levesque, 2000, p. 154).

A current popular culture example of this pattern comes from Indo-Canadian stand-up comic and actor Russell Peters. He is well known for his stand-up routine about child abuse and what he suggests "separates immigrant families from Canadian-born families." As part of his performance he asks his audience, "If they weren't born in this country, they will whoop your ass when you're growing up, won't they? Immigrant parents will beat their kids!" Peters has been both criticized and lauded for making light of issues of cultural relativism, cultural defence, racism, and stereotyping of immigrant families through this humour. However one views it, Peters raises the profile of the cultural stereotypes on which many continue to base explanations of child abuse.

SPANKING: PUNISHMENT OR ABUSE?

One of the most hotly debated cultural practices in Canada and around the world associated with child abuse is spanking (see Box 9.2). Spanking is a great example of the ongoing debate about the distinction between physical punishment and physical abuse and the role of cultural relativism. "Definitions vary, as one person's view of what constitutes abuse—'hitting'—is another person's method for disciplining her or his child—'spanking'" (Vine, Trocmé, and Findlay, 2006, p. 147 in McKay, Fuchs, and Brown, 2009, p. 210). These attempts at drawing distinctions is confounded by child protection mandates, children's human rights, and in Canada by s. 43 of the *Criminal Code of Canada* (Watkinson, 2009 in McKay, Fuchs, and Brown, 2009).

This news report speaks to the current social and legal positioning of children in Canada and the way in which the issue of physical punishment intersects with child protection and children's rights. Since spanking is an example of physical punishment, it is interesting to note that one of the findings of the

BOX 9.2   TO SPANK OR NOT TO SPANK?

"To Spank or Not to Spank?" This was a CBC News headline this summer as it reported on New Zealand reopening the debate with a nonbinding referendum. Although New Zealand criminalized spanking as a form of "parental discipline" in 2007, it was revisiting the question.

Twenty-four countries around the world have a full ban on corporal punishment for children—both at home and in school—and the United Nations Committee on the Rights of the Child has recommended that physical punishment of children in schools and families be prohibited. However, the defence of "reasonable correction" has been part of Canada's *Criminal Code* since 1892. Section 43 of the code provides parents, teachers, and caregivers—including babysitters and foster parents—a defence when they use corporal punishment as "reasonable force" to discipline children. In 2004, a Supreme Court of Canada case, *Canadian Foundation for Children, Youth and the Law v. Canada (Attorney General)*, ruled that section 43 does not violate the *Canadian Charter of Rights and Freedoms*, as it does not infringe a child's rights to security of the person or a child's right to equality, and it does not constitute cruel and unusual treatment or punishment. This decision upheld the rights of adults to physically discipline children between the ages of 2 and 12 years of age. Shortly after this decision, Liberal Senator Céline Hervieux-Payette introduced a private member's bill (S209) to eliminate section 43. Although the bill passed its third reading in the Senate in June 2008 and moved to the House of Commons for approval, the House never held a vote (CBC, 2009) (http://www.cbc.ca/canada/story/2009/07/31/f-spanking-discipline-debate.html).

In 2009, CBC's *The Current* revisited the issue and spoke to Canadian and Swedish spokespersons who debated the issue of whether criminalizing spanking has led to more harm within families by criminalizing "normal parental discipline" than the harm that may come from using physical discipline against children (CBC, 2009).

CIS-2003 was that "[p]unishment accounted for 75 percent of substantiated incidents in which physical maltreatment was a primary category for investigation" (Durrant et al., 2006, in McKay, Fuchs, and Brown, 2009, p. 210). Clearly the actual line between punishment and abuse remains murky.

Although the Supreme Court of Canada did not find section 43 a violation of a child's *Charter* rights, and did not prohibit it outright, it did limit the scope of the section by limiting the use of physical punishment based on the "severity, age and location on the child's body." As a result, neither children nor parents are fully protected. Children are not fully protected from physical punishment and parents are not fully protected from prosecution for imposing physical punishment. According to some (McKay, Fuchs, and Brown, 2009) this legislative compromise is tantamount to reinforcing for parents the belief that the physical punishment of children is an ethically necessary act. Watkinson (2009) explains that, in a recent study on the intergenerational transmission of the approval of physical punishment, the best predictor of approval is one's belief that it is necessary to uphold normative order (Durrant et al., 2008, in Watkinson, 2009, p. 223). According to Watkinson and others, the Canadian Supreme Court lost an opportunity to reduce the likelihood of physical violence against children. However, it is likely that this debate is far from ended.

THE GENDERING OF CHILD ABUSE, NEGLECT, AND VIOLENCE

In this final segment on child abuse in families, we look at gender in terms of the way in which child abuse impacts girls and boys differently. We also look at it in terms of our gendered response. Child neglect is often characterized as a breakdown in a relationship of care, and, by extension, as a breakdown of mothering (Turney and Tanner, 2001, in Daniel and Taylor, 2006, p. 427). Perhaps one of the reasons for this gendered assumption is because of the lack of research into the role of the father in child neglect. Mothers are usually assumed to be the perpetrators of neglect and intervention is expected of them. As with children who witness domestic violence, the prevailing assumption is that women are the last line of defence and, therefore the responsible party for breeches of it. Even when the father is perpetrating violence, the expectation is that the mother will assume responsibility for extricating herself and the children from the violence and their residence.

At first glance, patterns of child abuse may appear to be gender-neutral. The CIS found that the number of cases of child maltreatment are almost equal for boys (51%) and girls (49%) (Trocmé et al., 2005, p. 63). However, the type of maltreatment a child is likely to experience varies significantly by sex and age. While rates of maltreatment were similar for boys and girls up to 7 years old, there were more males among children aged 8–11 and more females between 12–15 years of age (Trocmé et al., 2005, p. 63). Alternatively, for almost all age groups, girls are more likely to experience sexual abuse (with the exception of children between the ages of 4–7 years when the difference is less pronounced) (Trocmé et al. 2005, p. 63). Similarly, the Statistics Canada 2008 report *Violence Against Children and Youth* found that the rate of sexual assault committed by family members on children was three times higher for girls than for boys (Statistics Canada, 2008b).

There is also research concerning the gendered impact this abuse and violence has on children, youth and eventually adults.

> Each child is unique and their reaction will vary according to age, gender, personality, socio-economic status, role within the family, the frequency, nature and length of exposure to violence, with the impact moderated or mitigated by a further set of considerations, such as relationship with parents and siblings and available supports (Hester et al., 2000; Kashani and Allan, 1998; Salcido Carter et al., 1999, in Holt, Buckley, Whelan, 2008, p. 804).

There is, however, persuasive evidence that boys' and girls' experience of abuse, violence, and the witnessing of it in their homes has a differential impact on boys and girls. Boys are more likely to replicate the role of the perpetrator while girls tend toward more internally directed aggression and are more likely to replicate the role of the victim (Gerwitz and Edelson, 2007, p. 157).

Beyond this pattern, there is the question of how gender is related to perpetration and victimization. Increasing attention is being brought to understanding this difference and the effects of gender socialization on offending and victimization. Despite the gains made for girls and women in the past century, many girls still grow up with the pervasive sense that they are not as important as boys and that they will still be responsible for home and family.

> Girls, at younger and younger ages, are continuously bombarded by cultural and media messages that focus on physically unattainable ideals of femininity that involve being thin, beautiful and sexual. Girls look around at the devalued status of women in society—the number of women living in violence, the high percentage of single mothers living in poverty, the wage gap between men and women, the lack of women in our political and governmental systems—and the images rebound on their own sense of self (Canadian Women's Foundation, 2005, p. 50).

These patterns have profound implications for girls' likelihood of victimization and response to it throughout their life course.

One example of the combined impact of gender socialization and exposure to violence in the family is the prevalence of dating violence (Ismail, Berman, and Ward-Griffin, 2007). Several researchers have examined the relationship between child abuse or maltreatment, adjustment problems, and dating violence. Males were more likely to perpetrate dating violence if they had witnessed spousal abuse between their parents, whereas adolescent girls were more likely to be victims of dating violence if they had been abused in their families of origin. A recent Canadian study on dating violence brings attention to the profound ways that gender shapes young women's experiences with respect to violence in dating relationships (Ismail, Berman, and Ward-Griffin, 2007). As the young women in this study reflected on their own experiences of dating violence, they began to think about how these experiences were linked to earlier violence that was a part of their lives. These young women talked about the amount of pressure they felt from their peers and families to have boyfriends as well as their inability to recognize violence in their dating relationships. These young women described the need to conform to widely held gendered stereotypes in order to be accepted by their peers, partners, parents, and adults in trusted positions. The net result was their determination to keep their boyfriends regardless of how abusive they might be. Through the young women's descriptions, the interrelatedness of dating violence, family environment, and gendered socialization became clear (Ismail, Berman, and Ward-Griffin, 2007, p. 471).

VIOLENCE AGAINST WOMEN IN INTIMATE RELATIONSHIPS

Prevalence

Despite decades of public education, women continue to be surprised to learn that being with one's family is more dangerous than being with strangers. Of course, it may be less surprising when women consider that they spend far more time with their families than with strangers and, for that reason alone, are statistically more likely be harmed by them. Yet it remains common for women to continue to consider strangers much more of a threat than they are especially when compared to those familiar to us.[5]

As discussed in the previous section, the term "family violence," is often used to refer to a wide range of abuse and violence occurring within families across the life course. Despite the gender-neutral language of a term such as "family violence," there is compelling evidence to show that the vast majority of family violence is gendered. An extensive body of research indicates that most physical familial violence is perpetrated by men *against* women (and children).

In its 12th annual report on family violence in Canada, Statistics Canada reported (using police-reported data) that more than half of the victims of family violence were victimized by their spouse and the overwhelming majority of these victims continue to be female. In 2007, more than 8 in 10 victims of police-reported spousal violence were female (2009, p. 25). In addition to the gendered nature of this violence, local, national and international figures point to the prevalence and seriousness (including injuries and other consequences) of this gendering. In 2006, Statistics Canada released a comprehensive summary of research on violence against women in Canada. It found that

- women in the territories experience higher rates of spousal violence than women in the provinces

- each year, one out of every four female university or college students in Canada experiences some variation of sexual assault

- over 86 percent of all criminal assaults in Canada are against women

- five times more women than men are murdered by their partners

- when women do kill their partners, it is most often in self-defence[6] or after years of abuse

- every second, a woman somewhere in Canada experiences some form of sexual violence (Johnson, 2006).

Additionally, a review of 11 Canadian studies of intimate partner violence (IPV) found annual prevalence figures ranging from 0.4 percent to 23 percent (Clark and Du Mont, 2003). Almost a quarter of couples experienced intimate partner violence in the course of one year (Clark and Du Mont, 2003). A number of community studies, mostly from North America, have shown on average, one in five couples experienced intimate partner violence (IPV) over a 12-month period (Field and Caetano, 2005) although wider ranges are produced by studies examining IPV rates over longer time frames than 12 months.

Over the course of the last 30 years much has been learned about relationship violence. Of particular significance in this process was the first national Canadian survey of women's experience of violence. In 1993, Health Canada commissioned Statistics Canada to conduct a landmark survey of women's experiences of male violence (Johnson, 2006). This Violence Against Women Survey (VAWS) involved telephone interviews with a nationally representative random sample of 12,300 women about their adult experiences of sexual and physical assault by men (among other related issues such as sexual harassment and fear of violence), including male partners, friends, acquaintances, or strangers (Johnson, 2006).

The VAWS, which focused exclusively on violence against women, has not been repeated. Instead, some of the same kinds of questions are now asked as part of the (self-report) victimization survey of the General Social Survey (GSS), which is repeated every five years in Canada. Violence by a spouse or partner is measured by asking a series of 10 questions about specific actions. This helps filter out differing interpretations of what constitutes violence. Here is a list of the questions respondents are asked:

> I'm going to ask you 10 short questions and I'd like you to tell me whether, in the past five years, your spouse/partner has done any of the following to you. Your responses are important whether or not you have had any of these experiences. Remember that all information provided is strictly confidential.

> During the past five years, has your partner:

> 1. threatened you with his/her fist or anything else that could have hurt you?
> 2. thrown anything at you that could have hurt you?
> 3. pushed, grabbed, or shoved you in a way that could have hurt you?
> 4. slapped you?
> 5. kicked, bitten, or hit you with his/her fist?
> 6. hit you with something that could have hurt you?
> 7. beaten you?
> 8. choked you?
> 9. used or threatened to use a gun or knife on you?
> 10. forced you into any unwanted sexual activity by threatening you, holding you down, or hurting you in some way?[7]

Figure 9.2   **SPOUSAL VIOLENCE TRENDS, FIVE-YEAR RATES, 1999 AND 2004**

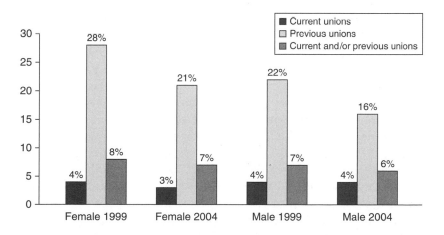

Source: Chart 1: Spousal violence trends, 5 year rates, 1999 and 2004, From: "What Are the Trends in Self-reported Spousal Violence in Canada?" by Jodi-Anne Brzozowski and Robyn Brazeau, Statistics Canada, General Social Surveys, 1999 and 2004, http://www.statcan.gc.ca/pub/89-630-x/2008001/c-g/10661/5200908-eng.htm.

Surprisingly, this recent Statistics Canada self-reported research on family violence suggested gender symmetry in patterns of intimate violence. As reported in July 2005 "an estimated 7 percent of women and 6 percent of men in a current or previous spousal relationship encountered spousal violence during the five years up to and including 2004" (Statistics Canada, 2005). The results of the 1999 and 2004 GSS indicate (as seen in Figure 9.2 above) that relatively equal proportions of women and men report spousal violence. Using these figures and other similar research, some researchers have been arguing that this is evidence of "gender symmetry" or an equal amount of female- and male-perpetrated violence against one's spouse. It is these findings of apparent gender neutrality that have lead to calls for gender neutral language such as "family violence," "spousal assault," and "intimate partner violence" (IPV). Meanwhile, those who see it as gender-specific continue to employ gender-specific terms such as woman/wife abuse and violence against women. However, as discussed below, the realities of family violence and abuse are in fact much more complex than either narrow position.

While the self-reporting rates may be similar for males and females, this very same Statistics Canada survey makes it clear that significant elements such as severity of violence (as evidenced in injuries), and level of fear are substantially greater for women than they are for men. For instance 19 percent of men indicated they suffered injuries, compared to 44 percent of women (Statistics Canada, 2005). Although there continues to be a debate about the extent to which there is an "equal" amount of violence perpetrated between spouses, the research itself indicates the contexts and motives structuring intimate violence are very different for men compared to women. This is especially true of consequences (notably, significance of injury) and level of fear which are substantially greater for women. It is well known that symmetrical data generated by versions of the Conflict Tactics Scale (CTS) does not tell us very much about why men and women use violence in intimate relationships (DeKeseredy, 2008, p. 1080). This draws our attention to the limitations of a gender-neutral perspective.

In addition to identifying the limitations of a gender-neutral approach, we must also be mindful of the limitations of a narrowly gendered approach, which tends to ignore other important variables such as race, age, disability, and so on. As Renzetti reminded us a decade ago, men and women also "do gender" differently and it is important not only to examine gender differences in IPV but also to ". . . take into account differences by race and/ or ethnicity, social class, sexual orientation, age and other social locating factors (Renzetti, 1999)" (2006, p. 1047). While trying to better understand the larger social, political, and economic context in which IPV occurs means more complex empirical and theoretical work on this issue, the results gleaned from such an intersectional approach offer more meaningful data in understanding prevalence, consequences, and responses to this violence locally and globally.

Violence Against Women Globally

Globally, "intimate partner violence" (IPV) has also been identified as the most common form of violence experienced by women according to a 2006 United Nations Report (United Nations, 2006). Estimates around the world range between 10 percent and 60 percent of women experiencing violence at the hands of their male partner at some point in their lives (Ellsberg and Heise, 2005, in Johnson et al. 2008, p. 33). A recent World Health Organization (WHO) "Multi-Country Study on Women's Health and Domestic Violence Against Women" (2005) found rates of 29 percent to 62 percent lifetime violence against women by male intimate partners in most sites in 10 countries (Minaker and Snider, 2006, p. 753). The International Violence Against Women Survey (IVAWS)[8] provides rates of intimate partner violence among women in nine countries ranging from 9 percent to 40 percent (Johnson et al. 2008, p. 38). On average, it seems that at least one in three women is subject to intimate partner violence in the course of their lifetimes (United Nations, 2006).

> *Violence by an intimate partner is one of the most common forms of gender-based violence, with population surveys suggesting that between 15 and 71 per cent of ever partnered women globally have been physically or sexually assaulted by an intimate partner at some-time in their lives (Garcia-Moreno et al., 2006, in Vyas and Watts, 2009, p. 577).*

As Rosenberg and Duffy explain, "evidence of woman abuse in intimate relationships is found almost everywhere. . . . Research indicates that one-third of women have experienced physical abuse at the hands of a male intimate" (Rosenberg and Duffy, 2009, 169). Rani and Bonu (2009) suggest that "the high prevalence of intimate partner violence directed toward women documented in both developing and developed countries (Heise, Ellsberg, and Gottemoeller, 1999) appropriately qualifies it as a "hidden and unacknowledged epidemic" (Coeling and Harnan, 1997) (Rani, Manju and Sekhar Bonu, 2009, p. 1371).

The above research helps to demonstrate that a significant element in the violence occurring in families is violence against women, and all women, regardless of class, race/ethnicity, age, religion, ability, or sexual orientation are in some sense subject to male violence (Rosenberg and Duffy, 2009, p. 161). In fact, after decades of speculation and assumptions about wife assault being more common in certain cultural or socioeconomic groups, the argument is now commonly made that woman abuse is found in all sociodemographic categories (Denham and Gillespie, 1998; Menard, 2001, in DeKeseredy, Schwartz, and Shahid, 2008, p. 283). Within this overarching social reality of risk, it is also clear that women in some definable categories are at greater risk of being assaulted by men than others and that there are important differences in women's experiences of gendered violence (Schwartz, 1988a as cited in DeKeseredy, Schwartz and Shahid, 2008, p. 283).

Theorizing Violence Against Women

As one would expect, research and analysis on "family violence" has evolved significantly over the past 30 years. Karel Kurst-Swanger and Jacqueline Petcosky (2003, p. 32) provide a simple way to make sense of the range of theories available. They distinguish "micro," "meso," and "macro" levels of analyses. Within these three levels they situate a number of theoretical models widely used to explain a specific kind of family violence.

A micro level of analysis of any social problem (including violence against women in relationships) focuses at the level of the individual. Micro analyses attempt to explain familial violence by examining the characteristics of the individual perpetrators and victims. Psychologists have identified numerous disorders and characteristics associated with "batterers" and "abused women." When the individual is the unit of analysis (as usual in mainstream psychology), the emphasis is on pathology or cognitive and personality "deficits" (Prilleltensky, 1989, as cited in Salazar and Cook, 2002). These theories tend to find the roots of violence in individual psychopathology or dysfunctional personality structures that are learned and shaped by early childhood experiences or biological predispositions (Dutton and Golant, 1995; O'Leary, 1993, in Mason et al., 2008). Personality disorders or dysfunctions, as well as mental illness, and alcohol and substance abuse are commonly used to explain the violence.

In spite of growing evidence of the limitations of such explanations, micro-level theories continue to enjoy credence in popular explanations of perpetrators and victims of family violence. It is common to read and hear things like, "What kind of a weirdo could do that?," "He's got an anger management problem," or "She must be crazy to put up with that." All of these direct our attention to mental pathology or deficits of the individual. As Gwen Hunnicutt explains, psychological and other individual-level theories used to explain the victimization of women are limited since they focus on "sick" people diverting us from attending to "sick" social arrangements (2009, p. 556).

The second level distinguished by Kurst-Swanger and Petcosky is the "meso" level of analysis. At this level, social problems are studied at the level of groups, and efforts to explain the problem focus on studying the people involved, their interactions with each other, and the environmental factors that affect the group (Kurst-Swanger and Petcosky 2003, p. 37). This is often referred to as a "social psychological perspective." Family systems theory and social learning theory are two prominent examples of meso level theoretical approaches. These theoretical approaches are interested in examining the actions of human beings as influenced by their interaction with their environment which includes situational factors, the most notable of which are "families." This branch of theory includes theoretical frames such as "traumatic bonding," "stress," "social conflict," "resource," "exchange," "social control," and "social learning."

According to Albert Bandura's (1973) social learning theory (which has been one of the most widely adopted theories on family violence) children learn aggression from their parents and reproduce this behaviour in their own adult relationships (O'Leary, 1988 in Mason et al., 2008). Social learning theory has also been referred to as the "intergenerational theory" and is a popular approach to explaining the impacts on children who witness violence against a parent. Despite their popularity, these meso analyses theories are also quite limited especially in terms of their inability to account for the subtle and complex ways in which every act of violence is embedded in a larger social organization (Hunnicutt, 2009, p. 556).

Kurst-Swanger and Petcosky's third level of analysis is the "macro" level. It explores social problems by looking at the larger societal structures and organizations that affect them. This level of analysis is often referred to as a "sociological" or "socio Bandura's (1973) cultural" perspective (Kurst-Swanger and Petcosky 2003, p. 37). Sociological scholarship on family violence first appeared in the literature in the 1970s (Breines and Gordon, 1983, p. 508). As a new approach to the phenomena, it began with dissatisfaction with the then dominant psychological explanations. Sociologists began with the assertion that "neither wife beaters nor their victims are necessarily crazier than nonviolent adults" (Gordon and Breines, 1983, p. 508). Other sociological researchers moved toward studying families as an institution and focused on social forces as causal factors in family violence. Theories including "feminist," "political economy," "culture of violence," and "environmental stress/strain" theories fit under the umbrella of this meso level of analysis.

Although feminist theory is identified as a meso level of analysis, there is a wide variety of feminist explanations of violence against women in intimate relationships. There are also discernable commonalities among feminist perspectives. They share the idea that violence against women is a social, political, and criminal problem, rather than an individual or family problem. Also shared is the focus on gender and its relationship to power. These elements clearly distinguish feminist analyses. Put succinctly, feminists work from the understanding that there is a direct connection between patriarchal social structures and the ideologies used to maintain them and the prevalence of male violence against women in general.

> ... [P]atriarchy is a sex/gender system in which men dominate women and what is considered masculine is more highly valued than what is considered feminine. Patriarchy is a system of social stratification, which means that it uses a wide array of social control policies and practices to ratify male power and to keep girls and women subordinate to men (Renzetti and Curran, 1999, p. 3).

Many feminists see patriarchy operating at the level of sociocultural "mythology" that supports implicit as well as explicit social control conventions, policies, and practices. Seen this way, patriarchy operates at a hegemonic level and is difficult to discern since it is interwoven with the taken-for-granted reality. Women can be expected to be "controlled" by males in both the family and society because patriarchy is foundational to the social order and pervades every level of society including the public and private sphere (Jasinski, 2001). The subordination of women is part of the definition of a patriarchal social order. It was not long ago when women and children were literally the legal property of men (Jasinski, 2001). Patriarchy and ownership gave men a socially legitimized moral and legal right to control this property using whatever means they felt appropriate. In a patriarchal society, women are considered legitimate objects of "correction" (for example, violence) when they are perceived as a threat to the social order and established power hierarchy. When violence is a legitimate means of maintaining the patriarchal social order, violence against subordinates is seen as the rather predictable result.

Patriarchies take a variety of ideological and structural shapes across the social landscape and do not exist as uniform systems (they vary across time, place, and material contexts) and the varieties are forever shifting as power relations change in concert with other key social changes (Hunnicutt, 2009, p. 568). Varieties of patriarchy are understood holistically, then, in terms of interlocking structures of domination. Patriarchal interests often overlap with systems that also reinforce property rights, and class and race privilege. According to many feminists, there is therefore a need for an "intersectional analysis" and a theory construction that allows for variation in dimensions of "dominance, power, and resistance" (Hunnicutt, 2009, p. 568) (cf. Crenshaw, 1994).

FEMINIST INTERSECTIONAL ANALYSIS

Feminist theorizing on intersectionality is not new[9] (see Crenshaw, 1994, and Hill-Collins, 1990, McCall, 2005), but it has become a central tenet of contemporary feminist thinking (Shields, 2008, p. 301). Some see it as the most important contribution of feminist theory to our present understanding of gender (Shields, 2008, p. 301). It has become particularly useful for understanding gendered violence.

Since the 1980s, feminist analyses of essentialist assumptions about gender increasingly have employed an intersectional perspective to understand gender in relation to other social identities, such as race, class, ethnicity and sexual orientation (Shields, 2008, p. 303). Intersectionality has become a basis for feminist theory, a methodology for research, and a springboard for social justice activism. It starts from the premise that people live multiple, layered identities that can be derived from social relations, history, and the operation of structures of power. People are members of more than one community at the same time, and therefore can simultaneously experience oppression and privilege as they move from realm to realm. Take this simple example—a person may be a respected medical professional at the office, yet suffer domestic violence at home. While she experiences privileges by virtue of her education and occupation, this does not make her immune from experiencing male violence given her gender and living in a patriarchal society.

Intersectional analysis aims to reveal these multiple identities, exposing the different types of discrimination and disadvantage that occur as a consequence of the combination of identities. It aims to address the manner in which racism, patriarchy, class oppression, and other systems of discrimination create inequalities that structure and reinforce the relative positions of people. It takes account of historical, social, and political contexts and also recognizes unique individual experiences based on one's identity (e.g., gender, race, class, age, ability, sexual orientation etc.) (AWRID, 2004, p. 1). Applying intersectionality to intimate violence means carefully analyzing how racism, social class inequality, sexism, ableism, ageism, and heterosexism affect both the causes and consequences of intimate violence (Renzetti, 1998, p. 123 in Brownridge, 2009b, p. 11).

Intersectionality and Victimization

As with child abuse, many social and economic factors impact women's risk of or vulnerability to violence and these same factors affect the causes and consequences of women's experiences of intimate violence. Applying an intersectional perspective recognizes differing vulnerabilities and tries to understand and explain why some groups are more at risk of violence than others. We now turn to a brief look at the way in which some groups of women are seen to be affected.

The Feminist Alliance for International Action (FAFIA) identifies poor women as well as young women and girls, women suffering from mental illnesses or addiction, women with disabilities, and immigrant women as particularly likely to be victimized (2008, p. 28). Research on different populations of women identifies social and political (rather than individual/psychological) factors associated with higher likelihoods of victimization. Intersectionality seeks to understand the larger context of social policy and victimization. Feminist analysts see this as a prerequisite for adequately addressing and perhaps preventing and eliminating such violence. As discussed below, social context and the connection between relationship violence and larger issues of oppression and inequality are seen as the distinguishing features of these women.

VIOLENCE AGAINST WOMEN WITH DISABILITIES

Women with disabilities are one of a number of populations that are distinctly vulnerable to violence (Brownridge, 2009a, p. 1705) Like women without disabilities, most women with disabilities are victimized by their intimate partners (Brownridge, 2009a, p. 1705). ". . . [W]omen with disabilities are more likely to experience physical and sexual violence (Brownridge, 2006; Martin et al.,

2006; Powers et al., 2002; Smith, 2008); increased severity of violence (Brownridge, 2006; Nannini, 2006; Nosek et al., 2001); multiple forms of violence (Curry et al., 2003; Martin et al., 2006; Nosek et al., 2001); and longer duration of violence (Nosek et al., 2001)" (Powers et al., 2009, p. 104).

In Canada, the DisAbled Women's Network (DAWN) reports that the incidence of abuse is 20 percent or higher in the developmentally disabled and deaf community (DAWN). They also report that women with mental illnesses face less access to services, such as women's shelters, due to a lack of awareness and acceptance of mental health issues (FAFIA, 2008, p. 35).

DAWN argues that "social attitudes" and more specifically "ableism"[10] (which refers to the broader social prejudices against other-abled individuals) toward persons with disabilities is one of the biggest factors increasing the likelihood of violence. DAWN outlines a number of examples of the way in which the current social context "handicaps" women with disabilities:

- They tend to be viewed and treated as children, as lacking intelligence.

- They may be trained to be compliant and are sometimes punished for assertiveness or for challenging authority figures. This is in direct contrast to the street-proofing taught to many children in schools.

- Women with disabilities are considered to be nonsexual and are often not given sex education, which can result in an inability to distinguish between abusive behaviour and normal or necessary forms of touching.

- They may be considered incompetent witnesses by police and the courts, particularly if they have difficulty or require assistance in communicating.

- When they do report abuse, they may not be believed (Dawn, n.d).

Clearly, understanding the unique factors that contribute to women with disabilities' victimization has important implications for social and public policy responses (Powers et al., 2002; Saxton et al., 2001).

VIOLENCE IN SAME-SEX RELATIONSHIPS

Scholarship has been slower to focus on same-sex intimate partner violence (SSIPV).[11] As it evolves, the social context of violence in Lesbian/Gay/Bisexual/Transgender/Queer (hereon LGBTQ) relationships is also seen as a powerful factor, which helps to explain SSIPV. Intersectional analysis helps illustrate that gender is not always the primary locus of oppression in understanding violence.

Janice Ristock (one of a few well-known researchers on this issue; see Chapter 5 of this text) argues that, in spite of all the important work done by feminists to address male violence against women, the "gender-exclusive" framework (that focuses on the roots of violence within sexism and patriarchy) ends up misunderstanding (if not, ignoring) violence in the LGBTQ population. She argues that same-sex partner violence requires an understanding of the connection between relationship violence and homophobia, biphobia, transphobia, and heterosexism along with other forms of phobia-based oppression including sexism, racism, and classism (2005, p. 3). Anahi Russo suggests that a framework of intersectionality expands a gender-based analysis of violence and in this way considers the relationship violence in relation to all systems of oppression. By examining differing contexts, researchers are better able to recognize the different spaces and ways in which violence occurs and the way in which violence is linked to hierarchies of inequality and necessary social justice efforts (Ristock, 2005, p. 10).

Although many of the tactics used in same-sex abusive relationships are the same as those used in abusive heterosexual relationships, a larger social context reveals the effectiveness of some "unique" abusive tactics (Pattavina et al., 2007, p. 377). These uniquely effective tactics include ". . . threats to reveal the sexual or gender identity of a partner to one's boss, landlord, or family member; threats to jeopardize custody of children because of a person's sexual or gender identity; threats to jeopardize immigration because of sexual orientation, and/or threats to reveal the HIV/AIDS status of a partner" (Ristock, 2005, p. 4).

Some research suggests that lesbians are affected by interpersonal violence (IPV) at rates similar to heterosexuals (that is, 25%–50%) (Lockhart et al., 1994; Owen and Burke, 2004, as cited in Eaton et al. 2008, p. 697).However, Statistics Canada data report that the rate of spousal violence among those who identify as gay or lesbian was twice the rate of reported violence experienced by those who identify as heterosexual (15 percent versus 7%) (Statistics Canada, 2005, p. 8). Moreover, such data needs to be cautiously interpreted for the same reasons that lead to the success of the unique abuse tactics discussed above. LGBTQ violence is less likely to be reported to the police or to mainstream social service agencies precisely because of the larger fear that coming out will carry worse penalties in homophobic social context.

VIOLENCE AGAINST IMMIGRANT WOMEN

While research on violence against immigrant and visible-minority women is also relatively scarce, some significant findings are available. One review of the U.S. literature (Raj and Silverman, 2002) found that 30 percent to 50 percent of immigrant women have experienced IPV, and this proportion may be increasing (Mason et al. 2008, p. 1400).[12] Various researchers have drawn similar conclusions that violence against women is one of the most common victimizations experienced by immigrants (Davis and Erez, 1998; Erez, 2000; Raj and Silverman, 2002, Merali, 2009). However, interpreting the data is complex. Canadian findings suggest that rates of IPV are lower among immigrant women compared to Canadian-born women (Cohen and Maclean, 2003, in Mason et al., 2008) but that, interestingly, the immigrant woman's risk increases over time (Hyman, Forte, Du Mont, Romans, and Cohen, 2006, in Mason et al. 2008, p. 1400).

An intersectional theoretical analysis is a common tool used to help explain and understand the social forces that shape experiences across immigrant groups (Hyman, Guruge, and Mason, 2008). "[In identifying racial/ethnic differences in research on family violence], we must consider that racism, sexism and other forms of oppression can exacerbate the situation and such violence is likely only one of the forms of abuse that members of marginalized groups experience" (Malley-Morrison and Hines, 2007, p. 947). Various social structural influences (such as poverty, limited educational opportunities), historical influences (for example, history of forced slavery and migration), and systematic oppression must all be considered when exploring the rates at which different groups experience family violence as well as their willingness to seek help for it (Malley-Morrison and Hines, 2007, p. 947).

Immigrant women's experiences of violence are certainly not homogenous just as their social class, educational background, language abilities, and so on will vary enormously. However, one significant and common issue faces immigrant women: their immigration status. For instance, limited host-language skills, lack of access to dignified jobs, uncertain legal statuses, experiences in their home countries, and a general lack of culturally acceptable alternatives to living with their abusers are unique factors for many immigrant women (Hass, Dutton, and Orloff, 2000). New research by Merali has examined violence and abuse on Canadian immigrant women after changes were made to Canadian family sponsorship policies (2009). Although recent changes were made specifically to improve the situation for immigrant women in Canada, her findings are consistent with others (Shirwadkar, 2004; Kang, 2006) who also found that changes to sponsorship policies and procedures have not improved the plight of non-English-proficient women (Merali, 2009, p. 334). Due to language barriers, these study participants were completely reliant on third-party interpretations of the nature of sponsorship. The relaying of the conditions of sponsorship by their husbands led to the sometimes-deliberate miscommunication of the sponsor and sponsored person's rights, limitations, and residency status. It also led to the omission of important protections that exist for the women. Consequently, the women did not recognize any rights they had apart from their right to perform domestic duties. Their lack of awareness of their rights and status seemed to make the non-English-proficient South Asian women vulnerable to various types of human rights violations (Merali, 2009, p. 334). Even more specifically, immigrant women's legal dependency (created in part by immigration laws), may limit their access to resources, employment, social services, and even protection under the law (Erez, Adelman, and Gregory, 2009, p. 46).[13]

Again, a predictable reluctance on the part of immigrant women to report violence implies that statistics are likely to under represent the extent of the problem.

ABORIGINAL WOMEN IN CANADA

The extent of violence against women among Canadian Aboriginal communities is also less well known than it is for the general population of women. Obstacles including geographical isolation, generational ties to the land, language barriers, and cultural differences can isolate victims of violence, which in turn make it difficult to get a clear picture of victimization rates (Campbell, 2007, p. 58). Statistics Canada research indicates that Aboriginal people are three times more likely to be victims of spousal violence than are those who are non-Aboriginal (21 percent versus 7%) (2005, p. 8). A number of provincial surveys also indicate that the incidence of family violence among Aboriginal people is considerably higher than that of the general population. These studies also suggest that Aboriginal women are further victimized by more severe incidents. For instance, homicide statistics indicate that they are eight times more likely to be killed by their partner than are non-Aboriginal women (Trainor and Mihorean, 2001).

As discussed around the issue of child abuse and neglect, a toxic mix of colonization, the forced institutionalization in residential schools, racist and sexist practices of the Indian Act, poverty, victimization, and criminalization along with alcohol and drug abuse have all contributed to a climate that exacerbates family violence. Despite recent policy initiatives and apologies from the federal government, Aboriginal communities continue to be plagued by child and youth suicide, family breakdown, alcohol and drug abuse, poverty, and unemployment. All of these factors interweave with patterns of Aboriginal family violence (Campbell, 2007, p. 59).

ABUSE OF OLDER ADULTS

Like "family violence" in general, elder abuse[14] is increasingly recognized here and internationally as an important health and social problem. "It is an important facet of the family violence problem as well as an intergenerational concern, and a health, justice, and human rights issue" (Lowenstein, 2008, p. 278). Canadian studies suggest that approximately 4 percent of seniors experience abuse or neglect (O'Connor et al., 2009, p. 158). While financial abuse is generally identified as the most common form of abuse perpetrated against seniors, spouses (and husbands in particular) are most likely to physically abuse while strangers or offspring are more likely to abuse through finances/resources (O'Connor, 2009, p. 158). See Box 9.3. According to Statistics Canada's 2009 Family Violence research,

- Senior men (163 per 100,000) had a higher overall rate of violent victimization compared to senior women (114 per 100,000). However, senior women had higher rates of violent victimization by a family member (52 per 100,000) compared to senior men (43 per 100,000).

BOX 9.3   EXPLAINING ABUSE OF OLDER ADULTS

In the past, the most popular explanation for abuse of older adults was that it was provoked by stress on the person providing long-term care for the more dependent older adult. Recent research shows that the dynamics between dependent individuals and their caregivers are much more complex.

The most common explanations of abuse of older adults focus on the following:

- *A web of dependent relationships*—physical, emotional, and financial, between the victim and abuser. Research findings are inconsistent. Not all dependent seniors are abused. Some studies even suggest that abusers are more likely than nonabusers to be dependent on their victims.

- *Traits of the abusive caregiver*—An impressive amount of research has linked mental health problems and social characteristics of caregivers to abuse. One example is that abusers are more likely than nonabusers to have alcohol or other substance abuse problems.

- *Situational stress*—Caregiver stress related to long-term care of an older adult sometimes leads to abuse. The failure of stress-reducing interventions (e.g., home care assistance, respite care) to reduce abuse has led to less emphasis on the singular importance of caregiver stress.

- *Transgenerational family violence*—Children from a long history of family violence "getting back at" a parent. The limited research on this theory suggests that it explains child abuse much more than senior abuse.

- *Social isolation*—Isolation has not been established as a cause of abuse, but abused older adults are more likely to have fewer contacts with friends and family members than are nonabused older adults.

- *Pervasive societal power imbalances*—Individual experience is inseparably linked to social forces and institutional practices that may support power imbalances in families (e.g., ageism or sexism).

Source: The National Clearinghouse on Family Violence. (nd). *Abuse and Neglect of Older Adults: Overview Paper Family Violence Prevention Unit, Health Issues Division, Public Health Agency of Canada.* Health Canada www.phac-aspc .gc.ca/nc-cn. Reproduced with the permission of the Minister of Public Works and Government Services Canada, 2010.

- Spouses and adult children were the most common perpetrators of family violence against senior women, while adult children were most often the accused in family violence against senior men (Statistics Canada Family Violence, 2009).

In Canada, about one-half (53%) of homicides against older women and one-quarter of those against older men are committed by their spouses or ex-spouses (Statistics Canada, 1999, in Sev'er, 2009, p. 280).

Like child abuse and IPV, senior abuse is thought to be seriously underreported (Sev'er, 2002, p. 281) for many of the same reasons (such as fear of retaliation, dependence on the abuser, the shame and stigma of being a victim, the fear of not being believed). As well, the underreporting of the abuse of older adults is seen as at least partly attributable to strong norms establishing the family as an inviolably private sphere. There is a strong cultural expectation that family matters will be kept within the family. Intervention is seen as interference (Sev'er, 2002, p. 281).

As in the populations previously mentioned, the social context or social forces contributing to the abuse of older women in relationships include sexism and ageism. Some researchers claim that elder abuse is simply "wife abuse" that has gone old or that it is a new experience of abuse either in a long-term relationship or in a new one (Sev'er, 2009, p. 282). The intersection of "sexism" and "ageism" reinforces stereotypes and social expectations that discourage older women from making changes in their lives that would benefit them. For instance, older women are expected to care for their spouses at all costs, and leaving a violent relationship is not considered socially acceptable (Buchbinder and Winterstein, 2004, p. 25).

Older women are often in a no-win situation. On the one hand, societal norms encourage them to feel responsible for keeping their family together regardless of the personal emotional, physical and financial costs they incur in doing so. On the other hand, they are seen as responsible for their own injuries (and even enabling the perpetrator and perpetuating the problem of intimate partner violence) if they stay in the relationship (Enander, 2010, p. 6).

Many scholars argue that abuse of older adults is also gendered and that the vast majority of perpetrators are men while victims are women. Some feminist analysts argue that gender and age combine to make older women one of the most disadvantaged groups in Canada and the United States because of the feminization of poverty. Statistics suggest that the poverty rate for elderly women is double the rate for elderly men and this increases the level of dependency of older women (Canada's Aging Population, 2002, in Sev'er, 2009, p. 283).

Some recent evidence points to a less significant split along gender lines in the over-80-years-of-age population (Sev'er, 2002, p. 283). While more work needs to be done in this area, some might argue that this is a sign that ageism eventually trumps sexism in contemporary Canadian culture. Age has been a significant variable to consider in our understanding of violence in families throughout the life course. However, it is clear from the literature that these are complex issues that require an ability to examine and understand the larger social, legal, political, and economic context. It is within this larger context that the impact of a range of variables (i.e., gender, age, race, sexual orientation, ability, and so forth) has on the prevalence, perception, resistance, consequences and response of violence in families in Canada.

CONCLUSION

This chapter has highlighted the difference between perception and reality about fear of victimization. Assumptions about the dangers of strangers and the safety of the family are both unsupported by the evidence. We have also seen that there are both shared and distinct features of violence in families. In short, it (like most social phenomena) is multidimensional, subtle, and complex. Different theoretical frames provide distinct ways of understanding familial violence. Feminist intersectionality is a powerful tool in interpolating perpetration and victimization in a broader social, cultural, and ideological context. It helps us address the powerful role that patriarchy, sexism, heterosexism, racism, classism, ageism, ableism, and so forth have on both perpetrators and victims of violence.

Despite increasing recognition of the global reach of the problem and emerging research and resources, there are still many gaps in our knowledge and understanding of violence in familial relationships—especially as we try to understand how it affects distinct subgroups. There is still much more research and theorizing required if we are to better identify, understand, respond to, and, ultimately, prevent violence in the sanctuary of our most intimate relationships. Armed with a realistic understanding of the gravity and extent of the problem and the hard work necessary to understand it, we may be better prepared to develop effective policy responses for the benefit of all.

Summary

- Our fear of victimization by strangers is inconsistent with the reality of violence in families. Confronting the varieties of abuse, neglect, maltreatment, and physical violence that children and adults experience in their intimate relationships through the course of their lives requires understanding and addressing of the larger social context.

- Specifically, the intersection of gender, age, class, race/ethnicity, sexual orientation, ability, and immigrant status are crucial lenses through which to deepen our understanding of policy response to violence in families.

- Feminist intersectionality is a powerful tool offering a broadly framed gendered perspective with policy implications for addressing violence in families by way of increased equity and social justice.

Notes

1. By definition, "police-reported violent crime" does not include that which goes unreported. Unfortunately, until we know more about the nature and extent of unreported violence, it is difficult to include it in statistics on crime (since if it is not reported or prosecuted as such, it is, by definition, not a crime). There is increasing research to suggest that unreported violence is a significant portion of possible crime in Canada (O'Grady, 2007).

2. There are many ways of defining a family. For our purposes we will simply say a social unit organized around someone with whom you have a spousal relationship.

3. "Child neglect includes situations in which children have suffered harm, or their safety or development has been endangered as a result of the caregiver's failure to provide for or protect them. This can include physical, emotional, medical, educational etc." (Trocmé et al., 2003, p. 41).

4. Very few people of any socioeconomic status openly and persistently maltreat their children but the stresses of poverty may be associated with increased likelihood of maltreatment occurring.

5. As discussed in the previous section on child abuse, part of the reason we fear "strangers" has to do with the ideology of the family that fosters a belief in it as a safe haven and a place of security. There are also evolutionary explanations that justify our commonly shared fear of the unknown (e.g., strangers). Treating "unfamiliar" things, animals, and people with caution and being wary of unknown threats promotes survival. We now realize that the unknown and unfamiliar things are not the only things to be feared. Survival among some women and children could be promoted with a more extensive understanding of known and familiar (in this case familial) threats.

6. Self-defence has been construed more widely especially after the Supreme Court of Canada case of *R. v. Lavallee*, 1990, which highlighted the reality that, especially for women who have been in long-standing abusive relationships, leaving can be more dangerous than staying. In the case of Angelique Lavallee, it was choosing between options literally posed to her by her husband who told her the night she shot him "it's either kill or be killed" (*R. v. Lavallee*, [1990] 1 S.C.R. 852).

7. Text excerpt from: Johnson, Holly. 2006. *Measuring Violence Against Women: Statistical Trends 2006*, online: Statistics Canada, http://www.statcan .gc.ca/pub/85-570-x/85-570-x2006001-eng.htm and "I'm going to ask you 10 short questions and I'd like you to tell me whether, in the past five years, your spouse/partner has . . . ." under the Methodology section, under the heading "How violence is measured using victimization surveys". Direct link to "Methodology" section: http://www.statcan.gc.ca/ pub/85-570-x/2006001/4054095-eng.htm.

8. The IVAWS is an internationally comparative project that incorporates a standardized methodology and has as a primary focus the strengthening of legal measures and improving criminal justice responses to violence (Johnson et al., 2008, p. 15).

9. It has been traced to ". . . Black feminist responses to the limitations of the accumulated disadvantage model (e.g., Mullings, 1997; Nakano Glenn, 1999) and the recognition that the intersections of gender with other dimensions of social identity are the starting point of theory (Crenshaw 1994/2005)" (Shields, 2008, p. 303).

10. Used to describe effective discrimination against people with disabilities in favour of people who are not disabled.

11. This is in part because it challenges the underlying heterosexist feminist paradigm.

12. National immigration statistics suggest that approximately 25 percent to 30 percent of immigrants arriving in Canada annually are family members of Canadian citizens or permanent residents. This amounts to between 62,000 and 65,000 people per year (Citizenship and Immigration Canada, 2005 in Merali, 2009, p. 321). The majority of family members sponsored to come to Canada by Canadian citizens or permanent residents are spouses, with a disproportionate number of them (60%) being wives (Citizenship and Immigration Canada, 2005 in Merali, 2009, p. 321). Half of the sponsored family members entering Canada come from developing nations in the Asia Pacific region (Citizenship and Immigration Canada, 2005 in Merali, 2009, p. 321). Every year, approximately 250,000 immigrants and refugees arrive in Canada, with 60 percent of recent immigrants coming from Asia and the Middle East (Citizenship and Immigration Canada, 2003 in Mason et al., 2008, p. 1400). According to the 2001 census, Toronto received the highest of immigrants of any city in Canada, where immigrants represented 44 percent of the population, a proportion higher than that found in Miami (40%), Los Angeles (31%), or New York City (24%) (Citizenship and Immigration Canada, 2003 in Mason et al., 2008, p. 1400).

13. Prior to the introduction of Canada's new *Immigration and Refugee Protection Act* in 2002 (Citizenship and Immigration Canada, 2002b) sponsored persons were excluded from access to any government financial or social assistance for the 10-year duration, as well as from immigration and settlement assistance provided to independent immigrants or refugees (Lamba and Wilkinson, 1998, in Merali, 2009, p. 322). As Merali explains, two seminal Canadian research studies on sponsored women's experiences conducted in 2001 revealed that the sponsored women revealed signs of helplessness in cases in which their husbands became barriers to their integration in Canada. They clearly did not understand their status as sponsored persons in Canada and did not seem to see any way to change their experiences or to access help (Husaini, 2001; Merali, 2009, p. 322).

14. For an overview of the issue of elder abuse and neglect in Canada see Podnieks, 2009.

Critical Thinking Questions

1. How would you explain the distance between popular conceptions of victimization (e.g., fear of stranger violence) and the much higher likelihood of familial violence?

2. In what ways is violence in families "gendered"?

3. How is the language we use to talk about violence within families related to understanding and responding to this violence?

4. What does an intersectional analysis of violence within families offer?

5. How might the "cultural defence" argument affect minority families?

Websites

Canadian Child Welfare Research Portal
http://www.cecw-cepb.ca
> The Canadian Child Welfare Research Portal provides up-to-date research on Canadian child welfare programs and policies. This website has been designed to be a searchable clearinghouse of information for child welfare professionals, researchers, and the general public. It provides links to past and current Canadian Incidence Studies (CIS) on child abuse, neglect, and maltreatment as well as links to the Research Watch, which tracks and produces concise reviews of articles on child welfare.

Ontario Women's Justice Network
http://www.owjn.org
> The Ontario Women's Justice Network (OWJN) promotes an understanding of the law with respect to violence against women, providing accessible legal information to women and their supporters in a manner that reflects the diverse experiences and realities of women. OWJN contains information on relevant legal issues, including written law (legislation) and case law (court decisions).

Canadian Women's Foundation
http://www.cdnwomen.org
> The Canadian Women's Foundation (CWF) is Canada's only national public foundation dedicated to improving the lives of women and girls. The Canadian Women's Foundation brings together organizations to share research, skills, and the most promising practices for ending violence against women, moving low-income women out of poverty, and empowering girls. The CWF website provides links to publications such as the *Girls in Canada* report.

The Canadian Network for the Prevention of Elder Abuse (CNPEA)
http://www.cnpea.ca
> The Canadian Network for the Prevention of Elder Abuse (CNPEA) is dedicated to the prevention of the abuse of older people in Canada. The website provides information to raise awareness of key issues around abuse and neglect in later life and to assure older adults are treated as full citizens in Canadian society. The website is intended to help people access and share information on abuse and neglect issues in later life, as well as learn more about what is being done across Canada to address this important health, social, and legal issue.

Suggested Readings

Nico Trocmé, Bruce MacLaurin, Barbara Fallon, Della Knoke, Lisa Pitman, and Megan McCormack. 2006. *Understanding the Overrepresentation of First Nations Children in Canada's Child Welfare System: An Analysis of the Canadian Incidence Study of Reported Child Abuse and Neglect* (CIS-2003). Toronto: Centre of Excellence for Child Welfare.

> This report compares children of Aboriginal heritage with non-Aboriginal children included in the CIS-2003 in an effort to better understand some of the factors contributing to the overrepresentation of Aboriginal children in the child welfare system in Canada. High levels of caregiver, household, and community risk factors are highlighted as reasons for the overrepresentation. The finding that neglect is the primary type of child maltreatment experienced by Aboriginal children calls for a reorientation of child welfare research, policy, and practice to develop culturally sensitive and effective responses. Effecting change also calls for a much greater emphasis by child protection authorities on the structural factors contributing to child maltreatment among Aboriginal children such as poverty, poor housing, and parental substance misuse.

David Hubka, Wendy Hovdestad, and Lil Tonmyr. 2009. "Child Maltreatment in Disney Animated Feature Films: 1937–2006." *The Social Science Journal*, 46 (2009) 427–441.

> This article analyzes 46 Disney films between 1937 and 2006 for child maltreatment content. All child and adolescent characters were counted and coded for age, role type, and incidents of child maltreatment, following US *National Incidence Study of Child Abuse and Neglect* (NIS) criteria. A total of 561 incidents of child maltreatment were identified among the 1,369 child characters in the films. A total of 26 of the 42 (62%) main child characters were maltreated at least once. Findings are discussed in the context of previous research. Implications of the findings for understanding potential effects on film viewers' understandings of issues around child maltreatment are outlined.

Joanne C. Minaker and Laureen Snider. 2006. "Husband Abuse: Equality with a Vengeance?" *Canadian Journal of Criminology and Criminal Justice*, 48:5, 753–780.

> This article presents a case study of the newly discovered problem of "husband abuse," which the authors argue exemplifies the complexities of neo-liberalism, neo-conservatism, and feminist engagement with the criminal-justice state. The authors argue that the myth that men are battered as often as women as well as the claim that male and female partners are equally prone to violence resonates with discourses of equality and reinforces constituencies promoting criminal-justice "solutions" to all social problems; the result is equality with a vengeance.

Elizabeth Podnieks. 2009. "Elder Abuse: The Canadian Experience." *Journal of Elder Abuse and Neglect*, 20: 2, 126–150.

> This article discusses elder abuse in Canada from a historical perspective, as well as current legislation, model programs, and research initiatives. The article suggests that abuse and neglect of older adults occurs in all

Canadian communities and solutions require the coordinated efforts of society at large. Amelioration entails more than a legislative approach. Prevention of this growing problem is a social responsibility that requires networking and collaboration between different disciplines in all sectors of the community.

Aysan Sev'er. 2009. "More than Wife Abuse that Has Gone Old: A Conceptual Model for Violence Against the Aged in Canada and the US (Report)." *Journal of Comparative Family Studies*, 40(2): 279–293.

This article suggests that we need to take a more reflexive position on the values of the societies we have created. While it argues that Canada and the United States take pride in themselves as societies of individual rights and freedoms, and their "moral" leadership in the global community, and in being states of law and order, they also tolerate inequities, inequalities, and injustices in the areas of gender, race/ethnicity, and age. These destructive societal attitudes create a fertile ground for ageism. In light of the demographic shifts in life expectancies, these archaic attitudes and behaviours need serious re-evaluation in the context of human rights.

References

Appel, A. E. and G. W. Holden. 1998. "The Co-occurrence of Spouse and Physical Child Abuse: A Review and Appraisal." *Journal of Family Psychology*, 12(4): 578–599.

Armitage, A. 1995. *Comparing the Policy of Aboriginal Assimilation: Australia, Canada and New Zealand*. Vancouver: UBC Press.

Association for Women's Rights in Development (AWRID). 2004. "Intersectionality: A Tool for Gender and Economic Justice." *Women's Rights and Economic Change* 9 (August): 1–8. http://www.awid.org/eng/Issues-and-Analysis/Library/Intersectionality-A-Tool-for-Gender-and-Economic-Justice (accessed April 20, 2010).

Baker, Linda and Peter Jaffe. 2007. *Woman Abuse Affects Our Children: An Educator's Guide*. Queen's Printer for Ontario. http://www.lfcc.on.ca/Educators_Guide_to_Woman_Abuse.pdf (accessed April 13, 2010).

Bandura, A. 1973. *Aggression: A social learning analysis*. Englewood Cliffs, NJ: Prentice-Hall.

Barrett, Michelle and Mary McIntosh. 1982. *The Anti-Social Family*. London: Verso.

Bennett, Marlyn and Cindy Blackstock. 2002. "A Literature Review and Annotated Bibliography Focusing on Aspects of Aboriginal Child Welfare in Canada. First Nations Research Site of the Centre of Excellence for Child Welfare. First Nations Child and Family Caring Society of Canada Inc. 1-239." http://www.cecw-cepb.ca (accessed April 13. 2010).

Bilge, Sirma. 2006. "Behind the 'Culture' Lens: Judicial Representations of Violence Against Minority Women." *Canadian Woman Studies*, 25(1/2): 173–180.

Breines, Wini and Linda Gordon. 1983. "The New Scholarship on Family Violence." *Signs*, 8(3): 490–531.

Brownridge, Douglas. 2006. "Partner Violence against Women with Disabilities: Prevalence, Risk and Explanations." *Violence Against Women*, 12: 805–822.

Brownridge, Douglas A. 2009a. "Situating Research on Safety Promoting Behaviors among Disabled and Deaf Victims of Interpersonal Violence." *Violence Against Women*. 15(9): 1075–1079.

Brownridge, D.A. 2009b. *Violence against Women: Vulnerable Populations.* New York: Routledge.

Buchbinder, Eli and Tova Winterstein. 2004. "'Like a Wounded Bird': Older Battered Women's Life Experiences with Intimate Violence." *Journal of Elder Abuse and Neglect*, 15(2): 23–44.

Campaign 2000. 2006. *Too Many Children in Poverty for Too Long: Report on Child and Family Poverty in Canada.* Toronto: Family Services Association of Toronto.

Campaign 2000. 2009. *Report Card on Child and Family Poverty in Canada.* "Family Security in Insecure Times: The Case for a Poverty Reduction Strategy for Canada." http://www.campaign2000.ca (accessed April 13. 2010).

Campbell, Kathryn M. 2007. "What Was It They Lost?" *Journal of Ethnicity in Criminal Justice* 5(1): 57–80.

Canadian Women's Foundation. 2005. *Girls in Canada 2005. A Report Prepared for the Canadian Women's Foundation* by Calhoun Research and Development Shediac, NB with C. Lang Consulting, Toronto, and Irène Savoie, Chiasson Office, NB.

CBC. 2009. http://www.cbc.ca/canada/story/2009/07/31/f-spanking-discipline-debate.html

Citizenship and Immigration Canada. 2005. *Annual Report to Parliament on Immigration—2005.* http://www.cic.gc.ca (accessed April 12, 2010).

Clark, J.P. and Janice Du Mont. 2003. "Intimate Partner Violence and Health: A Critique of Canadian Prevalence Studies." *Canadian Journal of Public Health*, 94(1): 52–58.

Coeling, H.V. and G. Harnan. 1997. "Learning to Ask about Domestic Violence." *Women's Health Issues*, 7(4): 263–267.

Cohen, M.M. and H. Maclean. 2003. "Violence against Women." In M. Desmeules, D. Stewart, A. Kazanjian, H. Maclean, J. Payne, and B. Vissandjée (Eds.), *Women's Health Surveillance Report: A Multidimensional Look at the Health of Canadian Women* (pp. 45–47). Ottawa, ON: Canadian Institute for Health Information.

Crenshaw, K.W. 1994. "Mapping the Margins: Intersectionality, Identity Politics, and Violence against Women of Colour." In M.A. Fineman and R. Mykitiuk (Eds.), *The Public Nature of Private Violence* (pp. 93–118). New York: Routledge.

Cunningham, Alison and Linda Baker. 2007. *Little Eyes, Little Ears: How Violence Against a Mother Shapes Children as They Grow.* London ON: Centre for Children and Families in the Justice System. http://www.lfcc.on.ca/little_eyes_little_ears.pdf (accessed April 13, 2010).

Curry, M.A., L.E. Powers, and M. Oschwald. 2003. "Development of an Abuse Screening Tool for Women with Disabilities." *Journal of Aggression, Maltreatment, and Trauma*, 8(4): 123–141.

Daily Bread Foodbank. 2009. *Who's Hungry 2009: Key Findings* http://www.dailybread.ca/learningcentre/hungerstats.cfm?id=3-3 (accessed April 13, 2010).

Daniel, Brigid M. and Julie Taylor. 2006. "Gender and Child Neglect: Theory, Research and Policy." *Critical Social Policy,* 26(2): 426–439.

Davis, R.C. and E. Erez. 1998. *Immigrant Population as Victims: Toward a Multicultural Criminal Justice System.* Washington, DC: U.S. Department of Justice, National Institute of Justice.

Deckha, Maneesha. 2004. "Is Culture Taboo—Feminism, Intersectionality, and Culture Talk in Law." *Canadian Journal of Women and Law* 16: 14–53.

DeKeseredy, Walter S. 2006. "Future Directions." *Violence Against Women.* 12(11): 1078–1085 Department of Justice Canada. 2009. http://www.justice.gc.ca/eng/pi/fv-vf/facts-info/fv-vf/fv1-vf1.html# (accessed April 12, 2010).

DeKeseredy, Walter S., Martin Schwartz, and Alvi Shahid. 2008. "Which Women Are Likely to Be Abused? Public Housing, Cohabitation, and Separated/Divorced Women." *Criminal Justice Studies: A Critical Journal of Crime, Law and Society.* 21(4): 283–293.

Denham, D. and J. Gillespie. 1998. *Two Steps Forward . . . One Step Back.* Ottawa: Health Canada.

Disabled Women's Network (DAWN). http://dawn.thot.net/violence_wwd.html (accessed April 13, 2010).

Donnelly, A.C. (Ed.). 2002. *An International Movement to End Child Abuse. The Story of ISPCAN.* Carol Stream, IL:ISPCAN.

Dutton, D.G. and S.K. Golant. 1995. *The Batterer: A Psychological Profile.* New York: Basic Books.

Durrant, J.E., K. Covell, A. McGillivray, A.M. Watkinson, and J. McNeil. 2008. *"It Didn't Do Me Any Harm":* Explaining the Intergenerational Transmission of Approval of Child Physical Punishment. Department of Family Studies, Faculty of Human Ecology, University of Manitoba, Winnipeg, MB. Manuscript submitted for publication.

Durrant, J.E. and R. Ensom. 2006. *Joint Statement on Physical Punishment of Children and Youth.* Ottawa, ON: Coalition on the Physical Punishment of Children and Youth.

Durrant, J.E., L. Rose-Krasnor, and A. Broberg. 2003. "Predicting Maternal Use of Physical Punishment from Maternal Characteristics in Sweden and Canada." *Journal of Comparative Family Studies* 34: 586–604.

Eaton, Lisa, Michelle Kaufman, Andrea Fuhrel, Demetria Cain, Charsey Cherry, Howard Pope, and Seth C. Kalichman. 2008. "Examining Factors Co-Existing with Interpersonal Violence in Lesbian Relationships." *Journal of Family Violence,* 23: 697–705.

Ellsberg, M. and L. Heise. 2005. *Researching Violence Against Women: A Practical Guide for Researchers and Activists.* Washington, DC. World Health Organization. PATH.

Enander, Viveka. 2010. "A Fool to Keep Staying": Battered Women Labeling Themselves Stupid as an Expression of Gendered Shame." *Violence Against Women,* 16(1) 5–31.

Erez, E. 2000. "Immigration, Culture Conflict and Domestic Violence/Woman Battering." *Crime Prevention and Community Safety: An International Journal*, 2: 27–36.

Erez, Edna, Madelaine Adelman, and Carol Gregory. 2009. "Intersections of Immigration and Domestic Violence Voices of Battered Immigrant Women." *Feminist Criminology*, 4(1): 32–56.

Fatah, Natasha. 2008. "Who Will Speak for Aqsa Parvez?." CBC News Analysis and Viewpoint. http://www.cbc.ca/news/viewpoint/vp_fatah/20071214.html (accessed April 12, 2010).

Faulkner, Samuel S. and Cynthia A. Faulkner. 2004. "Poverty as a Predictor of Child Maltreatment: A Brief Analysis." *Journal of Poverty*, 8(1): 103–106.

Feminist Alliance for International Action (FAFIA). 2008. *Women's Inequality in Canada: Submission of the Canadian Feminist Alliance for International Action to the United Nations Committee on the Elimination of Discrimination against Women on the Occasion of the Committee's Review of Canada's 6th and 7th Reports.* http://www.fafia-afai.org (accessed April 12, 2010).

Ferber, Richard. 1985. *Solve Your Child's Sleep Problem.* New York: Simon and Schuster.

Field, Craig A. and Raul Caetano. 2005. "Longitudinal Model Predicting Mutual Partner Violence among White, Black, Hispanic Couples in the United States General Population." *Violence and Victims*, 20(5): 499–511.

Fournier, S. and E. Crey. 1997. *Stolen from Our Embrace: The Abduction of First Nations Children and the Restoration of Aboriginal Communities.* Vancouver: Douglas and McIntyre, Ltd.

Garcia-Moreno, C., H.A. Jansen, M. Ellsberg, L. Heise, and C.H. Watts. 2006. "Prevalence of Intimate Partner Violence: Findings from the WHO Multi-Country Study on Women's Health and Domestic Violence." *Lancet*, 368(9543): 1260–1269.

Gewirtz, Abigail H. and Jeffrey L. Edleson. 2007. "Young Children's Exposure to Intimate Partner Violence: Towards a Developmental Risk and Resilience Framework for Research and Intervention." *Journal of Family Violence*, 22: 151–163.

Gilbert, Ruth, Alison Kemp, June Thoburn, Peter Sidebotham, Lorraine Radford, Danya Glaser, Harriet L. MacMillan. 2009. *Lancet*, 373: 167–180.

Gupta, Rita Paul-Sen, Margaret L. de Whit, and David MacKeown. 2007. *Pediatric Child Health*, 12(8): 667–672.

Hass, Giselle Aguilar, Mary Ann Dutton, and Leslye E. Orloff. 2000. "Lifetime Prevalence of Violence against Latina Immigrants: Legal and Policy Implications." *International Review of Victimology*, 7: 93–113.

Heise, L., M. Ellsberg, and M. Gottemoeller, 1999. "Ending Violence Against Women." *Population Reports.* Baltimore, MD. John Hopkins University Press.

Hester, M., C. Pearson, and N. Harwin. 2000. *Making an Impact: Children and Domestic Violence: A Reader.* London: Jessica Kingsley Publications.

Hill-Collins, Patricia. 1990. *Black Feminist Thought: Knowledge, Consciousness, and the Politics of Empowerment.* New York: Routledge.

Holt, Stephanie, Helen Buckley, and Sadhbh Whelan. 2008. "The Impact of Exposure to Domestic Violence on Children and Young People: A Review of the Literature." *Child Abuse and Neglect*, 32: 797–810.

Hou, F. and G. Picot. 2004. "Profile of Ethnic Origin and Visible Minorities for Toronto, Vancouver, and Montreal." *Canadian Social Trends*, 11: 9–14.

Hunnicutt, Gwen. 2009. "Varieties of Patriarchy and Violence Against Women Resurrecting "Patriarchy" as a Theoretical Tool." *Violence Against Women*, 15(5): 553–573.

Husaini, Z. 2001. *Cultural Dilemma and a Plea for Justice: Voices of Canadian Ethnic Women.* Edmonton, AL: Intercultural Action Committee for the Advancement of Women.

Hyman, I., T. Forte, J. Du Mont, S. Romans, and M.M. Cohen. 2006. "The Prevalence of Intimate Partner Violence in Immigrant Women in Canada." *American Journal of Public Health*, 96: 654–659.

Hyman, Ilene, Tonia Forte, Janice Du Mont, Sarah Romans, and Marsha M. Cohen. 2009. "Help-Seeking Behaviour for Intimate Partner Violence Among Racial Minority Women in Canada." *Women's Health Issues*, 19: 101–108.

Hyman, Ilene, Sepali Guruge, and Robin Mason. 2008. "The Impact of Migration on Marital Relationships: A Study of Ethiopian Immigrants in Toronto." *Journal of Comparative Family Studies*, 39(2): 149–163.

Ismail, Farah, Helene Berman, and Catherine Ward-Griffin. 2007. "Dating Violence and the Health of Young Women: A Feminist Narrative Study." *Health Care for Women International*, 28(5): 453–477.

Jasinski, J.L. 2001. "Theoretical Explanations for Violence against Women. In C. M. Renzetti, J. L. Edleson, and R.K. Bergen (Eds.), *Sourcebook on Violence Against Women* (pp. 5–22). Thousand Oaks, CA: Sage.

Johnson, Holly. 2006. *Measuring Violence Against Women: Statistical Trends 2006.* http://www .statcan.ca/english/research/85-570-XIE/85-570-XIE2006001.htm (accessed April 12, 2010).

Johnson, Holly, Natalia Ollus, and Sami Nevala. 2008. *Violence Against Women: An International Perspective.* Springer: New York.

Kang, N. 2006. "Women Activists in Indian Diaspora: Making Interventions and Challenging Impediments." *South Asia Research*, 26: 145–164.

Kashani, J.H. and W.D. Allan. 1998. *The Impact of Family Violence on Children and Adolescents.* Thousand Oakes: Sage Publications.

Kempe, C.H., F. Silverman, B. Steele, W. Droegmueller, and H. Silver. 1962. "The Battered Child Syndrome." *Journal of the American Medical Association*, 181: 17–24.

Korbin, Jill E. 2003. "Children, Childhoods and Violence." *Annual Review of Anthropology*, 32: 431–446.

Kurst-Swanger, Karel and Jacqueline L. Petcosky. 2003. *Violence in the Home: Multidisciplinary Perspectives.* Oxford University Press. New York.

Lamba, N.K. and L. Wilkinson. 1998. "Legislated Inequality: The Uneven Consequences of Immigration Policy on the Economic and Social Integration of Immigrants in Canada." In A. Richardson (Ed.), *International Multiculturalism: Preparing Together for the 21st Century* (pp. 21–32). Edmonton: Kanata Learning Company.

Lavergne, Chantal, Sarah Dufour, Nico Trocmé, and Marie-Claude Larrivee. 2008. "Visible Minority, Aboriginal, and Caucasian Children Investigated by Canadian Protective Services." Child Welfare, 87(2): 59–76.

Levesque, Roger J.R. 2000. "Culture, Maltreatment and the Law." Child Maltreatment, 5(2): 146–160.

Lowenstein, Ariela. 2008. "Elder Abuse and Neglect—Old Phenomenon: New Directions for Research, Legislation, and Service Developments." Journal of Elder Abuse and Neglect, 21(3): 278–287.

Lockhart, L.L., B.W. White, V. Causby, and A. Isaac. 1994. "Letting Out the Secret: Violence in Lesbian Relationships." Journal of Interpersonal Violence, 9: 469–491.

Maiter, Sarah, Ramona Alaggia, and Nico Trocmé. 2004. "Perceptions of Child Maltreatment by Parents from the Indian Subcontinent: Challenging Myths About Culturally Based Abusive Parenting Practices." Child Maltreatment, 9: 309–324.

Malley-Morrison, K. and D. Hines. 2007. "Attending to the Role of Race/Ethnicity in Family Violence Research." Journal of Interpersonal Violence, 22: 943–972.

Martin, S., N. Ray, D. Sotres-Alvarez, L. Kupper, K. Moracco, P. Dickens, et al. 2006. "Physical and Sexual Assault of Women with Disabilities." Violence Against Women, 12: 823–837.

Mason, Robin, Ilene Hyman, Helene Berman, Sepali Guruge, Pushpa Kanagaratnam, and Lisa Manuel. 2008. "Violence Is an International Language: Tamil Women's Perceptions of Intimate Partner Violence." Violence Against Women, 14(12): 1397–1412.

McCall, L. 2005. "The Complexity of Intersectionality." Signs, 30: 1771–1800.

McDonald, R., E.N. Jouriles, S. Ramisetty-Mikler, R. Caetano, and C. Green. 2006. "Estimating the Number of American Children Living in Partner-Violent Families." Journal of Family Psychology, 20: 137–142.

McKay, S., D. Fuchs, and I. Brown (Eds.). 2009. "Physical Punishment in Childhood: A Human Rights and Child Protection Issue" in Passion for Action in Child and Family Services: Voices from the Prairies. Regina, SK: Canadian Plains Research Center: pp. 207–226. http://www.cecw-cepb.ca/publications/1120 (accessed April 12, 2010).

Menard, A. 2001. "Domestic Violence and Housing: Key Policy and Program Challenges." Violence Against Women, 7: 707–721.

Merali, Noorfarah. 2009. "Experiences of South Asian Brides Entering Canada After Recent Changes to Family Sponsorship Policies." Violence Against Women, 15(3): 321–339.

Minaker, Joanne C. and Laureen Snider. 2006. "Husband Abuse: Equality with a Vengeance?" Canadian Journal of Criminology and Criminal Justice (September): 53–78.

Mitchell, B.A. 2005. Canada's Growing Visible Minority Population: Generational Challenges, Opportunities and Federal Policy. Ottawa, ON.

Morrow, Marina, Olena Hankivsky, and Colleen Varcoe. 2004. "Women and Violence: The Effects of Dismantling the Welfare State." Critical Social Policy 24(3): 358–384.

Morton, Mavis. 1996. "Wife Assault and the Limits of Leaving: Individualizing a Social Problem." Dissertation Abstracts. Toronto: York University.

Mullings, L. 1997. On Our Own Terms: Race, Class, and Gender in the Lives of African American Women. NY: Routledge.

Nakano Glenn, E. 1999. "The Social Construction and Institutionalization of Gender and Race: An Integrative Framework." In M.M. Feree, J. Lorber, and B.B. Hess (Eds.), Revisioning Gender (pp. 3–43). Thousand Oaks, CA: Sage.

Nannini, A. 2006. "Sexual Assault Patterns among Women With and Without Disabilities Seeking Survivor Services." Women's Health Issues, 16: 372–379.

The National Clearinghouse on Family Violence. (nd). Abuse and Neglect of Older Adults: Overview Paper. Family Violence Prevention Unit, Health Issues Division, Public Health Agency of Canada. http://www.phac-aspc.gc.ca/nc-cn (accessed April 12, 2010).

Nosek, M.A., C.C. Foley, R.B. Hughes, and C.A. Howland. 2001. "Vulnerabilities for Abuse among Women with Disabilities." Sexuality & Disability, 19: 177–190.

O'Connor, D., M. Hall, and M. Donnelly. 2009. "Assessing Capacity in a Context of Abuse." Journal of Elder Abuse and Neglect, 21(1): 156–169.

O'Grady, William. 2007. Crime in Canadian Context: Debates and Controversies. Toronto: Oxford University Press.

O'Leary, K.D. 1993. "Through a Psychological Lens: Personality Traits, Personality Disorders and Levels of Violence." In R.J. Gelles and D. Loseke (Eds.), Current Controversies on Family Violence (pp. 7–30). Newbury Park, CA: Sage.

Ontario Children's Aid Society. 2008. "Signs of Abuse." http://www.oacas.org/childwelfare/signs.htm#neglect (accessed April 13, 2010).

Owen, S.S. and T. W. Burke. 2004. "An Exploration of Prevalence of Domestic Violence in Same-sex Relationships." Psychological Reports, 95: 129–132 (Author Abstract).

Pattavina, April, David Hirschel, Eve Buzawa, Don Faggiani, and Helen Bentley. 2007. "A Comparison of the Police Response to Heterosexual Versus Same-Sex Intimate Partner Violence." Violence Against Women. 13(4): 374–394.

Pinheiro, Paulo Sérgio. 2006. World Report on Violence Against Children. Secretary-General's Study on Violence against Children, United Nations. http://www.unviolencestudy.org (accessed April 12, 2010).

Podnieks, Elizabeth. 2009. "Elder Abuse: The Canadian Experience." Journal of Elder Abuse and Neglect, 20(2): 126–150.

Powers, L.E., M.A. Curry, M. Oschwald, S. Maley, M. Saxton, and K. Eckels. 2002. "Barriers and Strategies in Addressing Abuse: A Survey of Disabled Women's Experiences." Journal of Rehabilitation, 68 (1): 4–13.

Powers, Laurie E., Paula Renker, Susan Robinson-Whelen, Mary Oschwald, Rosemary Hughes, Paul Swank, and Mary Ann Curry. 2009. "Interpersonal Violence and Women with Disabilities: Analysis of Safety Promoting Behaviors." Violence Against Women, 15(9): 1040–1069.

Prilleltensky, I. 1989. "Psychology and the Status Quo." *American Psychologist*, 44(5): 795–802.

R. v. *Lavallee*, [1990] 1 S.C.R. 852.

Raj, A. and J. Silverman. 2002. "Violence against Immigrant Women: The Roles of Culture, Context, and Legal Immigrant Status on Intimate Partner Violence." *Violence Against Women*, 8: 367–398.

Rani, Manju and Sekhar Bonu. 2009. "Attitudes Toward Wife Beating." *Journal of Interpersonal Violence*, 24(8): 1371–1397.

Raphael, Dennis, Ann Curry-Stevens, and Toba Bryant. 2008. "Barriers to Addressing the Social Determinants of Health: Insights from the Canadian Experience." *Health Policy*, 8: 222–235.

Renzetti, C.M. 1998. "Violence and Abuse in Lesbian Relationships: Theoretical and Empirical Issues" in R.K. Bergeon (Ed.), *Issues in Intimate Violence*. Sage Publications, United States.

Renzetti, Claire. W. 2006. "Commentary on Swan and Snow's 'The Development of a Theory of Women's Use of Violence in Intimate Relationships.'" *Violence Against Women*, 12(11): 1046–1049.

Renzetti, Claire W. and Daniel J. Curran, 1999. *Men, Women and Society*. Allyn and Bacon, United States.

Ristock, Janice. 2005. *Relationship Violence in Lesbian/Gay/Bisexual/Transgendered/Queer (LGBTQ) Communities: Moving Beyond a Gender-Based Framework*. Violence Against Women Online Resources. http://www.mincava.umn.edu/documents/lgbtqviolence/lgbtqviolence.html (accessed April 22, 2010).

Rosenberg, Lisa and Ann Duffy. 2010. "Violence Against Women." In Nancy Mandell (Ed.), *Feminist Issues: Race, Class and Sexuality*, 5th ed. (pp. 161–196). Toronto: Pearson Canada.

Royal Commission on Aboriginal Peoples. 1996. *Volume 1: Looking Forward, Looking Back*. Ottawa: Canada Communication Group.

Salazar, L. and S. Cook. 2002. "Violence Against Women: Is Psychology Part of the Problem or the Solution? A Current Analysis of the Psychological Research from 1990 through 1999." *Journal of Community and Applied Social Psychology*, 12(6): 410–421.

Salcido Carter, L., L.A. Weithorn, and R.E. Behrman. 1999. "Domestic Violence and Children: Analysis and Recommendations." *The Future of Children*, 9(3): 4–20.

Saxton, M., M. Curry, L.E. Powers, S. Maley, K. Eckels, and J. Gross. 2001. "'Bring My Scooter So I Can Leave You': A Study of Disabled Women Handling Abuse by Personal Assistance Providers." *Violence Against Women*, 7, 393–417.

Sev'er, Aysan. 2002. "A Feminist Analysis of Flight of Abused Women, Plight of Canadian Shelters: Another Road to Homelessness." *Journal of Social Distress and the Homeless*, 11(4): 307–324.

Sev'er, Aysan. 2009. "More Than Wife Abuse That Has Gone Old: A Conceptual Model for Violence against the Aged in Canada and the US." *Journal of Comparative Family Studies*, 40(2): 279–292.

Shields, Stephanie. A. 2008. "Gender: An Intersectionality Perspective." *Sex Roles*, 59(5–6): 301–311.

Shirwadkar, S. 2004. "Canadian Domestic Violence Policy and Indian Immigrant Women." *Violence Against Women*, 10: 860–879.

Smith, D. L. 2008. "Disability, Gender and Intimate Partner Violence: Relationships from the Behavioral Risk Factor Surveillance System." *Sexuality and Disability*, 26: 15–28.

Smith, Ekuwa. 2005. "Nowhere to Turn? Responding to Partner Violence Against Immigrant and Visible Minority Women." Ottawa: Canadian Council on Social Development.

Statistics Canada. 1999. *Family Violence in Canada*. Canadian Centre for Justice Statistics: Highlights. Cat. 85-224-XIE. Otttawa: Government of Canada.

Statistics Canada. 2003. *The Daily*. Survey on Ethnic Diversity.

Statistics Canada. 2005. *Family Violence in Canada: A Statistical Profile 2005*. Kathy Aucoin (Ed). Ottawa: Canadian Centre for Justice Statistics. http://www.statcan.gc.ca/cgi-bin/af-fdr.cgi?l = engandloc = http://www.statcan.gc.ca/pub/85-224-x/85-224-x2005000-eng.pdfandt = Family%20Violence%20in%20Canada:%20A%20Statistical%20Profile (accessed April 12, 2010).

Statistics Canada. 2008a. *Canada Yearbook Overview (CYB) 2008: Children and Youth*. http://www41.statcan.ca/2008/20000/ceb20000_000-eng.htm (accessed April 12, 2010).

Statistics Canada. 2008b. *Family Violence in Canada: A Statistical Profile 2008*. Ottawa: Canadian Centre for Justice Statistics. http://www.statcan.gc.ca/pub/85-224-x/2008000/fv1-eng.htm (accessed April 12, 2010).

Statistics Canada. 2009. *Family Violence in Canada: A Statistical Profile 2009*. Ottawa: Canadian Centre for Justice Statistics. http://www.pdfdownload.org/pdf2html/view_online.php?url = http%3A%2F%2Fwww.statcan.gc.ca%2Fpub%2F85-224-x%2F85-224-x2009000-eng.pdf (accessed April 12, 2010).

Trainor, C. and K. Mihorean (Eds.). 2001. *Family Violence in Canada: A Statistical Profile 2001*. Statistics Canada, no. 85-224-XIE. Ottawa: Minister of Industry.

Trocmé, Nico, Barbara Fallon, Bruce MacLaurin, Joanne Daciuk, Caroline Felstiner, Tara Black, Lil Tonmyr, Cindy Blackstock, Ken Barter, Daniel Turcotte, and Richard Cloutier. 2005. *Canadian Incidence Study of Reported Child Abuse and Neglect—2003: Major Findings*. Ottawa: Minister of Public Works and Government Services Canada. http://www.phac-aspc.gc.ca/cm-vee/csca-ecve/pdf/childabuse_final_e.pdf (accessed April 12, 2010).

Trocmé, Nico, Bruce MacLaurin, Barbara Fallon, Della Knoke, Lisa Pitman, and Megan McCormack. 2006. *Understanding the Overrepresentation of First Nations Children in Canada's Child Welfare System: An Analysis of the Canadian Incidence Study of Reported Child Abuse and Neglect*

(CIS-2003). Centre of Excellence for Child Welfare First Nations Child and Family Caring Society of Canada, Ottawa, ON.

Trocmé, Nico, Marc Tourigny, Bruce MacLaurin, and Barbara Fallon. 2003. "Major Findings from the Canadian Incidence Study of Reported Child Abuse and Neglect." *Child Abuse and Neglect*, 27: 1427–1439.

Turney, D. and K. Tanner. 2001. "Working with Neglected Children and Their Families." *Journal of Social Work Practice*, 15(2): 193–204.

United Nations. 2006. "In-depth Study on All Forms of Violence against Women." New York: Author.

Vine, C., N. Trocmé, and J. Findlay. 2006. "Children Abused, Neglected, and Living with Violence." In R. Alaggia and C. Vine (Eds.), *Cruel But Not Unusual: Violence in Canadian Families* (pp. 147–176). Waterloo: Wilfrid Laurier University Press.

Vyas, Seema and Charlotte Watts, 2009. "How Does Economic Empowerment Affect Women's Risk of Intimate Partner Violence in Low and Middle Income Countries? A Systematic Review of Published Evidence." *Journal of International Development*, 21: 577–602.

Walsh, Christine A., Jenny Ploeg, Lynne Lohfeld, Jaclyn Horne, Harriet MacMillan, and Daniel Lai. 2007. "Violence Across the Lifespan: Interconnections Among Forms of Abuse as Described by Marginalized Canadian Elders and Their Care-givers." *British Journal of Social Work*, 37: 491–514.

Watkinson, Alison M. 2009. "Physical Punishment in Childhood: A Human Rights and Child Protection Issue." In S. McKay, D. Fuchs, and I. Brown (Eds.), *Passion for Action in Child and Family Services: Voices from the Prairies* (pp. 207–226). Regina: Canadian Plains Research Center.

West, C. M. 2005. "Domestic Violence in Ethnically and Racially Diverse Families: The "Political Gag Order" Has Been Lifted." In B. E. Richie, N. J. Sokoloff, and C. Pratt (Eds.), *Domestic Violence at the Margins: Readings on Race, Class, Gender, and Culture* (pp. 157–173). New Brunswick, NJ: Rutgers University Press.

Chapter 10

Aging Families

Julia Hemphill

LEARNING OBJECTIVES

In this chapter, you will learn that:

1. Canada's population is demographically old,

2. the old and their families are diverse. They differ along the lines of immigration status, "race," gender, sexuality, and individual biography oppressions that exist in early- and mid-life, continue into late life, and become exacerbated,

3. there are several theoretical frameworks through which families can be understood.

INTRODUCTION

According to LeGault (2010), a journalist for The Globe and Mail, Canadians are no longer considered "old" until they die. By this controversial statement, LeGault means that, with a growing proportion of the Canadian population over 65, the point at which one is officially "old" has been pushed further and further back, all the way to the grave. The cliché "30 is the new 20" obscures as much as it reveals about society's view of aging. On the one hand, the cliché tells us that society denies and resists the label "old." On the other hand, the cliché tells us clear age boundaries are collapsing as the life-course itself widens and expands. In this chapter, I explore the many ways in which aging is a social, material, and cultural process. My focus is on how alterations in aging have shifted family practices and what these shifts mean for family members.

> Canadian families are aging. Currently, there are more Canadians over the age of 65 than ever before. The proportion of old Canadians will continue to grow throughout the next few decades. Longer lives have meaningful implications for Canadian families. Aging is a key social process within the institution of the Canadian family, and indeed, other larger social institutions.

An aging population, resulting from factors such as higher life expectancies and lower mortality rates, indicates a privileged citizenry. Yet with the advantage of growing older in a relatively affluent and stable country come some challenges.

The purpose of this chapter is to present a critical sociological conception of what it means to age, and become labelled as old. We hope to help students gain an understanding of aging families, and also provide the necessary tools to critically understand aging in general as a meaningful sociological process. We begin by discussing what it means to "age". Second, we present some key demographic characteristics of an aging Canadian society. Third, we discuss theoretical perspectives of the social aspects of aging and old age. Fourth, we highlight aging and difference, by focusing on gendered and racialized aging. Fifth, we look at the body as a key site of aging, and theorizing about aging. Sixth, late-life relationships are considered. Care work and caregiving, fundamental dimensions of late-life relationships, will be central in this discussion.

Throughout this chapter, we stress "differences" among the old. The elderly are often studied as a homogenous group when, in reality, they are just as diverse as younger cohorts.

DEFINING "AGING" AND "OLD"

Aging is a "process, and an identity" (Hockey and James, 2001, p. 5). This process is as social as it is physical. Altogether, aged identities are constituted by structural, historical, ideological, and individual or biographical factors.

Structurally, the progression of aging is often marked with rites of passages occurring throughout the life-course. In early life, such rites of passages might include religious markers such as bar mitzvahs and first communions, while in later life normative events such as retirement and grandparenthood are instrumental in helping us to define our age-based identities (Calasanti and Slevin, 2001). "Old" or "senior" is most often applied to people who are 65 years of age or older because this age is associated with pension entitlements (Connidis, 2010, p. 3). For this reason, we will adopt this chronological point as an indicator of "old." We do so knowing that a chronological marker of "old age" is largely arbitrary.

Like "aging," the term "old" is socially constructed. Its meaning is tied to the particularities of our social locations. For example, our *historical* context contributes to our understandings of what it means to be old. Although our age is closely tied to our social identities in current mainstream Western society, historically it was comparatively less integral to an individual's social identity. In many European cultures, it was not until the 18th century when life courses became more diverse that chronological, quantifiable age came to be relevant in constructing our social identities. Life-course variability can be linked to many events and social patterns including changes in the age of marriage and childbirth. Because the ages at which such events occur have increasingly become more variable, and as the extent to which most people actually engage in them differs historically and cross-culturally, no longer can these rites of passage be linked to "a strict age chronology" (Hockey and James, 2001, p. 61). Age has become a highly significant feature of identity. The reality that lives have been increasing in duration also contributes to this salience.

Ideologically, individual engagement with, or resistance to, dominant discourses on aging constructs aged identities. A particularly powerful discourse on aging is "**ageism**." Originally coined by Robert Butler in 1969, "ageism" refers to a process whereby old people become defined as less than human. It "encourages viewing people not as individuals but as members of a social category" (Calasanti and Slevin, 2001, p. 19). Ageism changes forms over time. For example, at one time in Western societies, the old were stereotyped as "greedy geezers," while current ageist discourses might classify them as anxious, uneasy, unproductive, and fearful (Calasanti and Slevin, 2001, p. 20). This ideology is so powerful and often invisible that it pervades even the most critical academic work on aging. For example, scholars who study aging sometimes avoid using the adjective "old" and opt for "older." Although this distinction seems innocuous, using the term "older" is a way of avoiding the stigmas associated with the term "old." However, using "old" instead of "older" connotes more value for the elderly, as "older" reinforces the notion that the old should be thought about as if they were middle-aged, thus making them more acceptable. Saying "older" is analogous to referring to people of colour as "darker" (Calasanti, 2003, p. 16). Rarely is the socially constructed derogatory connotation of "old" challenged (Calasanti and Slevin, 2006, p. 3). The notion that an old population is inherently negative must be avoided, as the impact of this perspective is a distraction from efforts to productively understanding how Canadian families function and relate to one another in late life.

Finally, *individual* or *biographical* variables are also instrumental in constituting aging identities. For example, if a woman decides to become a mother later in life, she may not adopt an "old" identity until later than those compared to others in her age cohort. This point will be further illuminated later, when we discuss the various theoretical frameworks for understanding old age.

Above, we have presented the ideology of ageism. In addition to the historical context, as we shall see, the meaning of aging and "old" varies along the lines of "race," class, and gender.

CANADIAN SENIORS: DEMOGRAPHICS AND CHARACTERISTICS

Demographic information is key to understanding the characteristics of an aging population. Important features of aging families relate to the demographic makeup.

Statistical trends reveal that Canada's population is aging rapidly. As of July 1, 2009, the median age of Canadians is 39.5 years old. Ten years earlier, this figure was 36.4. Current estimates project that by the 2030s, the mean age will increase to 44 (*The Daily*, November 2009). This also means that Canada has more seniors. For example, although people over 65 years accounted for only 9.6 percent of the totally population in 1981, by 2005 this figure rose to 13.1 percent. Further, this figure is projected to rise to 24.5 percent and 27.2 percent in 2036 and 2056, respectively (Turcotte and Shellenberg, 2006, p.12).

There are key differences among Canadian seniors. For example, due to longer life expectancies, women are overrepresented among the 65 and older population. However, men are slowly starting to catch up to women in terms of old age. For example, by 2005, men accounted for 39 percent of this population, which represents a 2% percent increase from 1981. It is estimated that the longevity gender gap will continue to narrow throughout the next three decades (Turcotte and Shellenberg, 2006: p. 13).

In Canada, immigrants represent a considerably large group among seniors. In 2001, some 29% of individuals aged 65 to 74 and 28 of those aged 75 to 84 were immigrants, that is, they were not born in Canada and/or did not have Canadian citizenship at birth. By comparison, immigrants accounted for about 17 percent of the nonsenior population in 1981 (The Daily, 2001).

THEORETICAL UNDERSTANDINGS OF AGING

Like any other aspect of the family and social life in general, in order to study aging families a theoretical framework is essential. Social gerontology and the sociology of aging are disciplines that are data rich, but theoretically poor (Chappell, 2003, p. 33). Nonetheless, there are other useful frameworks through which we can understand aging families and their relations sociologically. In this section we outline **social constructionism (symbolic interactionism)**, **materialism, feminism, postmodernism**, and the **life-course perspective**. Each standpoint is valuable in different ways. For example, social constructionism is a largely, but not exclusively, micro-level theory, which allows us to consider how members of aging families create meaning. Materialism represents a macro-level theory, which allows us to consider how larger social structures such as the economy influence or shape the experiences of the old and their families. Finally, feminism, postmodernism, and the life-course perspective combine both macro and micro levels, taking into account the individual's interaction with larger social forces. These standpoints are not mutually exclusive, as many of them share and borrow ideas and concepts from each other.

Social Constructionist (Symbolic Interactionist) Perspectives

Symbolic interactionists believe that humans are active agents. This means that we proceed in self-determined ways, actively interpreting and processing our environments. At the same time, social structure plays a significant role in shaping our lives, identities, and experiences. We are simultaneously the products and the producers of society. Culture, economic situations, families, and socialization agents influence our choices yet do not unilaterally determine our choices, which are constantly being produced. This perspective helps us see how old people and their families might cope with, or navigate through, such social structures.

Further, symbolic interactionists also believe that our identities or selves are dynamic. Who we are is tied to our social situations, locations, and contexts. Since these are constantly changing throughout our lives, so too does the self. For social gerontologists (those who work in the field of **social gerontology**), this perspective is useful, because it helps us to understand how the process of aging alters our identities. Social constructionists focus on identity construction as a mutual process of structure and agency. For example, a symbolic interactionist recognizes the multiple identities that we occupy throughout our lives, the relationships between these positionings, transitions to other identities, and how individuals ultimately take up identities. This theoretical position will be further illuminated later when we discuss life-course perspective, as it builds upon constructionist theorizing.

Materialist Perspectives

Many economy-based perspectives of aging are conservative, and sometimes even alarmist in nature. Through these lenses, the old are seen as a burden or a threat to the economic health of a nation. Such perspectives dichotomize citizens as financially "dependent" or independent.

These ageist perceptions are also gendered and racialized; women and people of colour are perceived as being financially dependent upon the state, as well as upon family members. However, the experiences of many old people represent a challenge to these alarmist views, as they continue to work well into late life. This will be further highlighted later in our discussion of unpaid care work.

These alarmist perspectives are tied to concerns about the "dependency-ratio." This ratio compares the proportion of "working aged" individuals to those who are "too young" or "too old" to "work." An old population unbalances this proportion and, according to this traditional economic perspective, creates financial strains on the economy. Such strains, will lead to "a crisis of the welfare state" (Maynard et al., 2008, p. 2). As critical gerontologists point out, a lot of the work performed by the old is largely ignored, because it is mostly unpaid. Traditional, conservative perspectives often produce very narrow definitions of work discounting and devaluing multiple forms of important labour. Critical perspectives regarding aging and the economy differ vastly from conservative, alarmist views, as the old indeed do work. They often perform important unpaid work in the form of care work and volunteer work, while others continue to participate in the paid labour force well into late life. In fact, the notion that "retirement" is a universal and inevitable life stage is erroneous. Many Canadians cannot afford to cease their participation in paid labour. Further, it is important to consider to what degree grandparents are "retired" if they spend five days of the week caring for their grandchildren without pay.

When a critical materialist lens is used to analyze the lives of the old and their families in Canada, economic disparities are revealed. Materialists assume that those who have the most access to material resources, such as wealth and property, hold the most power in society (Mandell et al., 2008). Like other inequalities, economic disparities that exist throughout the early and midlife years become exacerbated in old age. Although Canada's aging population is relatively economically secure compared to earlier cohorts, and international data, systematic financial inequalities persist among certain groups. For example, women, especially those who do not have access to male wages, and foreign-born individuals, especially those who arrived in Canada during and since the 1980s, continue to be economically vulnerable in late life, compared to their male, Canadian-born counterparts.

Feminist Perspectives

In 1985, at an American Women's Studies conference, 65-year-old activist Barbara MacDonald publicly addressed the tendency for feminists to ignore or stereotype old women. MacDonald implored her colleagues to seriously engage with the issue of aging (Calasanti and Slevin, 2001, p. 188). Since 1985, much scholarship on gendered experiences of aging has emerged. However, the omission of old age as a significant area of study within women studies courses and programs continues to be a point of concern for many feminist scholars who work in the area of aging. The result of such neglect is a largely invisible age bias that is reproduced in subsequent generations of feminist scholars (Ray, 2006, p. 21).

Aging is a gendered process. Women constitute the majority of the old population. They also represent a devalued, invisible social group. As women age, their social inequality worsens. An aging woman faces more social consequences than an aging male. Such consequences are material, as women are much more likely to be economically insecure in late life. They are also social as the aesthetic of an aging woman is deviant. These oppressions are linked to women's gender and their age. When aging women possess other potentially stigmatizing identities along the line of "race," ability, sexuality, or class, this oppression worsens.

In Canada, we live in a culture of youth. The youthful ideal is more valued in women than men. Women gain a form of power, albeit precarious and temporary, from being youthful. This form of power translates into young women not building alliances with old women, because it threatens this power. In this way, the oppressions experienced by aging women, and implicitly recognized by young women, is very divisive.

Feminist perspectives will be revisited later, as they are instrumental in understanding how care work functions within in aging families.

Postmodern Approaches

The postmodern position is rooted in philosophy. Such thinking disrupts the assumptions of modernist "positivist scientific perspectives," which sees the social world as a predictable entity that can be understood through objective measures (McPherson, 1998, p. 83). In contrast, postmodernists see the social world as unpredictable and complex. They believe objectivity to be impossible in any discipline, especially when studying humans. Although it is difficult to provide an exhaustive definition of "postmodernism," there are several important defining characteristics of this perspective. First, postmodernists are highly skeptical of "tradition." No longer, if ever, do our lives follow traditional life stages. Because our social worlds have become increasingly complicated and heterogeneous, we cannot rely on traditional "life scripts" to provide meaning and structure to our lives. Rather, we have to construct our own "life scripts" and learn to live with the ever-changing and fragile nature of experiences (Polivka and Longino, 2002, p. 5).

Second, connected to a fluid life-course is the significance of meaning. Meaning is unique, and different people assign vastly different meanings to seemingly similar experiences. For example, consider how different the experience of becoming a mother at the relatively young age of 19 might be for a woman who has access to financial resources, education, and family support, compared to another woman who does not have such resources. The meaning of any event will be very different depending on the life circumstances and the personal meanings associated with that event. Meaning varies along several lines including, but not limited to, structural factors and biographical variables. Third, the "role of expert knowledge" lacks legitimacy among postmodern thinkers. Expert discourses cannot generate universal truths, because there are none. Fourth, like symbolic interactionism, such theorizing puts the role of human agency, or "free will" at the core of understanding the social world. Humans do not simply respond in uniform and predictable manners to life events. They actively define and interpret their lives, and act upon those personal definitions. This means that our social contexts, although powerful forces in shaping our lives, do not determine our lives. Fifth, postmodernism rejects essentialism. Essentialism refers to the belief that there are common characteristics among all individuals in a group and, due to those commonalities, such individuals' behaviours and beliefs are predictable. For example, assuming that all old people are senile, and all women are emotional represent essentialist statements.

Finally, postmodern thinkers believe that language is socially constructed, and extremely significant in terms of either developing or limiting our perspectives. For example, consider how the terms "productive," "work," and "dependence" might be used and understood by an individual who has a conservative, alarmist perspective regarding the old and the economy. These words might be confined to rigid economic understandings, whereas a critical feminist might understand these words differently. Specifically, while traditional economic perspectives of "work" are often confined to work that is done in the public sphere for pay; a feminist might define "work" more broadly, including unpaid labour, and work done in the private sphere. Thus, meaning is constructed and perpetuated through language, and language is constructed and perpetuated through its meaning. In short, language and meaning constitute each other.

Ultimately, modern approaches to studying aging see people's lives as a standard life cycle, marked by predictable life stages, and linear events such as graduating from university, getting a job, getting married, having children, and eventually retiring. However, postmodernists see life paths as much more multiple, variable, unpredictable, and complicated. Instead of "life stages," postmodernists see "life strands" (Skucha and Bernard, 2000, p. 31) or "ripples" (Mandell et al., 2008, p. 9). This imagery connotes that although there is some commonality in terms of life-event timing, life events often occur in a more chaotic, less predictable manner, are multiple and diverse, and have vastly different meanings for individuals.

Postmodernist research methods also differ from modernist methods. Modernist analysis of the life cycle often adopts psychology-based methods, and pays attention to developmental stages, biomedical models, and predictable life events. It is often macro in nature. Postmodern life-course analyses represent a sharp contrast. For example, in their book, Mandell et al. (2008) adopt a feminist postmodern life-course analysis. This approach entails listening to aging women's interpretations of their own lives, and deconstructing their narratives. The individual is the unit of study, so it is micro in nature. This method ". . . [captures] the complex interplay between structure, culture, agency, which taken together . . ." is instrumental in understanding the lives of aging women (p. 9). Also central to their analysis is the life-course perspective.

The Life-Course Perspective

The life-course perspective stresses both continuity and change. This lens encourages us to see how earlier portions of life are instrumental in shaping our experiences in mid- and late life. Building on symbolic interactionism, and postmodernism, life-course theorists define humans as active decision makers. They seek to understand the relationship between agency and social structure. One of the strengths of this particular perspective is that it considers several levels of analysis: micro (individual), meso (social space within which we live including the family), and macro (the impact of large, political forces such as economic, social, and historical forces).

Central to the life-course perspective are the four "Ts": trajectories, transitions, turning points, and timing (Connidis, 2010, p. 16). In brief, trajectories refer to long-term patterns occurring throughout the life-course. These include the multiple roles and statuses that we occupy throughout our lives. Transitions refer to points of change along trajectories. These include the normative changes in roles, such as the move from student to worker, and worker to retiree. In contrast, turning points represent dramatic and substantial changes along trajectory pathways, like, suddenly becoming a widow in early mid-life, or losing a child. Finally, timing is also a key concept within the life-course perspective. This concept fulfills two purposes. First, there are expectations regarding the timing and order of events occurring throughout the life-course. Second, understanding how historical timing affects individuals' life-course trajectories is important. Specifically, historical events and periods will likely shape people's lives in comparable ways. For example, women who entered adulthood during the late 1960s might find that the political climate produced by feminism's second wave influenced their expectations and aspirations such as their education, family, and career choices. In addition, 9/11 might represent a shared experience for children who entered adolescence around 2001.

Variability in the life-course has amplified over the past 30 years. Increased fluidity comes as a result of many cultural changes including changes within the fields of science and medicine including the emergence and use of certain technological "advancements" that complicate the life-course. Reproductive technologies such as in vitro fertilization disrupt the conventional course of life, and enable women to have children when they are well into, and even beyond, mid-life. In terms of an age-based identity, "older mothers" trouble common conceptions of what it means to be mid-life, which is ultimately an issue of timing. Becoming a new mother in one's 50s or 60s has implications for social identities, some of which are highly stigmatized. To be an "old mother" is to be a deviant mother (Friese et al., 2008, p. 66). Such disruptions within the life-course impact and further complicate the course of life for these mothers and their families. This is especially true if we consider that for many women, their mothers represent a reference point in terms of when they will identify themselves as an "old" woman (Ballard et al., 2005, p. 175). With or without the intervention of new reproductive technologies, mothers are becoming older. This will undoubtedly shape what it means to be old and aging for future generations. It should be noted that the proliferation and development of these technologies are directly related to women's shifting life-course trajectories. These technologies have become "necessary" as they facilitate women's attempts at timing life-course events, such as having children, in manners that are consistent with the pre-existing male career path. This topic will not be investigated here; however, it is important to understand how the variability of the life-course impacts the field of medicine, and thus women's bodies. This trend highlights the interactional nature of the relationship between individuals and larger social structures such as medicine.

Theoretical frameworks are essential to understanding the lives of **late-life** people. Most often, scholars will combine elements from different theories when analyzing late life. In the remainder of this chapter, we draw on and develop a combination of these perspectives when we discuss aging and difference, the aging body, and relationships within the family.

AGING AND DIFFERENCE

Traditional sociological and social gerontological understandings of becoming old and experiencing old age have primarily been seen through the lens of white, middle-class men's experiences (Orel et al., 2004, p. 3). However, considering the distinguishing characteristics of aging Canadians, this group is very diverse. As such, sociological investigations and analyses of old age must account for such diversity. In this section, we will highlight gender and race as significant organizing variables in late life. Before proceeding, it is necessary to point out that both gender and "race" are socially constructed categories. Gender is a social category based on the male/female sex dichotomy. It is performed, and is not biologically based; it is a social category. Likewise, "race" is a socially constructed identity. People become assigned to various racial groups through racialization. Racialization can be understood as

> ". . . the process by which we differentiate on categories based on race. The process of racialization involves the construction of specific images based on a set of assumptions or stereotypes according to certain races. It not only refers to a process of differentiation based on race but to an imposition of a racial character on a person or an action. We impose a racial character or context on a situation by interpreting, perceiving and experiencing events within a racial context . . ." (Mandell et al., 2008, p. 24).

In short, "race" is a social category; it is not biological. However, "if [people] define situations as real, they are real in their consequences" (Thomas and Thomas, 1928, p. 571–572). Subsequently, since "race," and gender are defined as organic and natural, they become sociologically meaningful categories, because people act towards them on the basis that they are real.

Just as our definitions of old age are temporally and spatially fluid, they are also dynamic in terms of social identities such as "race." For example, Yang and Levkoff (2005) argue that for African American men, the age of 55 represents an appropriate chronological age at which they might be considered old. This differs from the conventional age of 65. This suggestion is based on their comparatively shorter life expectancy, and increased probability of developing age-related ailments earlier in life in comparison to their white counterparts. The same is true for Hispanic American men. These men tend to work in jobs that are particularly harmful to the body, and thus lead to an increased possibility of disability and ill health earlier in life than their privileged white male counterparts (Calasanti and Slevin, 2001, p. 23).

Further, many life-course trajectories exist along ethnic and gendered lines. Consider the issue of marriage timing. African American females who do not go to college are less likely to marry compared to their college educated counterparts. The opposite is true for white women. White women with higher levels of education are less likely to marry, compared to white women with lower levels of education (Macmillan, 2005, p. 11). Marriage and marriage timing have an impact on the roles that individuals take up, which again is central to how we understand aging. These patterns remind us that life-course events are shaped by a multitude of social forces, depending on gender, "race," ability, class, sexuality, and other features of identity.

Variations in gender or sexual identities also influence how people see themselves navigating the life-course and subsequently becoming old. Compared to heterosexual people, for gay men and lesbians aging and becoming old have different meanings because the life-course is less likely to be characterized by the social markers associated with a **heteronormative life-course**. Markers such as getting married, having children, and becoming grandparents are less likely to have existed in the lives of older cohorts of LGTB people, although these events are becoming more common among younger cohorts (Hunter, 2005, p. 4). Clearly, social inequality, power and privilege, and prevailing notions of what is normal and deviant are integral to who is considered to be old or how "old" is seen and experienced. Ultimately "aging" and "old" are socially constructed. This is evidenced by the historical and cultural variations connotations of these terms.

Gendered and racialized experiences of aging will be highlighted throughout the remainder of this chapter, as the appreciation of difference is key to understanding aging, and aging families.

THE AGING BODY

The aging body is socially constituted as an object of contempt. As Featherstone, Hepworth, and Turner point out, the old body is more prone to "bodily betrayals," which can include the loss of control of one's bowels or bladder, but also refers to, the ". . . loss of cognitive and other skills . . ." which might lead to embarrassing social situations or impose activity limitations (1991, p. 376). These in turn lead to a subjective experience of lacking control. In addition to these potentially shame-eliciting "mechanical" problems, the aging body's appearance is often regarded as deviant and disgusting. As such, the body has become an important aspect of sociological work on aging. The body is also the physical site upon which others read multiple identities such as gender, age and "race." Work on the social significance of the body is often oriented within a postmodern perspective, but is underscored by feminism, materialism, and life-course frameworks.

A consistent and defining feature of postmodern approaches to the aging body is the metaphor of the mask (Featherstone, Hepworth, and Turner, 1991; Biggs, 1999; Ballard et al., 2005). The mask of aging has two functions. The first function of the mask, originally articulated by Featherstone, Hepworth, and Turner (1991), understands ". . . the aging process as a mask or disguise concealing the essentially youthful self beneath" (quoted in Ballard et al., 2005, p. 171). In this case, an aging appearance is not integrated into an old person's identity, but is at odds with their youthful perception of the self. Eventually, however, through self–other interaction, the identity as an old person emerges. Aging in this conception is a "threat to [one's] true identity[1] "(Ballard et al., 2005, p. 172). The significance of the aging body, according to this metaphor, is that it conceals the youthful person inside.

The second function of the mask in social gerontological literature is to insulate and protect the old person from an ageist society. In this account, age-resisting activities participated in by old people are construed as attempts to cope with ageist stereotypes. In such societies there is a moral imperative to maintain a youthful appearance. This is to say that there are social consequences to accepting one's identity as an old person, because we live in an ageist society. In order to cope with this moral imperative, people might colour their hair, spend excessive hours exercising, or undergo reconstructive surgery in attempts to manage physical-based stigmas around creating old identities. Because contemporary society provides very limited ways to take up the role of an old person, expressing the desire to remain young represents one of the most fundamental ways of managing old identities. So, the second function of the mask metaphor is that age-resistance activities are performed as a means of stigma management, and the body is the site upon which these strategies are performed. In the former account, the body is at odds with one's identity, while in the latter account, an ageist society is seen as marginalizing identities of old people. Considering that consumerism is a defining feature of postmodern society and that there exists a moral imperative to demonstrate that one is making an effort to appear young, marketing services and products that "preserve" or "create" a youthful appearances benefit greatly (see Box 10.1).

Feminism and postmodernism have a strained, but important relationship. Women's bodies and the moral imperative to "choose" to resist aging vis-à-vis consumerism represent a contentious topic where tensions between feminism and postmodernism are expressed (Ballard et al., 2005, p. 172). This also represents the tension between the postmodern and materialist position pointed out by various social scientists throughout the past two decades (see Featherstone, Hepworth, and Turner, 1991). It has also been challenged in several respects. These challenges are concerned with the meaning of the aesthetic, or the physical appearance of the self. For example, Sharon Wray (2007) takes issue with gender-based analyses put forth by such scholars. Featherstone, Hepworth, and Turner (1991) argue that women in particular resist the physical signifiers of aging vis-à-vis purchasing products intended to produce youthful bodies. Wray, using data from 38 interviews with mid-life British women of various racial backgrounds, confronts such gender-based theories by pointing out that although this might be the case for many white women, it certainly does not remain true along the lines of "race." She reports that the white women in her study are more likely to use hormone replacement therapy[2] and engage in other activities, which underscore their "personal responsibility to fight old age through consumption" (Wray, 2007, p. 40). In contrast, her discussions with British Caribbean women reveal that, for them, the embodied changes associated with mid-life are not considered to be as significant. For example, for many of these women, menopause represents a largely unmedicalized life stage, and mid-life is a largely indistinct period of time compared to how it is described by white women. For many economically privileged, white women, mid-life is a relatively more clearly defined life stage, and is often characterized by medical interventions such as hormone replacement therapy (Wray, 2007, p. 36). Ultimately, Wray believes that experiences of aging cannot be separated from individuals' historical, cultural, and social contexts. Further, she advises that

BOX 10.1 COUGARS: ALTERING THE IMAGES OF AGING WOMEN

Popular culture offers us multiple discourses on aging. These discourses are articulated in many ways and in many places, but one of the most blatant examples is that of the "cougar."

WHAT IS A "COUGAR"?

In a general sense, a "cougar" refers to a mid-life woman (approximately between the ages of 40 and 50), who seeks out romantic interactions with younger men. Examples of cougars are highly prevalent on television and in gossip blogs and tabloids. For example, a reality television show called *The Cougar* premiered American network TV Land in 2009. The premise of this show is akin to *The Bachelor* whereby a 40-year-old woman is confronted with a group of men in their 20s who vie for her attention, in the hopes of ultimately becoming her boyfriend. Further, the comedy *Cougar Town* premiered on ABC in the fall of 2009, and features actress Courtney Cox as Jules, a 40-something woman who systematically dates men in their 20s.

Other examples of the cougar in popular culture can be found in gossip magazines and Internet gossip blogs. Perez Hilton, a popular and notorious blogger who writes about the lives of well-known celebrities, often describes middle-aged women as cougars.

HOW DOES THE PHENOMENON OF THE "COUGAR" ALTER THE IMAGE OF MID-LIFE WOMEN?

What does the use and proliferation of this term say about how we view aging women? There are several ways to think critically about this label.

North American society denies that women, in particular, are sexual beings after a certain age. The image of the cougar, a woman who is no longer defined as youthful, might offer a critical stance on aging women's sexuality. However, it is important to note that cougars are relatively young, as women in their 60s and 70s are less likely to be defined accordingly. Also, the cougars featured in popular culture appear to be invested in the "mask of aging," as they are attractive by traditional beauty standards. In the case of *Cougar Town*, Jules spends copious amounts of time doing bodywork such as working out, applying makeup, and dieting.

Further, more often than not, cougars are often said to be on the prowl for younger men (Connidis, 2010, p. 140). "Prowling" connotes a predatory activity. To what degree is framing the sexual relationship between a young man and a mid-life woman in these terms problematic? Consider that there is not a male equivalent to the cougar phenomenon. Has Hugh Hefner ever been compared to an animal of prey? Perhaps it is the case that an equivalent relationship between a man and a woman is considered "normal," and thus goes unlabelled.

Finally, consider how the term defines a woman according to not only to her gender and age, but also her relationship to men. Is the term inherently sexist? Ageist?

Western-centric understandings of aging must not be taken for granted, as they will obscure the experiences of racialized women. Notably, this point regarding the uncritical use of Western-centric understandings of old age arises many times in literature on aging that seeks to account for diverse experiences of aging along the lines of ethnicity (Mitchell, 2005). Lastly, Wray points out that mid-life is not a homogenous life stage. In many cases sameness is stressed in studying this age group. She recommends that scholars and policy makers, who seek to understand aging in context, should stress diversity and difference in experience.

Ultimately, Wray believes that there has been very little work done that considers how ethnicity and culture affect the forms of agency an individual might express. First, although many aging women confront financial problems, a "poor quality of life" is not the inevitable result. Such women actively resist and negotiate a quality of life that is not totally dependent on access to material resources. Second, as articulated above, there exists a perception that in order to age "successfully," one must reconstruct a youthful body, identity, and social life. These perceptions produce a moral obligation for old women to do so. Last, the applicability of social gerontological concepts to old women who are of a variety of ethnicities must be problematized. Control and agency in old age are strongly associated with engagement in the social world, as opposed to the development of coping strategies (Wray, 2007).

Wray's study speaks to the bigger issue of ignoring marginalized women in gerontological research. According to Wray, such research must be conducted along the lines of difference instead of sameness. Western-centric views limit the information that can be collected because fundamental, and often inaccurate, assumptions about the aging experience go unquestioned; thus the data collected is incomplete (Wray, 2007). Her findings also highlight the value of employing a life-course perspective within social gerontology. For example, in earlier portions of the life-course, it is common for white, middle-class women to experience more dissatisfaction with their bodies when compared to women of African, Hispanic, and Asian descent (Altabe, 1996). These perceptions persist into old age, in part because earlier portions of the life-course shape later portions. If a life-course perspective is applied to racialized women, the homogenizing effect of masking theories might become more nuanced, and account for the experiences of non-white, non-middle-class women.

Ballard et al. (2005) also disrupt masking theories. Through interview data, they find that when women do attempt to mask their aging experience, they often do so for a relatively brief period of time, eventually "acquiescing" to the physical expression of an old identity. This finding is consistent among white women as well as women of colour (Ballard et al., 2005, p. 183). Thus, masking strategies, if employed at all, are taken up for only finite periods of time. As such, this metaphor is only partially useful in understanding aging experiences.

In short, the degree to which such theories are helpful in supporting and understanding the realities associated with aging and old age is debatable. This is especially true regarding people who are marginalized before entering old age. Masking theories are a useful manner in which to understand certain people's relationship to their body, at certain points, within the social context of ageism. However, as Wray points out, coping and resistance take on different forms according to one's ethnicity, as well as other features of identity.

LATE-LIFE RELATIONSHIPS AND THE FAMILY

As our lives become longer and our families age the relationships within families are characterized by change as well as continuity; in many ways families in late life interact in similar ways to earlier parts of the life course. However, there are new challenges in existing relationships and new relationships that develop in old age. Family members can expect to know each other for longer periods of time due to our longer lives. Romantic partnerships last much longer. For example, less than 100 years ago, life expectancies for Canadian men and women were 59 years and 61 years, respectively. As of 2005, the average life expectancy for men is 78 and 82.7 for women (Statistics Canada, 2010). This means that for Canadians who remain involved in life long partnerships, they can expect to spend around 20 additional years with their partners compared to the 1920s. Further, grandchildren can also expect to know their grandparents into their early adulthood (Connidis, 2010: 190). This additional time spent together does impact the nature of these relationships in many ways. In this section, I will discuss both intimate relationships and intergenerational relationships in late life.

A particularly useful framework through which to understand the relationships experienced by late-life people is "**structured ambivalence**." This perspective was originally developed by Ingrid Arnet Connidis in order to connect the macro and micro levels of the social world. Connidis says that structured ambivalence is complementary to feminist and life-course perspectives. This perspective allows us to see relationships within the family as being neither "bad" nor "good." Instead, this view helps us to transcend a dichotomous perspective by underscoring the reality that many familial relationships are characterized by feelings of "solidarity and conflict" (Connidis, 2010, p. 139). Mandell et al. (2008) use the metaphor of the "double-edged" sword to describe family connections and intimate relations in mid-life. For women, relationships with their families and their partners and other family members are often extremely fulfilling, loving, and rewarding. However, they are also characterized by pain and suffering (p. 66). Accounting for this ambivalence is a combination of family relations and social processes that are much larger than the family. Cultural expectations regarding certain familial roles pervade even the most intimate relationships. These expectations are gendered, raced, and economically produced. For example, women often feel the weighty social expectations attached to being female. There is a moral imperative for them to perform unpaid work. Because gender is a performance, there are certain roles that men and women are expected to fulfill. This is a substantial motivation that drives women to perform the majority of unpaid care and housework. Such expectations are moral in nature, and are particularly coercive. These powerful social discourses shape relationships that exist between romantic partners, and among relatives. This is an example of how social structures shape our decisions.

CARE WORK

Due to the structure of social policies, as well as the moral obligations to provide care within the family, families—namely women—provide the bulk of care work. For these reasons, we must examine late-life relationships with an appreciation of care work. Care work is a highly salient element in a discussion of the aging family, because it is often forgotten that the old perform much of the care work for the old. Although care working can be a positive and satisfying experience, it can also be stressful, costly, and largely invisible (Calasanti and Slevin, 2002, p. 146), thus producing the feeling of ambivalence.

Care work and caring obligations represent a structural force in late-life relations. Gender is at the core of the discussion, as women represent the majority of the recipients and the providers of care work in late-life families. This discussion will also be guided by the life-course perspective, as caring is a lifelong form of labour. Materialist, feminist, life-course, and postmodern approaches will also be implemented. Unremuncrated care work has material consequences and represents a disruptive life-course force particularly for women.

What Is Care Work?

Work is a particularly salient feature of family life and is characterized by gendered patterns. Women perform the majority of unpaid care work, which limits their opportunity to experience economic security in late life in several ways. First, care work, when done within the family is, for the most part, unpaid. Second, such work often necessitates a full or partial exit from paid work. One result of such care work is often the systematic disentitlement of women to certain old age benefits and a general inability to save money.

The term "care work" refers to a diverse and complex interaction. As such, it is difficult to define. Further, as many feminist scholars point out, there is a deficit of adequate language available to express the meaning of this work (Altschuler, 2001, p. 80). Ultimately, care work has a variety of different meanings depending on who performs the work, who receives the care, and the context in which the interaction occurs. Care work may be defined differently by both the carer and recipient if such work is remunerated (Altschuler, 2004, p. 153). When care work is defined in a very broad manner, it includes labour such as helping a recipient maintain his or her home and property and providing transportation to and from medical appointments. If conceptualized this way, many more men are likely to be defined as carers. Some theorists have pointed out that such labour is rarely considered to be care work, and that the omission of these tasks from understandings of care work is deeply problematic (Wilson, 2000, p. 126). Others include in their conception of care work the ongoing thought processes of care workers. Mason refers to these processes as "sentient activity," where a care giver, perhaps not consciously, considers the preferences and needs of the recipient (in Calasanti, 2003, p. 19).

Altschuler describes a similar aspect of caring that involves "anticipatory skills and thinking." This refers to remembering the schedules and individual wants and needs of family members and friends with whom one is involved in a care relationship (Altschuler, 2004, p. 155). Moreover, care work is sometimes defined in more narrow and specific terms. For example, Twigg defines care work as "working directly on the body [of a care recipient]" (Twigg, 2000, p. 173).

Ultimately, an understanding regarding the meaning of care work must take into account "instrumental" tasks, "bodywork" (Twigg, 2000, p. 173), and anticipatory cognitive processes, discussed by Wilson, Twigg, and Altschuler, respectively. That being said, there are significant differences in terms of intensity between these various components of care work. For instance, "bodywork" represents a very intimate form of care that Twigg argues, although at times pleasurable for both parties in caring relationships, is by nature "negative work" (Twigg, 2000, p. 175). Compared to a task such as transportation, which is a necessary and essential component of care work, working directly on the bodies of recipients is a more emotionally and physically intense experience. These differences in intensity should not be taken for granted. In addition, regardless of how broadly one defines care work, women ultimately perform such labour.

Women take on the majority of care work for many reasons, not the least of which exists on structural levels. Research about policy implicitly assumes that women will be doing the caring work, at all points throughout their adult life-courses. Often it is thought that without women available to provide support, elderly people will not receive care; despite the fact that when women are unavailable, men do provide such care (Connidis, 2002, p. 121).

Physical abuse represents the most reported form of elder abuse in Canada (Ogrodnik, 2009) (see Box 10.2). However, this should not suggest that physical abuse is the most common form. Rather, it tends to be more dramatic, visible, and relatively easily identified. Such abuse may be manifest in the form of hitting or beating an elderly person. Because the old body is often less resilient than more youthful bodies, severe physical injuries can be incurred with relatively little force. Further, sometimes the elderly are tied to their beds, or otherwise confined (Sev'er, 2009, p. 280).

In terms of reported physical violence, the elderly are more likely than other Canadians to be assaulted by a person known to them. Elderly women are likely to be physically abused by their spouse, former spouse, or adult children, while elderly men are most likely to be abused by their children (Ogrodnik, 2009).

Due to widely held ageist attitudes, and social stigmas around old age and sexuality, the sexual abuse of elderly people is largely ignored. Seniors who are most vulnerable to sexual abuse are those who are institutionalized and dependent on caregivers. Elderly people with dementia are particularly vulnerable to sexual abuse (Sev'er, 2009, p. 280).

BOX 10.2   ELDER ABUSE

On June 15, 2009, the government of Canada launched a national campaign covering the abuse of elders (Canada News Centre, 2009). The goal of this campaign is to raise awareness around the issue of elder abuse in Canada, as this particular form of abuse is largely hidden, and rarely discussed.

Although virtually every demographic is subject to abuse, the old are unique in many ways. Many of the elderly are dependent on others for their care. Dependency creates the conditions for secrecy because the power dynamics between the abuser and the abused favour the abuser. Second, the old are more likely than others to be physically or mentally impaired, which also produces disparate power relations, leaving the elder person in a vulnerable position. Such impairments limit the resources for support. Also, especially in terms of mental impairments, the elder might not have the capacity to identify that the abuse is occurring. Even if they are aware of the abuse, they might lack credibility, because they are mentally impaired. So, the same conditions that make them vulnerable to abuse also make coming forward, getting help, or confronting the perpetrator less likely. Third, late life is sometimes associated with social isolation, which can mean less support from family and friends. Such support is valuable in terms of helping an elderly person identify his or her experiences as abusive, and getting out of such a situation. Lastly, females are overrepresented among the old. Women, at all points in the life-course, are more vulnerable to abuse than men.

WHAT IS ELDER ABUSE?

The Ontario Seniors Secretariat (OSS) defines elder abuse as

> *Elder abuse, or the abuse of older adults, is often defined as any act or omission that harms a senior or jeopardizes his or her health or welfare. The World Health Organization defines abuse of older adults as 'a single or repeated act, or lack of appropriate action, occurring in any relationship where there is an expectation of trust that causes harm or distress to an older person' (Ontario Senior's Secretariat, 2009).*

Elder abuse can take place in the home, in other residential settings, or in the community. It is estimated that between 4 and 10 percent of Ontario's seniors experience some type of abuse.

This type of abuse takes on multiple forms, including psychological, physical, sexual, economic, and neglect (Sev'er, 2009). Psychological abuse occurs in the form of insults or dehumanization. Further, the old are abused psychologically when they are "ordered around," and prevented from making decisions about their lives, while still capable of doing so. Social isolation also represents a component of such abuse, which contributes to its overall obscurity (Sev'er, 2009, p. 280).

Economic abuse is very common in Canada (The Ontario Network, 2009). Economic abuse occurs when family members, friends, or care workers steal from the old, sell their property without consent, or remain in the residence of an elderly person without their permission (Sev'er, 2009, p. 281).

The neglect of an elderly person can be intentional, unintentional, or self-neglect (The Ontario Network, 2009). "Neglect" refers to a variety forms of abuse, including over- and undermedicating an old person, or failing to provide an old person with adequate nutrition, hygiene, or attention (Sev'er, 2009, p. 281). This form of abuse is common but very difficult to define, identify, and subsequently report.

In addition to these standard categories of elder abuse, critical race scholars working in gerontology point out that elder abuse takes on multiple forms along the lines of ethnicity. Using Chinese communities as an example, Tam and Neysmith (2006) argue that Western-centric understandings of abuse do not account for culturally specific forms of abuse. In Chinese Canadian communities, these researchers have identified "disrespect" as a key form of abuse. They contend that "disrespect" is not simply a form of "neglect" or "psychological abuse." In this cultural context, there are certain expectations regarding the treatment of the old by the young, which differ from mainstream Canadian expectations. Chinese culture emphasizes the "value and norm that dictates respect for elders" (Tam and Neysmith, 2006, p. 148). For example, referring to one's mother with any word other than "mother" is considered to be extremely rude, and, in this context, is accompanied by much emotional pain (Tam and Neysmith, 2006, p. 148). Further, old Chinese people, especially those who immigrated to Canada, require an emotional dimension of care work, which would not be recognized by white, native-born Canadians. In order to be content, many of them need culturally specific items, and food that would simply be dismissed as "trivial" by cultural outsiders. Such items might be familiar candy, or music. These cultural artefacts are comforting to many elderly Chinese people, who are dealing not only with aging, but also often with cultural isolation.

INTERGENERATIONAL RELATIONSHIPS

Longer lives have changed the family structure, as well as the nature of familial relationships. For example, parents will likely know their children as mid-life people, grandparents often see their grandchildren enter adulthood, and people in life partnerships often spend multiple decades together. Also, technological advancement in communication facilitates increased contact among family members via e-mails, text messages, and instant messages (Connidis, 2010, p. 8).

Further, 80 percent of women over the age of 65 have at least one grandchild (Connidis, 2010, p. 41). Over time, the nature of grandparent–grandchild relationships has come to be more emotional and autonomous. In such relationships, adult grandchildren exercise agency in terms of how "close" they choose to be with their grandparents. Altogether, these relationships are very flexible (Connidis, 2010, p. 190). Relationships between grandchildren and grandparents are most likely the first young–old relationships experienced by children.

These relationships fulfill several important dimensions. For example, these relatives provide children with an important source of information regarding their cultural and ethnic identities. In addition, grandparents often provide care for their grandchildren (Connidis, 2010, 192). These factors have the potential to facilitate closer and perhaps more complex ties between generations.

Although multigenerational dwellings or homes where more than two generations reside are very rare among Canadian households, many grandparents provide child care for their grandchildren (Connidis, 2010, p. 197), which is a significant source of intergenerational support. As of 2001, only about 4 percent of homes are characterized as intergenerational (Turcotte and Shellenburg, 2006, p. 139).

In the United States, grandparent-headed households where grandparents act as primary caregivers are becoming increasingly common (Landry-Meyer and Newman, 2004, p. 1005). For example, between 1990 and 1998 there was a 53 percent increase in children residing in grandparent-maintained homes. Significantly, three-quarters of the grandparents who act as primary caregivers are female (Calasanti and Slevin, 2001, p. 169). In addition to gender, ethnicity and social class are significant variables in terms of who is taking on such a responsibility. Often these grandparents are black as well as economically disadvantaged (Calasanti and Slevin, 2001, p. 170). There are several problems encountered by grandmothers who act as primary caregivers to grandchildren. It is quite common for them to have fair to poor health compared to other women their age (Chase Goodman and Silverstein, 2006, p. 1607). In addition, it might be the case that grandmothers who provide primary care are often dealing with problems associated with the various reasons that their own children are incapable of providing such care. These reasons may include illness, problems with the law, and death (Chase Goodman and Silverstein, 2006, p. 1605). Grandparents who provide primary care are highly stigmatized, because their relationships to their own children are scrutinized by others, who blame them for not teaching their own children how to parent (Calasanti and Slevin, 2001, p. 170).

However, living together is only one form of grandparent-as-caregiver relationship. There are many other arrangements in which grandparents provide care. Grandparents often look after their grandchildren while their own children work outside the home. This work is gendered; grandmothers provide the bulk of the care work. In Canada, it is estimated that 20 percent of children of preschool age are cared for by their grandmother while their own parents participate in paid work (Connidis, 2010, p. 197).

Relationships between children and the grandparents are significant. These relationships challenge many ageist assumptions, such as the notion that the old are "unproductive," and "burdensome" to the economy.

INTIMATE RELATIONSHIPS IN LATE LIFE

Defining "intimate relationships" is difficult as there are competing meanings associated with this term. Most relationships within the family are characterized, at least in part, by intimacy. Indeed, mothers and fathers are often intimately involved with their children. Such intimate ties might come in the form of care work. During childhood, siblings also often have intimate ties, perhaps in the form of a shared space, like a bedroom. However, consider Anthony Gidden's conceptualization of a "pure relationship":

> The term "pure relationship"... refers to a situation where a social relation is entered into for its own sake, for what can be derived by each person from a sustained association with another; and which is continued only in so far as it is thought by both parties to deliver enough satisfaction for each individual to stay within it (Giddens in Connidis, 2010, p. 53).

Although this definition is somewhat problematic, especially if we consider factors such as having children, and the obligation to provide care, it is useful in terms of developing a basic understanding of what distinguishes "intimate" relationships from other family ties.

Other texts might simply label this section "marriage in late life". However, this label is largely exclusionary, as there are a variety of romantic relationships, and subsequent living arrangements, that occur in late life. Such relationships also include, but are not limited to, same-sex relationships, cohabiting couples, and couples who live apart.

Nevertheless, most elderly Canadians live with a spouse, or a romantic partner (Connidis, 2010, p. 44). Thus, in terms of living arrangements, such relationships constitute an important family structure in late life. However, it is important to mention that elderly white people are more likely to be living in partnerships compared to black, Asian, and Aboriginal people, who are more likely than their white counterparts to be living with other kin (Connidis, 2010, p. 44).

MARRIAGE IN LATE LIFE

With old age come more complications and change. Marriages[3] along the life-course are characterized by continuity and change (Mandell et al., 2008), meaning that while some aspects of marital relationships remain stable, others are variable. Aging married couples often experience new challenges in late life. For example, the retirement of one or both spouses might lead to strained interactions. When a male partner retires from paid work in a household where the female partner either works part-time, does not work for pay, or has retired at an earlier point, women often experience a loss of personal space, whereby their male partner "gets under their feet" (Fairhurst, 2003, p. 32). This tension is connected to the disruptions in the everyday routines of the female partner. A new stage of life, such as retirement, although thought to be a time of relaxation, and more leisure time, has the potential to be very stressful. This point also calls into question the degree to which a woman, who performs unpaid labour in the home, ever does retire. Marital relationships in late life highlight Connidis's conception of "ambivalence." Specifically, within such marriages there exists a complex combination of emotions, which are structurally produced. Often, women find themselves balancing caring obligations, personal desires and love.

Love and affection are also very crucial dimensions of most marriages. In late life, married people are likely to engage in sexual activities (Riggs and Turner, 1999, p. 204). Sexually active seniors subvert cultural notions of aging, and are often considered "perverse." As a result, some elderly people might feel guilty about their own sexual desires and activities (Riggs and Turner, 1999, p. 203). Although sexual intimacy often represents a continuous aspect of married life, there are some challenges as adults enter late life. Part of this challenge is connected to the higher probability of physical illness, which is an obstacle for many forms of physical intimacy. For many couples, when one partner falls ill, sexual intimacy tends to "fizzle out" (Riggs and Turner, 1999, p. 205)

Also shedding light on how sexual intimacy or affection might "fizzle" in marital relationships, Mandell et al. (2008) point out that men and women are exposed to specific and rigid discourses about romantic life. These discourses suggest that romantic love entails "attaching and giving" themselves to another person. Yet, another powerful, and contradictory discourse, stressing the connection between love, personal satisfaction, and individualism is also operating. So, while the former promotes selflessness, the latter promotes self-absorption (p. 68). These contradictory and powerful discourses provide a precarious framework for building romantic love. For both same- and opposite-sex partnerships, the ideal of love is elusive. Dominant conceptions of "fairy tale" romance and love do not account for the effects of social forces such as sexism, ableism, financial insecurity, and racism, which permeate and structure our most intimate relationships (Mandell et al., 2008, p. 69).

In addition, in late life it is spouses who provide the majority of care work if one of them becomes ill. Since women often remain in good health, and live longer than their male counterparts, this means that women are performing the majority of such labour. Underscoring this point, care work continues into old age and limits many women's access to leisure time. As a consequence, the popular conception of retirement is rendered unobtainable. Nonetheless, recent research suggests that for some women, late life is a time of resistance to the powerful gendered expectations associated with care work. Altschuler argues that women, as they age, do not necessarily become more "assertive," but that many more do become "self-protective" (2001, p. 92). Several of the old women she interviewed reported that they had learned to see themselves as deserving of support in the form of care. She also identifies a variety of reasons for the increase of "self-protective limits" among the old women in her study. Some of these include events such as seeing others resist caring duties, becoming a lone parent, and returning to school (Altschuler, 2001, pp. 93–94). In their study on LAT (living apart together) relationships, Swedish researchers Borrell and Ghazanfareeon Karlsson (2003) provide a fascinating example of these "self-protective limits" among old women.

LAT relationships, which are initiated by old women, are characterized by emotionally close bonds with male partners and separate residences. In LAT relationships, there is no potential for a shared residence in the future (Borrell and Ghazanfareeon Karlsson, 2003, p. 48). These relationships, often occurring in old age after events such as divorce and widowhood, in many ways represent women exercising self-protective limits. Partners involved in LAT relationships often eat, sleep, and spend time together. Within these unions, it is common for males to help their female partners maintain their residence by making repairs around their homes. Likewise, females often prepare meals for themselves and their male partners. However, each maintains an autonomous physical and social space. This space helps partners draw emotional boundaries. For example, when confronted with a hypothetical situation in which their male partner falls ill, most of the females in the sample reported that although they would be willing to provide care work, such care would be limited (Borrell and Ghazanfareeon Karlsson, 2003, p. 56). It may be that these female-initiated relationships represent one method of resisting the obligation to become completely immersed in the care for a sick or dying partner.

SAME-SEX RELATIONSHIPS

Same-sex relationships in late life share some of the same characteristics as heterosexual partnerships. However, there is considerably less scholarly work on late-life same-sex partnerships. This is due in part to the stigma experienced by older gay men and lesbians. Old gay men and lesbians "confront double invisibility" (Connidis, 2002, p. 83). Not only do they face social stigma for being old and gay or lesbian, but also most of them had to deal with severe homophobia when they were younger. One available mechanism for coping with such stigma is to conceal their sexuality). Because earlier parts of the life-course shape late life, even in cases where same-sex couples have ceased to conceal their sexuality the experiences and emotions associated with early stigmatization continue to affect individuals as they age (Connidis, 2002, p. 83).

Further, this population has largely been ignored by researchers due to homophobic attitudes within the discipline of social gerontology. Considering that women have only recently been meaningfully included in these studies, the inclusion of late-life gay and lesbian experiences does not as of yet constitute a well-developed area of interest among scholars. As Connidis points out, gay, lesbian and trans couples are often omitted from life-course studies, and rarely is the life-course perspective adequately applied to these couples. Family ties change and evolve throughout the life-course. Heterosexism often represents a significant bias within social gerontological research. For example, it is rarely appreciated in such work that "coming out" is not a singular event. Rather, "coming out" enacts a process of ongoing renegotiation within families. Ultimately, excluding these couples from a meaningful life-course analysis implies that gay and lesbian couples are not so much contributors to a family but members who "require additional or unique attention" (Connidis, 2002, p. 81).

While there is a lack of attention paid to gay and lesbian couples in terms of the division of care work in late life, it has been noted that gay and lesbian couples often rely on "fictive kin," which includes close friends, for care

(Calasanti and Slevin, 2001). In addition, they create supportive care networks, which suggests that the division of caring labour may be differently distributed compared to heterosexual couples (Connidis, 2002). In terms of instrumental care work, such as housework, one study suggests that within gay and lesbian partnerships, each individual spends similar amounts of time performing these duties (Kurdek, 2007). Understanding the patterns that are prevalent in nonheterosexual relationships in late life is an important component of understanding marginalized experiences of aging.

Gay men and lesbians are gendered. Consequently, their relationships in late life are also gendered. There is some evidence to suggest that lesbian relationships in late life may be similar to heterosexual marriages, while their male counterparts' relationship may be structured in very different ways. Lesbians tend to have committed and monogamous relationships, while gay men are more likely to have relationships characterized by a greater degree of independence (Connidis, 2002, p. 85). Gender differences like these shape how couples relate to each other in old age. Furthermore, just as sexism, ableism, and racism enter into heterosexual relationships, and contribute to structured ambivalence, as well as threaten the "ideal" notion of love, so too does homophobia.

Interestingly, because late-life same-sex couples are far less likely to be legally married, it has been suggested that they might be more likely to "prepare" for the death of their partner because they are highly conscious of their "second-class citizen status." Because they experience elevated levels of legal and social discrimination compared to their heterosexual counterparts, they are forced to actively understand their legal rights, and pursue avenues toward ensuring their potential future as widows and widowers. Such preparations can be both legal and informal (DeVries et al., 2009). Informally, aging lesbian and gay couples might be more likely to secure fictive kin within their communities to ensure company and care in late life. Formally, these couples appear to be more likely to seek legal counsel in terms of having secure wills. These measures are not necessarily undertaken by people in heterosexual marriages, because these supports are often taken for granted.

In short, late-life gay and lesbian relationships are both different from and similar to early and midlife relationships. They also share similarities with heterosexual relationships. However, homophobia represents a powerful influence throughout the life-course and into late life. As such, it contributes to structured ambivalence within same-sex relationships.

SINGLEHOOD IN LATE LIFE

Singlehood, which in the context of this chapter refers to late-life individuals who are never married or partnered, divorced, widowed, or separated, is a virtual inevitability in late life. Although the divorce rate is considerably low among old people compared to young people, it will become increasingly common (Connidis, 2010, p. 105). There has also been an increase in the number of older people who are divorced, yet the numbers are quite small (Connidis, 2002, p. 109). Future groups of elderly people will have to deal with the continuing implications of divorce, single parenthood, remarriage, and stepparenting. In the future, being single will be more common, and will be less associated with childlessness (Connidis 2002,, p. 109). In cases where couples do not divorce or separate, one will eventually enter widowhood. In most cases, women will be single in old age.

Of Canadian women aged 75 to 79, more than half are widows. Men are less likely to experience this life stage due to their shorter life expectancies and the tendency for men to marry younger women (Chappell, 2003, p. 105). Widowhood for women is associated with economic insecurity in late life. Being single has material consequences for women in all stages of the life-course, but because oppression worsens in late life, single old women are especially vulnerable. Here, we will focus on the relationship between single-hood and economic consequences, particularly for women.

Li (2004) finds that women from all income brackets, who become widowed in old age, experience a drop in income compared to earlier portions of the life-course. His findings are based on examining the income among women 65 years of age and over, between 1990 and 2001, using data from Statistics Canada data. He points out that many of these women are clustered just above the low income cut off (LICO).[4] As such, they are dangerously close to experiencing poverty according to this measure. Li believes that this is significant, as it would require a very little amount of financial support to elevate them from the lower income bracket. In a more recent study, Bernard and Li (2006) find that men who have lost their wives are also more likely to experience economic hardship. Thus, not being in a heterosexual relationship in old age is associated with a decrease in economic security for both men and women.

Gaszo (2005) looks at the poverty of unattached senior females. She turns a critical perspective toward the intertwining of informal structures that shape the earlier portions of women's lives, and the formal policies of the Canadian retirement income system. She points out that throughout their paid working lives, women make less money than men, perform more unpaid work, and are thus denied the necessary benefits to supplement their incomes. This presents a significant hurdle in terms of saving money for "retirement." Women who are single in late life are particularly vulnerable, as they have no access to male wages.

Late-life single people engage in sexual activity. However, there are some challenges to having an active sex life. For example, for late-life singles who live in nursing homes, the issue of privacy is at stake. It has been argued that nursing homes offer very little personal, private space. Frequently, seniors who live in old age facilities have only curtains to protect their privacy and, even if they do have a door, it often common practice for it to be left open. It is also commonplace for aides and nursing home employees to walk in and out of seniors' rooms unannounced and without knocking. As a consequence, single people who do wish to have sexual relations are often unable to do so, because they haven't an autonomous living or sleeping space (Lowell, 2009).

Widowhood is far more likely to be experienced by women. This life transition is accompanied by much pain by both men and women. However, research suggests that women tend to cope with widowhood more effectively than men (Maynard et al., 2008, p. 108). After the loss of one's spouse in a heterosexual relationship, both men and women have to adopt new roles in order to survive. For example, many women have to take up the management of their financial affairs, as such work is traditionally dealt with by the male partner (Maynard et al., 2008, p. 157). Further, in cases where women become widowed after dealing with their spouse's terminal illness, a period of anticipatory grieving and loss precedes their partner's death. As such, there is sometimes an element of relief associated with their partner's passing. Nonetheless, many women continue to feel guilty and depressed after such deaths (Connidis, 2010, p. 109). Such ambivalence, as we have seen, is common in many transitions throughout the life-course.

CONCLUSION

Canada is demographically old. Aging is a social process. Subsequently, the structure of, and the processes within, Canadian families alter substantially. The family is a significant context for aging individuals. Longer lives alter the structure of and the processes within the family. In order to understand aging individuals and their families, it is necessary have to adopt a broad perspective, relying on a combination of the various frameworks outlined above.

Of particular importance is that social inequalities that are apparent throughout earlier portions of the life-course become more pronounced in old age. Ageism itself is an oppressive discourse. This is why we have chosen to stress the homogeneity of the old and their families.

It is important to think about the potential of the relationships between the old and the young; the young ultimately benefit. Although the young may be reluctant to meaningfully engage with the old due to an implicit fear of power loss, this creates divisions and serves to deny the young the opportunity to learn from the old. For these reasons, an awareness of social inequalities must be at the core of social gerontology.

Summary

- Canada's population is aging. This has implications for the structure of, and the processes within, Canadian families.
- The definition of "old" is socially constructed, fluid, and dynamic.
- Demographically, Canada will continue to become older. Women continue to outlive men.

- Aging can be understood through a combination of various theoretical frameworks, including: social constructionism (symbolic interactionism), materialism, feminism postmodernism, and the life-course perspective.

- Diversity and difference must be at the core of how we understanding aging. The old are a homogenous group in terms of gender, "race," immigration status, ability, and sexuality. Oppressions experienced earlier in life follow individuals into old age. When other forms of oppression are also experienced in the context of ageism, they intensify.

- The body factors significantly both in terms of our personal experiences of aging, as well as in general perceptions of what it means to be old.

- Longer lives have an impact on family relationships. The structure of the family alters in old age. Care work is a key form of labour within late-life family relationships. The old are the recipients as well as the providers of care work. Care work is also gendered.

Notes

1. The notion of a "true identity" is socially constructed. Symbolic interactionists believe that we have multiple identities, which are never settled. However, the notion of a stable self is pervasive within dominant understandings of the self.

2. By 2001, most women had stopped using HRT. At this point, links between this therapy and heart disease became publicized (Worcester, 2004).

3. Although same-sex marriages are becoming more frequent among younger generations, older gay couples are less likely to be married. So we have put them in a separate category.

4. The LICO is one of many measures of poverty in Canada. It represents an income cut-off point where it is assumed that people will experience economic insecurity. There is no singular measure of poverty, and the LICO is a highly disputed measure. However, it is often used when measuring poverty in Canada.

Critical Thinking Questions

1. Can you think of examples of ageism in Canadian society? How can we challenge this ideology?

2. Do you think that ageism intensifies other forms of oppression (e.g., racism, sexism, and homophobia)?

3. How do longer lives affect relationships within the family?

4. What kinds of perceptions exist around aging bodies?

5. Does Canadian culture fear aging?

6. How is old age socially constructed?

Websites

The Vanier Institute of the Family
http://www.vifamily.ca
> The founders of The Vanier Institute of the Family believe that a strong and healthy family is at the core of a strong and healthy society. The goal of this institution is to help facilitate positive family life by raising awareness about the issues confronted by Canadian families. The researchers are invested in building understandings of, and advocating for, Canadian families. The institute's intention is to contribute to sound social policies, employment, and other institutions that are supportive of Canadian families.

Social and Economic Dimensions of an Aging Population
http://socserv.mcmaster.ca/sedap/
> Social and Economic Dimensions of Aging Population (SEDAP) is located at McMaster University and is funded by the Social Sciences and Humanities Research Council of Canada (SSHRC). SEDAP is a six-year program (running from January 3, 2005, to April 1, 2011) aimed at producing research that contributes to our understandings of the economic impacts of an aging Canadian society. The work produced by this program outlines some of the challenges associated with the Canadian age structure, and also debunks myths about the financial dimensions of an aging society.

Suggested Readings

Nancy Mandell, Susannah Wilson, and Ann Duffy. 2008. *Connection, Compromise and Control: Canadian Women Discuss Midlife*. Don Mills, ON: Oxford University Press.
> These authors explore how mid-life women construct and assign meaning to aging identities, as well as negotiate their roles within their families.

Ingrid Arnet Connidis. 2010. *Family Ties and Aging*, 2nd ed. Thousand Oaks, CA: Sage Publications.
> Connidis provides an overview of Canadian families, paying close attention to diversity of family structures and configurations.

Sharon Wray. 2003. "Women Growing Older: Agency, Ethnicity, and Culture." *Sociology* (3): 511–527.
> Wray studies the connections between ethnicity, gender, and self-determination in old age. She argues that "difference," not "sameness" should be at the core of social gerontology.

References

Afshar, Haleh, Myfawny Franks, Mary Maynard, and Sharon Wray. 2008. *Growing Older: Women in Later Life, Exploring Race and Ethnicity*. New York: Open University Press.

Altabe, Madeline. 1996. "Ethnicity and Body Image; Quantitative and Qualitative Analysis." *International Journal of Eating Disorders*, 23(2): 153–159.

Altschuler, Joanne. 2001. "Meaning and Centrality of Caring Activities Among Older Women." *Journal of Women and Aging*, 13(3): 79–100.

Altschuler, Joanne. 2004. "Meaning of Housework and Other Unpaid Responsibilities among Older Women." *Journal of Women and Aging*, 16(1/2): 143–159.

Ballard, Karen, Mary Ann Elston, and Jonathon Gabe. 2005. "Beyond the Mask: Women's Experiences of Public and Private Ageing During Midlife and Their Use of Age Resisting Activities." *Health*, 9(2): 169–187.

Berger, Ellie and Margaret Denton. 2004. "The Interplay between Women's Life Course Work Patterns and Financial Planning for Later Life." *Canadian Journal on Aging*, Supplement: S81–S95.

Bernard, André and Chris Li. July 2006. *Death of a Spouse: The Impact on Income for Senior Men and Women*. Administrative Data Division and Income Statistics Division Catalogue Number 11-621-MIE- no. 046: Ottawa.

Biggs, Simon. 1999. "The Blurring of the Life-course: Narrative, Memory and the Question of Authenticity." *Journal of Aging and Identity*, 4(4): 209–221.

Borrell, Klass and Sofie Ghazanfareeon Karlsson. 2003. "Reconceptualizing Intimacy and Ageing: Living Apart Together." In Sara Arber, Kate Davidson, and Jay Ginn (Eds.), *Gender and Aging: Changing Roles and Relationships* (pp. 47–63). Philadelphia: Open University Press.

Calasanti, Toni. 2003. "Masculinities and Care Work in Old Age." In Sara Arber, Kate Davidson, and Jay Ginn (Eds.), *Gender and Aging: Changing Roles and Relationships* (pp. 15–28). Philadelphia: Open University Press.

Calasanti, Toni and Kathleen Slevin. 2001. *Gender, Inequalities and Aging*. Walnut Creek, California: AltaMira Press.

Calasanti, Toni and Kathleen Slevin. 2006. *Age Matters: Realigning Feminist Thinking*. New York: Routledge.

Canada News Centre. 2009. "Government of Canada Launches Elder Abuse Awareness Campaign." http://news.gc.ca/web/article-eng.do?m=%2Findex&nid=458809 (accessed April 13, 2010).

Chappell, Neena. 2003. *Aging in Contemporary Canada*. Toronto: Prentice Hall.

Connidis, Ingrid Arnet. 2002. "The Impact of Demographic and Social Trends on Informal Support for Older Persons." In David Cheal (Ed.), *Aging and Demographic Change in a Canadian Context* (pp. 105–132). University of Toronto Press.

Connidis, Ingrid Arnet. 2010. *Family Ties and Aging*, 2nd ed. Thousand Oaks, CA: Sage Publications.

Dentinger, Emma and Marin Clarkberg. 2002. "Informal Caregiving and Retirement Timing Among Men and Women: Gender and Caregiving Relationships in Late Life." *Journal of Family Issues*, 23(7): 857–879.

de Vries, Brian, Anne M. Mason, Jean Quam, and Kimberly Acquaviva. 2009. "Recognition of Same-Sex Relationships and Preparations for End of Life and Lesbian and Gay Boomers." *Sexuality Research and Social Policy: Journal of NSRC*, 6(1): 90–101.

Fairhurst, Eileen. 2003. "New Identities in Ageing: Perspectives on Age, Gender and Life After Work." In Sara Arber, Kate Davidson, and Jay Ginn (Eds.), *Gender and Aging: Changing Roles and Relationships* (pp. 31–46). Philadelphia: Open University Press.

Featherstone, Michael, Michael Hepworth, and Bryan Turner. 1991. *The Body: Social Process and Cultural Theory*. London: Sage.

Friese, Carrie, Gay Beker, and Robert D. Nachtigall. 2008. "Older Motherhood and the Changing Life Course in the Era of Assisted Reproductive Technologies." *Journal of Aging Studies*, 22: 65–73.

Gazso, Amber. 2005. "The Poverty of Unattached Senior Women and the Canadian Retirement Income System: A Matter of Blame or Contradiction?" *Journal of Sociology and Social Welfare*, 32(2): 41–62.

Goodman, Catharine Chase and Merrill Silverstein. 2006. "Grandmother Raising Grandchildren: Ethnic and Racial Differences in Well-being among Custodial and Coparenting Families." *Journal of Family Issues*, 27(11): 1605–1626.

Hilton, Perez. 2010. www.perezhilton.com (accessed April 12, 2010).

Hislop, Jenny and Sara Arber. 2003. "Sleep as a Social Act: A Window on Gender Roles and Relationships." In Sara Arber, Kate Davidson, and Jay Ginn (Eds.), *Gender and Aging: Changing Roles and Relationships* (pp. 186–203). Philadelphia: Open University Press.

Hockey, Jenny and Allison James. 2003. *Social Identities across the Life-course*. New York: Palgrave MacMillan.

Hunter, Ski. 2005. *Midlife and Older LGBT Adults: Knowledge and Affirmative Practice for the Social Services*. New York: The Hawthorne Press.

Kurdek, Lawrence A. 2007. "The Allocation of Household Labor by Partners in Gay and Lesbian Couples." *Journal of Family Issues*, 28(1): 132–148.

Landry-Meyer, Laura and Barbara M. Newman. 2004. "An Exploration of the Grandparent Caregiver Role." *Journal of Family Issues*, 24(8): 1005–1025.

LeGault, Michael. 2009, January 22. "The New Definition of Old: Dead." *The Globe and Mail*. http://www.theglobeandmail.com/news/opinions/the-new-definition-of-old-dead/article1441291/ (accessed April 21, 2010).

Li, Chris. 2004. *Widowhood: Consequences on Income for Senior Women*. Analytical Paper, Analysis in Brief, Catalogue No: 11-621-MIE2004015. Ottawa: Statistics Canada.

Lowell, Marina. 2009. "Nursing Homes and Sex." Toronto Nursing Homes. http://www.torontonursinghomes.com/news/4-news/87-nursing-homes-dont-allow-sex.html (accessed April 13, 2010).

Macmillan, Ross. 2005. "The Structure of the Life Course: Classic Issues and Current Controversies." *Advances in Life Course Research*, 9: 3–24.

Mandell, Nancy, Susannah Wilson, and Ann Duffy. 2008. *Connection, Compromise and Control: Canadian Women Discuss Midlife*. Don Mills, ON: Oxford University Press.

Martin Matthews, A. and L.D. Campbell. 1995. "Gender Roles, Employment and Informal Care." In S. Arber and J. Ginn (Eds.), *Connecting Gender and Ageing: A Sociological Approach* (pp.129–143). Milton Keynes, UK: Open University Press.

McDonald, Lynn. 2006. "Gender and Family—Major Dimensions of Retirement Research." *New Frontiers of Research on Retirement*. Ottawa: Statistics Canada. http://www.statcan.gc.ca/pub/75-511-x/2006001/ch/5203542-eng.htm (accessed April 21, 2010).

McPherson, B.D. 1998. *Aging as a Social Process*, 3rd ed. Toronto: Harcourt Brace.

Mitchell, Barbara A. 2005. *Canada 2017: Serving Canada's Multicultural Population for the Future*. Canadian Heritage, Multiculturalism. http://www.pch.gc.ca/multi/canada2017/7_e.cfm#1 (accessed July 18, 2008).

Murphy, John W., Luigi Esposito, and Charles F. Longino Jr. 1999. "The Relevance of Multiculturalism for Aging." *Journal of Aging and Identity Politics*, 4(4): 223–229.

National Advisory Council on Aging. 2005. "Seniors from Ethnocultural Minorities: Seniors on the Margins." http://dsp-psd.pwgsc.gc.ca/Collection/H88-5-1-2005E.pdf (accessed April 13, 2010).

Ogrodnik, Lucie. 2009. *Family Violence in Canada: A Statistical Profile*. Statistics Canada. http://www.statcan.gc.ca/bsolc/olc-cel/olc-cel?catno=85-224-XWE&lang=eng (accessed April 13, 2010).

Ontario Seniors Secretariat. 2009. "Elder Abuse." http://www.culture.gov.on.ca/seniors/english/programs/elderabuse (accessed April 13, 2010).

Orel, Nancy, Ruth Ford, and Charlene Brock. 2004. "Women's Financial Planning for Retirement: The Impact of Disruptive Life Events." *Journal of Women and Aging*, 16(3/4): 39–53.

Polivka, L. and C.F. Longino. 2002. "Commentary: Aging Politics and Policy in Postmodern Society." *Journal of Aging and Identity*, 7(4): 287–292.

Ray, R. 2006. "The Personal Is Political: The Legacy of Betty Friedan." In T.M. Calasanti and K.F. Slevin (Eds.), *Age Matters: Realigning Feminist Thought* (pp. 21–45). New York and London: Routledge.

Riggs, Ann and Bryan S. Turner. 1999. *The Expectation of Love in Older Age: Towards a Sociology of Intimacy*. In Marilyn Poole and Susan Feldman (Eds.), *A Certain Age: Women Growing Older* (pp. 193–208). St. Leonards, Australia: Allen and Unwin.

Sev'er, Aysan. 2009. "More than Wife Abuse That Has Gone Old: A Conceptual Model for Violence against the Aged in Canada and the US." *Journal of Comparative Studies*, 40(2): 279–296.

Shakeri, Shemirani Farimah and Deborah L. O'Connor. 2006. "Aging in a Foreign Country: Voices of Iranian Women Aging in Canada."*Journal of Women and Aging*, 18(2): 73–90.

Silverman, Myrna, Esther Skirboll, and Joy Payne. 1996. "An Examination of Women's Retirement: African American Women." *Journal of Cross-Cultural Gerontology*, 11: 319–334.

Simmons, Beverly A. and Myra J. Betschild. 2001. "Women's Retirement, Work and Life Paths: Changes, Disruptions and Discontinuities." *Journal of Women and Aging*, 13(4): 53–70.

Skucha, Julie and Miriam Bernard. 2000. "'Women's Work' and the Transition to Retirement." In Miriam Bernard (Ed.), *Women Ageing: Changing Identities, Challenging Myths* (pp. 23–39). London, UK: Routledge.

Statistics Canada. 2010. "Indicators of Well-Being in Canada." http://www.hrsdc.gc.ca/.3ndic.1t.4r@-eng.jsp?iid=3 (accessed April 12, 2010).

Tam, Sandra and Sheila Neysmith. 2006. "Disrespect and Isolation: Elder Abuse in Chinese Communities." *Canadian Journal on Aging*, 25(2): 141–151.

The Daily. 2009, November 27. "Canada's Population Estimates: Age and Sex." http://www.statcan.gc.ca/daily-quotidien/091127/dq091127b-eng.htm (accessed April 12, 2010).

The Ontario Network for the Prevention of Elder Abuse. 2009. "About Elder Abuse." http://www.onpea.org/english/elderabuse/formsofelderabuse.html (accessed April 12, 2010).

Thomas, W.I. and Dorothy Swain Thomas. 1928. *The Child in America: Behaviour Problems and Programs*. New York: Knopf.

Tuelle, Emmanuelle. 2004. *Old Age and Agency*. Hauppauge, NY: Nova Science.

Turcotte, Martin and Grant Schellenberg. 2006. *A Portrait of Seniors in Canada*. Statistics Canada, Social and Aboriginal Statistics Division, Catalogue no. 89-519-XIE.

Twigg, Julia. 2000. *Bathing: The Body and Community Care*. London, UK: Routledge.

Ungerson, Clare. 2005. "Carework and Feeling." *The Sociological Review*, 53(s2): 188–203.

Veall, Michael R. 2007. *Which Canadian Seniors Are Below the Low-Income Measure?* SEDAP Research Paper No. 186.

Wilson, Gail. 2000. *Understanding Old Age: Critical and Global Perspectives*. London: Sage.

Worcester, Nancy. 2004. "Hormone Replacement Therapy (HRT): Getting to the Heart of the Politics of Women's Health." *NWSA*, 16(3): 56-69.

Wray, Sharon. 2003. "Connecting Ethnicity, Agency and Ageing." *Sociological Research Online*, 8(4), http://www.socresonline.org.uk.ezproxy.library.yorku.ca/8/4/wray.html

Wray, Sharon. 2003. "Women Growing Older: Agency, Ethnicity, and Culture." *Sociology*, 37(3): 511–527.

Wray, S. 2007. "Making Sense of Mid-life: Ethnic and Cultural Diversity." *Journal of Aging Studies*, 21(1): 31–42.

Yang, Frances M. and Sue E. Levkoff. 2005. "Ageism and Minority Populations: Strength in the Face of Challenge." *Generations* (29)3: 42–48.

GLOSSARY

Numbers in parentheses refer to the chapter(s) containing the main discussion of the term.

acculturation
a process whereby a person new to the social environment gradually adopts the values, norms, and behaviours prevalent in that social environment. (4)

ageism
a form of oppression, whereby the old are defined as deviant and less than human. Ageism promotes and justifies the exclusion of the old from meaningful participation in society. The consequences of ageism are economic, psychological, physical, and social. (10)

agency
the capacity of individuals and groups to think and act voluntarily. (4)

alter-activism
a form of political-oriented advocacy that is distinguished from others forms because "alter-activists" are highly networked, connected on a global level, and reliant on and shaped by technology in ways that earlier generations of activists were not. (3)

anti-oppression work
work that is committed to ending oppressive hierarchal social relations and larger systems of oppressions such as racism, sexism, classism, and heterosexism. (5)

anti-racist feminism
a branch of feminist analysis that considers racialized power relations as significant, along economic (social class) relations and gender (patriarchal) relations. (4)

astronaut families
migratory nuclear families that act as a family unit even if separated by distance and over time. (4)

Atlantic slave trade
the practice of the colonial era (from 1441 to the 19th century) whereby black slaves from Africa were transported in ships across the Atlantic, primarily to Europe and North America. (4)

bisexual
a person who is physically and emotionally attracted to both genders or who expresses fluidity in his or her attraction to a particular gender. (5)

black loyalists
Black runaway slaves, loyal to Great Britain, who arrived in Canada from the United States. (4)

blended family
where the children of either one or both spouses from a previous marriage/relationship live with the couple, in addition to the children they may have from one another. (8)

capitalism
a particular kind of economy. In a capitalist economy, most people work for others in return for a wage or salary and a small portion of the society owns most wealth. (6)

Centre for Contemporary Cultural Studies
an academic centre founded in the 1970s at the University of Birmingham, England, where the

researchers and theorists explored the roles of hegemony and counter-hegemony in modern society. In particular, they tended to focus on the ways in which resistance to hegemony and challenges to the dominant groups were embedded in popular youth culture. (3)

civil rights movement
the political activation of black people and their supporters, in the 1960s and the 1970s, to combat racism. (4)

cohabitation
two people living together. Cohabitation does not create a common-law marriage unless the couple holds themselves out to the world as spouses through mutual consent of the parties to the relationship as one constituting a marriage; both parties are of legal age to marry; and both partners are qualified to be married (of legal age/have parental consent, being unmarried, and being of sound mind). (1)

colonialism
economic and political domination of a region and its people by a foreign power. (4)

come out
identify oneself as LGBT or Q. Coming out is a multifaceted process that involves realizing one's own LGBT or Q identity and can include disclosing that identity to family members, friends, teachers, employers, or the media. (5)

common-law marriage
also called de facto marriage, informal marriage, or marriage by habit and repute. It is legally recognized as binding in some countries as a marriage even though there is no legally recognized marriage ceremony or civil marriage contract. (1)

compulsory heterosexuality
the system of thought that says heterosexual relationships are the only good and natural ones, and that all other kinds of relationships ought to be suppressed for the good of society. Compulsory heterosexuality works in part by prescribing strict gender roles for men and women. (5)

counter-hegemony
like "hegemony," also developed by Gramsci, refers to the potential for marginal groups to fight back against the forces that oppress them—challenging and mocking powerful dominant institutions. (3)

cultural broker
a person who translates and explains features of a social environment to people who have limited experience with that environment. (4)

cultural defence
a term used to suggest that an accused has used culture as part of a legal defence to help explain and or justify his or her behaviour. For example, it has been seen in some cases as a way to condone male violence against women and children in minority groups. (9)

cultural model of violence
an explanation of violence based on presumed cultural traits. (4)

cultural vessel
a person responsible for carrying on and transmitting core cultural values and practices. (4)

depression

a term used by economists to refer to a prolonged recession. While a recession occurs when the economy fails to grow for six months; a depression may last years. The so-called Great Depression of the 1920s lasted from about 1928 to 1938 and was reflected in unrelentingly high rates of unemployment and poverty. (6)

determinism

beginning with structural functionalism in the 1950s and closely followed by materialism or political economy, these two determinist theories see individual behaviour as a result of social structures, including social institutions, laws, and norms. Family structures are seen as determining individual behaviour within families. If something is wrong with an individual's actions, according to functionalists, the family structure is to blame and, according to materialists, the economy is the culprit. (1)

disenfranchisement

the denial of economic (working) and/or political (voting and political organization) rights. (4)

Divorce Act, 1968

the first federal divorce law in Canada; it standardized and unified the divorce legislation across the provinces and the territories. The 1968 act also helped to secularize divorce, and bring the process a step closer to a no-fault-based system by introducing the category of marital breakdown. The actual no-fault legislation had to await the 1985 liberalization in Canadian divorce laws. (8)

domestic labour

all those activities required to maintain a home and care for people who live in it. It involves at least three distinct types of work: housework, managing household economics, and caregiving. (7)

double day of work

a concept rooted in socialist feminism, pointing out that women under capitalist patriarchy perform a double day of work, one paid (wage work) and the other unpaid (domestic work). (4)

dual-earner family

the typical economic family structure today. In the majority of Canadian families there are two wage-earners, typically husband and wife (common-law or married). (6)

economic class immigrant

a person immigrating to Canada as a wage earner. (4)

economic globalization

the mass movement of peoples around the world in search of work; along with capitalism—the neoliberal consolidation of global resources—it forces individuals to put aside their personal desires and contribute to the collective enterprise of building families and earning a living. (1)

failure of intimacy

primarily the concern of women when they do not achieve the emotional closeness that they desire in their romantic relationships. (2)

familialism

a dominant or hegemonic discourse, the grand narrative of familialism provides a cultural and social definition of what families are and should be. As both an ideology and a set of customary practices, familialism constitutes the "heart and soul" of our culture. (1)

family class immigrant
an immigrant to Canada sponsored by a family member who is a permanent resident of Canada. (4)

family values
a system of thought developed by socially conservative faith communities that signifies "family values" as "straight, conventionally gendered married people with children." This discourse has been used in a range of faith communities and media campaigns to oppose progress in LGBTQ family rights. (5)

family violence
often used as an umbrella term to include different forms of violence and/or abuse throughout one's life within a familial relationship. (9)

family wage
a wage paid to a male worker deemed sufficient to support an economically dependent wife and children. (1, 7)

feminism
those espousing feminist standpoints believe that gender is one of the most significant organizing variables in social life. They believe that the ideology of sexism is associated with various forms of women's oppression, including economic, psychological, physical, and social. (10)

feminist political economy
a theoretical orientation with a strong methodological subscript. While attending to power relationships as embedded and reflected in economic

arrangements, this perspective is also cognizant of the diverse and intersecting social inequalities (including gender, ethnicity, age, sexual orientation, and so on) that affect our social existence. (6)

Frankfurt School of Social Research
a German school of social research that was founded in 1923 and that became best known for critiques of modern capitalism. The school's leading theorists, Theodor Adorno, Max Horkheimer, and Herbert Marcuse, fled from Nazi Germany and played an important part in analyzing mass culture and control through culture in North America. (3)

gay
a man who is physically and emotionally attracted to other men. The word can also be used to describe men and women who have primarily same-sex desires. (5)

gender-based analysis
an analysis that focuses on gender relations and how sexism and patriarchy operate. In the field of violence this analysis would examine the strong pattern of male violence against women. (5)

gender variant
those who identify their gender outside the gender binary system of male and female, who may be fluid with gender presentation, or who simply may not conform to conventions of gender identity or gender expression for their birth sex. (5)

generation gap
a presumed situation of antagonism between parents and children, based on different life experiences. (4)

globalization

the economic, political, social, and cultural integration of the countries in the world, through increased trade and communication networks. (4)

golden age of capitalism

the postwar period from about 1946 to 1976. During this period, rapid economic expansion was coupled with dramatic improvements in wages and standard of living. (6)

good jobs

the distinction between those jobs that are well paid, highly benefited, secure, and allow for advancement and training, and those jobs that lack all or most of these characteristics i.e., bad jobs. (6)

hegemony

a term developed by the early 20th-century Italian revolutionary Antonio Gramsci; refers to the ways groups in power (such as upper classes) are able to maintain their privileged position by developing strategies to ensure that marginal/oppressed groups consent to their power. (3)

heteronormative life course

the assumption that biological females partner with biological males, and that these partnerships will produce a series of predictable events such as marriage, and childbirth. This concept is routed in the more general ideology of heteronormativity, which systematically renders invisible the life courses of gay, lesbian, transsexual, and queer people. (10)

heteronormativity

another name for the discourse of compulsory heterosexuality. The term "heteronormativity" draws attention to the "norming" functions of the language conventions, institutional structures, and social practices that assume and enforce (only) heterosexuality as normal. (2, 5)

heterosexism

the assumption that everyone is or should be heterosexual and that only heterosexual relationships are natural, normal, and worthy of support. These assumptions are systemic and institutionalized. (5)

heterosexual

a person who is physically and emotionally attracted to people of the opposite sex and not to people of the same sex. (5)

heterosexual, nuclear family

a living arrangement that includes only a woman and a man and possibly children. (7)

homophilic

a term coined by Jesse Bernard (1985) that describes nonsexual, same-sex friendships. (2)

homophobia

1 a system of thought that supports compulsory heterosexuality by representing same-sex relationships as sinful, unnatural, and generally inferior to straight ones. Homophobia used to be reinforced by all the key institutions of society through measures such as silence about LGBTQ lives in the school system, condemnation in religion, and prohibition in law. It is still very active, though in much reduced form, through the continued efforts of socially conservative faith communities. (5);

2 the negative attitudes, stereotypes, and prejudices that still exist in society about individuals who are not heterosexual. It is most often directed at LGBTQ people or people perceived as LGBTQ but is also used to harass heterosexual individuals. (5)

human rights

a system of thought that says all human beings deserve to be treated with equal dignity and accorded equal rights. A key idea of human rights discourse is that marginalized populations need the active protection of the state. Human rights discourse is central to the Canadian *Charter of Rights* and provincial human rights codes, and features prominently in public school education. It is historically rooted in philosophy and law, and has become especially powerful as an official movement in response to the gross abuses of human rights in World Wars I and II. (5)

ideological assumptions

taken-for-granted, widely shared cultural ideas that profoundly influence our perceptions and behaviour. (2)

immigrant/permanent resident

people permitted entry to a nation state from other nation states, for the purpose of living there indefinitely. (4)

income-generating work

the activities involved in making a living, such as running a business, farming, fishing, or earning a wage or salary. (7)

indigenous/Aboriginal

people who have historically populated a geographic area prior to the more recent arrival of other peoples. (4)

internal colonialism

the continuation of colonial relations in the post-colonizing period, through subjugation of indigenous peoples. (4)

intersectionality

a sociological theory that examines how various social and cultural categories of discrimination interact on multiple and often simultaneous levels, contributing to systematic social inequality. Rather than seeing forms of oppression as separate, intersectional analysts see race/ethnicity, gender, religious, nationality, sexual orientation, class, and disability as creating an interlocking system of oppression. (1, 5, 9)

intersex

a general term used to cover many different situations in which a person is born with reproductive or sexual anatomy that does not seem to fit typical definitions of male or female. Often intersex people are subjected to surgical procedures as newborns or in early infancy to remove sexual ambiguity. These procedures can negatively alter and affect their adult lives. (5)

intimacy

a desirable goal for romantic relationships involving emotional and sexual closeness. (2)

Intimacy Discourse

dominant rhetoric about romantic relationships that constructs our ideas about what intimacy is, and how, where, and with whom it can be achieved. (2)

intimacy work

the efforts that people, typically women, expend with the goal of achieving emotional closeness in their romantic relations. (2)

involuntary part-time workers

those workers who are employed on a part-time basis (less than 30 hours per week) but who indicate they would prefer full-time work. In the new economy, especially in periods of recession, more and more part-time workers are part-time simply because they are unable to locate full-time employment. (6)

labour of love

coined by Meg Luxton, refers to the traditional gendered idea that sees femininity as synonymous with domestic labour. In this usage, domestic labour is not concept-ualized as "work" but rather seen as tasks freely undertaken by women on behalf of their partners and children as a demonstration of their "love" for family members. (7)

lesbian

a woman who is physically and emotionally attracted to other women. (5)

LGBTQ

an acronym for "lesbian, gay, bisexual, transgender, transsexual, two-spirit, queer, and questioning" people. (5)

LGBTQ rights/same-sex rights

a system of thought that says LGBTQ people are human beings and deserve equal rights. This discourse is in conflict with the discourse of family values, in which LGBTQ rights are depicted as (undeserved) "special rights." (5)

life course

both a theory and a perspective but is also used in a general way to refer to a person's life cycle and one's passage through life defined by stages or sequences of significant life events. (9)

life-course perspective

way of thinking that encourages us to see that our lives do not proceed along the lines of predictable, homogeneous life stages. Rather, our lives are characterized by variability and fluidity. Biographical, historical, and social differences account for the diversity of life courses. Central to the life-course perspective are the four "Ts": trajectories, transitions, turning points, and timing. (10)

lone mother

the female parent who retains the legal and/or functional custody of her children following pregnancy out of wedlock, divorce, or death of a spouse. (8)

lone parent

the parent who retains the legal and/or functional custody of the couple's children following divorce or death of a spouse. (8)

materialism

emerging from the writing of Karl Marx, materialists examine how economic systems shape and stratify social relationships, as well as how social relationships shape and stratify economic systems. (10)

materialist feminists

socialist or materialist feminists see women's inequality within the family as mirroring their inequality within society. Their maternal roles as nurturing caretakers pushed them away from economic independence, thus guaranteeing their dependence on male wages for subsistence. As dependent subordinates, women left themselves open to potential financial, emotional, and physical mistreatment. (1)

matriliny

the counting of significant family connections through women's/mothers' family lines. (4)

monogamy

the notion that one man should be married to one woman. (1)

moonlighting

the practice of taking on an additional job, typically part-time, in order to supplement the wages from a day job. (6)

multiple/hybrid identities

the co-existence of elements from different cultural environments, within a person. (4)

multiple jobholding

related to the practice of moonlighting but refers to the increasingly common phenomenon of workers holding more than one job. For example, a worker will take several part-time jobs since he or she is unable to locate a full-time job. (6)

neglect

the practice of a caregiver who fails to provide the basic necessity of life such as adequate food, sleep, safety, supervision, clothing, or medical treatment. (9)

neoliberalism

a moral, economic and social philosophy that promotes individualism, competition, and global freedom of marketplaces as conditions under which individuals engage in paid labour. (1)

new economy

term applied to the changes in economic arrangements that emerged out of advances in information technology and economic globalization that occurred in the latter part of the 20th century. (6)

othering/othered

the practice of depicting a group of people as different and inferior in biology and in culture. (4)

parental leave

in Canada, both parents have the right to take parental leave in order to spend time with their newborns. A "parent" includes a birth parent, an adoptive parent, and a person who is in a relationship of some permanence with a parent of the child and who plans on treating the child as his or her own. This includes same-sex couples. Most jurisdictions in Canada provide for unpaid parental and adoption leave in their labour standards legislation, with the exception of Alberta, which does not cover parental leave. (7)

PLUR

an acronym referring to the philosophy of peace, love, unity, and respect, which is embraced by some youth in the rave culture. (3)

points system of immigration

the Canadian practice for selecting permanent residents, whereby points are assigned to applicants based on education, age, work experience, language skills, and family already residing in Canada. (4)

polygyny

the practice of a man having many wives. (4)

postfamilial family

a phrase coined by Elizabeth Beck-Gernsheim (1999) to signal the way in which people are able to choose their family relationships more now than in the past. (2)

postmodernism

a reaction to modernist thinking, it rejects the notions of objective truth, predictability in social life, the role of expert knowledge, and essentialist categories. These thinkers are interested in the relationship between meaning and language. (1, 10)

precarious (marginal) employment

in the new economy, more and more work is not secure. The proliferation of contract work as well as part-time employment both reflect a marked shift toward work that is experienced as lacking long-term security. (6)

queer

a formerly derogative term that has been reclaimed in a positive way to reflect the diversity and breadth of sexual and gender identities. Sometimes used as an umbrella term to include anyone who is not heterosexual or conventionally gendered, it can also include people who are attracted only to the "opposite" sex but who reject the term "heterosexual" as oppressive and refuse to identify with it. (5)

questioning

a person who is unsure of his or her sexual orientation or gender identity. (5)

racial socialization

the practice of instilling in young people pride toward their racialized group. (4)

racialization

the social construction of "race" to categorize a group of people and used to explain their behaviours. (4)

racialized families

processes by which individuals and groups of people are viewed through a racial lens, through a culturally invented racial framework, and come to be defined as different and are subjugated to unequal and differential treatment. (1)

rave

a culture of youth whose members are renowned for their interest in computer-generated techno music, the use of amphetamine drugs, and attendance at all-night parties known as raves. (3)

remittances

contributions in money and goods sent between family members separated by migration. (4)

residential school system

the practice in North America from the late 19th century to the 1960s, of separating indigenous children from their families, to educate them and indoctrinate them in the ways of the dominant culture. (4)

resiliency

the thriving of a person or a group of people in adverse conditions. (4)

romantic love

idealized or sentimental love. (2)

satellite children

children who live apart from their parents due to migration. (4)

second-generation immigrants

individuals who are born in a country, to parents who immigrated to that country. (4)

seniority rights

the union principle that the individual who has worked longest in a workplace acquires specific rights as a result of his or her longevity on the job. Typically, for example, in the event of layoffs, more junior workers lose their jobs first and senior workers are the last to go. (6)

severe time-crunch stress

a personal state in which time pressures are so extreme that the individual indicates, in terms of his or her responses to specific questions, that he or she feels severely time crunched. (6)

Shari'a

the religious stipulations on the basis of the interpretations of the Qur'an (holy book of Islam) about male and female relationships/ marriage that governs orthodox Muslim groups. (8)

singlism

the stereotyping and stigmatizing of people who are single including those who are divorced, widowed, or never been married. (1)

slavery

the ownership of a human being by another human being, typically for use as unpaid workers. (4)

social constructionism (symbolic interactionism)

a micro-level sociological framework that focuses on how humans develop, construct, and share meaning. This paradigm recognizes that humans simultaneously shape, and are shaped by, social structures. (10)

social determinants of health

a model that seeks to explain the health status of groups and individuals based on features of their social environment, including their position in social hierarchies. (4)

social gerontology

an interdisciplinary field, it examines various social aspects related to the old, and an aging population. Social workers, sociologists, psychologists, and disciplines in the field of health contribute to social gerontology. (10)

social location

the multiple positions (gender, race, class, sexual orientation, age, etc.) that a person occupies. (9)

social reproduction

the view that social class is reproduced intergenerationally as a result of structural factors such as capitalism and patriarchy; the activities required to ensure the day-to-day and generational reproduction of the population. (7)

social safety net

the variety of government-based services that are intended to provide support and assistance to members of a society when they confront extreme personal difficulties and setbacks. For example, employment insurance, disability allowance, social welfare support, and subsidized housing figure prominently in the social safety net. (6)

socialist feminism

a theory that adds to the political economy (Marxist) perspective by considering gender relations as a significant power hierarchy, linked with social class relations. (4)

step family

a family in which at least one of the children in the household is from a previous relationship of one of the parents. (8)

straight

a person who is sexually and emotionally attracted to someone of the so-called "opposite" birth sex; heterosexual. (5)

structural model of violence

an explanation of violence based on pressures from, and/or changes in, people's social environment. (4)

structured ambivalence

emerging from the life course perspective and feminism, this theoretical framework helps us to understand relationships within the family as being neither negative nor positive, but a combination of "solidarity and conflict" (Connidis, 2010, p. 139) which shape personal responses as well as emotional and social bonds. This perspective bridges micro and macro levels of the social world, helping us to understand how social structures shape familial relationships. (10)

temporary foreign worker

a migrant who is allowed temporary residence for the purposes of work, and cannot bring family members along. (4)

the political economy perspective

also known as Marxism, a perspective that considers the economic organization of society into social classes is the most important basis for inequality. (4)

transgender or trans

a person who feels his or her gender identity as man or woman does not match his or her biological sex or who reject the binary gender system altogether and prefers not to be identified in its terms. "Trans" is also sometimes used by people who "play" with gender-crossing without feeling any deep inner sense of discomfort with the assumption of male masculinity. "MtF" (male-to-female) and "FtM" (female-to-male) are two of the common ways trans people describe themselves. (5)

transnational families

the continuation of family patterns and relations over distance and migratory separation. (1, 4)

transphobia

the negative attitudes, stereotypes, and prejudices that exist about individuals whose gender identity or gender expression does not conform with the gender traditionally assigned to their biological sex. (5)

transsexual

a person who experiences intense personal and emotional discomfort with his or her assigned birth sex. Some transsexuals pursue treatments (i.e., sex reassignment surgery and/or hormone therapy) to physically alter their body to correspond with what they feel their true sex is. (5)

Two Spirit

some Aboriginal people identify themselves as Two Spirit rather than as lesbian, gay, bisexual, or transgender. Historically, in many Aboriginal cultures two-spirit persons were respected leaders and medicine people. Two-spirit persons were often accorded special status based upon their unique abilities to see the world from both male and female perspectives. (5)

un-benefited work

work that lacks all or many of the benefits that have been associated with employment. For example, un-benefited work may lack pension, disability, sick leave, and health benefits. Since benefits comprise a significant component of a wage packet, the erosion of these elements mark an important downward shift in work compensation. (6)

underemployment

when a worker holds a job that does not make use of his or her skill or educational credentials. For example, a waitress with an M.A. is underemployed. (6)

violence

although the concept of violence has been used to include a variety of criteria including an act or omission, intent, or harm, it can also be used generally to refer to a way to physically, sexually, or psychologically harm others. (9)

visible minority

a term used in Canada to refer to racialized groups, criticized by the United Nations as stigmatizing. (4)

youth culture

the historical emergence of a set of beliefs, values, attitudes, norms, styles, and tastes associated with the younger (teen) segment of the Canadian population. (3)

INDEX

Note: Figures and tables are indicated by f or t, respectively, following the page number.